*Belonging in the two Berlins* is an ethnographic investigation into the meaning of German selfhood during the Cold War. Taking everyday life in the divided Berlin as his point of departure, Borneman shows how the practices of kin, state, and nation were constructed through processes of mirror-imaging and misrecognition. Using linguistics and narrative analysis, he compares the autobiographies of two generations of Berlin residents with the official version of the lifecourse prescribed by the two German states. He examines the relation of the dual political structure to everyday life, the way in which the two states legally regulated the lifecourse in order to define the particular categories of self which signify Germanness, and how citizens experientially appropriated the frameworks provided by these states.

Living in the two Berlins constantly compelled residents to define themselves in opposition to their other half. Borneman argues that this resulted in a *de facto* divided Germany with two distinct nations and peoples. The formation of German subjectivity since World War II is unique in that the distinctive features for belonging – for being at home – to one side exclude the other. Indeed, these divisions inscribed by the Cold War account for many of the problems in forging a new cultural unity.

D1457225

*Cambridge Studies in Social and Cultural Anthropology*
*Editors: Ernest Gellner, Jack Goody, Stephen Gudeman,*
*Michael Herzfeld, Jonathan Parry*

86

Belonging in the two Berlins

*A list of books in this series will be found at the end of the volume*

# BELONGING IN THE TWO BERLINS

## Kin, state, nation

JOHN BORNEMAN
*Assistant Professor of Anthropology,*
*Cornell University, Ithaca, New York*

CAMBRIDGE
UNIVERSITY PRESS

Published by the Press Syndicate of the University of Cambridge
The Pitt Building, Trumpington Street, Cambridge CB2 1RP
40 West 20th Street, New York, NY 10011-4211, USA
10 Stamford Road, Oakleigh, Victoria 3166, Australia

© Cambridge University Press 1992

First published 1992

Printed in Great Britain by Redwood Press Limited, Melksham, Wiltshire

*A catalogue record for this book is available from the British Library*

*Library of Congress cataloguing in publication data*

Borneman, John.
Belonging in the two Berlins : kin, state, nation / John Borneman.
    pp.    cm. – (Cambridge studies in social and cultural
anthropology)
Includes bibliographical references and index.
ISBN 0 521 41589 6. – ISBN 0 521 42715 0 (pbk.)
1. Ethnology – Germany – Berlin.   2. Kinship – Germany – Berlin.
3. National characteristics, West German.   4. National
characteristics, East German.   5. Berlin (Germany) – Social
conditions.   6. Berlin (Germany) – Economic conditions.   7. Berlin
(Germany) – Social life and customs.   I. Title.   II. Series.
GN585.G4B67   1992
305.8'009431'55 – dc20   91-34054   CIP

ISBN 0 521 41589 6 hardback
ISBN 0 521 42715 0 paperback

*For*
SALLY FALK MOORE

# Contents

# Figures

# Tables

# Acknowledgments

It is a genuine pleasure now to have a chance to express my gratitude to those individuals who in unique ways contributed to this work. First and foremost, I thank all the Berliners who shared their experiences with me. Without my conversations with them, I would really have nothing to say. My undergraduate intellectual mentor at the University of Wisconsin, David Adamany, first inspired me, little beknownst to him, to think critically about law as a social and historical process. My riding (yes, not writing) instructor during my non-academic years, Betty MacLane, taught me how to observe. Eight years later, at the University of Washington, Andreas Teuber and Daniel Lev encouraged me to see political theory and comparative politics anthropologically, and then told me that I belonged in social anthropology. Following their advice, Charles Keyes first tutored me in this new home, in a course on Paul Ricoeur and the model of the text as social action.

My initial field research for this project was in part supported by grants from the International Research-Exchange Board (IREX) and Fulbright-Hays in East Berlin, from the Krupp Foundation and Social Science Research Council – Berlin Program for Advanced German and European Studies in West Berlin. Return research trips for related projects were funded by IREX, the German Marshall Fund, and the Spencer Foundation, all of whom I thank for their support. In Berlin, I benefited greatly from the attention of Dr. Ilona Stolpe, who steered me through a legal maze, and from my friendships with Jürgen Lemke, Michael Weck, Robin Ostow, and Heinz Bude, who thought with me even when the route seemed sure to lead to a cul de sac. Correspondence with Liisa Malkki during fieldwork was indispensable, as was an ongoing conversation with Scott Long, who provided key moments of insight and intellectual momentum. Finally, I remain indebted to Sally Falk Moore, Stanley Tambiah, and Charles Lindholm, my mentors at Harvard University, where I received my training in anthropology.

Special thanks for the hospitality of faculty and staff of the University of California at San Diego, where I made final revisions on this manuscript. Especially, I am grateful to Michael Meeker in helping me through some of the problems I encountered at that time; and to Roy D'Andrade and Fred Bailey for suggestions on the postscript. Of the readers for Cambridge University Press, I wish to acknowledge and thank Michael Herzfeld for his acute editorial suggestions. In preparation of the final manuscript, Joe Masco and Michael Weck provided invaluable assistance, made possible by a grant from the Center for German and European Studies at the University of California, Berkeley. Beyond these specifiable debts, I wish to express deep appreciation collectively to my dear friends and colleagues, both here and abroad.

# Introduction

**Fieldsite**

Berlin is the ultimate postmodern space. It enjoys a shifting (until recently declining, now rapidly expanding), heterogeneous population, a discontinuous and ruptured history, old communists, young right-wing neo-Nazis, aging Red Army sympathizers – and, through the duration of this study, four foreign occupation armies "protecting" two opposed political and economic systems. I moved to Berlin in 1986 to study the relation of its dual political structure to everyday life. At that time little did I foresee the autumn revolution of 1989, when the desire for unity and continuity of the German *Volk*, for oneness, overwhelmed the diversity and duality of culture and politics, when Berlin's chameleon nature, its refusal, or inability, to fix its political, cultural, or economic organs, caught the world by surprise: the people of Leipzig and East Berlin spearheaded a peaceful revolution, presaging an about-face in the city's, and Germany's, identity, as well as the end of the Cold War era. Berlin's fluidity, its lack of final closure and essence, does not anomalize its place in history, however, but rather elevates it to an apotheosis of our time. More than perhaps any other city, it has periodized and shaped twentieth-century history in the West: 1914, 1939, 1989.

It took slightly less than a year to complete the about-face begun in the fall of 1989, transforming Berlin from a dual organization, a structure of two moieties (halves) within a tribe, into the (whole) capital of a nascent empire, suturing together its halved corpse composed of mangled limbs and appendages so out of place, so absurdly placed, as to mimic Picasso's wildest fantasies of dismembered bodies. The Wall, that until November 9, 1989 sliced through the heart of its old center and encircled the western (so-called free) half, both parodied, and raised to paradigm, the liminality of boundaries: it simultaneously excluded and included, proving its own necessity while demonstrating its permeability. Dismantling the Wall, and what followed from that, German unification, was by no means foreordained. The forty-year division of Berlin, and that of Germany, much like the Cold War which that division symbolized, had its own momentum, and had developed its own behavioral rules and cognitive structures, unlikely to give way and disappear so quickly as a solid wall. This study is a history of some of these structures of division and belonging from the time when Berlin was two. It was completed in the final years of their disintegration, shortly before the Cold War era attained historical closure and the status of self-conscious myth.

For two and a half years, 1986–1989, I conducted fieldwork in East and West Berlin, listening to life stories and histories of events, researching the legal history of "kinship policy" in the two German states. Drawing upon this fieldwork, I analyze the "life constructions" contained in autobiographies of two generations of Berlin residents and compare them to the preferred version of the lifecourse offered by the two German states in their legal texts. In applying ethnographic methods and social anthropological frameworks to the study of residents in a large central European metropolis, this study will probably challenge readers more than exhaust them, pique more than define, and perhaps irritate more than satisfy. It contains all the characteristics of an experiment: deriving its knowledge from actual participation, blending the personal and empirical, reaching provisional and tentative findings.

Central to this examination are changes in naming practices and classification schemes, for which this study itself may serve as an appropriate example. Anthropological accounts derive coherence from rendering something foreign, such as names and categories, into something familiar. Even when the object of description – whether person, process, or structure – initially lacks coherence in its own cultural setting, it is the anthropologist's task to come up with names and an ordering scheme that enables someone alien to it to grasp the particulars at hand. This task of making the object of study coherent – impracticable even in "cold" island cultures where boundaries have an appearance of timelessness and fixity – seems increasingly intractable to contemporary anthropologists who now perceive their local objects as active agents involved in national struggles, world markets, and transnational organizations.

Yet lending coherence and familiarity to culture is only part of the task of an anthropological narrative. A second and equally essential task is to understand *how* the inchoate is made coherent and *how* the exotic is made familiar. The porousness of Berlin's borders and the kaleidoscopic identity of its natives, a dynamism of place and person not found in most anthropological fieldsites, makes Berlin an attractive place to study processes of coherence-building. For the very diversity within and of Berlin has been a challenge to statesmen and social engineers, from Otto von Bismarck to Helmut Kohl, whose goal has been to bring these differences into line, to arrest and control their activities, to create out of human chaos a classical unity, a linearity of time, a uniformity of space. Berliners in this century, however, as well as the nations and states to which they belong, have not been able to delineate themselves by exclusive characteristics within stable boundaries; they have been undergoing constant transformations that have both antedated and followed abrupt changes in political and social life.

This study of Berlin, then, will not be a dissection, from a single vantage point, of continuity and change within a coherent culture. Native categories of Berliners as well as my own descriptive units are shifting significations given meaning through temporal action in a context. During the course of my fieldwork, the two German states bought from and sold Berlin property to each other, individuals changed citizenship in the middle of their lifecourse, and shortly after the end of my stay in Berlin, one state annexed the other. These changes were part of a dialogue, however distorted and coercive at times, whose meaning for those on one side of the Wall made sense only with respect to the meanings on the other side, which in turn made sense only when considered in the global context of the Cold War.

### Dual organization, politics, culture

Contrary to assumptions that East and West Germany were independent systems capable of being separately analyzed, the two Germanies are to be understood only in terms of their relations as parts of a whole. Beginning with the Russian and American/Western Allied occupation of Germany in 1945, the Berlins took on characteristics of a dual organization, that is, with moieties developing a matching, *a*symmetrical dual classification of the universe. Anthropology, inspired by the classic essay *Primitive Classification* by Emile Durkheim and Marcel Mauss, first published in 1903, has an illustrious history of trying to explain the cross-cultural practice of dualistic forms of thought and organization, often reducing political, aesthetic, and economic classificatory schemes to derivatives of women exchange at the level of cross-cousin marriage. Lévi-Strauss (1958) contributed to this debate by showing how marriage exchange was linked to a dualistic world view, based on what he attributed to a universal tendency to use binary oppositions in classification.[1] We need not fully agree with Lévi-Strauss' attribution of cause in order to argue for continued use of the concept "dual organization." Most analyses of moieties considered dual structures merely at one point in time and only in their cultural manifestations, without an adequate account of the political factors that create and sustain them over time.[2] It seems likely that all such structures throughout history were created for political reasons, however obscure those original struggles are to us today.[3]

The Germanies, from 1945/1949 to 1989, provides us with a rich historical example of the attempted construction of such a dual organization, one that began in 1945 with an occupation by two foreign, ideological opponents, who in 1949 created dual political organizations. This 1949 political–territorial division drew its justification from competing conceptual paradigms of social–cultural organization (socialism versus capitalism). Each state tried, in turn, to create its own cultural ideal in an intimate process of mirror-imaging and misrecognition.[4] Due to an increasing asymmetry in economic power, East Germany built the Wall in 1961 to provide a protected space for its utopian experiment. By the mid eighties the economic asymmetry had increased, notwithstanding the Wall, and those aspects of dual organization already created outside the state sphere began to crumble rapidly. In 1989 the political experiment came to an abrupt end. On October 3, 1990, the two states and societies completed formal governmental unification.

Political structures, such as states, are often studied by experts as something reified, autonomous, and causally connected to "culture." Yet they are part of a cultural order, formed historically, not to be viewed as part of a natural order, independent of and somehow opposed to culture. They get their meaning from contemporary culture and give meaning back to it; they are legitimated in a myriad of ways in everyday life much as they also shape life, in the extreme case by formally legalizing or criminalizing sets of practices. During the Cold War it was generally assumed that social and cultural formations were coterminous with or existed within states, and that states determined the boundaries of meaning systems. (In East Germany, an individual who tried to cross state boundaries without prior approval was officially called a *Grenzverbrecher*, border criminal.) This impoverished understanding of politics both mirrors back to the class of modern politicians their own grandiose notion of self-importance, their sense that they determine boundaries, as well as confirms and reproduces the importance of the social scientist and journalist who fixates on this reified, narrow notion of politics presuming that s/he is studying what is significant.

States, and the inter-national order they are said to represent, are recent cultural inventions, merely 200 years old; their autonomy is always constrained by the culture in which they exist. Certainly the fact that one of the two states I studied – throughout the eighties considered the tenth-strongest economic power in the world – has now dissolved itself, indicates how much governments, regardless of the power they exercise and of their own sense of self-importance, are dependent for meaning on a particular cultural ordering. This in no way denies the fact that all states try to monopolize the rules and terms controlling the reproduction of culture. Nonetheless, we may be witnessing a major transformation on a world scale in the "national order of things" (I am borrowing the felicitous phrase from Lisa Malkki 1992), for states are increasingly limited in their sovereignty by other competing cultural creations, such as bureaucracies, pan-national drug cartels, multi-national corporations, inter-national markets, the European Community, and cosmopolitan and local ethnic identities. Whatever the results of this process, states are and will remain part of cultural orders, and thus capable of being understood using the same analytical tools we use for other cultural artifacts.

**Authority and structure**
Unlike a "history" that fundamentally derives its authority from a chronologically enclosed past, my authority in this book stems primarily from the fact that I was there for the telling of the story. Although my sources are heterogeneous, many of them purely historical and not anthropological in nature, they are made to serve my ethnographic account, not, as many a historian would be prone to, made to serve a chronological narrative. In the past several decades old antagonisms between history and anthropology have considerably dissolved. Not only do the practitioners in the two fields borrow from each other, but it has recently become the vogue for anthropologists to avoid the contemporary fieldwork setting and engage in a necro-anthropology, escaping

into a past colonial encounter between ethnographer and native, or between the West and the Third World, rather than directly confronting the ubiquitous processes of colonization in the present or in the First World. This movement has further blurred distinctions between the two disciplines.

Yet, I would argue, the most significant shift within anthropology has not been the putative "break" fomented by its marriage with history as past, but rather is located in the re-examination of its authority and a reappropriation of the traditions of its practitioners: an attempt to remain true to a science of the study of all humankind while at the same time overcoming anthropology's tawdry origins as a tool of Western empire-building. This necessarily involves renouncing the forms of authority that sustained this project. By bringing northern European and Western civilizations under an anthropological gaze, ethnographers confront most directly the dilemma facing contemporary science as a whole: they deprive themselves of authority derived from the power asymmetry between scientist and subject, ethnographer and native, the privileged First World and underprivileged Third World.[5] Thus "the field" for anthropology no longer remains a particular place in the southern hemisphere inhabited by illiterate dark-skinned peoples, nor is it a space – in which we are forever confined – where past generations of ethnographers did their fieldwork. It has incredibly broadened in scope, and the locus of authority lies not in the reproduction or critique of past colonialism but in very present systems of domination.

Along these lines, we might say that the oppositions most often attributed to history and anthropology, in that the former prioritizes diachrony and the latter synchrony, or the former "unfurls the range of societies in time, the other in space" (Lévi-Strauss 1966: 256), are less significant than the fact that both historian and anthropologist construct their objects in the present. But, while both anthropologists and historians construct accounts mediated by the historical time of the writing, the ethnographic account distinguishes itself from the historical by privileging its *historicity*: the "having been there" in dialogue with the living other during the construction of at least part of the history about to be told.

The credibility of my account, therefore, must ultimately rest neither on any particular asymmetry nor on any claims of exclusive access, but on my ability as an anthropologist to interpret experience during the Cold War from an experience-near present, constructed in a dialogue between myself and the actual participants about whom I write.

Following the onslaught of the revolution of 1989, this Cold War dialogue is also historical, i.e., subject to a *before* and *after* coding, and hence enclosed in a fixed chronological period, a category for historiography, much like the "middle ages," the "renaissance," "antiquity," and the "eighteenth century." That my object of study has now fortuitously become a historical category alters the exclusivity of my account (for this period is now open to historians also), but it does not fundamentally alter the nature of my account's authority, that is, ethnographic authority derived from the particular dialogic relationship I established with East and West Berliners in the years 1986 to 1989.

I begin chapter 1 with a description of my entrance into the field and the dialogic space in which I worked. Additionally, I give a schematic overview of the issues dealt with in the book, their relation to my fieldsite, to anthropology specifically, and to social science generally. Chapter 2 focuses on how I know what I know, or rather, how I came to know what I wrote. Chapter 3 summarizes the demographic context; chapter 4 engages in a comparative analysis of the history of kinship law. Chapters 5 through 8 present the life constructions of two generations in the two Berlins; they are not ethnographically self-contained narratives, for generations invent themselves only upon reflection about difference and context. Hence each generational narrative informs (on) the other, and my own story is constructed with this in mind. Chapters 5 and 6 examine transformations in kinship in East Berlin; chapter 7 and 8 analyze kinship transformations in West Berlin. Chapter 9 presents final conclusions in a discussion relating marriage to family and nation. Finally, the postscript is about events subsequent to this study: the collapse and dissolution of the East German state, the unification of Berlin, and the refiguring of a united Germany.

# 1

# Naming, categorizing, periodizing

In fact history is tied neither to man or to any particular object. It consists wholly in its method, which experience proves to be indispensable for cataloguing the elements of any structure whatever, human or anti-human, in their entirety. It is therefore far from being the case that the search for intelligibility comes to an end in history as though this were its terminus. Rather, it is history that serves as the point of departure in any quest for intelligibility. As we say of certain careers, history may lead to anything, provided you get out of it.

Claude Lévi-Strauss, *The Savage Mind*
© University of Chicago Press (USA and Philippines) and
George Weidenfeld and Nicholson Ltd, 1966 [1962].

Ordnung muß sein. Das weiß man schon von klein.
(Order is all. We learn that when we're small.)

German aphorism

## Entering Berlin

Upon entering one of the border zones that divided the Germanies, either along the Elbe River, or between East and West Berlin, the first question put to you by the East German border guards was: "Where are you going?" The answer revealed not only intended destination, but also political standpoint and understanding of postwar history. The question would elicit simultaneously a name, a categorization, and a periodization. I encountered this situation on September 1, 1986, as I "entered the field" – the anthropological euphemism for going to live with the people one is about to study. That morning my West Berlin friends had wished me luck in leaving Berlin and going to East Berlin. My point of entry was Checkpoint Charlie. I was already quite aware that responding to the border guard's question with "East Berlin" would undoubtedly result in a correction: "This is Berlin, GDR, not East Berlin." If I said, "East Germany," I would be insulting my hosts, for this name implicitly questioned the legitimacy of the German Democratic Republic as a state by raising the then-heretical concept of *Wiedervereinigung*, reunification of the nation. If I said "the German Democratic Republic," it would have sounded as if I was mocking them, for they used only the initials: the GDR. The correct answer would have been simply "Berlin." I was leaving Berlin and preparing to enter Berlin. Caught between innocence and ignorance, I avoided the question, handed over my papers, and told them that I was part of an official research exchange program and in fifteen minutes was supposed to meet the Director of International Relations for Humboldt University at the Ministry of Higher and Technical Education in Marx-Engels Platz 2.

These conflicts and confusions over naming and periodizing, while consciously poignant in the case of the divided city of Berlin, are neither unique to the contemporary Germanies nor to the era of the Cold War. Classification schemes are always sites of political contestation.[1] To name is never neutral; it involves description and evaluation, it categorizes. The organization of history is precisely such a struggle concerning the legitimation of particular classificatory systems. Chronologically ordered sequences, the usual device of the historian, are themselves quite arbitrary, based on prior assumptions about the significance of events. "What makes history possible," writes Lévi-Strauss in his

Figure 1. The two Berlins, 1989.

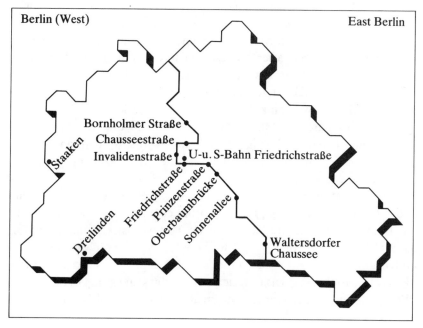

famous attack on Sartre, "is that a sub-set of events is found, for a given period, to have approximately the same significance for a contingent of individuals who have not necessarily experienced the events and may even consider them at an interval of several centuries. History is therefore never history, but history-for" (1966: 257). Historians order events into stories that often purport to be impartial accounts, but are not since they are always based on the perspective of particular actors. Ultimately, the historian chooses what and for whom s/he will narrate. In this study, I, as the inscriber, analyst, interpreter, will be classifying selected conflicts over naming, categorizing, and periodizing between 1945 and 1989 in Berlin.

The initial question, "Where are you going?", put to me by the border official was intended to elicit less my destination than my point of departure. And my point of departure suggested to the border guard an answer to the more important question, "To whom do you belong?" Belonging, in turn, is a cultural identity, dependent on familial, social, and political membership, or, expressed in analytical terms: kinship, nationness, and citizenship. As an American driving into the GDR with a West German automobile and a Dutch license plate, why did the border guards let me in? Since I am neither German nor a GDR citizen, how could I claim belonging?

Simply answered: I was part of a research exchange system. At one level, I was being exchanged, as *Austauschobjekt*, object of exchange, though only temporarily, for a GDR citizen who was sent for the same period of time to the United States. Even more significant, I was part of an exchange of words: after my research stay I would return home and represent the GDR in my work, much as their researcher would represent the United States upon his/her return home. This makes obvious sense if we think briefly about the basic rule of exchange systems, formulated by Marcel Mauss (1925) and Claude Lévi-Strauss (1949), that societies exchange three items: words, women, and goods. The Germanies applied a sex-neutral rule: they exchanged words, people, and goods.

Indeed, the major difference between West German–GDR and USA–GDR exchange lay precisely in the category "people." Whereas the two German states traded many words for words and some goods for goods, they did not trade people for people – and herein was the source of tension: they disputed each other's citizenship. Both states presented themselves to the world as proprietors over the same group of nationals. West Germany went so far as to claim all citizens of the GDR as its own, and even regularly bought them from the East. The people exchange was known in West Germany as *freikaufen*, to buy the freedom; East Germany called those exchanged *Verräter*, traitors. This aspect of German–German trade was troublesome precisely because of competing postwar claims over who belonged to whom – or more precisely, over kinship categorization – and its relation to the legitimacy of the German states. As an American scientist, I belonged to an East German category – the exchange of knowledge – that since the early seventies had become legally organized and regularized.

My official entry into West Berlin, on July 1, 1987, occurred under a quite different set of circumstances and financial arrangements. Whereas I was welcomed into East Berlin as an *Austauschobjekt*, I found my way into West Berlin as part of a *Wiedergutmachung*, reparations program. Americans continued to enjoy, some forty years after the Allied victory and German defeat, a special status in West Berlin and West Germany, not primarily, as is often thought, because of the *Befreiung*, the liberation from Nazism, but, more importantly, because we had saved them from the "Bolshevik menace," from the fate of their fellow nationals in the GDR. Although the German–American relationship changed considerably in the postwar years, it remained characterized by German deference to the American plan to make West Germany into the front line defense against so-called communist encroachment. This pattern of deference was institutionalized during the Cold War.

In return for this gift of Freedom to the West Berliners, I was part of a do-good, reparations program to attract bright, young social scientists (I was officially dubbed part of the *Führungskräfte*, leading elite!) to research about Germany in the Federal Republic. My stay in West Berlin was an unequal exchange – no West German was being sent to the USA for a comparable period of time – financed by West German money, primarily Krupp and Volkswagen. The term *Wiedergutmachung* came into currency in the postwar period to describe payments to victims of Nazi policies. A reparation payment, like any other form of restitution, cannot do away with the initial deed that created the debt or obligation to the victim, but it does recompensate to some extent by appeasing the injured party, rebalancing the debtor/creditor relationship. To be sure, neither the Americans as a group nor I personally were victims in the same sense that other groups were "victims of fascism." Yet the parallel holds at the level of exchange: in my case, the payment was not for the war years, but for the early postwar years in which the United States had reinvested in West Germany.

My guises as an *Austauschobjekt* and as part of *Wiedergutmachung* established the international contexts within which I constructed relationships with people in Berlin. *Wieso bist Du hierher gekommen?*, "Why did you end up here?" and *Was machst Du hier eigentlich?*, "What are you doing here?", were the questions put to me most frequently in both Berlins. For East Berliners, I was an equal exchange in a scientific program; for West Berliners I was being repaid for the largess of my state. My ethnographer's persona, while perhaps easier to identify than those of other fieldworkers, was, at the same time, shaped by processes intrinsic to the practice of social science. Much like the people we study, we cannot escape being identified by the cultural and historical contexts of the groups to whom we belong any more than the individuals studied can separate themselves from their groups. "Understanding," writes Hans Georg Gadamer, "always implies a pre-understanding which is in turn pre-figured by the determinate tradition in which the interpreter lives and which shapes his prejudices" (1979: 108).

We, as anthropologists, are *emplotted*, to apply the word Hayden White (1973) coined for a different context, by our natives. We are understood as narrators in a plot that encapsulates some version of the history of our group, and we are framed by that particular historical narrative which we personally did not write. "The history of the individual is never," asserts Pierre Bourdieu, "anything other than a certain specification of the collective history of his group or class" (1977: 86). This "specification," we might add, is one that both the native and the anthropologist make about each other. The kinds of interactions, forms of observation, and nature of dialogue informing my study developed in interplay with this larger context, limiting what I as anthropologist was able to learn and hence how I wrote up the native.

**Renaming the Germans**
Nowhere during the Cold War did the two Germanies fight more tenaciously with each other than over the naming of who and what were to be German. Naming and categorizing are always contested acts because they are essential sources of power in the construction of local, national, and international loyalties. Reconstruction of all three loyalties involved the creation of a new sense of Germanness, an issue of the utmost international importance following the defeat of "the German nation" and the collapse of the Third Reich in 1945. Postwar leaders had the dual tasks of using already existing symbols to reunite and rebuild a devastated land, and of distancing themselves from any symbols that

might be associated with "Nazism." The German nation, which had first reached a kind of political unity with the founding of the Kaiserreich in 1871, was now, merely seventy years later, equated with fascism and all that was evil.[2] Germans had blood on their hands. But unlike Lady Macbeth after her murder of Duncan, they could not exclaim, "Out, out, damned spot!" For what spot, precisely, was to be wiped out? Part of the ambiguity, or one might even say, the *aporia*, of the situation was that nobody knew exactly what fascism was – a precise definition of the term continues to escape us today – and therefore what aspects of nation, of Germanness, were to be stamped out. The Allied Occupation Forces, much like the Germans, differed among themselves about the relationship between Germanness and fascism, about how to go about what in the East came to be known as *die Umerziehung*, reeducating the Germans,[3] and in the West was referred to either as reeducation or *die Entnazifizierung*, denazification.[4] The immediate and long-term responses and strategies of the Allies corresponded more to their own national experiences and needs than to those of the Germans.

For people in the Soviet Occupied Zone, the postwar experience

Figure 2. Germany and Berlin at the end of World War II.

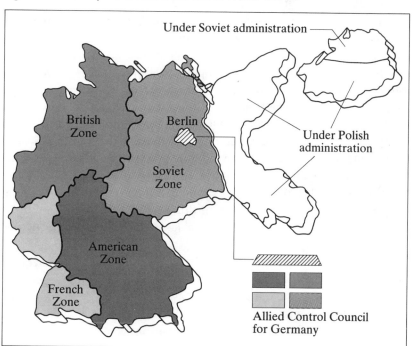

involved an initial, radical break with traditional German "national identity" concepts, and a rigorous enforcement of the four basic principles of the Potsdam Accords: demilitarization, denazification, democratization, and demonopolization. After 1949, the newly constructed socialist state traced its legitimacy back to two failed German revolutions, of 1848 and 1918–1919, and to the successful Russian October Revolution of 1917. The 1848 experience was far removed in time, the 1918–1919 failure was of a radically different kind of urgency, and the 1917 Russian Revolution was not viewed as a German national experience by those living between the Elbe and Oder–Neiße Rivers.

For people in the Western zones, an initially confused and contradictory occupation policy regarding the Potsdam directives had achieved a degree of coherence by May 1947, in that the Cold War assumed precedence over attempts at internal reform.[5] The Federal Republic of Germany, founded in September 1949, one month before the GDR, traced its legitimacy back to the failed liberal-democratic Weimar Republic of 1918–1933, and to a full and speedy integration, *Westintegration*, into Western (foremost American and British) democratic, economic, and military alliances.[6] A general amnesty and rehabilitation of all Nazis in December 1950 marked an official end, to all intents and purposes, of the attempt at denazification in West Germany.[7]

The building of new "nation(s)" and "states" proceeded via continual comparison and contrast between ideologically opposed models, now divided by the Elbe River. This postwar territorial division was also complicated by the Four-Power occupation of Berlin, the former imperial capital, geographically situated in the heart of the Soviet-occupied eastern zone. The American, British, and French occupation forces (renamed protection troops) remained stationed in West Berlin, until 1990 a walled city of ambiguous status located in the middle of a sovereign, enemy state. After the founding of the two states, leaders in the Federal Republic could continue appealing to the issue of national reunification and simultaneously strengthen their own power base, for they assumed that a reunification of the two territories would result in absorption of the eastern part into a liberal-democratic state of the American ilk.

From the start, the perspective from the Soviet Zone was quite different. The Soviets, in comparison to the other Allies, made the greatest sacrifices in the war against the fascists. They had been the object of a four-year annihilation campaign by the Germans – "scorched earth" meant mass murder (over 22 million dead) and physical devastation of the land. German attitudes toward "the Russians" did not change overnight; if anything, the unexpected defeat embittered them even more. Thus the Soviet and the new German leaders in the eastern territories insisted upon, as a precondition for reunification, a strict carrying out of the Potsdam Accords. The other Allies and the West Germans, however, resisted, to varying degrees, each aspect of the accords. Moreover, to the extent that the new leaders in the East also referred to a united Germany, *Gesamtdeutschland*, they made it difficult to build a state with a distinctive set of national loyalties separate from West Germany.

Accordingly, when leaders on one side would appropriate an historical category, those on the other found it necessary to reject that employment for themselves in order to avoid the conventional meanings associated with the contested word or phrase. For example, when western leaders enacted a surprise currency reform in June 1948, the Soviet occupation forces responded with a year-long, and ultimately unsuccessful, blockade of West Berlin. As the victorious West Germans continued to label their currency the *Deutsche Mark*, often shortened to D-Mark, the eastern leaders were forced to create a new currency, which they called *Deutsche Mark der Deutschen Notenbank*. Soon it became clear that the West German state was and would remain the economically and politically stronger of the two, and the GDR began to yield to the Federal Republic in the use of the "German" designation. In 1964, East German officials shortened the currency name to *Mark der Deutschen Notenbank*, merely legitimizing the everyday speech convention of D-Mark (for West Germany) and Mark (for the GDR). The label used for the inferior East currency, *Mark der Deutschen Demokratischen Republik* or simply Mark, was legally inscribed in 1967.[8] It is no coincidence, then, that the apogee of the many symbolic acts uniting the two Germanies in 1989–1990, even before the formal dissolution of the East German State, was the elimination of the East Mark and its replacement by the West German D-Mark in the GDR.

Disputation over naming at the national level, as in the example of the Currency Reform of 1948, has direct consequences for international and local politics. The victor in such a contest can claim success only when international actors (other states and multinational organizations) and local actors (their own nationals) affirm their choice of names by utilizing them in everyday discourse. These two contexts, of international and domestic legitimacy, were acutely significant for the two postwar German states, for both contexts could call into question their fragile sovereignty. It should be kept in mind that prior to the twentieth century Western states developed within a historical process unique to their societies. The two German states founded in 1949, contrariwise, were artificial products, fictions of an international order given a kind of virgin birth by their superpower patrons; they were in no way indigenous creations, although their legitimacy was often dependent on their passing as such. In family law, as in other domains, both states initially sought to legitimize their legal reforms by claiming they spoke, not only for their particular half (nation), but for all of Germany.

The position of West Germany on the relation of the nation to the state, written into the *Grundgesetz*, Basic Law, of 1949, has always been simple: there is only one German nation into which one is born (with minor exceptions) and this nation needs and has only one legitimate state, the Federal Republic. The preamble to the Basic Law even obligates the Federal Republic "to protect the national and state unity of Germany," by which is meant all Germans in the territory of the former German Reich. East German leaders had a more difficult time with the concept of a German nation, for they claimed an identity based primarily on international, socialist ideology. For the first twenty-five years of the state's existence, East German leaders argued for a Germany ultimately reunited, but, as declared in Article 1 of the 1949 Constitution, only in a "socialist state of the German nation." Article 8 of the 1968 Constitution retained the insistence on a Germany united under a socialist system, but notably also recognized "two German states" with equal rights. Thereafter the state also began to speak as if it had its own (separate) nation.

In 1974, the leadership changed the Constitution accordingly, omitting the phraseology from Article 1 and replacing it with references to one "*Volk* of the German Democratic Republic," consisting of "a socialist state of workers and farmers." The ruling Socialist United Party (SED) thus rejected all connections with German nationness within a single German state, preferring to reimagine themselves as cultural Germans inhabiting a socialist state. They reasoned that socialism had been achieved in a mere twenty-five years, and that the nation was now socialist as opposed to capitalist.

By the mid 1980s the leadership had reversed itself again, reclaiming elements of German history, in particular Frederick the Great, Bismarck, and the Prussian tradition, as their own. Their efforts to legitimate themselves by grounding the state in a past national identity, one that relied on tradition, came too late, however.

All along for domestic reasons both the GDR and West Germany had to pay obeisance to *Wiedervereinigung*, the potential reunification of the two territories – hence the vacillations of the East German regime. But by the early fifties it was already apparent that if it did ever come to fruition, reunification would threaten the existence of the East German regime as well as change the power structures of West German political parties. Since the ruling SED in the East was not able to plan an economy that could keep pace with the Federal Republic, whatever political legitimacy it attained on other fronts just as quickly disappeared into the quicksand of its growing economic swamp. By 1961 the leadership decided to contain its population by force in order to maintain the territorial division initially conceived as a temporary political solution.

In this process of mirror-imaging, the two states fabricated themselves as moieties in a dual organization. The catchphrase in the West was "integration into the West"; leaders pointed the finger at the "totalitarian East Zone," and simultaneously embraced many formal aspects of the liberal-democratic model of their occupation forces, above all free-market capitalism and parliamentary democracy. In the East, policy was initially directed toward negation of what the Germans in the Third Reich had been; leaders depicted themselves first and foremost as anti-fascist and anti-war. Very soon, however, they began to represent themselves in positive terms – as democratic and socialist – and began to take on concrete and enduring characteristics, often borrowed from the Stalinist model of the Soviets. In this battle of state-building, the concrete practices of past Nazism quickly dropped out of contention as the mirror-image against which the present was viewed. Furthermore, the fight was asymmetrical from the start: the Western Zones/FRG initiated every major confrontation – Currency Reform, state founding, remilitarization, NATO/Warsaw Pact formation – leaving the smaller and weaker East Zone/GDR with little choice but to respond and oppose.

Much as nineteenth-century socialist theory was a response to capitalist practice, the proposal for a socialist GDR was a response to the actually existing capitalism in West Germany. In only one domain did Eastern leaders take the initiative, and that was in kinship reconstruction. Yet these reforms brought the GDR minimal advantage, for the quickly developing Cold War created new anxieties among the populace that soon dampened whatever enthusiasm initially existed for structural reforms of any sort. In West Germany, the desire for stasis and normalization was expressed in the very successful 1950s campaign

slogan of the conservative Christian Democrats: "No Experiment."
Western Allies themselves quickly lost interest or even turned hostile to
efforts at internal domestic reconstruction, which they began to assoc-
iate with communist totalitarianism and to contrast with the already
existing patriarchal–bourgeois structures. Nazism and its relation to
authoritarian structures of domestic life quickly became taboo in both
private and public life in the West.

## Changing topography

This book is centrally concerned with the relation of the state to
everyday life. It focuses on patterns of belonging during a forty-four-
year period, 1945–1989, within a divided Berlin, and proceeds by
comparing the commentaries about belonging of individuals and states
as they interact with each other. The relation of states to local
communities finds its most direct articulation at border sites such as
Berlin, where the development of national boundaries is most ambiguous and thus of marked strategic importance to the state. If states are
more centrally defined by their territorial than their political sovereignty, as Peter Sahlins (1988) has argued about the border between
France and Spain, then the city of Berlin (West) was an inherently
destabilizing factor for the East German state, always challenging its
political sovereignty. At such border sites not only do states challenge
each other's commentaries by disputing significations, actions, and
territories, but also citizens in their everyday lives arrive at their own
significations and needs, contesting these among themselves as well as
disputing the official versions put forth by the state. In this book I shall
be moving between levels that are usually either conflated or framed
separately – state, nation, generation, and practice. Because of the
continual oscillation between different perspectives and action domains,
I may predispose the reader to a feeling of vertigo. Such is the nature of
belonging, however, that it is more a signification that shifts than a
property that adheres, more a meaning revealed in movement than a
character viewed in repose.

The ability to name or categorize, as the examples in the previous
section indicate, becomes significant when the name indexes a category
of belonging, when the name serves to classify either a category of
ownership or membership. Kinship categorization is one way, perhaps
the generic way, of getting from naming systems to patterns of belonging. This explains both why anthropologists have long argued that
kinship is a primordial system of signification and why kinship systems

show such tenacity over time. Kinship never dies.[9] At the same time, though, kin membership is an arena of political conflict where meanings are disputed and changing. Contrary to *Notes and Queries on Anthropology* (1912), the charter text for ethnographic fieldwork, kinship as a system is not readily demarcated from economic, religious, and governmental domains.[10]

This book argues that kinship membership is the topos on which "nationness"[11] is mapped. Because kinship is a constitutive element of nationness, it indexes categories of belonging essential to a state's claim to legitimacy in representing a nation. Hence, during the Cold War kinship in Berlin remained the major social field of political contestation between the Germanies. I follow the transformations in kinship practices by examining the categories of belonging in life histories of two generations of East and West Berliners. In their reconstructions individuals order experiences around the repetition of specific *experiential tropes*, which then draw on *master narratives* provided by the state. Both analytical terms are explained in more detail in the next chapter. These master narratives unite individuals as a generational group and demarcate them from other generations. A narrative analysis of state edicts and autobiographies brings the state and everyday life into the same interpretive frame, allowing for a dynamic, experience-based understanding of the ongoing processes of differential nation-building and state legitimation in the two Berlins.

For Berliners, kinship categorization was perhaps of even greater significance, at both the personal and the political levels, than it was for other West or East Germans. The significance of kinship was not due to divisions generated by the Berlin Wall – to the rest of the world *the* symbol of familial, national, and international division. The imagined political communities comprising East and West Germany *antedated* the building of the Wall. Division of the city by the Wall in 1961 was, in essence, a result and consequence of national-ideological and familial disputes growing out of the dual state structures; the Wall did not create them. It did, however, heighten the consciousness about and politicize the issue of family membership.

At the personal level, Berliners experienced the conflicting claims on belonging more immediately than other Germans, simply because they lived on the border, either walled-in or walled-out from the other half of their city. At the political level, both states looked to kinship categories as a quasi-natural model for the structuring of nationality and citizenship. Because the two states publicly contested each other's membership categories, Berliners were quite aware of the arbitrary, political nature of belonging and therefore active in manipulating the official classifications. Categories of belonging, including terms such as "relative," "family occasion," and *deutschstämmig* (of German descent), were frequently invoked catchwords in fights between the two states and their citizenry concerning allowable, legitimate, and preferred kin relations.

The city of Berlin, as former national capital and arguably the only German metropolis, was the major site where the two states competed for control over visions and representations of the future of the German nation(s), functioning both as an object of contestation and an arena in which allegiances were contested. West Berlin, cut off from its main territorial center (West Germany) and from its cultural *habitus* (Western Europe), was reduced to a city on the periphery, a mere stage for power displays emanating from elsewhere, its political status dependent on the politics of the superpowers, its economic feasibility on the goodwill of West Germany. Only in the domain of *Kultur* could it make its own history. East Berlin operated under many of the same constraints, but with two major differences: it had gained stature by becoming the capital city of the GDR in 1949, and by the mid seventies had become the economic showplace of the European socialist world. Both of these distinctions, however, were more important to the leadership than to the East Berlin populace, for the two saw their reflections in different mirrors; the state looked East to Moscow for direction and support, the people looked to West Berlin.

Much as the lives of its residents underwent a series of transformations since World War II, so did the topography of Berlin. On May 8, 1945, the Soviets occupied Berlin and it lost its status as capital city of the Reich. In everyday speech, Berlin was reduced from *Reichshauptstadt* to *Reichstrümmerstadt*, from Capital of the Empire to Capital of Rubble. On June 5, 1945, the United States and Britain traded with the Soviets their conquered parts of Saxony, Thuringia, and Mecklenburg for parts of Berlin, and on July 3 and 4, they occupied their zones in Berlin. The French entered their Berlin zone four days later. Although this initial geopolitical mapping persisted through 1989, the cultural significations of this topos were unstable and changed radically. After the postwar division of Central Europe into American and Soviet influence/control zones, Berlin lost its traditional meanings within the prewar Central European cultural–political configuration. It simultaneously gained new significance, however, as *Frontstadt*, the site of the Cold War, with its appropriate East (Soviet-dominated) and West

(American-dominated) parts, and was quickly reterritorialized, materially and ideologically. The West was soon the rich zone, the East the "poor brother"; the West called itself free, the East democratic and socialist.

But while the West may have been economically stronger than the East, West Berlin no longer had a secure political status. West Berlin politicians thus latched on to their special meaning for the Cold War, hoping to secure the loyalties of the Americans and West Germans, and to integrate the city into the newly constituted Western European political–cultural–geographical entity. During the Berlin Blockade in 1948, soon-to-be Mayor of West Berlin Ernst Reuter passionately called on the Berliners to fight for their freedom, the enemy threat coming from the "Pankow Regime" in the other half of their city. West Berliners were exhorted not to use the GDR-owned S-Bahn, not to work in the East, and not to have their hair cut or to buy food in the East. East Berliners, at the same time, were being exhorted to become socialists: to contribute to the construction of the new society, to involve themselves in official organizations, and to avoid any contact with people from "the West." *Einheit*, unity, was the divisive buzzword most frequently appealed to on both sides.

Minimally until the building of the Wall, then sporadically thereafter, Berliners were squeezed by a continuous vacillation between a policy of *Abgrenzungspolitik*, demarcation, and a policy of integration: either you are my opposite or you become who I already am. Everyday life intersected with politics everywhere in Berlin; both states began contesting all action domains. The surreal nature of the division of the city as it affected everyday life in the mid fifties is described in a report written for *Süddeutsche Zeitung* on December 9, 1955, by Gabriel Müller out of Berlin:

For some of those [visitors from West Germany], East Berlin already lies behind the Ural Mountains and they think that the Iron Curtain is a real wall that cuts across the city of a million residents. The Berliners have become used to this condition in the seven years since the division . . . [She offers the following example.] Herr Nonberliner wants to cross over again at Potsdamer Platz to West-Berlin, but he has both West and East money with him; he can be penalized for having both. At least theoretically. In reality, the West visitor can travel on the street cars, use the telephone, or go to the theater in the Soviet Sector only for East money, but only for West money can he have a cup of coffee for 1 Mark 20 Pfennig [$5.00] in an East Berlin restaurant. He is not able to buy anything in the East shops, whether that be a bread roll or a fur coat, neither with West nor with East money.

The West German visitor shakes his head. It appears to him uncanny, the things that one can eat only with the forbidden West money, and the forbidden East money with which alone one can pay to ride on the streetcar.

Cars are going back and forth from West to East and East to West through the Brandenburger Tor. Is, then, the traffic at least not divided? West cars may go to the East, but East cars cannot leave the "democratic sector." Only a few artists, doctors, or engineers who live in West Berlin but work in the Soviet Sector have a special approval certificate, which they must show everytime they cross the border . . .

Only one time in the history of the divided city did the Iron Curtain actually go through the whole city: That was the 17th of June, 1953.[12]

Since the June Barricade was removed, the traffic in the Four Powers city is again free . . . One can cross approximately 100 streets along the 40 kilometer border between West Berlin and the East Sector. And one can use a bicycle on six or eight crossings. There is only one thing a West Berliner cannot do: He cannot telephone any of the 1.2 million East Berliners. The cable was cut three years ago . . .[13]

Neither Berlin could indefinitely rally loyalty around its Cold War status. By the early fifties, West Berlin was also calling itself the showcase of the West, a reputation based on ostentatious displays of consumer wealth. The foremost symbol of *West-Konsum* is KaDeWe, the mammoth Luxus-Tempel at Wittenberg Platz on Ku-Damm, fully destroyed during the war and reopened in 1950. KaDeWe, which alone employs 2,400 workers, offers in its grocery section, for example, 1,800 kinds of cheese, 400 kinds of bread, and 150 different sorts of ham. East Berlin, after becoming capital city in 1949, moved onto the itinerary of statesmen, even though initially only *Ostblock* statesmen. At the same time the Federal Republic turned its back on Berlin (West) and situated its capital in the small, provincial town of Bonn.

The rather clear and opposed political self-representations of the two halves were initially much less clear and oppositional in the everyday practices of the populace. Yet the odd fixation during the fifties upon the imagined Iron Curtain, described in the account of Gabriel Müller, became a self-fulfilling prophecy. The building of the "real wall" by the East Germans, then, should have come as no surprise; it was, in fact, a realization of what already had been a divided community in the political imagination of the residents. Yet those imagined differences, it should be stressed, were more ideological than political in nature. Only after 1961 were the two halves completely demarcated into moieties – ideologically, politically, and in praxis. Thereafter membership in the political system became the a priori legal principle of classification, taking precedence over all other memberships.

A visit to the city in 1949 by the Berlinophile, W. H. Auden, resulted in the following perspicacious lines (1979: 193–194):

Across the square,
Between the burnt-out Law Courts and Police Headquarters,
Past the Cathedral far too damaged to repair,
Around the Grand Hotel patched up to hold reporters,
Near huts of some Emergency Committee,
The barbed wire runs through the abolished City.

Behind the wire
Which is behind the mirror, our Image is the same
Awake or dreaming: It has no image to admire,
No age, no sex, no memory, no creed, no name,
It can be counted, multiplied, employed
In any place, at any time destroyed.

Is it our friend?
No; that is our hope; that we weep and It does not grieve,
That for It the wire and the ruins are not the end:
This is the flesh we are but never would believe,
The flesh we die but it is death to pity;
This is Adam waiting for His City.

Auden's lines are touching in their lament for what was "abolished" and telling in their refusal to believe that "the wire and the ruins are . . . the end." His obsession with "barbed wire" was, of course, a projection of a

Figure 3.  The Wall, December 1989.

truly divided Berlin that did not yet exist. The border remained porous until 1961; people passed back and forth with relative ease.

In a visit to Berlin in 1958, Carlo Levi focused on Auden's suspicion that "behind the mirror, our Image is the same." He crossed the border many times daily, seeing

in the two Berlins – pathetic sisters of inner bondage . . . Each of the two parts seemed to have chosen what the other had forsaken . . . Like actors, they took on the looks and desires of those who wanted them to be opposed. They faced each other like two champions of different cultures, without any possible contact. But they were champions of the same mold. Whoever observed them without their arbitrary and make-believe fierceness, realized that in that very arbitrariness, in that fierceness, in that nonexistence, in that desperation, they were identical.                                                                    *(1962: 126–130)*

Certainly the Berlins were identical in their artifice, in their determination to portray duality; but then, in this they were simply exaggerated versions of much of the rest of the world. Moreover, whereas duality is not a characteristic of all cultures, artifice is. All cultural performances worth taking note of contain elements of ingenious trickery. And to the extent that the Berlins took on the divisions of the Cold War, they were simply Cold War culture writ large.

The barbed wire and the Wall notwithstanding, in the seventies the two states reconciled themselves to normalizing the situation, hence steadily readjusting the mutually exploitative relationship between the Berlins. West Berlin had long been a hot spot and a thorn in the side for politicians in both German states, but it also functioned as a fulcrum in forcing the two states to communicate with each other. Since neither German state could ignore West Berlin, they were continually confronted with each other's presence in, or by, that part of the city. This was much less true for the majority of West and East German citizens who lived outside the Berlins. Their relation to *die drüben*, those over there, as the other side was called, was based on pure fantasy. For the West Germans, the connection rested on a projection of the meaning of Germanness onto the other: *Ossies* were a mirror-image, a replica waiting to join them in a whole Germany. For the East Germans, fantasies of the West were formed primarily by images from West German television: *Wessies* are the desired other, richer, more successful, more powerful.

Although East Germans could not easily ignore the alien, forbidden city in their midst, West Germans could, precisely because for them the city was a distant territory in an enemy state. Moreover, the vast majority of West Berliners adjusted to living in their territorial anomaly by avoiding travel in East Berlin and the GDR; many younger West Berliners never visited the East, some crossed the border only to travel to West Germany or southern Europe. Hence the irony before the opening of the Wall was that while contact between the two states increased over time, contact between the citizens decreased with age. For a growing number of younger West Germans, Berlin became a theoretical, abstract issue, a political topic and not a living city. The West German government almost wholly subsidized grade-school trips to West Berlin, thereby hoping to keep younger generations aware that West Berlin was, in effect, part of their republic. Yet by 1988 most West German grade-school classes preferred traveling to Italy, Spain, or Greece rather than to West Berlin.[14]

The nature of differentiation between the cities changed over time, determined in large part by state goals, though the surreality of it did not. During my fieldwork in Berlin several aspects of the changing modes of relationship between state policy and everyday practice seemed most perverse. Official East German maps of its territory did not color in West Berlin. Their maps of subway and street-car lines showed West Berlin as a self-contained blank, diminished in size with no streets and no entry points from the GDR. West Berlin maps, on the other hand, reduced East Berlin, wherein the old city center lies, to the margin of the larger city, decentered but still connected to the whole; the territorial boundary between the two halves was but lightly marked (see figures 4 and 5).

In West Berlin, one could legally buy East German Marks at the rate of between five and ten to one, but it was illegal to carry these marks into the GDR. For West Berliners, it was illegal to buy any goods at the GDR-owned and run Intershops in the West Berlin U-Bahn station at Friedrichstraße, which was also the most frequently used border crossing between the two cities. Yet these shops existed solely for the East to obtain Western currency from West Berliners. For West Berliners, the purchase was legal only if they were returning from an official trip to the East with proof of the compulsory one-to-one 25-Mark exchange. East Germans called this a "minimal exchange"; West Germans complained bitterly about it, and called it a "forced exchange."

Down-and-out West Berlin drunks bought their liquor from the Intershops at Friedrichstraße, rode the (at that time GDR-owned) S-Bahn through West and East Berlin until it closed, then often slept in

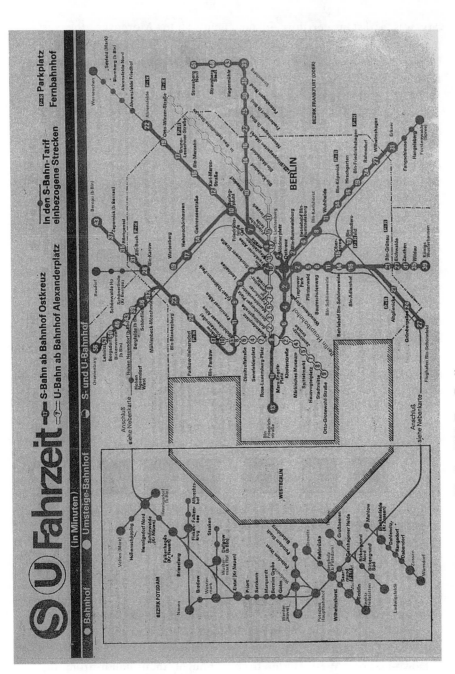

Figure 4.  U- and S-Bahn map of Berlin, 1988, East Berlin.

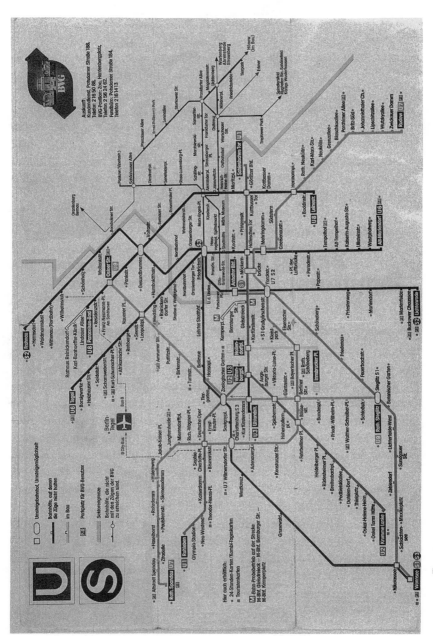

Figure 5.  U– and S-Bahn map of Berlin, 1988, West Berlin.

the Friedrichstraße station (which lies in East Berlin territory) until the subway reopened in the morning. If the drunks seemed to be the West's curse on the East, or at least on its major border crossing, the East cursed (or blessed, depending on one's point-of-view) West Berlin by sending/selling its dissidents there. West Berlin, not to be outdone, disposed of nearly all its garbage in antiquated East German dumps (West Germany refused to share with the GDR its most recent technology). The East German "Worker and Farmer State," as it officially called itself, was paid well, of course, in coveted Western currency for undergoing the humiliation of poisoning its own population with West German and West Berlin pollutants.[15]

**Constituting meaningful subjects**
Since the introduction of modern kinship studies in anthropology by Bronislaw Malinowski and E. R. Radcliffe-Brown, ethnographers have investigated the relationship of kin groupings to economic and political organization. Although kin definitions have often been (wrongly) viewed ahistorically, meaning having nothing to do with *periodization*, they have nonetheless been observed to be integral to *categorization* schemes that determine patterns of belonging within social groups. This means that conflicts over the right to name and categorize are generally agreed to be primary instances of power conflicts within social groups. Anthropologists have thus routinely classified societies according to their kinship structures, often using as their unit of analysis naming systems. It is kinship patterning, according to a basic anthropological axiom, which is the decisive factor of societal organization for non-Western peoples, the vertebra of traditional political systems. Yet nearly all academics, including most anthropologists, exempt contemporary Western societies from this axiom.

British legal scholar Sir Henry Maine and classicist George Grote initially formulated the notion that kinship-based polities, organized along the lines of descent and exogamy, were superceded by a territorial state which ordered property relations. This belief was later popularized by the pioneering American anthropologist Lewis Henry Morgan in his influential study *Ancient Society* (1877).[16] Rather than viewing the process of kinship formation and nation-building dialectically, this particular logic, reproduced in one form or another by subsequent generations of scholars, argued from a linear, evolutionary perspective. Meyer Fortes and E.E. Evans-Pritchard, for example, in their pathbreaking introduction to *African Political Systems*, nonetheless followed

Maine and Morgan exactly in arguing that there were two types of societies, one with states and one stateless, the former characterized by "centralized authority, administrative machinery and judicial institutions – in short a government," the latter by the *lack* of those institutions (1940: 4). State-centered societies were organized by a territorial principle, stateless societies by kinship. The conclusion drawn from these assumptions was that if one were to concentrate on social groups organized under a state, then kinship must be left behind.[17]

Social scientists of European societies readily grant, therefore, that kinship was a major political factor in an earlier time, perhaps prior to the eighteenth and nineteenth centuries, in the epochs before states and national groupings began occupying the landscape. The key variables in this organizational shift, according to most theorists, were the advent of the state following the French Revolution, and the subsequent appropriation of "the nation" by the state as its most powerful organizing principle. Since then, moreover, changing forms of economic organization have supposedly resulted in new forms of loyalty, membership, and belonging not based on kin membership. In their discussions of national patterns of belonging, most political scientists and sociologists have defined nationality as this new determinant of modern belonging, and have defined this in terms of ideological persuasion or "opinions" about state and/or national loyalties, avoiding more substantive, intersubjective definitions related to practices.[18]

According to this research paradigm, the "nation-state" and "everyday life" are defined as ontologically separate domains, so that the political is what happens on a large scale and the domestic or everyday (often called "civil society") is what happens on a small scale. States, so the conventional wisdom goes, produce policies not people. Domestic life is considered primarily an intra- or inter-individual affair handed on from one generation to the next, and if at all affected by the state, only by policy from without. The empirical link between state activities and everyday life has been difficult to infer precisely because of the academic division of labor between policy studies of *objective conditions* on the one hand and individual interaction studies of *subjective meanings* on the other. Both states and individuals are, after all, coeval cultural constructs; they belong in the same frame.

Contemporary anthropologists, too, with some important exceptions, have contributed to this schema by refusing to make the leap from naming systems at the local level to larger patterns and contexts of belonging, such as citizenship. The renowned British anthropologist

Ernest Gellner, for example, who has made important contributions to the analysis of kinship and of the state, has consistently refused to link the two domains when dealing with the modern West. Instead he prefers to examine how a holistic, "universal high culture" within a politically centralized state spawns a voluntaristic form of nationalism, leaving the relation of kinship (and everyday life) to nationness and to the state entirely aside.[19]

From this putative schism between everyday action and the state the conclusion often drawn is that domestic life, the traditional object of anthropological study, is non political, thus trivial. Given this definition of domains, most research on the state is so general that it cannot account for the specifics of daily life, and most research on everyday life is so narrowly defined that it cannot account for the role of state agents in its construction. One way out of this dilemma, I suggest, is to situate at the center of study not the state and individual or the political and everyday as discrete actors or domains of investigation, but to shift focus to the *constitution of meaningful subjects*.[20] The object of study, then, is neither objective conditions nor subjective meanings, but instead the *meaning of the subject*.

How, with what mechanisms, did the two German states try to produce different subjects in the postwar Berlin, and what particular subjectivities have been constructed? Three interlocking subjectivities are particularly important in the postwar dispute over Germanness: kinship, nationness, and citizenship. Moreover, it is precisely around belonging to a nation that kinship and the state come together in a single frame.

Given the widespread suspicion that German fascism grew out of authoritative state and family behavioral models, postwar reconstruction of the domains of kin, nation, and state has been a particularly sensitive and thoroughly politicized affair. Through what kind of kin policy did the two states seek to name, periodize, and categorize the subject so as to control the terms in which belonging to the nation were constituted? I am defining kinship substantively, as the structuring of belonging patterns to realize specific kinds of everyday relationships which follow a particular trajectory over a lifecourse. This definition enables us to take into account the historicity of belonging patterns, for it avoids fixing the definition of kin to a specific set of affinal or consanguinal arrangements. Recent fights among scientists and politicians concerning the definition of "families" are not innocent disputes about naming an empirical reality, but, in fact, are attempts to impose a rigid, unchanging meaning on living structures that are multiform, historically sensitive, and in practice exceptionally fluid over a life-course.[21]

Everyday relationships and interaction routines that are unique to a particular group form the basis for feeling *zu Hause*, at home, in one place and not in another. To feel at home is to be among kin. This *zu Hause*-identity is created only when an individual experiences a particu-lar set of lifecourse meanings enabling him or her to belong to a group demarcated from other groups. Over time such everyday relationships become the criteria for national identifications, for a sense of nation-ness. This hypothesis is much in agreement with the argument of Norbert Elias (1978) that European national distinctions and loyalties initially grew out of routinized everyday behaviors. But unlike Elias, I shall argue that in postwar Berlin the dissemination of interaction routines partakes more of a concentric diffusion across and between groups than a hierarchical flow from upper classes to those at the bottom. In other words, class structure and the will of elites influence but do not play a determinative role in regulating the diffusion of models for everyday relationships.

In the modern world system of nation-states, the ultimate long-term legitimation of a particular nation-state grouping, such as the French or the Swiss or the Americans, is wholly dependent upon the extent to which that state can claim to represent a specific national identity unique to it, meaning that it has people with characteristics it can call its own. The discourse about kinship, inscribed in autobiographical accounts, indexes these very characteristics, the categories of belonging essential to nationness. Accordingly, although the Federal Republic and the GDR came close to full diplomatic recognition, to recognizing each other's existence as sovereign states, they continued to fight over the nature of the nation, the signification of "German."

At the national level, the struggle over control of meaning concerns making people's life constructions coterminous with periodizations given by the state, which then uses the classification schema that grows out of this periodization to characterize the society within its borders. The state seeks thereby to "institutionalize the lifecourse" (Kohli 1985: 1–29) of its citizens.[22] If citizens periodize and categorize their own biographies in ways congruent with the model lifecourse projected by the state, they legitimate their state's claim to represent them. To the extent that the two German states were successful in differentiating the lifecourse of their citizens from those in the other Germany, they created a congruence between personal narrative histories and the state's version of history. In this double maneuver with regard to nation-building – demarcation by the states from each other and congruence between their accounts and those of their citizens – states legitimate their respective claims on a nation. In short, states are successful in nation-building when they (re)create a unique group which retells its history in categories and periods congruent with those used by the state in its own accounts.

The conversation about the nation between states and citizens, marked throughout by coercion due to essential power asymmetries, rarely produces the clear victory that many states would like to claim. Moreover, the state is not the only societal instance encountered by the individual, nor do its interactions, when compared to those of other institutions, such as churches or schools, produce the most predictable outcome. Yet precisely because the dialogue is so distorted by the effects of power and so intense due to sustained interactions over a lifecourse, it generates constant self-deception (often telling each other exactly what one wants to hear) and paradox. The unpredictability of the outcome does not detract from its significance, but infuses the interaction with the affect peculiar to an experiment in operant conditioning.

Furthermore, the power asymmetry does not work in one direction, for a state may claim a monopoly on the uses of space and the instruments of violence, but an individual has more control over the uses of time and the instruments of reflection. To account for how this nation is constituted in interaction, we might here map the useful distinction made by Michel de Certeau between tactics and strategies onto individuals and states. He writes, "[Strategies] conceal beneath objective calculations their connection with the power that sustains them from within the stronghold of its own 'proper' place or institution," while a tactic is "a calculus which cannot count in a 'proper' [a spatial or institutional localization]. The proper is a victory of space over time" (1984: xx, xix). State strategies, embodied in powerful legal and political commentaries, are never, as we shall see, able to uniformize the lifecourse of their citizens. But they do set the aesthetic and ideational framework in which experiences are categorized and periodized. Only in interaction with the state's narrative do individual experiences gain coherence by obtaining a group, *ergo* generational, identity.

States regulate the lifecourse with the use of normalizing strategies that define the particular categories of the self which can be said to signify Germanness. Following Michel Foucault (1981), these strategies involve the use of three analytically separable techniques: of signification, communication, and self. At the level of signification techniques, the two states intended to create differently valued objects (both people and things) through oppositional naming of similar experiences. The fight over significations was most clearly exemplified in such terms as *Flüchtling* (refugee) in the West counterposed to the fabricated label *Umsiedler* (resettler) in the East, used to name the 12 million individuals who were driven or fled from their homes in the East Prussian territories between 1944 and 1950; or *übersiedeln* (verb: to move), used until 1961 in the East to describe the act of moving from one Germany to the other, thereafter taken over by West Germany as the noun *Übersiedler*, with the GDR then using the noun *Verräter* (traitor) to describe their citizens who emigrated. West Germans also use the word *Aussiedler* (emigrant) for *Volksdeutsche* (people of German blood living in Eastern Europe or the USSR, not including the GDR) who are trying to "return" to West Germany; those who moved to West Germany after the Helsinki Accords in 1975 are called *Spätaussiedler* (late emigrant). And with the tremendous increase in 1988 of *Aussiedler* from Eastern Europe (primarily Poland), West German officials began using *Zuwanderer* (immigrant) to distinguish those *Aussiedler* people resettling from the other German state. Resettlers from East Germany – because, according to the FRG Basic Law, they had a constitutional right to West German citizenship – received special economic benefits once in West Germany.

The economic history after the founding of the two postfascist states serves as a salient example of counter-periodization, with *Wirtschaftswunder* (economic miracle) in the West counterposed to *Aufbau* (construction) in the East. Or in the domain of experiential naming, the particular individuals who suffered during the Nazi period in ways that make them deserving of special postwar treatment were called *Verfolgte des Naziregimes* (persecuted by the Nazis) in the West counterposed to *Opfer des Faschismus* (victims of fascism) in the East.[23] This endeavour to create new significations often revolved around fights over the meanings of the same words, such as "democracy" and "freedom," or the same product labels, such as "made in Germany." And it extended, of course, to the meaning of German citizenship and the evaluation of German culture.

At the level of communication techniques, the struggle between the two states focused on the regulation of new relationships to others. This involved defining both the terms and content of a relationship, with whom specific types of relationships are legitimate. Equal rights for the sexes, for example, meant something quite different for the two states, though that meaning steadily changed. In the East, it initially meant first and foremost equality in the fields of education and work. Until the seventies in the West, so-called natural differences between the sexes were used to justify sex-specific legal and policy positions maintaining unequal treatment of men and women. Oppositional policies regarding NATO and Warsaw Pact integration also had direct consequences for relationships across international borders, manifested in, for example, marriage preference policies that made it difficult to marry a citizen of another country, and doubly difficult if that country did not belong to the same military block as one's own. Communication techniques also focused on redefining the relations of partners to each other or parents to children through, for example, refusing to recognize legally *Lebens-gemeinschaften* (non-marital partnerships), redefining "parental authority," or coining the term *alleinstehende Eltern* (single parents) in order to establish a legal relationship with non-married caretakers of children.

Self techniques were contested at more banal domains through periodizing and naming the subjective experiencing of lifecourse stages. What were, precisely, children, youth, mothers, married women, or retired people? What legal status did individuals have as they took on particular categories of self? Were all children, for example, supposed to be equally supported in educational opportunities (as in the GDR), or was the opportunity dependent on the proof of early merit by the child or contingent on the amount of cultural and economic capital of the parents (as in the FRG)? And how did this early definition of the child affect his/her lifecourse trajectory? Or, for example, when a man and woman married, did they become married selves and part of a "family" (as was the final legal version in the GDR), set apart from other men and women who engaged in the same practices but did not marry? Or, was such a legal union of "marrieds" defined as a family only when there were also dependent children (as is the current legal version in the FRG)? At what point in time or under what conditions did such individuals lose their "family" status? Was it after divorce of a partner (as in the GDR) or after the loss of dependent children (as in the FRG)?

States prefer a particular set of self-transformations at any time, but this preference results not merely in individual acquiescence, as we shall see, but also in a calculated adaptation to such formally given state ends and categories. Do citizens seek to develop into the kind of person the state wants them to be? Do they narrate their lives the way the state expects them to? These three techniques, of signification, communication, and self, are separable only analytically. In practice, they often fold into each other, at times so harmoniously as to blur their distinctiveness; at other times, they separate so incongruously as to appear autonomous. Together, they were deployed to create the categories of self necessary to construct the desired genus of German kin, nation, and state.

Despite the international and national political contexts, the decisive fights over which words, which people, or which goods can be exchanged are carried on by local actors with local meanings. By assigning specific significations to words, people, and goods – through naming and periodizing – people construct their lives in terms of shared and meaningful categories.

Having used the conflict over naming, categorizing, and periodizing as my introduction, I shall turn to historical details as my point of departure. First, I must make a theoretical excursion not germane to my narrative. This excursion is not "out of history" – the high ground Lévi-Strauss, writing during the heyday of objective social science, had hoped anthropology could reach – but, in fact, is an attempt to historicize my own place in the narration. The next chapter clarifies the concepts and methods of the study.

# 2

# Clarification of concepts

## An ethnography of the nation

The classic statement on ethnographic method, by Bronislaw Malinowski, the father of modern fieldwork, that one must begin from "the native's point of view," is still considered, some seventy years later, an axiom of anthropological research. Like all axioms after seventy years of practice, however, it is now more a statement of the problem than its solution, more an orientation than an answer. Not only do natives differ among themselves and over time as to what things mean, but native symbology rarely has identical counterparts in the ethnographer's world. Ethnographers are now asking: "Whose life?", "What meanings?", "And when?", "Which ethnographer?" The issues that Malinowski avoided – periodization, categorization, and classification – are now central to anthropological writing and research.

In response to positivist ethnography – the attempt to record culture, in all its facets, holistically and for all time – many anthropologists have taken what Clifford Geertz (1974: 47–53) has dubbed an "interpretive turn."[1] A focus on disputed symbols and contestable meanings, or what might be identified as a hermeneutic anthropology, does not so much regress ethnography to a crisis in representation as force an understanding of representation as a research *aporia*, an insoluble problem.[2] The task, then, is not to overcome or bracket the problems of representation, but to examine their process of constitution and efficacy. Taking into account the constraints of representation, writes Steven Lukes, "yields perhaps the only 'objectivity' that is possible in much of social enquiry." Anthropologists cannot hide behind "perspective neutrality," he continues, but must write "accounts that are not merely theory but also perspective-relative, yet constrained by evidence that is as systematic and reliable as possible, and relatable to other perspective-relative accounts. In applying them, one may explain from some perspective what could not be explained from no perspective" (1982: 305). In the narrative that follows, the initial meanings may be theirs, but the final story is mine. How do I justify the arbitrary choices I have made, the partiality, contingency, and incompleteness of my account?

In this book I explore the constitution of meaningful subjects during the postwar period in the two Berlins; I do this through a comparison of processes of narrativization. This conflict over narrativization centers on control over the meaning of the lifecourse of citizens, what is in essence their nationness; it is an arena of contestation and cooperation between generations as well as between the state and its citizens. I proceed by examining the narrative construction of the preferred lifecourse of citizens by the two German states and then compare these state commentaries with the life constructions of two generations in the two Berlins. Hence several comparisons are at constant play in my account: law and autobiography; state and citizen; a generation born before the war and one born after the war; East Berlin and West Berlin; GDR and FRG.

Five concepts are essential to my organization: experiential trope, master narrative, life construction, generation, and state. All of the information gathered and perspectives presented in this text are derived from individuals dealing with their own actual experiences, either in their own words or taken from my observations of their interactions, and from legal texts and policy statements. Individuals and states do not include all experiences or events in their stories, but rather select out specific nodes which are for them most significant in constructing a coherent narrative. Periods and categories are the devices used to structure narratives; together they make up what I shall call *experiential tropes*.

Tropes achieve their full meaning not at an individual level, but as part of a generational gestalt. Because they are themselves of indeterminate meaning, their potential polyvocality allows for different individuals with dissimilar experiences to utilize the same trope to figure a life story. It is only in their relation to the totality of a life, however, in their *emplotment* over time, that they become meaningful through regular appeals to *master narratives*. The state, in constant interaction with its citizens, seeks to unite these disparate experiential tropes into a single frame, a shared history of the nation; it does this by providing its own preferred master narratives, which can be found in legal texts, thereby legitimating (or failing to legitimate) both culturally and politically the nationness of the group. In sum, master narratives serve as public matrices for the creation of collective conscience; they give an over-arching meaning to a series of experiential tropes, and hence are politi-cally contested frameworks for constructing historical accounts.

Subjective, experience-based accounts of everyday meanings draw upon master narratives to form what I shall call *life constructions*. The life constructions are, in turn, significant for this study in that they reveal the relevant structured and structuring categories specific to a *generation*. In my written text, I do not follow the life of specific agents or events; instead, I classify practices (behaviors and understandings) of individual agents most significant for social continuities and discontinuities over time. These experiences are characteristic of a particular generation; hence individual lives are described and explained only insofar as they exemplify alternative responses to the problems of a generation. Before explaining these terms in more detail, let us examine the relationship between political narratives (the state's version of the lifecourse) and autobiography (the individual's version of the lifecourse).

### Law and autobiography

Remembrances, like those embedded in law or autobiography, take place within a Western culture that prides itself on the value of accurate reflection as a proper method of recovering the past. Yet legal texts and individual histories, which both derive their authority from what they say about social identities and therefore the meaning of the nation, are based on a very selective reading of events. In fact, "forgetting," writes Ernest Renan, "I would even go so far as to say historical error, is a crucial factor in the creation of a nation, which is why progress in historical studies often constitutes a danger for [the principle of] nationality" (1990: 11). It seems to be the case, therefore, that selectivity and significance, not universality and objectivity, are the principles behind remembering and forgetting in the construction of legal and individual narratives insofar as they are engaged in nation-building.

In their autobiographies, citizens select events and experiences not on the basis of some abstract principle of truth but rather because they are assumed to be significant for their lives. Unlike law and policy texts, personal recollections rarely attempt to divide history into discrete categories of political and domestic life, into a set of objective circum-stances and subjective responses. When people tell their life histories, they do not make the distinction between "historical knowledge" that is somehow true and what they say as mere opinion. On the other hand, lawyers and politicians often think of their texts as brute data that is not domestic and subjective, as somehow "objective" and therefore based more on knowledge and less on opinion. Yet the writers of law and policy, much like autobiographers, initially also apply principles of selection and significance, not those of universality and objectivity, when deciding what to address. Thus neither autobiography (memoirs) nor History proper (documents of state) is written based on knowledge accumulated primarily because of its objectivity or accuracy. Rather, the two textual genres share in common the characteristic of being human cultural artifacts that take the form of narratives. They (per)form by selectively fashioning diverse experiences into a form assimilable to structures of meaning and thereby, as Hayden White has argued, translate something *known* into something *told*. The relation of these two textual genres to narrative also has a history, though, to my knowledge, not yet written.

I suspect that history would assume the following plot: by the middle of the nineteenth century in the West the two activities of telling a personal history and telling the history of the group took on mutually exclusive characteristics. Succumbing to the pressures of state-building, historians began to naturalize national groups, writing for them nearly species-like histories. "The national state became the ultimate verity," writes Michael Herzfeld. "The state, the ultimate reification of social and cultural identity, displaced folklore with *Folklorismus*. In short, the totalizing ideologies of the era reduced the vagaries of social experience . . . to an intransigently invariant cultural *form*" (1987: 13–14). These "totalizing ideologies" were not new to European history, we might add, for other instances of institutionalized power, such as religion, village and city authorities, family and clan, were always attempting to reduce social experience to invariant forms. Yet Herzfeld is correct in noting how the state's narrative authority began to displace and subsume other voices.

During this period of state-building, individuals, on the other hand, were said to tell stories and remember folklore; their personal histories were contradistinctions to, parallel to but separate from, the history of the nation. European history, told from the perspectives of particular states, became increasingly a tool for nation-building and the consolidation of state boundaries (see Anderson 1983). As history became the captive of politics in its narrowest sense, personal accounts of common folk were increasingly regarded as bothersome, heretical, or dangerous, for they always threatened to contradict official accounts. To relegate personal accounts to the domain of folk wisdom and opinions rendered them safe; as such, they made no claims to speak for the present interests of the polity. In other words, the discourse of the state became knowledge, the discourse of the citizen became opinion.

Even before the founding of the German state, Hegel pronounced such a distinction in discourse types in defining the object of history:

> History combines in our language the objective as well as the subjective side. It means both the *historia rerum gestarum* and the *res gestae* themselves, both the events and the narration of the events. (It means both *Geschehen* and *Geschichte*.) This connection of the two meanings must be regarded as highly significant and not merely accidental. We must hold that the narration of history and historical deeds and events appear at the same time; a common inner principle brings them forth together. Family memorials, patriarchal traditions have an interest confined to the family and the tribe. The uniform course of events under such conditions is not an object for memory. But distinctive events or turns of fortune may rouse Mnemosyne to form images of them, just as love and religious sentiments stimulate the imagination to give shape to an originally formless impulse. But it is the State which first presents subject matter that is not only appropriate for the prose of history but creates it together with itself.
>
> *(1953: 75–76)*

For Hegel, there could be no history without the state to organize its narrative; families and clans, or as he goes on to say, "revolutions, migrations, and the wildest transformations," are "without objective history because they lack subjective history, records of history" (1953: 76).[3] In other words, a "political mode of human community," comments Hayden White, "made a specifically historical mode of inquiry possible, and the political nature of this mode of community . . . necessitated a narrative mode for its representation" (1984: 5). The advent of the state, as Hegel and White make clear, did indeed open the space for a narrative about History. And the opening of this space effectively created the illusion of a separation between public and private, between the political state and civil society.

It was this division that Marx, in "On the Jewish Question," most perceptively criticized:

> Where the political state has attained to its full development, man leads, not only in thought, in consciousness, but in *reality*, in *life*, a double existence – celestial and terrestrial. He lives in the *political community*, where he regards himself as a *communal being*, and in *civil society*, where he acts simply as a *private individual*, treats other men as means, degrades himself to the role of a mere means, and becomes the plaything of alien powers. The political state, in

relation to civil society, is just as spiritual as is heaven in relation to earth . . .
[In civil society] where [man] appears both to himself and to others as a real
individual he is an *illusory* phenomenon. In the state, on the contrary, . . .
man is the imaginary member of an imaginary sovereignty, divested of his real,
individual life, and infused with an unreal universality.        *(Tucker 1972: 43)*

This sacralization of the state's voice went hand-in-hand with
privatizing the voices of "communal beings," so that the state, from its
celestial position, ultimately gained a legitimate monopoly on voice in
historical representation. Yet both the object and subject of the state's
narrative is the nation, and the history of this nation, as an object of
representation, can be told from quite different perspectives, including, of course, from that of "a real individual" in his terrestrial
existence.

We might radicalize White's insight on the relationship of the
political community to its mode of historical representation by going beyond metahistorical accounts of the "political," and question altogether
the assumption that historiographers of the state offer a privileged or
particularly insightful representation of the nation. National history
resides in many sources, including, e.g., autobiographies. Though
much can be learned from descriptions of national communities based
on historiography, they remain one step removed from the original
official narrative of the nation: the inscriptions of the state, formed by
its literature of laws and policy. The discourse of political history
should, accordingly, not be restricted to the narrative of historians and
the commentary of politicians, but rather also be extended by
definition to their common sources – the narrative formed by laws and
state-sanctioned norms that attempt to shape the nature of belonging
patterns, and the narrative formed by the citizens' autobiographies of
their lifecourse. As I will illustrate in chapter 4, the official state
discourse can also be found directly in changing legislation, in the
evolution of legal norms formulated by states in their attempts to
shape the lifecourse of the nationals they claim to be their own.

Current interest by historians and philosophers in everyday life, kin
history, and oral stories is one attempt to recover individual remembrances either submerged or ignored largely because they had a
tenuous relationship to the political community. In confronting state
history (the mythmaking apparatus of national communities) with the
autobiographies of citizens (the object of History), my account will
not, however, try to judge the correctness of any particular story.
Instead I attempt to portray, through a kind of deep-figural analysis of

two genres of narratives, the relation of competing forms of narrative classification to the cultural and political legitimation of nation-building.

Narratives of both states and individuals are cultural fictions whose intent is to endow real events with mythical meanings. For the former they are allegories of group life, for the latter they are allegories of self. Neither account is a mere chronicle, for, while periodization is an essential aspect of the narration, there is an indefinite number of ways to order a sequence of events. Rather, chronological aspects of the narrative serve to construct a particular story; the story is not in service of the chronology. "Events are made into a story," explains White about how events take on meaning, "by the suppression or subordination of certain themes and the highlighting of others, by characterization, motific repetition, variation of tone and point of view, alternative descriptive strategies, and the like – in short, all of the techniques that we would normally expect to find in the emplotment of a novel or play" (1978b: 47).

Furthermore, the choice of periods and categories is not fixed by any universal rule, but is itself a product of imaginative constructions. Official state strategists as well as historians by trade must submit to the same rules of construction, the same *allegoresis*, as must individual citizens, for they all seek to construct coherent narratives with claims to represent something real – that is, a truth claim "not merely for each of its individual statements taken distributively, but for the complex form of the narrative itself" (Mink 1978: 143–144).

This claim to truth cannot be defended by any accepted procedure of argument or authentication, for neither the self nor the national community has a past with a narrative structure of its own to be discovered; the narrative itself simultaneously describes and constitutes the history. Here, in the relationship of narration to the past, we come to an important difference in the two types of stories. Because I had first to construct the two textual genres (autobiography and state accounts) in the field before I could determine their relation to one another, I encountered in writing an unexpected consequence of my particular ethnographic method:[4] the individual reconstructions, in the telling and writing, are retrospective accounts (genealogical narratives) from 1986–1989 back to 1945, whereas the state's history is already presented to me as a written reconstruction (historical narrative) of future-oriented sequential policy maneuvers by the two states from 1945–1949 to the present. With the benefit of hindsight the autobiographies are inscribed as linear accounts; with the pretension of foresight law reveals disconti-nuities. Unlike an individual, a state has, of course, no memory by which it can reconstruct anything. It cannot at any point in time tell you its history, though historiographers may take it upon themselves, often with state approval, to do so.[5]

The process which brings genealogical and historical narratives together into the same frame, that makes them dynamic and is a precondition for their effects, is neither their telling nor their writing; instead, we must look at them as works that are read. "The work," writes Wolfgang Iser, and under this term we can subsume both law and autobiography, "is more than the text, for the text only takes on life when it is realized, and furthermore the realization is by no means independent of the individual disposition of the reader – though this in turn is acted upon by the different patterns of the text. The convergence of text and reader brings the literary work into existence" (1989: 434). Rather than ask how laws are formulated and enacted, I ask about their virtual readings: what range of processes they support and how they are appropriated in specific ways over time. I use legal texts to reconstruct serially and chronologically the state's biographical plan for its citizens, and I use autobiographical accounts and interviews with citizens to assemble everyday life constructions.

A second consequence of my narrative choice is that individual and generational life constructions appear more static than the legal histories, when in fact they are not. The culture or symbol-in-the-making aspect of policy stands out, whereas the individuals appear, on the whole, to appropriate symbols almost mechanically and to confer meaning to objects without signs of the personal struggles and difficulties that necessarily accompany the process of making something meaningful. If I had relied more on participant observations or compared individual reconstructions from different times, my own narrative might appear less confident. Instead I listened to people's accounts of their histories, and I contextualized these primarily by relying on other historical documents. Their accounts await not a quantification or falsification, but a proper historicization either through reinterviewing them at another time or through archival work on their earlier life constructions. These methodological constraints necessarily limit this study to processes of meaning attribution; it only occasionally sheds light on processes of meaning-in-the-making.

The texts used in this investigation all deal with *historical* as opposed to *fictional* events, in that they make claims to represent experiences that really happened. I have not used what are known as purely literary accounts or fiction. The meaning and significance of these texts over time, their *cognitive* force, is not, however, based on a function of their "factuality," but rather, of their narrative form. It is in form that historical accounts resemble fictional ones and resort to the same linguistic conventions as do poets, playwrights, and novelists. I am not, however, thereby setting history against fiction in the nineteenth-century manner of identifying the former as truth and the latter as non-truth or myth. Rather, the narrative elements of historical texts are precisely the key to their interpretation. They do not hinder an understanding of what really happened, but indeed make it possible to apprehend experiences, rules, and events. In other words, linguistic devices give narrative form to stories, whether state or individual versions, without which they would be meaningless. The fact that individuals and groups think of themselves linguistically, namely, allegorically – that they themselves are allegoric constructions – does not make them any less real. It makes them comprehensible.

On the other hand, autobiographical narratives and policy texts share with each other, as *against* fictional accounts, a more rigorous truth claim regarding contents or the exactness of the details of the story. Given this genre-specific claim to historicality, they are read differently by the public, assigned a different status because the horizon of expectations and cognitive rules of the reader are based on the reception aesthetic at the time of reading (cf. Jauss 1970: 7–37; Iser 1974). Since Western culture holds the distinctions between fiction and non-fiction to be valid, people construct and read accounts that, in fact, do take into consideration the truth claims regarding content. Therefore, when I have not used my own observations or interviews in this monograph, I have resorted to citing only those texts holding to a more stringent rule as to the historical accuracy of the experience.

Following White, I am employing a tropological reading of historical narratives. White defines tropics as "the process by which all discourse *constitutes* the objects which it pretends only to describe realistically and to analyze objectively" (1978a: 2). He isolates four master tropes (metaphor, metonymy, synecdoche, irony), which, he argues, are universal linguistic devices that prefigure narratives (1973).[6] While agreeing generally with White that a tropological analysis concerns itself with a figurative interpretation, it may be useful to concentrate less on formal linguistic genres and to introduce a distinction between trope and master narrative. First, if we arm ourselves with a more narrowly metaphorical definition of trope – as a figure of speech, word or phrase, sentence or verse, which amplifies or embellishes experience – we can take into account the historicality of our discoveries by locating the tropes in the stories at hand. Second, we can attribute the metonymic, integrative function, or modes of emplotment, as White calls them, to master narratives.

In a stimulating analysis of the "mission of metaphor" in culture, James Fernandez argues that tropes provide the means for the "metaphoric cross-referencing of domains," and thus function to integrate culture by "providing us with the sensation of wholeness" (1986: 25).[7] This "cross-referencing of domains" is a metaphoric process for the individual insofar as disparate objects are brought together into a coherent (cosmological) whole through comparison and contrast. But a second function of tropes, performed at a group level, is a metonymic and integrative one. A trope, or metaphor, partakes in an integrative function not merely by translating between domains to bring about cosmological coherence at the individual level, as Fernandez illustrates, but also shapes individual experience into something socially shared by forming with other tropes the constituent parts of a coherent whole. This whole, I would argue, can never be arrived at through the accumulation of individual experiences, which then differentiate or unite individuals by means of metaphorical cross-referencing. It is also necessarily constituted by social constructs, such as the state, that are phenomenologically independent of and prior to the individual. The relationship of part to whole, or of experiential trope to the lifecourse of a member of a nation, is established through metonymy; it is an integrative function performed not by tropes themselves but by the way in which they obtain meaning through appeals to master narratives.

Rather than narrowing emplotment modes, as does White, to the four archetypes of Northrop Frye (romantic, tragic, comic, and satirical), we can uncover master narratives within the repertoire of the culture (and for this study, generation) in question, and hence remain in a more dialectical relationship with our texts as ethnographer and reader. Instead of merely identifying the genre in the legal story and autobiography waiting to be found, we can first isolate the tropes that structure the narrative, and second, analyze how they are emplotted in a series of transformations over time, obtaining meaning by appeals to common master narratives.

**Experience, life construction, generation, and narrative**
Let us now elaborate the specific analytical units that organize the ethnographic part of this study. I will return to the analysis of legal texts in chapter 4. The life constructions are also always reconstructions, since

they are based either on recollections of experience, related orally or in a written narrative, or on my observations, reconstructed after the interaction with the aid of those who were present. Not all experience refers to something other than itself, and hence not all experience, even when capable of being verbalized, becomes a trope in a narration. Additionally, much is left out of personal narratives which can be inferred from the contexts of experiences; these silences and omissions can also serve as tropes in a life construction. Furthermore, the significance of experience changes as it is reevaluated over time, and each recollection can produce a slightly or radically different retelling. I am not concerned with the veracity of any particular version, but with its significance, from today's perspective, in structuring the lives of a generation. The truth-value alone of an experiential trope does not determine its significance for a life, since individuals rarely construct lives that turn around an obligation of truth. In fact, many experiences obtain significance only through lies, distortions, and misrepresentations. In short, a reconstruction revolves around self-allegorization processes, meaning references to ideals of self obtained by reflecting back upon a narrated, perspectival history; it does not revolve around principles of abstract truth obtained with reference to some neutral and universal principles of recovery.

Experiential reconstructions, like most forms of knowledge, become narratives in the telling, either consciously or unconsciously. Individual narratives share similar figurational devices, that is, they are constructed with reference to the same experiential tropes. The coherence of the life reconstruction lies not in the plot produced by the chronology of experiences, but instead in the *emplotment* of those experiences in a story made coherent by appeals to common master narratives. Master narratives function to enable individuals to order their experiences around the repetition of specific tropes by integrating the lifecourse into a coherent story, hence constituting a meaningful subject. To the extent that the same master narratives are appealed to by different subjects, they become instruments for producing social and possibly national cohesion; subjects then unite as a generation, and they demarcate themselves from other groups. To the extent that the same master narratives are utilized by both the citizens and the state, they are indices of state legitimacy. Thus, life reconstructions, in their generational specificity, index the ongoing processes of differential kin, nation, and state-building in the two Berlins.

I am examining individual life constructions not to ascertain sets of fixed personality attributes or psychological types, but to uncover the generative logic of the lives of a generation. These lives realize themselves in a continual process of transformations (see Bude 1987: 80). For this study, the individual life is interesting not because of its statistical typicality, but because of its *prototypicality* for a generation. There are particular individual life constructions that are better examples of the generational category, that is, *prototypes*, than are others (see Lakoff 1987: 68–85).[8] Two principles informed my selection of individuals for life constructions: (1) to illustrate the range of practices rather than the mean, mode, or ideal-typical practice, and (2) to reveal the historical and cultural specificity of practices rather than to disclose a set of universal, timeless, "necessary and sufficient" conditions for membership in a category. The dynamic aspects of any set of practices are more apparent on the borders of experience than in the center; thus, in describing the range of practices, I often incorporate what might be statistically peripheral experiences. Yet practices at the edge are the motors for historical change, precisely because they are in some kind of contradictory relation to *doxic* experience (Bourdieu 1977: 164–171). And it is precisely to this border that states look when writing their laws, when formulating the "proper," for what obeys societal norms is not in need of regulation. Only in contradiction do practices become self-referential: they turn back on social processes to explain what they are not, and in this process, clarify what in fact they are.

I am using the notion "generation" merely as a heuristic device. It roughly correlates with the political chronology of this century, although there are individuals who do not belong to their chronological generation. Two Berlin generations in the postwar period structure this study. Generation I reached adulthood during the Third Reich (most of its members were born between 1910 and 1935). The lifecourse of Generation II was shaped primarily within the postwar period (most born between 1940 and 1955). The two most frequently employed uses of generation are to make it either coterminous with shared chronological origin (cohort: age grading or shared year/decade of birth) or with shared lineage (genealogical membership).[9] Neither of these conventions offers much promise for analysis of social groups in Berlin; first, because age is merely one form of ranking, and by no means the most significant, and second, because concepts such as lineage or family membership, while applicable in some domains (such as inheritance in West Berlin or education in East Berlin), nonetheless vary in significance across generations, across social classes, and over an individual lifecourse.

Karl Mannheim (1982: 509–565), in his seminal essay on generation, turns to this concept to reveal "the dynamic of historical development." He is concerned more with dynamic than with structural aspects of generation, although there is no reason to consider these aspects as separate or contradictory, for the processes that constitute generations contribute to both stability and change. What holds a generation together, according to Mannheim, are similarities in feelings, behavioral norms, and connectedness. Generational disposition/storehouse refers to the objective conditions and environment in which a generation lives, the given, determinative limits and opportunities for a life to unfold. Generational unity means those publicly understood, subjective interpretations collectively and similarly responded to. Generational coherence refers to hidden connections within a specific group which hold it together, such as feelings and orientations. It is the second and third characteristics with which I am concerned.

For Mannheim, as for myself, a generation is determined not by the shared problems of the time, but by the responses to these shared problems and objective conditions (e.g., war, poverty, geographical resettlement, change in political regime). Objective processes become part of life constructions only through subjective interpretations. Meaning is not a thing that adheres in events, but always involves weaving those events into a story that is meaningful *to us*. Both what really happened and individual interpretations of this – what in literary study, following the Russian Formalists, is often distinguished as *fabula* and *sjuzet*[10] – are continuously undergoing revisions as they interact with each other. We might look at the generational narrative as a plot of the lifecourse, a highly mediated text created by the dynamic between objective conditions, or what supposedly really happened (*fabula*), and interpretations of reality (*sjuzet*), a discourse that is continually being reconstructed as it is retold.

What Bourdieu (1977) calls *dispositions* and Gadamer (1975) calls *prejudice* shape and limit our horizons in the perception of actual events and happenings. One carries dispositions and prejudices into all interactions, but dispositions do not force specific actions; they merely incline one to act in a certain way, or delineate a range of possible activities from which to choose. The horizon may be more or less elastic, but it has a generational specificity to it. Generations, then, situate the life history in a group context; they create the possibility for historical thought and category membership in two ways: metonymically (by shared contiguity) in providing identity through shared experiences within a group over time, and metaphorically (by differentiation) in demarcating between groups who experience the same historical time differently. As such, they are indispensable organizational devices for both the Germans and my study of them.

## Method

Berlin became my home from September 1986 through January 1989. I returned twice during semester and vacation breaks from my teaching schedule for an additional five months of fieldwork during 1989. And after completing this study, I was in Berlin again for parts of the months of January, March, and December 1990. During my entire stay, divided nearly equally between the two parts of the city, I enjoyed living in apartments in both centers: in the East, near Alexander Platz, in the West, initially near Kurfürstendamm in Wilmersdorf, thereafter in Kreuzberg, Section 61.

Doing fieldwork in modern urban settings, such as Berlin, necessarily entails the development of new methods sensitive to the historical space and place in which the research is done. Like all fieldwork studies, mine is not replicable because the knowledge obtained is tied to a specific set of fieldwork conditions (everyday life in the Berlins during the waning years of the Cold War) which are not likely to reproduce themselves. My own ethnographic approach was, however, peculiarly suited for understanding the range and historical specificity of the practices I studied. This anthropological angle of vision is limited most by its inability to determine the typical or "average" practice, or to comment authoritatively on the distribution of practices. I might counter, however, that the "average person" (genderless, classless, ageless) depicted in much social-science literature does not empirically exist, but is always extrapolated or abstracted from "real data" by one or another kind of scientific cunning.

Anthropologists in particular have a long tradition of looking for the average or typical when describing their "tribe," or "culture," of sacrificing the diversity of everyday life for a theoretically inspired pursuit of the classical and the banal. Hence the use of the singular: Franz Boas did "the Kwakiutl," Bronislaw Malinowski did "the Trobriander," Margaret Mead did "the Samoan," and E.E. Evans-Pritchard did "the Nuer," to name but four of the most renowned. Totemically appropriating the name of the group studied, or, in extreme cases, first subsuming the group's local identity into a continental one, resolves two problems: it lends the anthropologists an aura of native authenticity (they become one of the boys), and it establishes their ethnographic authority (they were there).[11]

When anthropologists describe the peoples they study, they now studiously avoid assuming that the groups are monolithic, genderless, isolated, and historically inert. In other words, the assumption today is that all places and peoples are in some sense multicultural. Yet it is often thought by people outside the field of anthropology that ethnographic methods are most appropriate for the study of "primitive" or less complex, "Cold" societies in the Third World, and ill-suited for historically conscious or "Hot" societies in the First World. Furthermore, the nearly unanimous agreement among social anthropologists that the primitive never existed has radically altered neither the way the discipline is viewed by others, nor where and whom anthropologists generally study.

I take the object of anthropology to be the same as that of other social sciences; as formulated by Max Weber, to seek "knowledge of the cultural significance of concrete historical events and patterns" (1968: 67). In examining cultural significance, Weber hoped to obtain knowledge of historical phenomena. By historical, he meant to ask how something is "significant in its individuality." This point has been further elaborated by Hans-Georg Gadamer:

[The] true goal [of historical knowledge] – even in utilizing general knowledge – is to understand historical phenomenon in its singularity, in its uniqueness. Historical consciousness is interested in knowing not how men, people, or states develop *in general*, but, quite on the contrary, how *this* man, *this* people, or *this* state became what it is; how each of these *particularities* could come to pass and end up specifically there.                              *(1979: 116)*

My object, then, is historical knowledge of the particular subjectivity of East and West Berliners during the Cold War, a subjectivity with universal significance but certainly unique in its compositions.

If we are bound to explain the past in terms of present interests, we are engaged in a history of the present, or, as Foucault states, a genealogy of knowledge "to reveal the relations that characterize the temporality of discursive formations" (1972: 167). Because anthropological knowledge is based on fieldwork, it is distinguished by a present-orientation much more than other disciplines. This is precisely the strength of its approach. Whereas Clifford Geertz (1973: 23) writes, "ethnographic findings are not privileged, just particular" I maintain that any scientist – someone doing oral history, for example – can gather more particular information. What other studies often lack is the privileged access to the present obtained through intensive fieldwork. That access makes possible a unique contribution of anthropology to historical consciousness, one informed by its own history.

During the course of my fieldwork, each private encounter proved in itself a unique experience, as no person is reducible to a fixed list of personality or system traits. And how could I be disappointed? My goal was, after all, to discover both the singularity and particularity of each personal history. In both parts of the city I put myself at the disposal of a wide range of individuals with different ideologies and identity structures. Something arose out of each meeting that, to my anthropologically trained eye, longed for inscription. On my second evening in Berlin, GDR, a friend of a friend of a friend took me to *zur letzten Instanz*, the oldest bar in Berlin, where we were seated at a table with three young apprentices. One was university bound, studying for the *Abitur*, one was a mason, presently washing windows, the other a mechanic. They were very excited about meeting an American, and inquired of my friend if they could ask me questions. Then came a flood of queries concerning rock music, about which I know nothing. Then they tried politics, and the *Abitur* candidate, who had lived in Sweden with his parents (his father was a diplomat), asked me what I thought of Honecker's Peace Initiative. I replied that I didn't know enough about it, but that there was an amazing amount of propaganda about it: there seemed to be a poster announcing peace on every streetcorner in the center of *Berlin, die Hauptstadt*. The discussion turned to weapon systems and why the Americans had so many – "Beats me," I said – before one of them provocatively asked why I felt the need for both the MX and a new generation of Cruise missiles. My friend of a friend of a friend responded: Americans don't keep missiles in their homes.

That sort of encounter and dialogue typified my subsequent fieldwork in public places in the East: easy to come into contact with strangers, mixed publics in terms of occupation and status, primarily if not exclusively male-only bars. Most of the women I got to know I had to meet at arranged times and usually at home; I also observed them at shopping centers. The reason was rather simple: most of the women had children; many were single; when married, they still took primary responsibility for childcare. In contrast to my position in the East, I did not enjoy any automatic exoticism in the West. On both sides of the Wall people who had reached adulthood before the war (Generation I) treated me with deference and respect. Among people under fifty in the

West (Generation II), there was often some reserve and skepticism about greeting an American, in part a remnant of the anti-Vietnam-War sentiment from the late sixties, and in part the result of a negative association with the 30,000 American troops and supporting personnel who still exercised extensive occupation rights (including the right to open private mail, tap telephone conversations, and have relative immunity from West German criminal law). Moreover, people in large cities in capitalist societies between the ages of twenty and fifty tend to be very busy and have little free time for curious strangers. Groups of friends in West Berlin tend to be small, closely knit together, and closed to outsiders. Eventually, a comparable form of hospitality to that I had experienced in the East was extended to me in the West.

I proceeded in my fieldwork by focusing on a succession of single problems for short periods of time, asking people as I befriended them such bewildering questions as the history of the meaning of *Kumpel* in the East or *Wohngemeinschaft* in the West. I would note the use of frequently repeated words or concepts in texts, listen for them in conversations, or simply ask people to distinguish a *Kumpel* from a friend or lover or whatever other categories they used. Naturally, I also steadily observed interactions. At some point I would be satisfied with my answer, or frustrated that I couldn't go any further, and then turn to another problem. Once I was satisfied that I had established a trusting relationship with someone, I would return to people's homes to interview them individually. Altogether, I recorded forty-three full-life histories and some part of hundreds of others. We would start with an agreed-upon theme, such as *Kinderwunsch* (wish for a child), parenthood, household history, history of legal encounters, educational experiences, and the interview would most often, but not always, branch out into related topics, such as sexuality, marriage, family history, work. I also conducted many short interviews by asking people to retell to me an event or episode to which they had referred at some prior meeting. I would take copious notes during the interview and reconstruct them that evening in more detail.

After seven months in the GDR, I selected five individuals for tape-recorded interviews. These ethnographic interviews distinguished themselves from journalistic or sociological ones in several ways: I knew the individuals quite well before we began taping; I did not have a catalogue of essential questions; I did not interrupt them except to ask for examples, details, or clarification; and I yielded to my interviewees the power to close the interview, either on that day or after several such encounters. My final selection of discussion partners included a single mother, happily married mother, married man, single man, and widow. I promised them anonymity and, except for one person (who requested that I use her real name), that I would not publish the interview as a whole unit. I selected these individuals because they exemplified a range of experiential patterns prototypical for a generation. I wanted some complete narrative life histories, which would themselves be reflectively evaluative and sequentially ordered. I began the interviews with the question, "How do you periodize your own history?" I had already put this question to many other individuals in other contexts; it always elicited both a periodization and categorization. A third set of interviews I conducted, arranged by my advisor at the law school in Humboldt University, included twenty-eight formal interviews with academics and researchers at Humboldt University, The Akademie der Wissenschaft, Institut für Staat und Recht in Babelsberg, and Karl-Marx University in Leipzig. These discussions were mainly to inform myself on the literature available, on official perspectives not yet published, and to obtain an historical perspective on policy developments; they were not tape recorded.

Following similar procedures, I put the same questions to my discussion partners in West Berlin. After thirteen months of living in West Berlin, I selected five people for tape-recorded interviews. They included the same categories of persons as in the GDR, except that the married man was selected in part because he was also a father (the man in the East was a divorced father, remarried but without children in his current marriage). I did not conduct any interviews with experts or officials, as published texts on policy proved sufficient for my needs.

There were several groups, or cultures, if you like, that I avoided becoming more than peripherally involved with in both East and West, for the reason that I had a natural affinity to them, and I feared they would draw me away from exploring the range of practices. In both cities, I tended to avoid intellectual or academic culture and the expatriate community. Since my official affiliation with the Berlins was through universities, I was obliged to partake in a number of university events. Since I was an expatriate, I came into contact with many other interesting foreigners living in the two cities. I did not want these particular communities in either city to color my perceptions; hence I made a sustained effort to enter into non-academic communities and to befriend non-expatriates.

While in West Berlin, I visited my friends in East Berlin on the average once a week, but several times for stays up to a month. During my last six months of fieldwork, I was writing-up, and I often shared my interpretations with people I knew. Many had experienced me only as ethnographer and friend, and were not used to my role as critical anthropologist. I found their reflections and criticisms, in turn, always helpful, and incorporated them into my writing by revising my accounts.

The nature of my dialogues was always generation specific, sometimes gender specific, and in West Berlin, class specific. Men of Generation I were, on the whole, frustrating discussion partners for me. They insisted on repeating their life events in a very fixed format, as if they had memorized a way of narrating their lives from which they were incapable of deviating. The idea of an interviewer injecting a comment intending to prod them into reflecting back upon what they were saying seemed foreign to them, as if I were destroying (which I was) the rhythm of their performance. Certainly many understood my interjections, which were nearly always requests for clarification and not contradictions, as lack of respect for their authority. Women of Generation I, especially in the West, were interested in telling me their stories, often with tremendous openness and at times, like their male peers, with a fixed narrative structure. After my first eighteen months of fieldwork, I began doing systematic library research, and discovered recently published interviews and life histories of Generation I in both cities. After checking on the accuracy and method of these studies, either by meeting the authors or asking others who knew them, I decided to utilize them and to focus the remainder of my ethnographic work on Generation II. Hence I often cite published interviews of Generation I, using material from my own encounters only when it contradicted the already-published accounts or when no published material was available to me.

I had easy access to men and women of Generation II, due largely to the fact that I am of their age cohort. In East Berlin, I came into private contact with members of all classes and social groups, from cleaning women to children of Central Committee (ZK) members. It proved quite difficult for me to obtain access to working-class members of this generation in West Berlin. When I tried bars, the men seemed to take offense to my status as someone "educated"; as the evenings wore on, they also became increasingly inarticulate as they got drunk. Middle-class family men and their wives most often stayed home and watched television in the evening, an activity that makes me nervous. I attribute my lack of access to the working class of West Berlin as due to the class-specific nature of communities and life-styles in West Germany/West Berlin. Also, given the tremendous mobility of the postwar population in West Berlin, the city contained a multitude of communities with no common bonds to each other. They all lived in the city for very different reasons: some stayed because they were born there (or born in the East), many moved there from West Germany to avoid the army, to go to school, to enjoy the counter-culture, or to obtain tax breaks. The fact that Berlin is unique does not, however, make my study less valid, though it does make it an extreme case of East and West German nation-building.

As I began work with Generation III, born approximately after 1960, I discovered a plethora of excellent "youth studies" in both Germanies, and again, did not desire to repeat them. Additionally, I realized after several interviews that members of this generation had not yet lived long enough to narrate the kind of evaluative, sequential history that marked the narratives of Generations I and II. My method was more suited for adults than for youths. The aspect of crystallization of experience through reevaluation over time, and of appeals to master narratives for coherence in the troping of experience, seemed missing from their accounts. Ultimately I could not trust that their "life constructions" had already taken form. For these reasons, I ended up concentrating in my ethnographic work on the life reconstructions of Generation II and drawing more from historical work on the reconstructions of Generation I. I have omitted a discussion of Generation III from this study.

Table 1 lists the numbers and kinds of contacts I had with people in the two Berlins, including only those individuals whose experiences I drew from for this study. It is meant only as an orientation, for since each encounter was unique, any attempt to typologize them is to some extent arbitrary. Furthermore, since "data and analysis are inextricably intertwined," as David Schneider (1980: 123–124) forcefully argues, no absolute number of informants of a particular kind could possibly be trotted forth to prove that my analysis is based on "objectively verifiable facts," whatever those may be in the human sciences. At most, I can claim that I became acquainted with a wide range of individuals whose identities cross-cut their own criteria of personal signification (age, sex, class, and political ideology). The argument based on an evaluation of this "data" is itself a part of the data, since it was formed during (and thus influenced by) the process of data collection.

I list as "well-known" those individuals for whom I can identify political party membership, occupation, family status, and parental history. I knew these individuals minimally for a year and, for those of Generation II, rarely would a month go by without some sort of

Table 1. *Classification of discussion partners in East and West Berlin*

|                     | East Berlin |    | West Berlin |    |
| ------------------- | ----------- | -- | ----------- | -- |
| Well-known          |             | 95 |             | 54 |
| Gen. I              | 20          |    | 6           |    |
| Gen. II             | 54          |    | 26          |    |
| Gen. III            | 21          |    | 22          |    |
| Acquaintances       |             | 52 |             | 11 |
| Brief acquaintances |             | 48 |             | 45 |
| Total               |             | 195 |            | 110 |

interaction. I include among "acquaintances" those individuals of Generations I and II who told me of their occupation and family status along with some other aspects of their life, so that they appear as names mentioned more than once in my fieldnotes. Finally, among "brief acquaintances," I include those individuals, of Generations I and II only, whom I met at some event, after which I wrote down some comment.

This book will from here onwards be organized around the analytical terms outlined above, beginning with a chapter on the comparative demography of postwar Berlin. I follow this with a comparative analysis of state narrative strategies, before moving to a separate analysis of life constructions in East and West Berlin.

# 3

# Demographics of production and reproduction

The physical reproduction of the population, and thus the nature of kinship patterns, has been a recurrent, central anxiety of German states. This preoccupation also holds true for the governing bodies in Berlin in this century, where demographic patterns have been intensely distorted by male deaths and massive population relocations resulting from one cold and two hot wars. Policymakers and social scentists have perceived these postwar demographic changes as in part both cause and result of peculiarities in kinship patterns. One of the major problems in interpreting this demographic data is that the ambiguity and multisemic nature of local statuses and their interrelationships are lost when they are absorbed into abstract, universalistic categories. And since "some classes of events can be more easily conceptualized [in demographic terms] than others," as François Furet states, events are reduced to categories "stripped of the layers of meaning that each civilization has in its own way given them" (1984: 60). This is especially true for kinship classifications or, as everyday speech has it, families and their members. The cognitive categories constituting kinship – the units demographers take to have empirical equivalents – are frequently viewed as ahistorical and isomorphic with the practices they are said to name.

This chapter will analyze selective demographic data that bears on the comparative constitution of postwar kinship patterns in the Berlins. Not all of the numbers presented are comparable, for sources often cite different statistics, and both states and individuals at times deliberately falsify or distort the presentation of data. In addition, East and West Berlin were anomalies or distortions in their own right, frequently representing the extreme case of patterns and processes in the GDR and the FRG. East Berlin was also much better integrated into East

Table 2. *Berlin population, 1939–1988*

|  | West Berlin | | East Berlin | |
|---|---|---|---|---|
| Year | Total (in millions) | % women | Total (in millions) | % women |
| 1939[a] | 4,323.7 | 54.2 | – | – |
| 1946 | 1,967.7 | 59.6 | 1,164.6 | 59.2 |
| 1950 | 2,146.8 | 57.6 | 1,189.5 | 57.4 |
| 1960 | 2,204.2 | 57.6 | 1,071.7 | 57.1 |
| 1970 | 2,122.3 | 55.9 | 1,085.4 | 55.3 |
| 1980 | 1,899.3 | 54.6 | 1,152.5 | 53.8 |
| 1986 | 1,869.6 | 54.0 | 1,236.2 | 53.0 |
| 1988 | 2,047.1 | 53.3 | 1,284.0 | 53.0 |

[a]Number for Greater-Berlin
*Sources: Statistisches Jahrbuch Berlin; Statistisches Jahrbuch der DDR;* Winkler 1990

Germany than was West Berlin into West Germany. Nonetheless, when statistics for the city are not available, I resort to those for the larger unit of which it is a part, that is, for the state. With this caveat in mind, I will note when the Berlin statistics radically differ from those of the states to which they belong.

**Population base and labor policy**
Between the beginning of World War II in 1939 and the end of the war in 1945, the population of Berlin declined, through death and flight, by 35 percent. In 1945, the Allies divided the city into four sectors, with the three Western Allies appropriating 54.6 percent of the land containing 64 percent of the population, and the Soviets appropriating 45.4 percent of the land containing 36 percent of the population. The population in all four of the occupied zones grew until 1948 (see table 2), in large part due to the influx of refugees, primarily from the *Ostgebiete* and *Sudetenland*, land yielded to the Polish, Soviet, and Czech states. Thereafter, both Berlins experienced a relatively stable population in absolute numbers, although the content was in constant flux until the mid 1970s. At that time the population in East Berlin began to increase slowly again, while that of the GDR as a whole as well as of West Berlin and the FRG continued to decline.

The Berlin population was additionally skewed, in comparison to that in the rest of Germany, by the large percentage of children, women, and the elderly. These three groups were not capable of immediate incorpo-

Table 3. *Employed women as a percentage of working-age women, 1939–1985[a]*

| Year[b] | FRG | GDR |
|---|---|---|
| 1939[c] | 49.7 | 49.7 |
| 1950, 1955 | 43.8 | 61.2 |
| 1960, 1965 | 47.5 | 76.2 |
| 1970, 1975 | 47.4 | 86.5 |
| 1982, 1985 | 51.0 | 91.0 |

[a]These statistics are not exactly comparable, for the two states use different categories. East German statistics include students, and mothers taking the paid baby-year; West German statistics often hide unemployed or part-time, employed women or women who work without legal contracts (before 1977, women who worked unpaid for their husbands). Minimally, they illustrate the number of housewives compared to women working in the public domain.
[b]When two years are listed, the first applies to the FRG, the second to the GDR.
[c]This percentage applies to the former German Reich.
*Sources: Vierter Familienbericht* 1986: 71; *Demographische Prozesse* 1984: 23; Gysi and Speigner 1983: 33

ration into the workforce, for obvious reasons: the elderly were too old, the children too young, and the women unskilled. East Germany encountered the additional handicap, up to the building of the Wall, of steadily losing working-age men to West Berlin and the FRG. This presented the East Germans with a more immediate task of incorporating working-age, primarily unskilled women into the labor force. In 1945, women comprised 63.2 percent of the Greater-Berlin population, declining in 1950 in East Berlin to 57 percent, in 1980 to 54 percent, and in 1986 to 53 percent (with these figures 0.6 to 1.0 percent higher in West Berlin).

Partly because of this steady flow of people from East Berlin/GDR to West Berlin/FRG, policy in the East was oriented, from the start, not only to integrating women fully into the labor force, but also to advancing them into the ranks of skilled labor. Most of these women, lacking education and training, and also with greater constraints on their time (due to childcare), were integrated into unskilled jobs; thus although some women reached the top of most industries, most women held lower-status positions. On the other hand, West German policy was structured around using women as a reserve labor pool and sending them back to the home when no longer needed (a policy model that

Table 4. *Aging patterns in the FRG and the GDR, 1970 and 1983*

| Ages (years) | FRG | | GDR | |
|---|---|---|---|---|
| | 1970 | 1983 | 1970 | 1983 |
| 0–15 | 23.2 | 15.9 | 23.3 | 19.3 |
| 15–60/65[a] | 60.1 | 66.2 | 57.2 | 63.8 |
| 60/65+[b] | 16.7 | 17.9 | 19.5 | 16.9 |

[a]Ages 15–60 for women, 15–65 for men.
[b]Ages over 60 for women, over 65 for men.
*Source: Materialien* 1987: 259–260

Table 5. *Non-working plus non-employable people as a percentage of working-age, employable people in the FRG and the GDR, 1970 and 1983*

| | 1970 % of total | 1983 % of total |
|---|---|---|
| FRG | 66 | 51 |
| GDR | 75 | 57 |

*Source: Materialien* 1987: 259–260

later came to structure the attitudes toward *Gastarbeiter*, guest workers). As table 3 reveals, the number of working women in West Germany steadily declined through the 1950s, not reaching the old wartime high again until the 1980s. The employment rate for women in West Berlin, however, was always considerably higher than in West Germany. In 1984, for example, only 51 percent of working-age women in West Germany were employed, compared to 62.2 percent of working-age women in West Berlin. On the other hand, the full-employment policy of the East German government produced a steady and dramatic increase in the public employment rate for women, by 1985 reaching 91 percent, the highest in the world.

By 1988, women made up 48.9 percent of the total labor force in East Berlin, 43.4 in West Berlin. Of those working part-time (usually meaning less prestigious, more mechanical work), women comprised 60 percent in the GDR, and 75 percent in West Berlin. Women in the GDR, like their West German counterparts, were concentrated in menial and non-skilled jobs. The general rule in both Germanies was that women worked in the service sector and men in production. Yet in

Table 6. *Unemployed people in West and East Berlin, 1946–1986*

| Year | W. Berlin | E. Berlin/GDR |
|------|-----------|---------------|
| 1946 | 96,700 | 56,665 |
| 1950–1952[a] | 286,472 | 107,162 |
| 1958–1955 | 80,468 | 43,634[b] |
| 1960 | 33,251 | 5,644 |
| 1962 | 12,173[c] | — |
| 1969 | 31,858 | — |
| 1980 | 30,488 | — |
| 1982 | 68,584 | — |
| 1986 | 84,813 | — |

[a]When two years are listed, the first applies to West Berlin, the second to East Berlin.
[b]The numbers for 1955 and 1960 listed under East Berlin apply to the unemployed in the entire GDR, including East Berlin.
[c]No statistics are available for East Berlin or the GDR after 1960, but it is understood that full employment characterizes the situation since 1958, and thereafter the few unemployed are not comparable to unemployed in capitalist systems (for explanation, see *DDR Handbuch* 1985: 63–64).
*Sources: Berlin in Zahlen* 1947; *Statistisches Jahrbuch für die Bundesrepublik.*

the GDR, more women had the opportunity to complete advanced qualification courses, increasing from 5 percent in 1949 to 78.9 percent in 1983, equalling that of men; the number of women with official qualifications in West Berlin lies somewhere less than 30 percent. (*Demographische Prozesse* 1984: 24; *Berliner Statistik* 1950–1989: 296–297).

Another significant aspect of population composition and labor policy is the unusual age-distribution following the war. This distribution has long-term effects, in that, coupled with a low rate of population growth (in comparison to prewar growth) and an increase in longevity, a disproportionately large percentage of the population in both states will soon be in retirement with a correspondingly small percentage working. Statistics from 1970 and 1983 (tables 4 and 5) illustrate several patterns common to the two states.

Table 4 demonstrates how the number of children has decreased as a percentage of the population in both countries, with a greater decline in the FRG. Table 5 reveals that the total non-working, non-employable part of the population (children and elderly together who need state support), while significantly decreasing between 1970 and 1983 in both states, has comprised a much higher percentage of the postwar popula-

Table 7. *GDR citizens (*Zuwanderer*)
who resettled in West Berlin, 1950–1986*

| Year | Total number of citizens |
|------|--------------------------|
| 1950 | 76,821 |
| 1953 | 317,603 |
| 1954 | 114,435 |
| 1959 | 76,313 |
| 1960 | 109,383 |
| 1961 | 103,507 |
| 1962 | 6,179 |
| 1970 | 3,701 |
| 1975 | 4,028 |
| 1980 | 3,204 |
| 1986 | 2,468 |

*Source: Statistisches Jahrbuch Berlin*

tion in the GDR than in the FRG, still more than half of the population and expected to increase in the future. Also of importance demographically, but not illustrated in these tables, is the much higher proportion of women among the elderly, who outlive men by an average of 6.5 years in the FRG, 5.7 in the GDR (*Materialien* 1987: 266). The life expectancies of the populations in both states remained relatively similar until 1975, when those in West Germany, both women and men, began to live substantially longer than their peers in the East.

West German labor policy, especially with regard to West Berlin, had its own idiosyncrasies. Because of West Berlin's insecure political status, many large and many small industries vacated Berlin during the 1950s for West Germany. This exodus stopped only with the building of the Wall, after which West Berlin began to receive more generous financial support from the Federal Republic. The sudden drying up of the reserve labor pool coming from East Berlin/East Germany caused industrialists in the early seventies to begin importing foreign labor from the Mediterranean region. The Wall secured and stabilized the economic situation for both Berlins. In 1988, over 52 percent of the total city budget of Berlin came from federal subsidies. In addition to various subsidies to families, select groups, and companies, every person employed in West Berlin received a tax-free bonus of 8 percent on his/her gross income.

Table 6 lists the numbers of unemployed in East and West Berlin.

Table 8. *Age-breakdown of persons resettling from the GDR to the FRG, 1970, 1982, and 1989*

| Age group | % of total | | |
|---|---|---|---|
| | 1970 | 1982 | 1989 |
| Children under fifteen years | 2.2 | 13.3 | 23.2 |
| Persons of employable age[a] | 18.5 | 52.9 | 73.8 |
| Persons of retirement age | 79.3 | 33.8 | 3.0 |

[a]Employable age is defined as 15–60 for women, 15–65 for men. Retirement age is over 60 for women, over 65 for men.
*Sources: Materialien* 1987: 268; Winkler 1990: 38

Despite the lack of a full-employment policy in West Berlin, the city reached nearly full employment soon after the building of the Wall (see table 6). By the late 1960s, the number of unemployed had again tripled, and under Christian Democratic Union rule in the 1980s the numbers tripled once more. For the whole of the GDR, by 1958 full employment had, to all intents and purposes, been reached. In fact, by 1952, the number of unemployed for the whole of the GDR was less than the number for West Berlin alone.

Up to 1962, resettlers and refugees from the East played a critical role in supplying labor for the West German *Wirtschaftswunder*. Tables 7 and 8 detail the number and composition of these resettlers. Table 7 shows the number of resettlers and refugees to West Berlin; table 8 reveals the changes in age-breakdown of resettlers from the GDR to the FRG between 1970 and 1982.

Between 1948 and 1989, the number of resettlers to West Berlin/FRG from the GDR totaled 3.9 million. After 1953, West Berlin was the first stopping point for well over 80 percent of them, who often then made it their home. They constituted a tremendous loss for the GDR: over 50 percent of these people were younger than twenty-five; less than 10 percent were of retirement age. Each successive refugee flood included more people of working age, as we can see in table 8.

Building the Wall in 1961 ended the steady drain on the East German economy, but at the same time created new labor shortages for the expanding West German economy. The percentage of men leaving since then was approximately equal to that of women leaving. In another respect, however, the composition of the resettlers between 1970 and 1982 did change, with over 66 percent being children or people of

Table 9. *Growth in employed guestworkers in the FRG (including W. Berlin), 1950–1980 (in thousands)*

| Year | Yugoslavian | Spanish | Turkish |
|------|-------------|---------|---------|
| 1950 | 0 | 0 | 0 |
| 1955 | 1.8 | 0.4 | 0 |
| 1961 | 16.4 | 44.2 | 6.7 |
| 1969 | 331.6 | 206.9 | 332.4 |
| 1973 | 673.3 | 286.1 | 893.6 |
| 1980[a] | 632.0 | 180.0 | 1,462.0 |

[a]After 1980, the numbers decline slightly and shortly thereafter stabilize.
In 1986 in West Berlin, the total number of foreigners (including guestworkers) was 1,964,084, slightly less than 10 percent of the population.
*Sources:* Esser 1985: 133; *Miteinander Leben* 1986: 76

working-age and 34 percent retired people, compared with only 21 percent children and employables and 79 percent retired people in 1970. In the 1989 flight, these shifts in the composition of resettlers and refugees were even more exaggerated, working strongly to the benefit of West Berlin/West Germany and to the disadvantage of the GDR.

As the number of East Germans moving to West Germany dwindled, they were replaced by Mediterranean workers. Three groups of guest-workers are examined in table 9. Guestworkers increased very slowly until 1954, stabilized until 1964, then rapidly increased from the mid 1960s to 1973. After 1980, the number of guestworkers declined slightly and thereafter remained constant.

**Partnership**
Partnership patterns can not be precisely determined from demographic statistics because the statistical categories used are based on legal relationships between kin, defined either by shared blood or marriage, while in practice these terms are polysemic, not limited to their legal definitions. Census categories that define the individual in terms of marriage and legal parental status ignore affectual and sexual relations, cohabitation patterns, and forms of property dependence not legally recognized. Furthermore, marriage, divorce, and birth statistics can not be read as continuous, since they are derived from different generations over time, hence they apply to different lifecourse trajectories. Despite these limitations, a combination of demographic indicators points to some of the significant changes in the meaning of kinship.

Table 10. *Marriages and divorces in East and West Berlin, 1945–1986*

| Year | West Berlin | | East Berlin | |
|---|---|---|---|---|
| | Marriages | Divorces | Marriages | Divorces |
| 1945[a,b] | 20,028 | 11,235 | — | — |
| 1946 | 20,903 | 24,998 | — | — |
| 1947 | 26,396 | 21,179 | — | — |
| 1951, 1955 | 19,636 | 7,724 | 10,896 | 3,006 |
| 1961 | 21,641 | 4,445 | 11,523 | 3,018 |
| 1969 | 17,898 | 6,371 | 16,932 | 3,300 |
| 1975 | 14,505 | 7,100 | 17,012 | 4,576 |
| 1980 | 11,883 | 5,559 | 16,403 | 4,771 |
| 1984 | 11,941 | 6,052 | 23,324 | 5,119 |

[a]When two years are listed, the first applies to West Berlin, the second to East Berlin.
[b]Statistics for 1945–1947 apply to Greater-Berlin.
*Sources: Statistisches Jahrbuch Berlin; Statistisches Jahrbuch der DDR; Berliner Statistik* 12/87

### The meaning of marriage and divorce for partnership and procreation

Table 10 illustrates the changing meaning of marriage and divorce in the two Berlins. Despite a slightly declining population in both cities (approximately the same number but not the same people), in the years after the war and before the founding of the states the number of people who married and divorced increased. This was a period of tremendous population movement, with many refugees and prisoners-of-war moving to Berlin. Between 1948 and 1960, in both Berlins the number of marriages declined slowly, divorces declined rapidly. Thereafter we are looking at statistics that apply to Generation II. The number of people marrying in West Berlin declined until the 1980s, and then remained stable; in East Berlin marriages continued to increase yearly.

After 1960 in East Berlin, 1963 in West Berlin, divorces began to increase again, doubling in the next ten years, with the most intensive increase after 1968. Divorces peaked in West Berlin by 1970, then levelled off in the 1980s; in East Berlin, they continued to increase. These divorce averages are consistently higher for the Berlins than for the GDR and FRG. In 1986, the divorce rate was 70 percent higher in West Berlin than in West Germany, and of those who married, in 40 percent of the marriages one of the partners had already been married. In 1985, approximately 33 percent of all marriages in the GDR ended in divorce; the number was 40 percent in East Berlin.

The conclusion we can draw is that marriage patterns for Generation I are quite similar, but divorce patterns differ (with fewer in West Berlin, in large part because of the significant role of the *Hausfrauenehe*, housewife marriage, in holding marriages together in the FRG). Partnerships take on different meanings for Generation II, however. For the latter group, in West Berlin from 1964 to 1975, many people avoided marriage, and thereafter few sought it out; by the end of the sixties (preceding the change to no-fault divorce), members of Generation II began divorcing in greater numbers. In East Berlin during this same period, the number of both divorces and marriages increased. After 1975, we are additionally dealing with marital statistics of a third generation.

The fact that marriage *and* divorce rates were much higher in East Berlin and East Germany illustrates the more frequent use of legal institutions to legitimize partnership relations in the East, a pattern of serial legal partnership. In the GDR, the number of marriages during this period had increased from 7.7/1,000 in 1970 to 8.0/1,000 in 1984. The marriage frequency for 1984 was 35 percent higher in East Germany than in West Germany. On the other hand, the decline in the number of marriages in the FRG, from 7.3/1,000 in 1970 to 5.9/1,000 in 1984, indicates a general increase in avoidance of legal interactions having to do with partnership. These marriage and remarriage statistics must be interpreted together with the divorce rate, which increased in both states between 1970 and 1983, from 1.3/1,000 to 2.0/1,000 in the FRG, from 1.6/1,000 to 3.0/1,000 in the GDR. That indicates a 50 percent higher divorce frequency in East Germany than West Germany (*Materialien* 1987: 265). We can conclude that in East Germany the processes of constituting and dissolving partnership were increasingly accompanied by legal ceremonies wherein the state played a role in legitimating changing statuses; in West Germany, partnership processes were increasingly private affairs in which the state was avoided.

Family experts and demographers in both Berlins estimate that 50 percent of all first marriages will end in divorce. The length of the marriage is decreasing as well (*Familienbericht* 1987: 63; Heyl 1986: 10–36). The age at first marriage has gone up in West Germany, down in East Germany, again traceable directly to marriage incentives in the East. In 1970 in the FRG, the average marital age for men was 25.6, for women 23.0, *increasing* by 1982 to 26.6 for men, 23.8 for women. In 1970 in the GDR, the averages were 24.0 for men, 21.9 for women, *decreasing* by 1982 to 23.7 for men, 21.6 for women. While an increasing number of people in both Berlins tend to marry more than once, the absolute percentages are greater in East Berlin.

Another trend true for both Germanies is for the woman to be the partner asking for the divorce. For example, from July 1946 to 1947 for Greater-Berlin, 32,291 people divorced; of these divorces 4,535 were initiated by the man, 4,912 by the woman, and 11,598 by both (some divorces were decreed by the courts without either party taking the initiative against the other). By 1985, 66 percent of all divorces in West Germany, and 75 percent in East Germany, were initiated by women, a generation shift indicating the increased autonomy of women of Generation II in comparison to their mothers.

### Children born out of wedlock

If we turn to the patterns of children born out of wedlock, we see partnership, marriage, and divorce in yet another context. In 1945, 31.8 percent of all children were born out of wedlock. This rate dropped precipitously in the following years, ranging between 14 and 18.5 percent up to 1961, which approximately periodizes the childbearing years of women of Generation I. In West Berlin, the number of illegitimate births dropped even more (now those of Generation II), to a low of 12.7 percent in 1970, before climbing to a high of 20.7 percent in 1986; in the GDR, the number declined until 1966, and then began increasing, reaching 23 percent in 1980, 33.8 percent in 1985.[1] For Generation II, the decision to have a child has become increasingly separated from the decision to marry, a process more pronounced in East Berlin/GDR than in West Berlin/FRG. In East Berlin, the increase in the number of children born out of wedlock parallels the breakdown of marriage as a legal institution that legitimates children. Partnership there was practiced increasingly as a separate institutional domain, and the decision to have a first child was something the woman increasingly decided without consideration of her partnership status. Unlike their East German counterparts, West German women, however, often listed as the major reason for marriage the fact that they were pregnant. They saw marriage primarily as a preparatory legal act for parenting, and only secondarily related to partnership.

By 1986 in East Berlin approximately 93 percent of all women became mothers and, in 1986, approximately 48 percent of all first births were to unmarried mothers. Since some 80 percent of all women who have a second child are married, it is likely that the decision to have a second or third child is tied to the stability of partnership expectations. The

Table 11. *Nuclear family status in West Berlin, 1950–1986*

|        | Status (% of total) | | | |
|--------|--------|---------|---------|----------|
| Year   | Single | Married | Widowed | Divorced |
| 1950   | 36.1   | 47.7    | 11.9    | 4.3      |
| 1964   | 33.0   | 48.9    | 14.0    | 5.0      |
| 1975   | 33.6   | 45.3    | 13.8    | 6.7      |
| 1986   | 39.5   | 41.4    | 11.3    | 6.8      |

*Source: Statistisches Jahrbuch Berlin*

Table 12. *Nuclear family status in the GDR, 1964–1988*

|        | Status (% of total) | | | |
|--------|--------|---------|---------|----------|
| Year   | Single | Married | Widowed | Divorced |
| 1964   | 11.74  | 72.46   | 12.59   | 3.21     |
| 1975   | 14.86  | 67.58   | 12.69   | 4.86     |
| 1983   | 17.56  | 64.42   | 11.36   | 6.66     |
| 1988   | 18.20  | 63.80   | 10.60   | 7.40     |

*Sources: Statistisches Jahrbuch der DDR; Winkler 1990: 17*

pattern is somewhat different in West Berlin, where only 80 percent of all women have children,[2] and minimally 10 percent fewer women than in the East (I cannot determine the precise number) decide to have a first child without a husband (see for West Germany, Schütze 1988: 95–112, Nave-Herz 1988: 71–72; for East Germany, D. Meyer 1987: 79–92, Hoffmann, 1987: 98–112).

*Family status*

Tables 11 and 12 compare the changes in family status in West Berlin with those in East Germany. These statuses for East Berlin were unavailable to me, although I have been told that the differences between East Berlin and the GDR are not so great. The tendencies are similar for both West Berlin and East Germany, although much more pronounced in some categories in West Berlin. Basically, the number of marrieds and widowed has decreased over time, the number of singles and divorced has increased. In West Berlin in 1986, marrieds make up only 41 percent of the total; in East Germany in 1988, they still comprise a hefty 64 percent. The number of singles has always been high in West

Berlin, increasing from 33 to 39.5 percent in the last twenty-two years; the numbers are much smaller in East Berlin, but the increase – nearly 60 percent over the same period – is much greater.

The most significant aspect of partnership ignored by marriage and divorce statistics is the *Lebensgemeinschaften* (LG) forms of partnership without marriage, including what in English is often called "domestic partnerships." The LGs have been a constant and widely practiced form of postwar partnership in Berlin. The 1987 West Berlin report from the Senator for Youth and Family (*Familienbericht*) calculatedly avoided using the word in its report, instead referring to "new household types" (p. 21), which presumably includes both LGs and *Wohngemeinschaften*, living-together arrangements usually larger than two. The 1986 report of the West German government (*Vierter Familienbericht*: 36) did mention "non-married *Lebensgemeinschaften*," but then again confused them

Figure 6. Size of German/FRG households from 1900 to 1981.

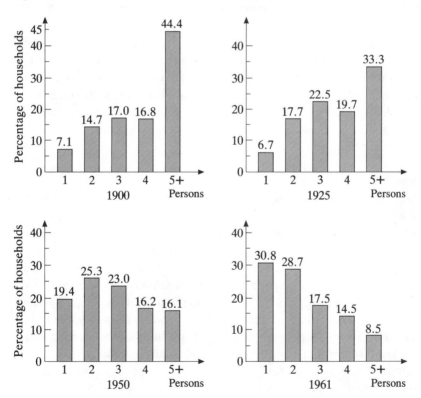

with households, estimating that they comprised but 2 percent of all households in the entire republic. More importantly, this report noted the increasing number of people living in and the changing generational meaning of an LG. LGs tripled in number between 1972 and 1984, and of the estimated 136,000 LGs in 1972, most were comprised of people over fifty-six years old, whereas in 1982, the majority of partners in LG were under thirty-five years old (see also Meyer and Schulze 1988). This means that models of a specific generation are carried on not only through the appropriation of tradition by groups that succeed them, but can also influence the generation that *precedes* them. In this case, I suspect many members of Generation I were already living in LG before a word existed for them, and that Generation II only legitimated them in popular consciousness by supplying a name.

During my stay in the GDR, the LG was much discussed by demographers and lawyers. The 1981 census revealed 10 percent of all households to be LGs, a figure believed to be abnormally low. A 1982 unpublished study by the Institut für Sociologie und Sozialpolitik estimated that 28 percent of all unmarried mothers between eighteen and thirty-five lived in LGs. Of these women, 46 percent intended not to marry and 54 percent indicated that an LG was a temporary arrangement. For this second group of women, scientists often attributed the decision to postpone marriage as most probably related to favorable policy measures for single mothers (Dorbritz 1987: 33; Büttner 1987).

**Household types**

Data on households, while quite incomplete, shows some dramatic changes over time. Figure 6 shows the changes in household size from 1900 to 1981 in Germany and West Germany. Patterns in 1900 and 1925 are marked by larger households, with the modal household having five or more persons. Yet, even in these years one could ascertain the tendency toward smaller households, for in that interim the modal type (five persons or more) declined by 11 percent. By 1950, larger households had become the *least frequent* form; between 1950 and 1981, they decreased in number by another 50 percent. The household form that has increased the most since the beginning of this century, establishing itself as the modal form by 1981, was the single-person household, which increased from a low of 6.7 percent in 1925 to the present 30.8 percent of the total number of households.

Table 13. *Household types in West Berlin, East Berlin, the FRG, and the GDR, 1971 and 1981*

| Place/no. of people | Percentage of total 1971 | | | Percentage of total 1981 | | |
|---|---|---|---|---|---|---|
| | 1 person | 2–3 persons | 4 or more persons | 1 person | 2–3 persons | 4 or more persons |
| Berlin (W.) | 42 | 43 | 15 | 52 | 39 | 9 |
| FRG | 27 | 46 | 27 | 31 | 46 | 22 |
| Berlin (E.) | 34 | 48 | 18 | 33 | 48 | 19 |
| GDR | 26 | 49 | 25 | 27 | 50 | 24 |

*Sources: Statistisches Jahrbuch-Berlin; Statistisches Jahrbuch der DDR*

Running a close second (and the only other form to gain in popularity over time) was the two-person household, mostly childless, hetero-sexual couples.

The housing data from 1971 to 1981 illustrates first and foremost the dramatic increase in single-person households in both the Berlins and Germanies. On the other hand, this data also indicates the decline in practice of the "family" as traditionally conceived: married with children in a single household. Yet the Berlins show a much higher proportion of single-person households than do the two republics as a whole, although by far the greatest increase has been in West Berlin, where singles occupied 52 percent of the households in 1981. What should be emphasized about the household statistics is that they reveal very little about partnership forms. It is likely that many singles have stable partners with whom they do not reside; they maintain separate apartments in case the partnership does not last.

A second process pointed to by household figures is the changing nature of co-generational residence. In 1986, only 2 percent of all households in the entire West German republic contained people of three generations. Although no statistics are available for the GDR, East Berlin patterns are probably similar to those in West Germany, with the three-generational model being somewhat more frequent in the rest of the East German republic. Not only are the elderly increasingly living alone or together with other elderly, but given the low reproductive rates in the two republics, fewer adults below retirement age now live with children. Additionally, the three-child family represented as necessary to reproduce the population by the East German state explicitly, and the West German state implicitly, is in fact characteristic

Table 14. *Percentage of multi-person households, with and without children, in West Berlin, East Berlin, the FRG, and the GDR, 1981–1982*

| Household type/% | W. Berlin | FRG | E. Berlin | GDR |
|---|---|---|---|---|
| Without children | 52 | 36 | 47 | 49 |
| With children | 48 | 63 | 53 | 51 |

*Sources:* Schwarz 1988: 98; *Materialien* 1987: 272

of less than 10 percent of all family units in both Berlins. That leads us to the final section, on childcare patterns.

**Childcare**

Table 14 illustrates the relation of households with children to those without in the two Berlins and two Germanies. As of 1980, a majority (52 percent) of multi-person households in West Berlin includes no children; for East Berlin such households total 47 percent. Only 25 percent of the total number of households in West Berlin, substantially less than in West Germany, includes children. The rates for East Berlin and East Germany are much closer to those of West Berlin than they are to those of West Germany. In East Berlin, 74.4 percent of all children live with two officially defined legal parents (80 percent for the GDR), 25.6 percent live with a single parent, among whom 93 percent with the mother, 7 percent with the father. In West Berlin 78 percent of all children live with two parents (90 percent for the FRG as a whole), 22 percent live with a single parent, among whom 85 percent with the mother, 15 percent with the father. Given the strong legal status of the mother and weak status of the father in both states, it is not surprising that women presently play a much greater role in parenting than do men. This pattern is, again, more extreme in Berlin.

Lastly, let us turn to parenting and household structure. The average large apartment house in Berlin in 1981–1982 had minimally ten kinship units, of which 32.5 percent in East Berlin and 52 percent in West Berlin were single-person households. The average household size of the multi-person households is 3.0 in East Berlin, 2.7 in West Berlin (compared to 3.1 and 3.09 for the GDR and FRG, respectively), meaning that close to half of all multi-person households in both cities include no children. In 1985, of all new mothers in East Berlin, 48 percent were single, (33.6 percent in the GDR), compared to 20 percent in West Berlin (15 percent in the FRG). In East Berlin, nearly 47 percent of all multi-person households (mostly heterosexual couples in LG) have no children, and 61.5 percent of all mothers have only a single child. In West Berlin, 51 percent of all multi-person households have no children, and 54 percent of all mothers have only a single child.

Single mothers in the GDR had a preferred legal status (especially with regard to childcare and apartment allocation), whereas in West Germany their weaker status was not compensated for by the state. We can see that the explicit West German state policy of encouraging mothers to marry did in fact seem to reduce the increase in the number of women who chose to risk not attaching themselves to a husband before giving birth to a child. On the other hand, the explicit East German policy of strengthening state support for mothers, regardless of marital status, had the opposite effect on women, enabling them to become mothers without having a husband, in effect separating partnership from the decision to give birth.

In 1987, Wolfgang Speigner, the director of the demographic section of the Academy of Science of the GDR, forecast that: "We must deal with a stable procreative rate but sinking birth rate in the year 2000 . . . [and along with this] a decline in the total population" (1987: 15). The same kind of prognosis seems to hold for West Berlin and West Germany. But since the opening of the Wall in November 1989, the duality of the two systems has broken down, and German demographic patterns are now being shaped in a different context. Unification has resulted in a massive population transfer of more than one million people from East to West. Moreover, the united Berlin is a favorite site for Eastern European workers, some of whom merely come to work illegally, some of whom apply for citizenship. In the future, the united Germany could easily increase its working-age population if it relaxed immigration policy. It is likely, however, that unification will also entail a new hegemony for West German labor policy in the new republic. This means that policy is more likely to react to crisis situations and import "guestworkers" at a time of labor shortage than to rethink fundamentally the nature of Germanness and its relation to the reproduction of a population and culture.

# 4

# State strategies and kinship

## Strategies over time

Stated simply, my objective in this schematic overview of state strategies will be to write a history of family policy as a future-oriented narrative whose telos is to direct the citizen's lifecourse. This history disaggregates and contextualizes kin codes; it will not reduce the family and the state to simple control instruments or voluntarist arrangements. I will disaggregate law and policy by isolating the shifts in units or objects of state interest between 1945/1949 and 1989 and contextualize by relating kin strategies to the larger state goal of nation-building in the context of the Cold War. This type of analysis does not easily lend itself to praise or chastise the motivations of policymakers or states, who may well be aware of what they want but are rarely able to foresee the rules of the game in its entirety. Hence during the making of policy they are unable to predict fully the effects of their strategic moves, and therefore unable to close the narrative.

I will focus on three characteristics of postwar family policy:

1 On the historically arbitrary yet contextually constrained nature of strategies of kin restoration/construction during the Cold War. Both parts of Berlin and both states began with the same set of demographic circumstances (the same population, the effects of the same wars), yet the solutions proposed were rarely the same, and when they were, they took on different meanings.

2 On the alternating employment of signification, communication, and self-techniques by the states in the construction of institutionally typified and standardized lifecourses.

3 On the mirror-imaging and misrecognition (*méconnaissance*)[1]

inherent in East and West German domestic policy, illustrating how the Cold War affected the construction of even the most "apolitical" and romantic of objects, such as the child and the mother.

An analysis of the details of kin policies in the two German states obtains coherence only when we examine policies comparatively over time and then interpret the prescribed lifecourse in terms of state narrative strategies about nation-building. In other words, a history of family law, written from an anthropological perspective, is a history of narrative strategies engaged in by the state to influence the lifecourse of its nationals. These maneuvers ultimately aim to fix the meaning of kin relations essential to the constitution of citizens as subjects, meaning that the citizens themselves should preferably desire to structure their lives according to the official rules. To be sure, formal rules have a tenuous and complex relationship to actual kinship practices; rarely, if ever, are they isomorphic with one another. I describe practices for East and West Berlin separately in chapters 5 through 8.

In this attempt at nation-building – to define, regularize, institution-alize, and normalize the domestic practices of the self[2] – the state codifies and legalizes the desires for specific kinds of relations and specific kinds of selves. Running parallel to nation-building are pro-cesses of state formation. It is precisely around state formation that most academic work has been concentrated, on the development of "the state" as a set of autonomous, bureaucratic institutions with its own set of internal operational rules and actors.[3] Often scholars conflate nation-building with state-building, ignoring both the inter-action of states with the cultural practices out of which form is obtained as well as the everyday lives of the citizens that policy seeks to regulate. The legal texts and policy settings of a state obtain their full meaning not with reference to state formation, and not in the process of their enactment by policymaking bodies, but in the process of their being read or appropriated as formal codes by citizens. In other words, the authorship of legal texts and the ostensive references of the law (what it says) are less important than what it talks *about*. As Paul Ricoeur writes in his essay, "The Model of the Text": "What has to be understood is not the initial situation of discourse, but what points towards a possible world. Understanding has less than ever to do with the author and his situation. It wants to grasp the proposed worlds opened up by the references of the text" – by which he means the non-ostensive references of the law, the "something disclosed in front of it" (1981: 218).

Furthermore, once enacted by the state, laws are variously appropriated by citizens and thereafter take on a life independent of the motivations of the lawmakers and sets of institutional arrangements which gave them birth. This is not to say that the law is open to arbitrary reading, that its meaning is totally dependent on its appropriation, for the law itself imposes constraints upon possible interpretations. The interpretation of texts, "by virtue of the exactness of their situation in the world," writes Edward Said, "has already commenced, [they] are objects already constrained by, and constraining, their interpretation. Such texts can thereafter be construed as having need at most of complementary, as opposed to supplementary, readings" (1983: 39). Depending on how legal codes are appropriated, citizens then carry them around (in altered form) in their very subjectivities, as part of the "natural order of things," the *doxa* that makes quotidian life predictably and recognizably German for them. I refer to the strategies embodied in these codes, formulated by proto- and quasi-state actors as well as by official state representatives, as either "state strategies" or simply "the state." Hence, the central question posed is: what sort of "institutionally typified and standardized" lifecourse, what sort of belonging pattern, is envisioned by the law of two German states?

The movement from individual practices to a standardized lifecourse is not a process unique to Western social welfare states, but in fact can be found in some form in all societies, including stateless ones. Stanley Tambiah (1984), for instance, has demonstrated how the biography of the Buddha, standardized over time in written texts within Southeast Asia, now serves as a paradigm for sainthood among Thai forest monks. He shows how the movement from textual paradigm to life model for forest-dwelling monks is intricately connected to sources of power and relations between Thai society and polity. In a somewhat different but parallel fashion, I propose to look at attempts to standardize the lifecourse of Berliners, constructed in interaction with state models over a forty-year period. Control over this lifecourse, as argued in chapter 1, is necessary for the production of belonging patterns essential to modern states in (re)producing nations they can call their own. Kinship is the main social field in which this lifecourse is contested.[4]

The process of kinship construction is often narrowed, by anthropologists and historians of the family alike, to a consideration of relationships based on blood (consanguinity) and marital ties (affinity) (see

Table 15. *Narrative strategies of the East and West German states, 1949–1989*

| Forms/States | East Germany (GDR) | West Germany (FRG) |
|---|---|---|
| Strategy | | |
| 1949–1965/68 | Construction | Restoration |
| 1965–1989 | Sentimentalization | Desentimentalization |
| Emplotment | | |
| Aesthetic | Romantic | Satiric-lapsarian |
| Ideational | Integrational | Assimilational |
| Teleological | Egalitarian | Hierarchical |

Bourdieu 1977: 58–71). Historical shifts in the generative categories of both the "idiom of kinship" and aspects of self production are generally ignored. David Schneider (1984) argues that such a narrow definition of kin ends up replicating folk categories of blood and marital ties at the analytical level, limiting the analyst's purview to the ideational self-representations of an historically specific Western grouping pattern. If the analyst proceeds in this manner, s/he is likely to find and explain a reified mean or normative family that unavoidably excludes possible non-blood and non-marital ties also generating kin. Often these non-consanguinal and affinal ties are lumped together as "fictive" or "categorical" kin, a rather deceptive if not meaningless label since all kin are culturally constructed categories, thus by nature both "fictive" and "categorical." Even if the native him/herself or the native state, as in the case of the two Germanies, makes these distinctions, they serve a useful *analytical* purpose only when they explain the actual practice of households, partnerships, childcare, and self. This holy foursome in fact defines kin; it is its operation that "kinship theory," if there is such a thing, seeks to explain. I suggest, then, that we approach family constructions as a nexus of relationship and self-techniques always being constituted over time, rather than begin with the assumption that the family is a set of formal, already-constituted relationships handed on from one generation to the next.[5]

Comparative policy transformations are informed by fairly consistent use of master narratives, which the state inscribes as models that give form to the everyday experiences of the citizens. To orient the reader in the following analysis, we can summarize the narrative strategies of the two states in table 15. Because official discourse becomes detached from the conditions of its immediate enactment, it employs mechanisms within its historical narrative to insure a correct reading over time. These mechanisms are linguistic in nature, and function much as genre does for more conventional literary texts, to predispose a proper reception by controlling the range of meanings in the formal environment. The consistent use of different generative principles in a state's narrative gives a *specific form to policy* and a *unique emplotment to experiencing it*. In other words, even when the content of law or policy in the two states is nearly identical, it will be read differently depending on the specific linguistic devices of the state's narrative.

Accordingly, law and policy in the GDR exploited an aesthetic strategy of *romantic* emplotment and an ideational strategy of *integration* oriented toward egalitarian ends. Law and policy in the FRG exploit an aesthetic strategy of *satiric* emplotment along with a *lapsarian* (backward-looking) form and an ideational strategy of *assimilation* oriented toward hierarchical ends.

Let us explore in more detail the consequences of these narrative strategies. Differentiation by aesthetic form entails the use of romantic self-images and apperceptions for East Germany, of satiric self-images and apperceptions for West Germany. The use of a romantic or satiric mode has consequences for the way in which a narrative is figured and hence, as argued above, for the manner in which it is read; in this case, we are dealing with state narratives and possible reader-reception options as citizens appropriates legal codes in their everyday practices. Romanticism, defined by Northrop Frye in his classic work on genre theory as "the search of the libido or desiring self for a fulfillment that will deliver it from the anxieties of reality but will still contain that reality" (1957: 193), is an emplotment mode intrinsic to socialist republics.[6] Frye stresses how romance is tied to a utopian fantasy aimed at transfiguration of the everyday to restore some lost Eden or to anticipate a future one. Considered cross-culturally, common elements of romance include the implication of a total commitment that can bring about great self sacrifice, a transcendent personal identity that thrives on fantasy, and the construction of "an illusory world of absolute happiness and fulfillment" (Lindholm 1988: 6, 28, 34). Since the nineteenth century, the various socialist utopian schemes in Western Europe contain all of these elements.

Satire, on the other hand, is intrinsic to liberal republics with constitutions. It presupposes homogeneous, transcendental moral standards in order to ridicule vice in a supposedly stable society. Rather than transfiguring the everyday, as is the goal of romance, satire aims merely to substitute for the everyday a superior version of its present form.[7] Because it condemns corruption and decadence, "all satire," argues Theodor Adorno, "is [necessarily] blind to the forces liberated by decay." Although satire often identifies itself with the oppressed, continues Adorno, this is "especially [true for] those who in reality [are] no longer so." Identification of the West German state and its leaders with victims of fascism, as discussed in chapter 1, was a convenient aesthetic emplotment of experience, a satiric stance of identifying itself as victim while simultaneously incorporating former Nazis into a number of prominent positions in government and industry. Hence satire, maintains Adorno, while representing itself as "on the crest of progress," is never totally able to forsake its superior moral grounds, which tend to come from its alliance with authority (1984: 210–212). More specifically, this authority is grounded in the constitution. Armed with a lapsarian form (as in constitutional republics such as the FRG), satire will become more backward-looking over time in order to maintain its vision of humanity as invariant.

Working in the romantic mode, the GDR perceived its policies and citizenry in idealized form, as progressive, following a nearly sacred mission (fulfillment of the Five Year Plan). In the first several decades of the republic, state policy was aimed toward a future communist destiny; in the eighties, policy increasingly romanticized its early and present accomplishments. The Plan had primarily religious or communitarian functions, and only secondarily economic ones. Its meaning was less practical than visionary; or, in the terms of speech-act theory, it is to be understood at the illocutionary (performative) level rather than by its locutionary (propositional) or perlocutionary (consequential) meanings. In conformance with socialist principles, GDR leaders perceived their laws as performing both educative and configurative roles, simultaneously enforcing social rules and constructing them. The ruling Socialist Unity Party (SED) acted "in the interests of the working class and their allied classes and groups to lead and protect the socialist re-construction of the society" (*Kleines Politisches Wörterbuch* 1986: 796).

The FRG perceives its policies and citizenry in lapsarian form, under the rubric of a timeless constitution, "the Basic Law of 1949," which embodies permanent truths that protect the Germans from a fallen or degraded world (e.g., Nazism or communism). At the time of its adoption, politicians purposefully avoided calling the Basic Law a constitution, stressing in the preamble its provisional nature, and in Article 146 that a *Verfassung* would replace the Basic Law following a "free decision" of "the German people," ostensibly meaning after reunification. Legal scholars in the FRG, nonetheless, treat the Basic Law as a constitution.[8] They express a populist view of the role of law: law should not lead, but remain in accordance with or "reflect" the wishes of the majority – so long as these wishes are not *verfassungswidrig*, against the constitution (for a summary of family law, see Glendon 1989; Limbach 1988: 11–33; Willenbacher 1988: 141–166). For the FRG, it is not the community or Plan for the future that is worshipped but the Basic Law. In her study of constitutional democracies, Hannah Arendt rightly points to the religious nature of constitutions in such republics, how the worship of this document is intimately connected to the Roman concept of authority, a sense of being "bound back" to one's beginning. Although the power is given to the people, "the source of law," writes Arendt, "[resides in] the Constitution, a written document, an endurable objective thing" (1985: 157).[9] Using basically lapsarian argumentation, state officials have most often used the Office of Protection of the Constitution to declare illegal or to harass more future-oriented minority groups that have been critical of this origin (including peace and youth groups, pacifists, and communists), and not, as Arendt idealizes, "to prevent . . . the procedures of majority decisions from generating into elective despotism of majority rule" (1985: 164–165). Since the late fifties, the principles of *Verfassungsschutz* (protecting the constitution) and *Verfassungspatriotismus* (being loyal to the constitution) have taken on increased importance for West German identity-building, especially in times of conflict.

Ideational differentiation entails the use of integrative mechanisms with, to use Talcott Parsons' terminology (1951: 101–112), universalistic criteria and principles of achieved identity for East Germany, of assimilative mechanisms with particularistic criteria and principles of ascribed identity for West Germany. Following socialist ideology, the GDR provided standards that it *universalized* in its principles of membership: anyone could theoretically become a citizen of the socialist republic. Hence Germanness was also an achieved identity: it granted rights as well as requiring duties. In creating equal chances and equal rights for all, it de-differentiated social groups and special interest patterns and sought to integrate all its members on the single criterion of being socialist. This tendency to de-differentiate was strengthened at the systemic level after the securing of the borders in 1961, for a major concern of kinship policy was to assure the labor stability necessary for effective central planning.

Following liberal-democratic ideology, the FRG relies on membership principles that it *particularizes* in its policies: one is born *deutschstämmig*, of German blood. Hence Germanness is an innate or ascribed identity. In accordance with the norms of a pluralistic, class society, the FRG differentiates social groups and hierarchically assimilates people through policies applied non-uniformly to various interest formations. As the *Wirtschaftswunder* subsided in the early 1970s, the economic component of kin policy came to the fore, and, in contrast to the goal of labor stability in the GDR, the FRG pursued a strategy promoting more labor mobility. This, in turn, further necessitated a more differentiated and partial kin policy aimed at differently impacting various groups and classes within the population.

Although the two German republics have proceeded between 1949 and 1988 to reconstruct the family on the basis of radically different, often oppositional, assumptions about what constitutes families and about the legitimate role of family policy in the state's relation to its citizens, they both represent themselves as strong defenders of the family. In the constitutions that accompanied the foundation of the two states in 1949, the positions on the relationship of the state to the family are nearly identical. Articles 3 and 6 of the Basic Law of the FRG, and Articles 7, 18, and 30–33 of the Constitution of the GDR speak in very similar terms, that is, of the "special protection" to be accorded by the state to "marriage and the family," equal rights for men and women, special protection for mothers, "natural" childcare rights of parents, and equal rights for "children born out of wedlock."

This formal agreement on the importance of the family masks fundamental differences over its meaning and the proper narrative strategies used in its construction. In the rest of this chapter, the analysis of kin policy will center on explaining the following historical paradox: that until the 1970s, the "special protections to be accorded to marriage and family" in the FRG were based on a *sentimentalization of kinship* which, in turn, was dependent on an ideology of love and a *strategy of restoration*. This strategy crystallized around support for what was officially called the *Hausfrauenehe*, housewife marriage.[10]

Prodded by social protests around 1968, educational, legal, and economic reforms slowly shifted the kinship focus from love and a particular partnership form to economics and child-centered families. The opposite pattern holds true for the GDR: from 1949 to approximately 1965, educational, legal, and economic reforms placed the child at the center of a strategy of *kinship reconstruction* and *desentimentalized* the family and partnership forms. After 1965, love and sentiment were brought back into family law, and by the mid 1980s partnership in the form of a state-sanctioned marriage had become the legal focus of family policy.

In effect, the two states reversed themselves over time, adopting foci which their opponent had earlier embraced. Neither policy followed a linear trajectory. Yet, in the forty-four years of dual organization, the two states remained remarkably consistent in both style of self-representation and explicit nexus to kin policy. Regarding self-representation, the socialist state found it necessary to display itself, to herald its every maneuver and tactic in directing change; the capitalist state found it necessary to hide itself in order to foster an illusion of the autonomous consumer, to maintain that it merely follows the wishes of the majority and does not constitute them. Regarding the nexus to kin policy, the socialist state consistently sought to change the context, the public arena, in which kin is constituted, in one sense colonizing all public space; the capitalist state consistently sought to avoid public regulation, instead relying on "market forces" or agents acting in the private sphere (primarily advertising and consumer industries) to stimulate private desires into a particular public mold.[11] Despite differences in appearances and nearly simultaneous "incorporation of the contrary" into policy in the mid 1960s, the oppositional movements and self-constructs are discernible equally for both sides. Let us backtrack momentarily and examine the ideological context of state strategies.

**Ideology in the GDR**
Even before the founding of the two German states in 1949, postwar leaders in all of the occupation zones were concerned as part of the denazification process with constructing new models of citizen/state relations. Only leaders in the Soviet Zone, however, were also involved in writing new legal norms for kinship practices. For leaders in the East, the two reform processes went hand-in-hand. For those in the West, kinship codes (even when inherited from the Nazi regime) were considered private affairs of more concern to the church than the state. Hence they initially reformed only the most pernicious aspects of race, marital, and eugenics laws inherited from past German regimes, avoiding the more substantial changes until 1976. The dualistic, oppositional nature of Cold War thought penetrated every area of legal reconstruction, including that of family law.

Within days of the unconditional German surrender, the Soviet Military Administration (SMAD) began a radical transformation of the political and legal system in the Soviet Occupied Zone.[12] But unlike reformers in the Soviet Union after the October Revolution, they consistently supported the nuclear family as a unit. After 1949, GDR legal theorists and policymakers differentiated their reform from that of their West German counterparts, in that they refused to grant the family a "neutral corner," but instead saw the family as a "basic collective" that would work with other collectives – school collectives, the residentially organized *Hausgemeinschaften*, the work-organized *Brigaden* – to integrate individuals into the work process and the society. Early GDR theoreticians took their inspiration on state–society–family relations directly from Marx and Engels, supplemented by the work of Clara Zetkin (1960) on the role of women. While Lenin's theories of state development – e.g., the dictatorship of the proletariat, the leading role of the Party – were crucial for state–citizen theory and remained so through 1989,[13] Lenin had little to say about the family. Other socialist theories that centered around free love or alternate family forms were either totally ignored or summarily dismissed.

From the Marxist–Leninist perspective taken in the GDR, family forms and relationships were to be understood within the context of the total productive relations of the society.[14] The family itself, much as the society, was expected to develop progressively according to evolutionary principles. Engel's three stages of family forms corresponding to the evolutionary stages of civilization – group marriage for Savagery, pair marriage for Barbarism, and monogamy along with divorce and prostitution for Civilization – were taught in GDR schools, even through the period of my fieldwork.[15] With the advent of socialism, Marxist theoreticians predicted that the progressive elements of Civilization (such as heterosexual monogamy) would be strengthened; divorce and prostitution would disappear.

Although the very first writings coming out of the Soviet Occupied Zone in 1946 envisioned a family form that was nonpatriarchal,[16] that form still had an implicit late-nineteenth-century socialist moral base: monogamous, heterosexual couples who both work and raise children, who all love each other, where property (through inheritance and gender-specific wage dependence) no longer plays the organizing role. This vision remained at the center of GDR kinship codes. Yet, the content of this nuclear family form was radically redefined, specifically with reference to the relations of women to men within a marriage and their relation to work. An early GDR legal theorist, H. Nathan, argued that the new legal orientations would undermine two prior assumptions: first, that the "woman is predestined to perform the housework," and second, "that she will always be the weaker one" (1949: 102–103). In retrospect, these assumptions are particularly significant in that they do not allow the woman to define herself as victim. Rather, legal theorists assumed women of the future could and would attain the same educational qualifications and positions in the society as men.[17] Subsequently, women were encouraged, often even forced, to become active agents in public life in the postwar economic re-construction of the society, and not allowed to legitimate their usually inferior social statuses with arguments appealing to woman's nature or with appeals to the difficulty of overcoming a long history of discrimination. Nor were they allowed to retreat into motherhood. Recognizing that most working women were also mothers – many of them single mothers – Nathan, among others, argued that the status of mother must not be an impediment to women as workers. To carry through the logic of this argument, the state began erecting institutions to lighten the burden of parenting.

The lifecourse of Germans, as envisioned in GDR theory, while assumed to be teleological and progressive, was not to be gender-specific and could be subject to conscious individual and societal redirection. As we shall see in the next section, initial policymakers in the Federal Republic proceeded from opposite assumptions: they tried to strengthen traditional patriarchal–bourgeois marital roles by appealing to the naturalness of gender roles, and they denied any historical evolution in the development of the family. (If anything, leaders in the FRG argued that devolution characterized the postwar German family. Many observers were convinced the German family had broken down and was collapsing.)

**Ideology and the FRG**

The signing of the *Grundgesetz*, Basic Law, of the FRG in 1949, which guaranteed equal rights for men and women, was accompanied by an order that the contradictory passages from the *Bürgerliches Gesetzbuch* (Civil Law Code of 1896, hereafter cited as BGB) be amended or stricken by March 31, 1953. The Konrad Adenauer regime did not get around to studying the needed changes until October 1952, a mere six months before the Basic Law mandated that they be implemented. Since the existing legal provisions concerning property and family deviated significantly from the Basic Law, the task of how to equalize relations between the sexes fell to individual courts. Yet, even before the first reforms, the regime passed two laws with direct bearing on family–state and citizen–state relations. First, on June 26, 1951, membership in the Free German Youth (FDJ), the youth organization in the East, was declared unconstitutional; this prevented West Berlin/West German youth from partaking in common activities with youth in the East. Second, on November 22, 1951, the ruling coalition in the FRG proposed to make it unconstitutional to be a member of the Communist Party (KPD). Although this ban was not enacted until 1957 (at which time a new matrimonial property law was also worked out), it effectively stigmatized and hindered Communist Party members or those on the "Left" from partaking in many public activities in the FRG. Both measures had the desired *Abgrenzungs*-effect, that is, they made political loyalty to the state a priority over national or kin loyalties.[18] And both measures helped to create a new set of significations for old objects, that is, the Communists and their sympathizers effectively replaced Nazis as the correct, official oppositional figure or mirror-image for the construction of West Berlin/West German identity.

The 1953 reforms of the old BGB, Civil Law Code, were twofold: the reforms altered the two passages most antagonistic to women's formal equality (§1354 granting the husband sole right to make all family decisions, and §1628 and §1629 granting the husband sole legal standing for both marital partners) and created a new Ministry of the Family, to be headed by Dr. Franz Josef Würmeling, a conservative Catholic and member of the ruling Christian Democratic Union Party (CDU).

Much as Hilde Benjamin, the second Minister of Justice in East Germany (whose early texts we will examine in the next section) initially shaped the GDR family-law reconstruction, so did Würmeling initially shape the FRG family-law restoration. Würmeling's context, however, was quite different from Benjamin's in that he began four years later, aware that the GDR had already completed major structural reforms, and driven by a need to negate, or minimally oppose, the actions already taken in the East. The minority Social Democratic Party (SPD) – which controlled the city government of West Berlin at this time – initially opposed many of Adenauer's policies and skeptically viewed the creation of the Family Ministry in 1953. But they were excluded from ruling coalitions at the federal level until 1966 and until that time exercised little political initiative in this domain. Adenauer justified the creation of the Ministry not on conservative ideational grounds, but by an appeal to more neutral demographic or pro-natal needs, to deal with the "growing overly old population of the Germans" (Ruhl 1988: 119).

Würmeling clarified his tasks in a December 1953 Congressional speech: "The church [is] my best and most important protagonist in fulfilling my tasks . . . [which center around] inner, ethical renewal" (cited in Langer 1985: 110). The Evangelical (or Protestant) and Catholic churches had made their positions *vis-à-vis* reform quite clear in the years immediately preceding Würmeling's appointment. For example, with respect to basic equal rights between men and women, guaranteed by the Basic Law of 1949, the Evangelical church feared a devaluation of the "Christian Marriage," and the Catholic church feared a destruction of the "natural, Christian concept of order" (Ruhl 1988: 165–175). The goal then, shared by the Family Ministry and the churches alike, was not structural-economic reform, as was Benjamin's in the East, but a sentimental one: to restore the family to its former, honorable status. This restoration was also signaled by the national Supreme Court in its 1953 ruling on equal rights: partners would each contribute to the marriage "*what they were capable of,*" meaning "work outside the home" for the man and "housework and care for the children" for the women. Single women, working women, children, and non-marital relationships were ignored.

In his appeal to ethical renewal, Würmeling referred to the values of workmanship, tradition, readiness to sacrifice, and respect for Christian values. The state as such was not to interfere in the sphere of the family. That function belonged to the church, to which Würmeling ascribed an "independent" and "free" role in shaping the ethics and customs of the family. Instead of a state policy aimed at alleviating domestic tensions, Würmeling proposed that families play a foreign policy role: in their state-supported and secured private functions, they would be part of a general national defense effort and form a bulwark against communist influences. "A million innerly healthy families with correctly raised children," he wrote, "are at least as important a security against the threatening danger of the large families in the East as is all of our military security" (cited in Langer 1985: 110). For him, working women were a specific characteristic of communist countries, not something that belonged to the "Free World."

This simple model of family–state relations served, in effect, to affirm the *Hausfrauenehe*, housewife marriage, and to deny the need for structural economic changes, as propounded by the GDR (see Helwig 1982: 8). The 1955 report of the Federal Ministry for Family Questions made the connection explicit: "[If the] suction industry [the growing economy] continues to absorb women into the workplace, we must soon fear that in the near future the majority of all young mothers will be working outside the home. That will surely lead – certainly against the will of those involved – down another road to the same social order that already is regnant in the countries of the Eastern ilk" (*Familienlastenausgleich* 1955: 23).

One cannot overestimate the significance of the Catholic church in shaping family policy in the formative years of the FRG. Because of the ties between the church and Adenauer and Würmeling, church positions to a large extent became state policy. In any case, a strong division between church and state had never as such existed in German history. Still today, all West German citizens (and with unity, East Germans, 75 percent of whom identify themselves as atheists) must pay mandatory church taxes, unless they personally petition for a waiver. The Catholic church was perhaps the first large policymaking institution in the FRG to engage in *Abgrenzung*. Three months before the FRG declared itself a state, the "Holy Office" in the Western Zones closed its sacraments to communists. The German bishops based this decision on the assumption "that the representatives in Bonn of the socialist and liberal world-view have shown no understanding of essential Christian demands" (Hollenstein 1985: 238). Foremost among these demands were support for Christian morality and family life, embodied in laws forbidding premarital sex and homosexuality, birth control and abortion, making divorce prohibitively expensive and difficult to obtain, and mandating public support of parochial schools. Discussion of the role of the Catholic church in supporting Hitler and the Third Reich, including the signing of the Concordat between Hitler and the Pope in 1933, was avoided until the mid 1960s, and then forced on the church by dissident members (Hollenstein 1985: 240–241).

The Evangelical church in Germany positioned itself much more critically *vis-à-vis* its role in Nazi Germany and its relation to the East. It represented itself as engaged in *Brückenbildung*, bridge-building, between East and West, and fought against a quick integration of the FRG into a Western European/American alliance (Greschat 1985: 277–280). Protestant organizations were active in maintaining ties with groups in the GDR and worked together with other interest groups in organizing large demonstrations against the remilitarization of West Germany in 1954–1955. They were again active in resisting the introduction of atomic weapons into West Germany in 1957–1958.

Some Protestant groups put forth progressive policy positions oriented to recognition of changing family configurations and problems. They were, however, counterbalanced by the positions of other groups more in line with the Catholics, who "feared and worried about the collapse of customs." By the 1970s, the Protestant groups showed two non-complementary positions. One side argued for restoration, a position manifested in papers issued jointly with the Catholic Bishops, including, e.g., the "Law of the State and the Moral Order" (1970), "Basic Values and the Law of God" (1979), "Yes to Marriage" (1981). The other side argued for reconstruction, a position manifested in papers such as "Memorandum to Questions of Sexual Ethics" (1971), "Women in the Family, Church, and Society" (1979), and "Marriage and Non-Marital Arrangements" (1985). (For a discussion see Keil 1988: 198–221.)

Having explored the ideational background against which the two states enacted specific laws to construct particular, oppositional model citizens, I will now turn to an examination of the evolution of legal codes.

### Hilde Benjamin's key text

For the first twenty years after the war, the GDR took the initiative in formulating new kin codes. West German reactions to these changes were primarily of three sorts: to ignore them, to dismiss them as forms of East Zone Communism/totalitarianism, or to define their own law in opposition to East reforms. A seminal 1949 legal text entitled "Suggestions for a new German Family Law" (1982: 160–175), written by Hilde Benjamin, the soon-to-be Minister of Justice, defined the initial terms of debate. Because of the centralized, hierarchical nature of policymaking in the GDR, Benjamin was able to shape single-handedly legal reform. A detailed analysis of this one text allows us to decode initial state strategies, to uncover the range of meanings in the proposed legal reconstructions of the lifecourse. Published sixteen years prior to the first GDR Family Law Book and shortly before the founding of the two states, this article anticipates nearly all of the developments which were of concern in subsequent years.

Benjamin addresses the family law of a single *Deutschland* and writes of a united German constitution, *gesamtdeutsche Verfassung*. Her suggestions are situated within the context of German history, specifically of the suggested family-law reforms in the Weimar period, in both 1924 and 1931/1932. And, she draws upon the late-nineteenth-century work of the German communist and feminist, Clara Zetkin.[19] Her intentions in this text, as well as in other family-law reforms until 1965, are not to engage in *Abgrenzung*, demarcation from West Germany, but to push for pan-German reform. What are the theoretical needs behind a new family law, she asks, and what is the status of the current law? Two primary areas are to be addressed in the new family law: "equal rights of the woman as wife and as mother, and new nonmarital rights."

### Mothers

"The legal codification of the position of women not only concerns the woman," argues Benjamin,

but also influences the position of the man, and the relation of both woman and man to the children. And it is crucial that everyone affected by these questions, both men and women, reflect upon them, and that they themselves take positions. Our new laws should not be the work of lawyers, who sit behind their desks – not even when these lawyers are women – rather, they should be the result of a broad democratic exchange of views.

For a reader familiar with only the GDR of the 1970s and 1980s, Benjamin's pleas for more democracy and citizen initiative seem incongruent. Her goal, as well as that of other East German legal reformers, was to mobilize the population for the grand task of *Aufbau*, construction. She knew the regime would fail if it could not rally the people behind it.

In the remainder of her article, and indeed, as we shall see, in the remainder of her work and in the general development of family law in the GDR, the law was formulated from the perspectives of wife, mother, child, woman, and man. Lawmakers ignored the perspective of the father and those of other kin, such as sibling, uncle, aunt, or grandparent. The rights of the father and husband, which were central and all-encompassing in the BGB of 1896, along with those of other relatives, were either altogether removed from the law or balanced with those of working women and mothers. This change in perspective, giving working women and mothers legal rights, singles out the female as mother and worker for a variety of forms of state support, while the male as father loses his signification. By the mid 1970s, as we shall see, women's concerns had again been equated with those of "the family" – their status as workers was falsely assumed secured – and the man's status *vis-à-vis* the family had been legally marginalized. The new legal code had rectified the major disparities along gender lines, but it had not made family law neutral with regard to gender.

### Workers

Already in 1949 women were playing a major role in the GDR labor force. Benjamin concludes that whereas women had already been

granted equal rights politically, and were active equal partners economically, this was not yet true in terms of their *bürgerliche*, civil, rights;
women now needed "the realization of the same legal equality in the
area of civil rights." The precondition of this development was that
women acquired professional skills, "which would root them in the
society and secure their independence." This did not mean that they
would be forced to work, says Benjamin. She offers the example of
pregnancy as a time when they need not work (although women are
not to be excluded because of pregnancy). It is important, she argues,
to establish in the consciousness of women that their independence is
self-evidently based on their role as qualified workers. Benjamin
admits that many women were resisting this step, claiming that it was
not in their interest to learn a profession. Her description of the
objections of two women is worth quoting in its entirety:

A woman who had heard a Leipzig radio program on women's equal rights
wrote to me, "How can a woman demand the same rights as a man? A woman is
a woman and not a man-woman, *Mannweib* . . . As a woman I will forego these
public rights, and so will the many other women who think like I do."
    Another woman indicated, "If a man entirely provides for his wife and family,
then the woman should see her task in the household and as a mother." And a
man expressed, "As men, we do not marry women so that they then still must go
off and work, rather, we would like to lead a family life."

The fears expressed by the women and the man in these letters are
unique to this first postwar generation. Many women feared that by
making work outside the home part of their identity, they would end up
losing their position, i.e., becoming a *Mannweib*: losing their femininity
along with their identity as mothers and homemakers. Although many
of these women had been working outside the home throughout the
Nazi period, the vast majority were poorly trained and worked for low
pay; many had been forced to go to work for the Nazi cause. Postwar
governmental attempts through ideological arguments to involve
women in the labor force were thus often viewed with extreme
skepticism, if not openly resisted.
    Benjamin concludes that what lies behind this position is the fear of
the double burden both of having to work outside the home and of
having to do all the household duties. The solution to this, she argues, is
more childcare facilities: kindergartens and after-school care; and better
public facilities: laundromats and convenient shopping centers to lessen
housework.

Soviet Occupation Order No. 253 in 1946 had initiated the re-construction, by giving women in the Soviet Zone (outside Berlin, which was ruled by all four Allies together) legal claim to "equal pay for equal work," and Order No. 20 in 1948 extended these rights to women in the Soviet sector of Berlin. These orders were heartily resisted by many men, complains Benjamin, and were difficult to enforce because women suffered both from having poor qualifications and from being overburdened in the home.

Women's inferior legal status, surmises Benjamin, would become clear to them through their own experiences. Despite legal changes, however, many women continued to suffer forms of legal discrimin-ation, and as an example, she points to the uneven property divisions resulting from divorce proceedings: men continued to get the larger share of property after separation.

*Wives*
In the second part of the article, Benjamin deals with the current legal status of married women, which was fixed in legal codes in 1896, enacted in 1900 in §1353–1362 BGB: "The marital partners are bound to one another in a partnership between two people, *Lebensgemeinschaft*." She agreed with this formulation: it will "be the same in the future," but, she says, the content will change, and this with regard to the meaning of "obligation to live together." The BGB intended that the man make all the decisions concerning marital life, that he determine both the apartment in which and place where the couple lived together. The future marriage, she says, will involve working women, not the "only-a-housewife," *Nur-Hausfrau*. This means that in the future the woman cannot be forced to share a residence with her husband. The example she offers is that women seeking further qualifications may be required to live in another city, a right that should be circumscribed only when the household separation of woman from man and family leads to a "damaging of the duty to a marital union." At that point the man has a right to make a claim on the woman's time, she writes; however, this must be balanced against the fact that there are forms of "being together" other than shared residence, such as shared weekends or shared vacations.

Benjamin makes several categorical distinctions here that had pro-found consequences for subsequent GDR law. First, she removes the legal connection between household and partnership, maintaining that household form is no concern of the law. Second, she defines the family form ahistorically, without taking into consideration that the content of the relationships will change. She elevates as model family interests embodied in for-life heterosexual partnerships, consecrated in a legal (marital) contract. With this simple definition, she makes problematic all relationships that cannot obtain this legal form (regardless of similarity in content), such as nonmarital partnerships, single parents, same-sex partnerships, intergenerational family units, and communal or cooperative arrangements of loving and parenting.

Benjamin's purpose in mentioning the content of the heterosexual partnership – that cross-sex partners need not necessarily share a residence – is to make the legal institution of marriage flexible enough to fit contemporary forms of practice, to bring antiquated law into line with the current practice of two working spouses. Living apart or in different household forms, as we shall see in the next section, was a necessity for many partners in the first twenty-five years of the GDR, often precisely for the reason she gives in the example: women and men were simultaneously seeking careers and qualifications. Many of the marriages about which she speaks, however, ended in divorce. Benjamin did not take this into account, nor did she imagine giving the stamp of legality to other forms of partnership or dependency. Her interest in the flexibility of content within heterosexual marriages was not matched by a flexibility about the form. Except for her innovation on household structure, she remains rigidly tied to the old BGB formal family model – one man, one woman, married for life, with children.

Her legal definition politicizes nonnuclear and nonmarital partnerships in two ways. First, they are placed outside of the law, meaning outside of legal protection and legal oversight, and second, individuals not living in the state-sanctioned relationship (marriage) are defined oppositionally. Notwithstanding her many innovative suggestions, Benjamin was proposing a fixed legal model of family relations that over time had less and less to do with actual practices.

Nonetheless, in the same stroke as Benjamin strengthens the formal marriage–family model, she also strengthens the power of a married woman who does not want also to fulfill the traditional roles of a wife. She proposes to eliminate the BGB §1356 Abs.1, which makes it the right and obligation of the woman to make the house a home, *gemeinschaftliches Hauswesen*. Paragraph 1356 Abs.2 makes it the obligation of the woman to do the housework: if her husband owns his own business, she is also obligated to work for him. If the woman does work for her husband, counters Benjamin, it should be only under the condition that she receive a taxable salary in return for her work. In addition, she repeats the argument that a partnership must mean the recognition of the right of the woman to her own residence, that she should not be obligated to live with the husband.

A final partnership problem that Benjamin problematizes is that of the woman's rights concerning changes in family name upon marriage or divorce. The woman should have the right upon marriage, says Benjamin, to maintain her maiden name, to add the maiden name to her husband's name, or to change to the husband's name. After divorce she should also be able to maintain this name. The BGB had made it necessary for the woman to change her name upon marriage, and after divorce she was obligated to retake her maiden name. All of these measures strengthened more the signification of working women and divorcees than that of wives.

### Parents and children

The final set of questions addressed by Benjamin concerns *elterliche Gewalt*, parental authority. The terminology itself is objectionable, she complains, and should in the future stress

equal rights for the child, meaning recognition of his personality. Rather than parental authority, [the concepts] protection and education should be brought to the fore . . . The rules concerning parental authority are the very middle point of our consideration, for until now this parental authority has been in reality not the authority of the parents, but the authority of the father. This is true even when the mother is the actual caretaker: she may raise, clothe, and care for the child, but she cannot be the legal representative of the child. She cannot, for example, contract for an apprenticeship for the child. And when the opinion of the parents differs, that of the father always takes priority.

In the case where a father died and the mother remarried, under the BGB the mother would upon the death of her husband lose her parental rights, and upon remarriage her new husband would then assume parental rights. Benjamin stresses how this right "must be exercised by both parents." In the instance where the parents disagree and cannot decide on the fortunes of the child, the decision should go to a *Vormundschaftsgericht*, juvenile/protectorate court. Under the new law, both parents would be equally obligated after a divorce to contribute to the financial support of the child.

Lastly, Benjamin addresses parental rights for the incomplete family, *unvollkommene Familie*, more specifically the single, self-reliant woman, *alleinstehende selbständige Frau*. Here, she wants to give the man and woman who are single parents the same kind of parental rights as couples have. Problems of single parents balancing childcare and career should be solved, she suggests, "through special accommodations for progressive social education in the schools, youth clubs and organizations." Special support for single mothers and full equal rights for "children born out of wedlock" were, in fact, legally codified in 1950, the year after Benjamin acknowledged their situation and status. This universalized the state's relationship to mothers and children, making their status no longer contingent on husbands or fathers.

As stated above, nearly all of her proposal was enacted into law in 1950. The major domestic significations to be created by kinship law in the postwar period were then already apparent: women as workers, women as mothers, and children as individuals with legal rights. The Federal Republic, on the other hand, did not begin changing its kin laws until 1957, and then quite reluctantly. In 1954, Benjamin, who in the meantime had become GDR Minister of Justice, wrote to the West German Minister of Justice Neumeyer proposing to meet with him to discuss a common reconstruction of kinship laws in order to keep open possible future reunification. Neumeyer refused to reply to her letter. His reaction was not untypical of West German leaders during the Adenauer era, who spoke loudly and incessantly of the need to "reunite Germany," but rejected every concrete proposal that might force them into a dialogue with the leaders in the East. The formal reason for his rejection was tied to what many (in the West) considered the overzealous campaign of Benjamin against former Nazis and political opponents in the East, many of whom were given death sentences. For this, she earned the nickname "Red Guillotine" (Benjamin 1966: 733).

**Comparative history of family law**
Keeping in mind the GDR reforms contained in Benjamin's key text, we can now examine in more detail the legal strategies of the two states as they created themselves. Benjamin's proposals were not only the basis for further developments of East German law, but also served as a mirror-image for initial developments in the Federal Republic. The West Germans themselves proceeded forward in a helter-skelter fashion, if not reluctantly, producing no standard text on kinship. Let us compare the strategies that attempt to shape the

lifecourse through three areas of kinship regulation central to citizens in the two republics: childhood and parenthood, partnerships, and family units.

### Childhood and parenthood

The GDR began to expand the rights of children as autonomous legal entities in the mid 1950s, the FRG first in the late 1970s. In East Germany, Benjamin's 1949 proposal to purge from the law the concept of *elterliche Gewalt*, parental authority – with all its connotations of parental ownership and the supreme authority of the father – was first enacted in 1956. Parental authority was then replaced with a concept of *elterliche Sorge*, parental care. After 1965, this concept was further refined to *Erziehungsrecht*, the right to raise. In West Germany, the concept of parental authority was utilized until 1979, whereupon a "parental care law" was passed. A 1957 parliamentary reform of the law retained the specification in the BGB that the father's decision would prevail in the event of disagreement between parents regarding the child. In 1959, the West German constitutional court declared this law unconstitutional (it contradicted the equal rights provision of the Basic Law), and thereafter policymakers remained silent until 1979. Both states gradually restricted the right of parents suspected of negligence or abuse to retain custody of children, although in neither state did children ultimately attain substantial rights with which they might protect themselves from parental abuse.

The GDR Constitution of 1949 guaranteed "children born out of wedlock," or "illegitimate children," equal rights and protection. The September 22, 1950 Mother and Child Protection Law accelerated the realization of these rights by strengthening the legal status of single and divorced mothers. It mandated the building of public institutions for child care and support, and established state-supported prenatal care for all pregnant women. These measures made substantive legal changes in that they addressed "the child" in a new way: as an entity with needs independent of parental wishes or capabilities. In order to provide equal chances for all children, the state engaged in a kind of affirmative action for children with special problems or for those who needed special protection (such as children with single mothers).

In their 1949 Basic Law, the FRG also had a provision to protect illegitimate children, but the law to put this into effect was not enacted until 1970. The 1950 GDR and 1970 FRG laws are not so dissimilar from each other. Their most basic reform lies in enabling children to inherit and to obtain financial support from their non-married fathers. They also redress the rights of mothers of illegitimate children by giving them the legal right to represent their children without control by juvenile authorities. Fathers of such children are given obligations (such as child support) but no rights unless they establish a legal relationship with the mother through marriage (Ansorg 1967; Stolpe 1986; Limbach 1988: 22, 23).

Support of children has increased equally over time in both countries, although the extent of support and timetable of enactments is quite different. Whereas the GDR began in 1950 to build *en masse* child-support institutions[20] as well as to establish an extensive system of transfer payments to families with children, the Western Allies in 1950 forbade payment of child support by the West German state, condemning it as part of the Nazi race laws and population policy.[21] The FRG began again with a child-support law in 1953, restricted to *Beamten*, civil servants, giving an employment bonus to workers with children. A November 1954 law addressed the general public, establishing a small sum for child support after the birth of the third child (and each child thereafter), and encouraging voluntary child-support payments to large families by individual companies. Throughout the 1950s, the FRG offered various forms of taxation relief for large families, but the major advance came first in 1961, with the enactment of a *Kindergeldkasse*, child-support fund. Child-support money along with other subsidies was thereafter given to families with two or more children. In 1969, a new taxation law offered deductions and subsidies to all families with children, as well as apartment and housing subsidies and financial support for education. This step, again, brought the FRG closer to the policy direction that the GDR had taken ten years earlier.

In a similar fashion, the GDR in 1958 extended child support beyond "large families" to parents of first-born children also, whereas West Germany enacted a comparable law first in 1975. During an economic downturn in 1982, a newly installed ruling coalition led by the Christian Democrats reduced the amount of money transferred per child, but the same coalition subsequently increased the amount several years later. Finally, a 1985 FRG law adjusted support for the second child and each thereafter to the income level of the parents; it also created differential taxation and rules for subsidies of different family types. Many of these rules parallel types of affirmative action for children of less advantaged parents that had been enacted in East Germany during the fifties (see Lüscher and Schultheis 1988: 244–245).

Throughout its history the GDR has maintained a consistent policy of expanding state child support, due both to its ideological commitment to children (in particular to those of the working class), and to its political calculation that increased vertical ties between the state and child would strengthen the child's loyalty to the regime. Policy therefore was more concerned with the child as such than with funneling money or benefits through particular family forms. Children's legal status, which before the war had been totally dependent on the wealth and marital status of the parents, became almost totally independent of these factors. In the early 1950s, an education policy that preferred children from working-class and farm families did result in discrimination against some children from the classes of bureaucrats and intelligentsia, who often then resettled to West Germany (see chapter 5). Given the continuous labor shortage in the GDR, however, this policy had the principal effect of increasing social mobility and thus the status of children who stayed and otherwise wouldn't have had a chance.

With the publication of the GDR Family Law Book in 1965 (hereafter FGB)[22] the state formalized new self-techniques of children and parents. The state had assumed that infrastructural re-construction, in the form of new and pervasive public institutions, was a precondition of social planning, and this work had by then been largely completed. New codes in the 1965 FGB added nothing new to parent–child relations. The periods in the lifecourse pertaining to children, youth, and parents were already clearly demarcated and delineated, as were their relations to one another. Rather than attempt to create new objects for policy or change the relations between those already in existence, the book lists the characteristics that should define the child, in other words, the techniques of the early self.

FGB §1, Section 2 describes the new child: (1) has a sense of responsibility for oneself and others, (2) has a collective consciousness and is ready to help, (3) is unyielding and goal-oriented, (4) is honest and decisive, (5) is courageous and steadfast, (6) is persistent and disciplined, (7) is respectful to the elderly and to their achievements and service (8) shows responsible behavior toward the other gender, (9) has healthy and industrious self. Curiously, these traits, while describing model children, are also directed to parents and all social institutions in their responsibility *vis-à-vis* children. They recode the child as a co-production, formalizing the 1956 shift in legal codes from *elterliche Gewalt*, parental authority, to *Erziehungsrecht*, the right to raise/educate. Parents then exercised a right, a privilege not automatically (or "naturally," as proclaimed in the FRG) granted them. Thus parents were to collaborate with the school, youth organizations, and other educative instances in raising the child toward what by 1965 was labeled a "socialist personality" (see Lemke 1980). As family and education expert Rosemarie Walther wrote in 1979: "Moral education in the family concerns itself with the building of elementary behavioral norms, which are also necessary for a communist education" (p. 728). Such formalization of behavioral norms can produce both compliance and resistance. In any case, it has one major unintended consequence: by identifying state goals unambiguously, it enables (and encourages) citizens to become more calculating in their relations with the state, increasing the general use of instrumental rationality both to subvert state models and to adapt everyday routines to them.

During the sixties and seventies in the Federal Republic, the state became a kind of phantom of the opera, appearing as arbiter, even reformer, in crucial moments of debate on family, education, or civil reform. Yet the locus of power was always somewhat dispersed, never so centralized and transparent as in the GDR. Hence "private" actors and groups from "civil society" – such as pharmaceutical organizations, physicians' unions, press conglomerates, automobile producers, political parties – often took the initiative in shaping the model lifecourse. And each of the *Länder* within the federation enacted different versions of policy.

*Control over reproductive rights*
Reproductive rights remain highly politicized in West Germany, especially in the light of the low birth rates and the oft-repeated concern that "the Germans are dying out."[23] Despite the fact that the East Germans faced the same set of concerns, reproductive rights were by the early seventies no longer a topic for political debate. When they do become political issues, debate most often focuses on the use of contraception and abortion. Abortion remained a criminal act in the GDR until 1972, with partial legalization in 1965; in the FRG until 1976. Abortion rights, along with the mass production of contraceptive devices in the sixties, significantly changed the way women directly, and as a result men, experienced the family, for these two rights switched the locus of control over family planning from men to women, enabling many women both to time and to limit the number of children, and to experience sexual pleasure with men without attaching intercourse to the fear of pregnancy.

In the Soviet Zone, a fairly liberal law was passed in 1945 outlining ethical and social conditions that would justify an abortion. The social criteria included family income, availability of room in the household, general health of family, and moral stance of parents (Obertreis 1985: 56). I was told by women that these criteria were interpreted liberally; yet for many women fear reigned until full legalization. The 1950 Mother and Child Protection Law, motivated partly by pro-natal interests, recriminalized abortion except when the birth would result in "actual damage to the health of the mother" (Obertreis 1985: 55–56). Throughout the 1950s and 1960s many women were performing abortions on themselves or finding doctors to perform them illegally. Those who were caught were arrested, along with their doctors, and imprisoned.

The GDR Ministry of Health was consistently a leader in fighting for planned parenthood, use of contraceptives, and abortion rights in the 1950s, but did not succeed in any formal legal change until 1965. This Ministry organized the first European congress on abortion rights in 1960, and in 1965 an ordinance was passed allowing abortions upon medical examination and doctor's approval. In 1972 legalization had much to do with rumors that West German jurists were planning a change in their own anti-abortion laws; the first state to pass a more liberal law, it was felt, would receive international accolades. The GDR *Volkskammer* vote on legalization was not unanimous, marking the first time in the history of the GDR that a law did not receive unanimous passage by the parliament. Since then, the decision to abort has belonged solely to the woman during the first three months of pregnancy; thereafter she must obtain the approval of a panel of gynecologists. Abortion is largely regarded as another means of birth control. In this legal history, women have been the sole objects of policy (Mehlan 1980: 54; Helwig 1982: 75).

In West Germany, Nazi laws criminalizing birth control and abortion for most women, and forcing other so-called racially inferior women to abort, were first nullified in 1960; abortion itself was not legalized until 1976 (on Nazi law and policy, see Mühlfeld and Schönweiss 1989; Bock 1986). Signed into law by Heinrich Himmler in 1941, these National Socialist laws made it illegal for women to possess any means (such as any knife over 12 cm. long) with which they could abort themselves, and likewise, illegal for doctors to abort women under any conditions (Dellile and Grohn 1985: 122–126). The infamous §218 of the BGB making abortions a criminal act remained in effect until 1977; thereafter the jail sentence was replaced with a monetary fine. It was most rigorously enforced in the 1950s, so that by 1959 there were approximately 5,400 cases of prison sentences for doctors, midwives, and nurses (most of whom themselves were women) in the Federal Republic/West Berlin. Between 1947 and 1953, more than one million illegal abortions were performed in the British zones alone. This comes to approximately one out of every five adult women (Dellile and Grohn 1985: 124).

Massive protests by West German feminists against §218 in the early 1970s, including busing groups of women to Holland where abortion was legal, finally resulted in a 1974 parliamentary decision to legalize abortion. At that time the Constitutional Court immediately declared the law unconstitutional (Helwig 1982: 74). A watered-down version of the law was approved in 1976, stipulating the medical, eugenic, ethical, and social conditions under which a woman could justify her decision. Policies varied greatly from state to state within the FRG, with Berlin having one of the most liberal laws. Still on the table was a 1988 Christian Democratic Union proposal by then Family Minister Rita Süssmuth which attempted to force women to go through three "advice sessions" before obtaining approval for an abortion (given the preponderance of male gynecologists and doctors, most likely three male judges). For the majority of West German women, however, the situation was less restrictive, and had been throughout the 1960s, for they could travel to doctors in neighboring countries (e.g., Holland, Denmark, Sweden) with more liberal abortion laws. Provided they had the money and time, they were not dependent on the status of West German "reproductive law" to control this part of their lifecourse.

By the mid fifties in the GDR, the Marriage and Sexual Counselling Service (ESB) openly promoted birth-control information and some reproductive control techniques, although the extent to which they reached a large public is unknown (Mehlan 1980: 54). Birth-control pills were not introduced until 1966, although other forms of contraception were available in the 1950s. In West Germany, most forms of birth control remained illegal until the mid 1960s, with each province having its own rules. This did not, however, prevent people from practicing birth control, much to the alarm of the West German Family Ministry. In 1957, the radically pro-natalist *Bundesministerium für Familienfragen* noted with alarm the growing number of abortions and miscarriages, yet simultaneously condemned the use of condoms. Use of condoms had doubled between 1950 and 1955, from 44 million to 88 million (Ruhl 1988: 133). By the early 1960s in many provinces of West Germany birth-control measures such as the pill had become popular, making less necessary "kitchen-table abortions" – referring to how, in order to avoid the law, many abortions were performed at home on the kitchen table. By the eighties contraceptives were readily available in both states and abortion was widely utilized as a form of birth control.

Like most negative sanctions that seek merely to repress and control, postwar attempts to increase births by penalizing women did not stimulate the birth rate. The legalization of abortion and birth control in itself had no long-term effect on demographic tendencies in either state. As illustrated in chapter 3, birth rates in the GDR remained stable before and after the legalization of abortion, though one can attribute the dramatic *decrease* in the number of miscarriages and deaths of pregnant women directly to the legalization (Mehlan 1980: 119–128).

Pro-natal interests in East Germany came to the political forefront in the 1970s around positive sanctions, including pregnancy leave, *Wochenurlaub*, and the so-called "baby-year." The GDR had already in the 1950s introduced the pregnancy leave (before birth) and *Wochenurlaub* (after birth), an unpaid period when the mother was not required to work. A woman on such an occasion (*Urlaub* means literally vacation) was called a *Wöchnerin*. The state introduced the baby-year initially as an "unpaid vacation" in the early 1960s. Not until 1972 did the state extend the *Wochenurlaub* to all mothers and begin to pay up to three months for mothers after the birth of a third child (with a free paid year for every child thereafter), after which the woman retained her old job with no loss of status. In 1976, this paid *Wochenurlaub* was lengthened to twenty-six weeks for mothers after the birth of the first child (and every child thereafter), and a full baby-year was extended to mothers after the birth of the second child, then in 1986 to mothers after the birth of the first child. The 1986 law also allowed the father or grandmother to take the full baby-year, and gave an extra half-year to the parent of a third child (and each thereafter) – thus significantly widening the definition of parent. In addition, it introduced an extra free day a month for all mothers of children under fourteen, and shortened the workweek for mothers from forty-three and three-quarters to forty hours. Finally, the 1986 law did away with the special privileges for single mothers, extending paid leave for mothers of sick children to married mothers.

The FRG and GDR both developed an extensive program for maternal vacations in the 1950s, intended to make mothering less burdensome. These programs, while not seeking to restructure parenting, actually reinforced the role of mothering and, by not recognizing the possible role of fathers in childcare, reinforced the absence of the father from child-rearing practices. In the 1970s, the FRG began to redress the burden on single parents through taxation reform. In 1972, the state, through tax reform, equalized benefits for single and married parents (previously, married parents had an advantage); and in 1979, it enacted tax exemptions for families with children (before then, marital status alone was sufficient to qualify). Also in 1979, the state passed a series of laws establishing paid pregnancy leave and *Wochenurlaub* for working mothers (much as the GDR did in 1972). The FRG introduced a baby-year first in 1985, simultaneously making it available for the husband or wife, with added benefits for single mothers (such as, e.g., money to start a household, apartment preference, rent subsidy, apartment furnishings).[24] West Berlin, most often in the forefront of social reform among the various self-governing *Länder*, had already enacted a baby-year in 1983, at that time also making it available to the father or mother. With the enactment of the FRG law, Berlin parents could take the first baby-year from the West German government and follow it with another nine months granted by the Berlin Senat.

*Children, youth, and lifecourse design*
In the FRG, the gradual turn away from the "housewife marriage" toward a concentration on the child began around 1973, when the Ministry of the Family began using the word "family" in its plural form, no longer committing the state to one type of family. By 1987, partnership forms were removed from the center, replaced by a focus on the child and the household. The *Familienbericht* of the Berlin Senat for Youth and Family begins their 1987 report with the statement, "the starting point for a definition of family is the parent-child relation" (12). The GDR, which had made the child central to family policy in 1950, moved in the opposite direction in the 1970s, toward a concern with family form. Anita Grandke, Family Law Professor at Humboldt University in East Berlin, states in a 1986 article that she understands the family not as a "social group with children," but as a group defined by marriage. Marriage, she says, takes on such critical importance because of its "role as the central link between the law and family relations" (129–130). In the FRG, on the other hand, legal links to the child and household were added to already existing strong controls on marriage, something discussed further in chapter 7.

     With reference to state narrative strategies, we can see that policy in both states has remained fairly consistent over time, although its object has shifted. In sum, the GDR strategy of construction, based on universalist assumptions that emphasize achieved over ascribed identities, introduced children as legal objects independent of the status of their parents; this policy has, then, consistently emplotted its young citizens in a romantic aesthetic, oriented toward full and early integration in an egalitarian society. This contrasts starkly with the FRG strategy, based on particularist assumptions that emphasize innateness over achieved identities, which structures the lifecourse quite differently for diverse groups of children, youth, and parents, thus making the entirety of the policy *unübersichtlich*, obscure. Child dependency on the parents remained relatively untouched in the FRG until after the turbulent late 1960s; while the subsequent educational reform allowed for more mobility of children in the education systei 1 through their own efforts, it also lengthened the period of dependence on parents by increasing the time spent in the stage called "youth," or in educational institutions where youths depend on some financial support from parents. Of course, the specific life design of particular children – for example, whether female or male, or from wealthy or poor families – depends greatly on parental wealth and social networks (see Jaide 1988; Zinnecker 1987).

The life design was quite different in the GDR, where, as we shall see in the next chapter, the state–child relationship became better and more tightly planned, more predictable, stable, and *transparent*, so that individual efforts of parents were no longer so significant in controlling the lifecourse trajectory. Childhood as a period in the GDR was lengthened to encompass the whole of the youth period, except that children became dependent on state agencies and not on parents. In 1988 GDR youth left educational institutions and entered the workforce (and thus brigades, collectives, and other social organizations) at the average age of 22.8, whereas their FRG counterparts made this step (and then into privatized work relations, with approximately 10 percent unintegrated into adulthood) first at the average age of 27.9 years. Because of the restricted role of East German parents in tracking the lifecourse of their children, the parent–child relationship was reduced to largely sentimental aspects, based on mutual love and affection, much as the state itself in the *Family Law Book* of 1965 had planned.

Childcare in both Berlins became increasingly a responsibility and privilege of the woman, though East German women received much more state assistance for this task than did West German women, who were often dependent on husbands or ex-husbands for financial support.

At the same time, childcare was less of a burden in the GDR than in the FRG, for the East German state took over many of the responsibilities and positively valorized the mother's labor, making it equal in worth to public work.

## Partnership

The changes proposed by Benjamin in her 1949 article, while centering on children and equal rights in the workplace, had radical consequences for partnerships. As in the domain of child–parent relations, West German policymakers tended to follow, react to, and oppose the East German policy of reconstructing the state's relation to couples. In both states, the recodification of partnerships proceeded incrementally and involved more of a direct interaction with partnership practices that proved resistant to state attempts at control than did the revalorization of children and parents. Strategies oriented to the control of partnerships discussed below include naming rights, equal rights, marriage, and divorce.

### Naming rights

Under §1355 of the BGB the family name was the husband's, which the woman was obliged to assume upon marriage. This code directly conflicted with the equal rights clauses of both the FRG Basic Law and the GDR Constitution. Policymakers in the GDR extended the principle of equal rights between the sexes to nearly every domain of kinship practices, including naming. Benjamin's 1949 suggestions for changes in naming laws upon marriage were enacted within the same year she proposed them. Since then, partners still must choose a joint name, but they could take the name of either the man or woman, or the woman could attach her name to that of her husband. Children of single mothers received the name of their mother, children of married women received the name that the married couple shares in common. The old rights of the husband were no longer at the center of the law.

The FRG found it difficult to reconcile the expressed goal of family unity through a common family name with the principle of equality, and thus resisted changing the old naming rights until 1953. Thus, from 1945 to 1953, a couple was forced to take the name of the man upon marriage. In 1953, the rule was changed so that the couple could choose either to take his name or they could create a double name with a hyphen. The wife could bring her name to the marriage only by making a public declaration at the time of the marriage, and the husband, moreover, was forced to go through a formal name-change proceeding if he wished to add the woman's name to his own. This law was amended in 1976, so that the couple could at the time of marriage choose either his or her name as the family name, or they could add his or her own name ahead of the marital name.

In March 1988, the other changes which had been introduced in 1949 in the GDR were put into effect in West Germany, the most important one being the right after divorce to take one's maiden name back. The FRG extended the possibility for a hyphenated name to more situations than does the GDR: upon marriage, whichever partner, regardless of sex, yields their pre-marital name to the "married couple" now has the right to use a hyphenated name, and thus retains as a private person their own name in a hyphenated form. Children must still take the single "family name" of the parents. One other naming practice continued to differentiate the two republics: in West Germany, the first name of the child must be taken from a list of approved names to make sure that it corresponded to his/her *correct gender*. Given the importance of gender distinctions for West German policy, an ambiguously gendered name would signal danger, perhaps leading to incorrect differentiation (see Douglas 1966). The only exception to this is the name "Maria," which can be used as the middle name for a male child. In the GDR, there were no gender-specific rules for naming children.

Two major similarities in naming practices united the states. First, partners upon marriage were not allowed to retain their individual identities, but had to assume through a common name a common identity as a new legal entity, with different entitlements and status from non-marrieds. Second, partnership was something restricted to two individuals of different sexes and genders, i.e., heterosexuals.[25] By denying legality to non-marrieds, and by further denying certain citizens the right to marry, both principles reinforce legal, heterosexual marriage as a technique of state control.

*Equal rights*
Equal rights between the sexes, as part of the egalitarian teleology of GDR law, was a basic generative principle of its family model. The preamble of the Constitution states that the "married pair are obligated to construct their relations so that both are able to avail themselves fully of the right to develop their abilities for their own use and for those of the society." A marriage is defined in the 1965 FGB as based on "mutual love, respect, and faithfulness, on understanding and trust and selfless

help for one another." Household duties are to be shared, as Benjamin initially insisted, by both the husband and the wife, so that the woman can also enjoy a career outside the home.

The idea of equal rights is also promoted by the Basic Law of the FRG, but it has since been interpreted as a private affair, the form of which is to be decided upon by the partners themselves. After much delay, an actual equal rights law was finally enacted in 1957, but the law essentially restated the centrality of the housewife-marriage model (Limbach 1988: 14; Helwig 1982: 48), meaning a partnership where the woman stayed home and the man had an occupation. Wives did not actually gain equal legal rights to independent work outside the home until Article 1356, which declared the wife's responsibility to run the household, was amended in 1976. This second marriage reform law, which went into effect in 1977, renounced any legal model that delineated a strict gender/sex role-division in a marriage. Thereafter, the state's position *vis-à-vis* equal rights between married partners has been to refuse any active role in redressing inequality, which the partners themselves are supposed to work out while respecting each other's interests as well as those of the family. As an FRG legal commentary to the 1976 law explains, "The equal rights clause does not obligate the married couple to live accordingly; they are still free to follow a partriarchal model" (*Münchener Kommentar-Wache*, cited in Limbach 1988: 18). Likewise, legal interpretations of equal division of labor in the household and responsibility for childcare have uniformly supported a view holding the woman responsible for household and family (Limbach 1988: 19; Vogel 1985: 120–121).

Both states also addressed equal rights with regard to inheritance and property law for married couples. Since 1955 in the GDR, the property that marital partners bring into a marriage was considered to be their own personal property (the BGB had given the man nearly all jural control over property), but the property accumulated after marriage was assumed to be common, regardless of how it was accumulated. There were some exceptions to these rules, but they were few. The idea behind the common-property concept was that the couple forms a social unit based on shared affections and not on property needs. Division of property after divorce was thus not a concern of family law, and the couple was most often told to settle the matter on their own. Property settlements were always separated from divorce proceedings, unlike in the FRG where the property settlement was an essential part of a divorce. An important factor enabling the GDR to separate property settlements from divorce law was the institutionalization of state supports for education and career training, as well as for childcare. The social standing of the parent after divorce was no longer dependent on the income of the spouse. Child-support payments after divorce in the GDR were in most cases limited to two years, for it was assumed that property dependencies would not play a significant role in tracking the lifecourse.

In the FRG, the rights of the man to dispose of property as he wishes prevailed until 1957, after which each partner retained the right both to property brought into the marriage and to that accumulated during the marriage. Married couples in the FRG can make contracts specifying what is shared and what not; thus no single arrangement (such as equal sharing) is mandated by the law if the couple has other wishes. Hence if a couple reaches the point of divorce, the inequality, financial and otherwise, between the partners brings added significance to how child support and financial dependence is settled.

*Marriage*
The assumption that a legal partnership exists only in marital form, held in common for most of the history of both states, has not always meant that the legal family presupposes a marriage. For the FRG, family law was, until the early 1970s, precisely oriented around the equation that marriage means family; thus if the family policy strengthened one unit, like marriage, it was assumed that the family was also being strengthened. The GDR, on the other hand, defined family policy until the early 1970s around the needs of children, in effect both broadening the definition of possible families and relegating marriage to an act of secondary significance. This all changed in the early 1970s. Anita Grandke, chairperson of family law at Humboldt University (East Berlin), summed up this new model as follows: "Family law [supports the constructions of a] historically new type of family . . . The Family Law Book distinguishes love as the basis for the construction and continuation of marriage, and it is on this basis that the specificity of this union derives its legal recognition and is given its basic orientation for societal and state policy" (1978: 159). Grandke thus makes explicit a syllogism which goes as follows: family = marriage, marriage = partnership, partnership = family. Children, oddly enough, are left out of this picture (unless they belong to a married partnership) and so, quite obviously, are single people, as well as the elderly or any kind of partnership not based on a heterosexual love marriage.

The FRG's policy in the 1950s and 1960s was focused, as argued above, toward a particular family model, organized around the housewife marriage. From taxation to employment to child-support policy, the woman was encouraged to marry and stay home, the man to marry and support a housewife and children. The one statistic pointing most directly to the continued efficacy of this model is the comparison of the number of working-age women employed in 1988 in the FRG (51 percent) compared to the number in the GDR (91 percent); at least half of these women have little choice but to live dependent on a husband. The *Zölibatsklausel*, celibacy clause, allowing for the dismissal of female public employees if they married, was, for example, still in effect for government policy until 1950 (Korinth 1988: 32). The common practice of firing single women who decided to marry was finally declared illegal in 1957, against the expressed wishes of Family Minister Würmeling and Justice Minister Dehler, in a court decision involving the nurse Irmgard Krüger and clerk Edith Mayer. The practice of firing these women was motivated primarily by the assumption that women upon marriage would (and could) rely on their husbands for support, which in turn would make them less dependent on their employers; single women were most easily manipulable (and thus capable of being workers) for they had no other sources of support (Langer 1985: 79, 80). The correlate assumption was that married women worked only to earn extra money for the family and not out of career interests. Yet the situation for single women in the 1950s and 1960s was in many ways worse than for married ones because unmarried women were accorded a lower social status. Although single women received priority (over married women) for jobs, they were given no legal recognition as heads of households and financial supporters of families. Following the tumultuous late sixties and the reforms of 1976, however, West German marital law has become much more differentiated, partly because an increasing number of people refused to legalize their relationships.

Partnerships not legalized through a state marital ceremony, practiced widely in both Berlins, have proven difficult to deal with for the two German states. Most often called *Lebensgemeinschaften* (hereafter LG), living-together or cohabitation arrangements, they include, among others, same-sex couples, heterosexual couples with and without shared sex, and couples with and without children. In the GDR, Grandke, as well as most other theorists, insisted that LGs are temporary test arrangements to prepare for marriage and not alternatives to it (1986: 132). Hence legal recognition of couples was conferred only on marital units, with special legal arrangements made for childcare units.

Legal theorists in the FRG also refuse to recognize, meaning to give legal rights to, the LG (Limbach 1988: 27–30). The reasoning against the LG in West Germany has consistently appealed to the immoral nature of sexual relations outside the marriage. A 1954 decision of the West German Supreme Court argues: "Because the law of morality prescribes marriage and the family as the obligatory mode of living, it follows that sexual intercourse should only come to pass within the bonds of wedlock. An act to the contrary constitutes transgression of an elementary norm of sexual propriety." As late as 1969, the same court reaffirmed this decision: "Sexual intercourse between unmarried persons in and of itself must be considered a violation of the law of morality" (both cited in Glendon 1989: 263–264). Treating unmarried, cohabiting partners as if they are immoral and "had deliberately chosen to have a relationship without legal consequences," writes Mary Ann Glendon, "inevitably works to the detriment of the more economically dependent partner," who nearly always is the woman (1989: 264). In East Germany, the lack of legal recognition for the LG had few economic consequences, but in a state where precious apartments, tax credits, and travel privileges were distributed according to a scale that put married couples on top, members of LG were notably accorded second-class status.

In both countries, however, the LG as a family form was widely debated, and it is likely that in the unified Germany some form of legal recognition, as already exists in, for example, Denmark, Sweden, and Holland, will be forthcoming. Although there were no regulations governing inheritance or property among LGs, there were regulations linking inheritance and child support. The legal father (meaning blood father) of a child born out of wedlock was obligated to pay child support if the mother so wished for an unlimited time in the FRG. He did not, however, automatically obtain any rights (such as access to the child) by doing so. This was the case since 1950 in the GDR, since 1969 in the FRG.

*Divorce*

In all of the Occupation Zones from 1945 to 1950, Allied and German authorities liberally granted divorces, most of which were occasioned by missing or dead husbands. The 1896 BGB legal principle of annulling marriages only when one of the parties could be determined to be guilty was replaced by a no-fault principle first in the GDR in 1955, then in West Germany in 1976. The 1955 GDR law also separated the issue of divorce from property settlement and child support, thus making the separation of the couple a relatively simple and quick procedure with minimal costs. Since 91 percent of the women in the GDR worked, and since women and men contributed nearly equally to the household budget of married couples, a wife had a very limited claim to support (maximally two years) from a husband upon divorce. If the pair had a child in common, they were both equally responsible for child support, regardless of which partner obtained childcare.

Reform of the 1944 divorce ordinance was first revised in West Germany in 1976, and then amended again in 1986. The 1976 law retained the principle of marriage as a *Zwangsverband*, a coercive union, which makes it difficult, costly, and time consuming to annul the marriage, even if the couple has agreed upon the terms of the divorce. Moreover, it eliminated most aspects of the judicial determination of "guilt" that not only affected issues of property division, but also determined whether one spouse was responsible for the other after divorce. In 1986, however, "fault was firmly reinstated as a major factor in maintenance issues," with the caveat that "the needs of any child of the couple must be met before the custodial parent's support may be curtailed" (Glendon 1989: 222). At the time of divorce, all issues of property division, inheritance, child support, and retirement pensions (in the FRG, unlike in the GDR, women's pensions are still frequently pegged to the income of the husband) must be settled with the aid of a professional lawyer. In the GDR, all of these issues were settled without the aid of a lawyer (unless the couple desired one, which was very seldom), and in any case not as part of the divorce proceedings.

In sum, how are we to see the development of the marital and divorce strategies of the two states? In West Germany marriage and divorce have been consistently deployed as positive and negative legal sanctions for a particular kind of heterosexual union. Over time, divorce law has become the more intricate and detailed of the two, or we might say, more appropriately, following Glendon: divorce law has become regulation of "the satisfactory resolution of the economic consequences of divorce" more than the fact of divorce (1989: 181). Certainly, this is to be expected in a capitalist state organized around the accumulation of private property. Incentives for marriage are primarily economic – home credit, marital credit, and taxation. In fact, the West German income taxation system favored significantly, in comparison with that of the GDR, married couples over singles (*Zahlenspiegel* 1988: 73).

In the GDR, on the other hand, divorce was no longer used as a coercive tool to keep people in marriages. But marriage itself increasingly became a (or the) policy tool which the state used to coax people into a particular family form. Grandke lists marriage as the precondition for four kinds of benefits given out by the state: (1) preference for an apartment together, (2) benefits related to work and free-time (such as sick leave when one partner is sick), (3) taxation benefits in the case where one partner is retired or the man gets veteran's benefits, and (4) marital credit, especially advantageous for couples with three or more children (1986: 145). Noticeably missing from the list are benefits related to motherhood or parenting (except for 4, i.e., large families), which were supported by the state independent of the partnership status of the parents. They were included, however, in the newly valorized unit of "the family."

### New valorization of family units

Over the years, policymakers in both states have been inconsistent in the meaning and relative significance they attach to the concept "family." The family law textbook of the GDR explains the relationship of the state to the family as follows: "State exercise of power means, in the final analysis, the creation and organization of organizations, the means by which the state exercises its necessary influence on the *family*, and the cooperation of the society, the state, and individual citizen for the development of *family* relationships" (*Familienrecht Lehrbuch* 1981: 26, my italics). The family unit to which the text refers has not remained constant over time. Initially, family policy was oriented to childcare units; by 1986, the family had been narrowed to marriage, and not to a "social group with children" (Grandke 1986: 130–132). The family itself does not constitute a nexus for a legal relationship, she argues. That role is played by marriage, which means, she admits, that neither sexual relations nor mother–child relationships are always going to be coterminous with the legal institution of marriage. The former is regulated only *vis-à-vis* laws forbidding sex with minors (in 1968, adult homosexuality was also legalized: in 1969 in the Federal Republic), the latter is regulated by other laws.

Such a clear statement of the relationship of the state to the family is absent in FRG texts, partly because of the decentralized nature of the polity (the different *Länder* also make their own kin laws), and partly because policy is in a more dynamic relationship with diverse political interest groups. It is therefore, on the one hand, more prone to reversals, and on the other, more likely to utilize covert or subtle means in order to maintain the myth of the autonomous family and the private sphere. From Family Minister Würmeling's concern with the housewife marriage and the nuclear family as a bulwark against "the threatening danger of the large families in the East" to the 1986 report of the Ministry of Youth, Family, Women and Health, the route has not been linear.

The 1986 ministry report was to address primarily the problems of "the elderly in the family," but the commission writing it found it impossible to restrict their considerations to a "precisely delineated nuclear family." To do so would have meant to ignore the needs of the majority of the elderly, who no longer live in this family form. The report thus pleads for the policy use of an "expanded notion of the family" that takes into consideration the "lived social network" of families (*Vierter Familienbericht* 1986: 14). The 1987 *Familienbericht* of the Senat for Youth and Family in Berlin seems to be unaware of this new tone at the federal level. This report defines family as "the parent–child relationship," and loftily summarizes as the goal of policy "[to provide] the family a protective space in which the personal relationships of each member can freely develop, in which neither the state nor others can meddle, a free space for the construction of one's own life according to one's own standards and sense of responsibility" (1987: 12).

For GDR policymakers in the early years of the republic, the family unit itself, when referred to at all, was defined in terms of a central feature – childcare – and not in terms of an exclusive set of characteristics for partners or married couples. Thus in 1950, objects of family policy included, e.g., large families (three or more children), single mothers, working women, and children. Except for large families, all of these categories were ignored, more or less, during the same period in West Germany, where the focus was on the housewife marriage, a "complete family" of a particular kind. Here we see another specific instance of the general strategy of integration in the GDR versus assimilation in the FRG. East Germany was concerned with integrating the different elements into the socialist whole, an operation in metonymy; West Germany was concerned with assimilating on the basis of likeness (to the *Hausfrauenehe*) similar elements into its whole, an operation in metaphor.

Not until 1965 did the GDR conceptualize the family around love and marriage – elements of partnership instead of childcare. In the 1950s, the concern was to restructure and integrate into societal processes specific types of relationships, in particular, and to reformulate the ethics of human communication, in general. The ethical appeals culminated in Walter Ulbricht's 1958 declaration of the socialist *Menschengemeinschaft*, a socialist human community, and a proposal for Ten Commandments of Socialist Morality and Ethics. An exercise in the secular cosmology-making of the atheist state (see Kligman 1988: 249–279), two of the commandments referred to the family: Commandment Eight, "To raise the children in the spirit of peace and socialism," and Commandment Nine, "You should lead a clean and respectable life and respect your family" (*DDR Handbuch* 1985: 918). With the issuing of these moral appeals, we see the beginnings of a shift in state strategy, from re-construction to sentimentalization. Wrapping itself in the divine silks of its arch-enemy, the church, the state valorizes *Kleinbürgertum*, the moral sentiments of the petty bourgeoisie: *Sauberkeit* (cleanliness), *Anständigkeit* (respectability), *Ordnungssüchtigkeit* (thirst for order), and *Autoritätsgläubigkeit* (worship of authority). The other eight commandments focused on individual–community relations; none of them addressed marriage.

Because the family is "the smallest cell of the society," as stated in the preamble to the *Familiengesetzbuch* of 1965, the entire corpus of law must be organized around "its respect, protection, and support." Linda Ansorg, head of the collective in charge of writing this text, explicated in 1967, "The protection of family law is enjoyed only by the legally grounded marriages recognized before the state. The socialist state does not support other family-like forms of cohabitation because these do not correspond to the moral and familial-political attitudes of the socialist society" (cited in Hille 1985: 37). Although this strategy was not fully articulated until the late 1970s, it marked a new tendency in the GDR: to concentrate on the family as a unit, a new signification with its own set of rights and privileges. Thereafter, the law no longer focused directly on reconstructing the techniques of the self (e.g., children, working women) or the techniques of relationships (e.g., parent–child, husband–wife). Working women, mothers, and children had been up to that point the central object of policy; men as fathers and husbands, and women as wives, had been devalorized.

The new valorization for the family as an object in itself and for itself was augmented with a new round of policies in 1972, and again in 1977 (see Dorbritz 1987: 159–175). Although the signification of each individual member of the family unit remained relatively unchanged, the new unit "family" acting as a whole became empowered. Publication of the *Familiengesetzbuch* signalled a slow process of revalorization of the husband and wife, a tendency not explicit until the 1980s, revolving again around pro-natal interests and a debate about *Kinderwunsch*, why women decide to have children. Policymakers, backed by social-science evidence, argued that the longer and more stable the relationship between partners, the more likely it was that women would decide to have more than two children (see Speigner 1987).

Up to the 1970s in West Germany, families as such were objects of policy primarily through ideological proclamation intent on delegitimating forms of kin other than those centered around the *Hausfrauenehe*, and through preferential taxation and housing benefits. Policy was oriented toward fixing the signification of individual members, and not to changing their status *vis-à-vis* each other. Between 1950 and 1954, four organizations were founded to lobby for restorative family policy: the nondenominational *Deutscher Familien Verband* and *Bund des Kinderreichen Deutschlands*, and two Christian groups, the *Evangelische Aktionsgemeinschaft für Familienfragen* and *Familienbund der Deutschen Katholiken*. Although these groups shared some basic ideas about what type of family they wanted to support, they never managed fully to centralize policy around their goals.

Financial grants to support marriages, called "family-founding" grants, did not become part of policy until 1962. First initiated after the building of the Wall as part of the "Berlin Help" of the West German government, policymakers justified them as a way to encourage (married) people to move to Berlin from the Federal Republic. Financed by the West German Ministry for Work and Social Policy, the aid took the form of a low-interest loan with an eleven-year payback period. To qualify, the marriage had to take place after the building of the Wall, at least one partner had to be living in Berlin within a year of the marriage, and at least one partner had to be in a first marriage (non-divorcee). If the couple had children, payback on the loan was subsequently reduced. Up to the end of 1963, 38,000 young married couples received aid of this kind (*Berlin ABC* 1965: 164).

By the late 1970s, direct grants and subsidies to family units were viewed as merely one part of family policy, which additionally offered financial aid and legal support to individual members. West Berlin was often the innovator among the various West German *Länder* in these programs. In 1976, the amount given for family-founding grants in West Berlin increased tenfold, and in 1979 the definition of family was extended to include single parents – meaning that children became a feature as central to the family as marriage. In 1982, the program was limited to parents under a certain income. And in 1984, legislators enacted a special West Berlin grant program for certain families, including pregnant women, parents of handicapped children, and single parents. After 1985, Berlin families were also eligible for rent subsidies, limiting the rent to 25 percent of the total net income of the family (additional rebates if children are part of the family), with the government subsidizing the rest. Within approximately one decade, 1973–1985 – a very short time indeed – West Berlin and the West German state stretched the definition of family to include a variety of living arrangements formerly excluded from policy. Most of the measures were aimed at childcare units, but justified as "family help."

*The elderly*
The one group rarely mentioned in family policy in either state is the elderly. State strategies oriented around either "marriage" or "children" will exclude by definition this group from the legal penumbra. In this chapter, I have avoided much discussion of aging policy largely because both states did little to construct old age other than to set it aside as a "retirement period" of the lifecourse. What retired people were supposed to do, however, was something the states only lately concerned themselves with. This situation was changing especially in West Germany as social scientists investigated this part of the lifecourse, and policitians, increasingly alarmed by rising state costs for retirement/ entitlement programs, begin to rethink the state's relationship to this group (e.g., see Kohli and Wolf 1986). In addition, the new West German Family Minister (as of December 1988), Ursula Lehr, a woman with expertise on aging (see Lehr 1984), vowed to intensify work in this area. The GDR had not shown such interest at the federal level.

In neither state were there significant state rituals demarcating retirement comparable to those for birth, youth, marriage, and death. Family and company retirement parties rarely involved forms of state support, although, to the extent the latter existed in the GDR, state support and industrial organization were closely intertwined. The age of retirement in West Germany is sixty-five for men and unemployed people, sixty for women, although men may also retire at sixty under special circumstances. In order to draw retirement pay one must have worked for at least five years. None of these rules apply precisely to *Beamten*, civil servants, who can collect retirement pay after five years, and if in a special class (e.g., military or police), can retire before sixty-five. In East Germany, the retirement age was the same as in the FRG, but with a minimum of fifteen years' work to qualify. The principle for both systems was that individuals who work collect retirement pay when they are old or no longer capable of working. In West Germany, the terms of this social contract are being questioned as long-term unemployment increases, and as the assumption grows that approximately 10 percent of the population will never find full-time work, therefore will be forever excluded from benefits for the elderly (see Offe 1988: 24). Moreover, FRG policy has a strong gender component: only 51 percent of all women work, many part-time, and increasingly many do not marry (hence they do not qualify for their husband's pension). Since most people were employees of the state in the GDR, and since the state maintained full employment since 1955, disparities between classes of elderly were not so marked as in West Germany.

Both states had several levels of retirement pay, but the principles rewarded varied: in the West, an abstract principle of achievement based on income generated in a lifetime was operative; in the East, achievement was based not on market criteria but on state consideration of the social utility of the work. In East Germany, there was a minimum retirement pay, and the difference between the highest and lowest pay was small, from 140 to 440 Marks. The few individuals who got more did so based on principles that tended to be political (rewarding, e.g., victims of fascism, widows of resistance fighters). In West Germany, there was a maximum retirement pay, and the differences between the highest and lowest were significant, from under 300 to over 2,300 DM. Those on the higher end of the pension scale were *Beamten*, state civil servants, and those who had enjoyed higher incomes during their lifetime (*Materialien zum Bericht* 1987: 573–585). Those receiving minimal pensions can apply for subsidies for rent, clothing, and utilities. Their problem is, however, that most who could qualify for such subsidies either do not know of their availability, or they are ashamed about receiving welfare. When the two states addressed the elderly specifically through "family policy," they also differed from each other in their emphasis. In the GDR, the stress was on keeping the elderly in their own homes and keeping them integrated in their old work unit (Runge 1985). In West Berlin, the emphasis remained on integrating the elderly into the family: "three generations under one roof" was the most recent slogan in Berlin (*Familienbericht* 1987: 25).

## Conclusion

Despite the dramatic domestic situation in Berlin after the war, the two opposed German states did not proceed out of a strategy of necessity. Although we can follow policy designs and trajectories during the Cold War and come up with reasonable accounts for their oppositions and reversals, we can also imagine other possible solutions. After forty-four years of such policy, the ensemble of kin regulations resembled each other in ways policymakers on neither side really desired (such as support for and social legitimation of unmarried mothers and children born out of wedlock, the increase in divorce), and at the same time were dissimilar in ways they intended from the start (such as the high ratio of qualified and employed women in East Germany compared to the low ratio in the FRG). At various times in the last forty years, both states enacted policies, ultimately more similar than different, that sought to change radically the signification of their citizens and the meaning of their lifecourse. Among the most significant of these shifts, we can include: creating children with independent legal rights, women as public workers equal to men, and rights for mothers independent of their kin status; eliminating many rights attached to fathers, decentering the privileges of married couples, and enacting no-fault divorce and bilateral inheritance laws.[26]

While, from today's standpoint, the policies in their totality may resemble each other, they differ in their aesthetic and ideational form-giving principles, as well as in the critical aspect of periodization: the timing of their enactment. Hence, as we shall soon see, people living during the same time in the two states experienced similar state strategies at different times in their lives. This contrary periodization created state-specific differences within a single lifecourse, thus demarcating the same generation by city-half or state (and often by gender) – to a considerable extent, creating different nations. It also intensified cohortal differences, thus demarcating generations from one another within a particular state and creating differences within single nations. Aspects of kin policy in which one side dressed itself were ignored by the other during the hot part of the Cold War, only later to be worn as if apparel of one's own invention. Bourgeois sentiment, for example, became by the seventies the major concern of marriage policy in the

East, while Marxist infrastructural reconstruction became the belated focus of state-supported childcare in the West. Neither state, of course, appealed to these designs in the making of its policy. Let us now turn from the state strategies embedded in laws and policy, what we can call the *official political discourse,* to the *discourse of practices,* the categories and tactics of everyday life. The next chapter explores the transformations in kinship practices in East Berlin.

# 5

---

# Victimization, political reconstruction, and kinship transformations in East Berlin: Generation I

This chapter begins the presentation of ethnographic material, shifting the focus from state strategies to individual tactics. In their autobiographical narratives, individuals reconstruct their lives with reference to ideals of self and not to principles of abstract truth. My objective here is to follow these self-techniques embodied in their personal histories. Though this account includes a range of perspectives, it remains necessarily quite partial. Therefore, one must be careful not to generalize to all Germans from the particular examples which inform my narrative. The life reconstructions in this section are based on stories of women and men of Generation I in East Berlin, born approximately between 1910 and 1935. Many members of this generation are no longer living; some now live in West Berlin. Additionally, I did not have equal access to all social and economic classes. As much as possible, I have tried to take these factors into consideration.

For members of Generation I in East and West Berlin the years from 1933 to 1945 were formative. Some had significant experiences during the Weimar years, and many had significant experiences during the Cold War. But what unites them most as a group are the twelve years they experienced, either in their late youth or as young adults, during the Third Reich. Yet belonging with reference to the Nazis, as supporter or nominal member, or even as someone in the resistance, is not a particular ideal self around which most people could construct an identity. In West Germany, the Nazi period was relatively taboo, in official and private discourse, for the first twenty years after the war. This was not the case in East German discourse, where an official narrative of resistance was cultivated. Socialism was defined in direct opposition to Nazism, indeed, as its negation, and provided one mode for a positive identity in East Germany, one that legitimated the state's narrative. Especially during the *Aufbau* phase, where an ideal of opposition to the past was linked to building a utopian future, people used this romantic emplotment provided by the state to integrate their own experiences into a meaningful and coherent narrative. For these individuals, romance with the *Aufbau* turned into nostalgia by the seventies, as the GDR stagnated economically and culturally. We may say that these people were basically motivated by a value-orientation, or to use Max Weber's terminology (1978: 24–26), by *Wertrationalität*, oriented by ultimate ends.

For those individuals who had no oppositional experience of their own from the Nazi period to draw upon, an accommodation with the state narrative was nonetheless possible, but not through the appropriation of this romantic narrative. Rather, these individuals, who basically did quite well for themselves during the *Aufbau*, acquiring new skills and steadily improving their standard of living, used the state and society instrumentally to achieve their own ends.[1] They organized their lives not around ultimate ends, but by using means-ends calculations, that is, to use Weber's other concept, their motivation was structured by *Zweckrationalität*, instrumental rationality. For these individuals, the GDR was never more than an instrument to be manipulated, and, as the state began to fail in its performance, especially when compared with West Germany, these people turned exceptionally bitter. Thus, they rode the wave of the revolution in 1989 as if they themselves had prepared the way for it, when, in fact, the time to change their allegiances was simply ripe, based on a rational calculation of their needs and position.

It is worth noting one other mode of identity formation, a positive one where the personal narrative legitimated that of the state. In this construct, individuals identify some prewar experience as socialist: either with communist/socialist opposition in the Weimar period, or resistance in the Nazi period, or even with communal life in a domestic group. By socialism they appeal to a working-together, a unity of purpose in a relatively egalitarian group, and a strong sense of belonging to an empirical community. Often these domestic experiences were in marked contrast to the terror of the Nazi regime, where extreme atomization and *Gleichschaltung* (the systematic destruction of old structures and loyalties) were the goals (Neumann 1942; Kershaw 1983). This source of identity, based as it is on a romanticized past and not on a present reality, gave individuals the strength (and illusion) of holding on

Table 16. *Narrative strategies of the East German state, 1949–1989*

| Strategy | |
| --- | --- |
| 1949–1965/68 | Construction |
| 1965–1989 | Sentimentalization |
| Emplotment | |
| Aesthetic | Romantic |
| Ideational | Integrational |
| Teleological | Egalitarian |

to a utopia yet to be fulfilled despite the nature of their own experience, which at times was in direct contradiction to their ideals.

Table 16 may serve as an orientation for the reader in following my account of how individuals construct their own narratives of belonging. It should be kept in mind that these master narratives of the state are appealed to by the citizen to construct coherent narratives out of their own disparate experiences. Since many narrative accounts of life under the Nazis have already been published, I am going to begin with stories about the end of the Third Reich and the beginning of postwar life. I will be isolating the experiential tropes – that is, periods and categories – most significant for organizing life constructions. For men and women of Generation I, postwar history usually begins before the end of the war; individual periodization rarely follows the state's chronological history. In accounts of the men,[2] the Third Reich frequently ends with being taken as prisoner of war (POW); in accounts of the women, reference to the Third Reich ends when they begin talking about Allied bombing attacks or their own refugee status outside Berlin.

**Households and the domestic group**
*Pragmatics of victimization and agency at the end of the war*
In the hope, or under the pretense, of supporting civilian resistance to the Nazi regime, the Allies began bombing residential areas of large German cities in March 1942. The first bombs fell on Berlin in January 1943, and as the raids increased in intensity, German authorities began to evacuate the city in July. By the end of 1944, approximately 1.9 million Berlin residents, over half of whom were children and youths, had become refugees.[3] Those citizens who remained in Berlin, primarily single women, widows, and a few old men, spent the last year of the war alternating residence between their partly damaged homes and under-

ground shelters. Soviet troops entered the city on April 25, 1945, and had to conquer the city house by house before the remaining German troops finally surrendered exactly seven days later. The most common and immediate reaction of adult civilian survivors to *die Erste Stunde* (GDR label: the first hour)/*Stunde Null* (FRG label: hour zero) had nothing to do with either their "capitulation" (as much West German historiography has it) or their "liberation" (as it is called in the GDR), but with a sensate observation – silence. No warning sirens, no gunfire, no airplane raids. Silence.

Auguste Ott, who remained for the last few months of the war in Berlin, remembered:

Despite everything that we had to live through, I had the most joyous feeling in May 1945 as I was again able to stand in the street. Glass splinters and debris were lying everywhere. But it was quiet – not a single gunshot, no more threatening airplanes, nothing. And I knew there would be no more alarm sirens. Once again, I could go to bed at night and sleep through the entire night. I stood on the street and thought, my God, I've done it, I've survived. That was a feeling that is indescribable.                *(Meyer and Schulze 1984: 83)*

The silence described by Auguste was to become a common response of her peers to many of the postwar problems they encountered. It is also a trope that reappeared regularly to structure their life histories. Being silent enabled them to think of themselves as a *tabula rasa* on which new meanings could be written. Their horrible past – *die Vergangenheit* – had been erased and was not to be recovered. Yet Auguste's "indescribable" feeling of "quiet" and the ability to "sleep through the entire night" was only one of several ways in which women experienced the end of the war. Her *élan* was by no means shared by all. "We were gathered in an underground shelter when the Russians entered our street. I was one of the first ones taken into the basement of the next house," explained Elke S., thirty-nine years old at the time. "No, no, I hadn't imagined that peace was going to be like that." Adult German women were considered spoils of war in the days following the Soviet march into the city. Reports of refugees from the already occupied Eastern territories included the most gruesome descriptions of rape, murder, and pillaging by the invading forces. Moreover, Nazi propaganda throughout the war tended toward hysteria in its particularly vehement portrayals of the Russians as a bestial, inferior race. Fear of the Red Army was one of the major reasons why many German women in Berlin could not experience the end of the war as the liberation it was meant to be, in retrospect, by their new state.

A Jewish woman who survived the war in hiding in Potsdam related how at the age of twenty-four she experienced the occupation:

For my mother and I, we didn't care who liberated us. Whether that was the Russians or Americans made no difference to us. Russian soldiers, many who were of Asian origin, came looking for girls. I was sick for the first three months of the occupation; my illness, in fact, saved me. But I remember one soldier coming in the house, and we were hidden in the attic. "*Wo Mädchen? Wo Mädchen?*" (Where girl? Where girl?) he repeated as he circled around the house constantly looking upstairs. It was horrible. Finally, my mother and I went to the authorities and told them that we'd been in hiding from the Nazis and were socialists. The officer said, "Thank God you've come. We've been waiting for people like you." But he also explained that he couldn't control the behavior of every soldier.

The Soviet army that initially conquered the Eastern territories apparently was quite different, less disciplined and more intent on revenge, from the army that later marched into Berlin. When the British, French, and Americans moved into Berlin three months after the Soviets, relations of German women to the occupying troops again changed. "If we saw Russians, we would run down the basement steps. If we saw Americans, we would run up the steps to meet them," reported Ingeborg L. The most notable and remarked-upon difference between the soldiers in the varying occupation forces was the smell: Americans smelled better, for their troops were much better provided for than the others. The Russians, being the poorest of the armies, smelled the worst.

I was often told in both Berlins that most of the women who became pregnant by Russian soldiers aborted the pregnancies. They did this privately and against the wishes of local authorities – there are no public records documenting this act of resistance to victimization. When Prior Heinrich Grüber and Professor Ferdinand Sauerbruch appealed to the Berliner Magistrat to allow abortions on ethical grounds, the Catholics and the communists united in rejecting the petition, the former on moral grounds, the latter for political reasons (Conradt and Heckmann-Janz 1987: 16). Already we can notice a conflict over narrativization: how one of the tropes of Berlin women after the war, their fear or actual experience of being raped, and their abortions, did not become part of the public narrative about the end of the war. This not-becoming-part of the official story was very much due to action by public authorities. In the West, the Catholic church, with the sanction of West Berlin political authorities, ended up ventriloquizing for these women, assuming a public voice emphasizing victimization by the Russians, the communists, the Cold War, denying them agency in dealing with rape. German leaders in the East, dependent on Russian authority, simply denied "it" had ever happened. In both cases, the ability of individual experience to take on generational meaning was limited, constrained, emplotted by political (master) narratives independent of the personal account. Only in the eighties, with the problematization of rape by young West German feminists, was this postwar trope recovered, brought into public discourse, and now even reread as part of the official story.

During the Cold War many Berlin women acquiesced to officialdom in narrativizing their experience, maintaining silence about the fact that their own praxis did not conform to the proper version of history. This discrepancy between story and practice becomes apparent only in recent recoveries, such as in the 1987 published account by East Berliner Frieda S., born in East Prussia in 1915: "Then I was with child. I must be honest with you," she pleads, indicating how in the past she had not been able to affirm, to be truthful to, her own experience, "I didn't want a child. I didn't really know where I was, when I returned to the farm. The farmer's wife helped me; she said, 'Freidel, don't have it! What will you do with the child? There's no purpose in it!' She then supported me. I aborted" (Herzberg 1987:120). Frieda S. focuses neither on the rape, nor the Russians, nor the "moral" consequences of an abortion. Rather, for her the issue was one of pragmatics: under those circumstances, what could she "do with the child?"

In narrative accounts one finds more East than West Berlin women who did decide to have children sired by members of occupation forces. This response may again have much to do with the official state policy in the East where, unlike the West, identifying the father and establishing the legitimacy of the child were downplayed in public discourse. Three East Berlin women of my acquaintance, Solja M., Sigrid B., and Sylka G., actually bore their children conceived by rape, one by a Russian, one by a Pole, and one by a Frenchman. Two of the women were already mothers, Solja M. of a girl, Sylka G. of a boy and a girl. All three raised their children as single mothers, simultaneously holding outside jobs. They maintain that they suffered no actual discrimination raising these children in the GDR. Their children confirmed these accounts.

*Return of the man and resignification of gender*
Many of the women and children who had been resettled in the countryside or small towns remained for more than two years in their

temporary lodging. Others, sensing the imminent Soviet invasion, returned in early 1945 to Berlin. At war's end 5 million Berlin apartments, over 55 percent of all residential space, had been destroyed: 31 percent of all apartments were totally destroyed, 30 percent heavily damaged, 30 percent mildly damaged, and 8 percent undamaged (Heimann 1985: 121; *Berlin ABC* 1965: 574). The damage in the Soviet-occupied part of Berlin was even greater, estimated at 65 percent of all residential space (*Zur Socialpolitik* 1984: 323). More than 400,000 of the homeless people were housed in emergency centers, including sports halls, schools, and subway tunnels. The domestic unit in this situation, then, was rarely coterminous with either family or kin groupings. Most residences included three generations, primarily women and children, often unrelated through marriage or blood. Some grandfathers were also present, although many men of their generation had been killed in World War I. One consequence of the population displacement was that in the year 1945 in Berlin, women outnumbered men by 63 percent to 37 percent.

The absent and longed-for kin, some already missing for twelve years, were the fathers and single men who had served as soldiers. Never to return were the victims of the extermination campaigns: Jewish Germans and gypsies. The vast majority of prewar Poles and other non-German ethnics, homosexuals, and the leadership of the anti-Nazi political opponents from the Weimar period returned in vastly reduced numbers. Nearly 4 million fallen German soldiers were also never to return. Of the 11.7 million German prisoners of war in May 1945, 4.5 million were released before the end of the year. By year's end of 1948, the British, American, French, and Belgian camps had released all of their prisoners. German POWs in Yugoslavia and Czechoslovakia returned home early in 1949. Soviet and Polish authorities released their prisoners, except for those accused of war crimes, in April and May of 1950.[4] The return of adult males to their households, anticipated with great expectation by all, was disappointing in most cases and resulted in increased hardship and domestic conflict for the female-dominated households.

Victimization permeates the memory of the last years of the war and the beginning of the occupation. Feelings of loss, waste, and powerlessness become a trope for the entire postwar experience. The dream of a reunited (and whole) family more often than not proved an illusion. Wives and husbands report that often they could hardly recognize each other. Communication between the soldiers/POWs and those at the homefront had been meager during the last years of the war, and neither party anticipated the havoc the war would play with their appearances. Many children had never even seen their fathers, and the early war photos which their mothers had repeatedly shown them no longer corresponded to the gaunt, cadaverous looks of the returning men. Likewise, the men were unprepared for the emaciated, weary appearance of the women. Moreover, because of cramped living quarters (frequently a single room and kitchen for three, often unrelated, generations, or two rooms and a kitchen for two mothers, grandmother(s), and children), spatial arrangements were subject to constant negotiation. Kitchens functioned simultaneously as bedrooms, and bedrooms and living rooms were not easily age- and sex-segregated. Given the importance to Germans of orderly spatial divisions in homes, the disorderliness and impermanence of arrangements was exceptionally stressful. The major adjustment and reintegration problems were not, however, a result of incommodious living space. They were brought on by different, sex-specific attitudes to authority, stemming from the profoundly disparate experiences of men and women during the Third Reich and the immediate postwar years.

During the final years of the Third Reich the practice of daily life – for men in military service and for women at the homefront – was a matter of improvisation centered around diametrically opposite survival strategies. The war inverted some of the significations attached to gender. Men in the Nazi military, like men in every military, were taught to follow unquestioningly the hierarchically given orders. (The high rate of desertion and massive number of executions in the last years of the war testify to the difficulty of creating such total submission.) Never to think independently, they were told, would eventually result in victory and a reassertion of German authority. For the many men who had until the last minute believed in a Nazi victory, the Nazi defeat marked more than a military and social capitulation, it meant the collapse of a cosmology.

Helmut K., born in 1910, reported about authority relations in the military:

Then I went to the lieutenant [to appeal a decision of the field marshal], who said to me, "When the field marshal says that something is black, then it is black, even when it is in reality white. You have to get used to this!" A soldier is not allowed to have an opinion. Because if each were to have his own opinion, then nobody would take the lead when he was sent to the front line against the enemy. If a soldier could think on his own, he'd say, "I'm not going there,

because I'll get shot if I do. This kind of thinking doesn't work here! We all have
to do what they tell us!"                                    *(Herzberg 1986: 204).*

Those men who survived the war ultimately did so in part by totally
yielding their individuality. As the war years stretched on and as the war
experience became not a series of quick victories, of *Blitzkriege*, but of
gruesome defeats, the soldiers experienced less camaraderie and with-
drew into themselves, what is retrospectively called "inner immigration." As more and more of their friends and comrades died, they
suffered from increased loneliness accompanied by feelings of abandon-
ment and isolation: they turned to personal survival strategies. The
opposite was true for the women: they were forced by circumstances to
assume leadership in the home and to integrate themselves into the
public economy. To survive meant constantly to improvise, to organize,
to think independently. Unlike men in the military, women's wartime
survival necessitated not a personal withdrawal, but an expansion of
exchange opportunities, an exploitation of kinship and residential
networks. While men were reduced to the role of mute objects, women
became economic entrepreneurs and single parents, the active con-
structors of their everyday lives. Hence immediately after the war men
and women exchanged their prewar gendered roles, at least those
written in the law and propagated as official models: men became
passive victims, women became active agents.

*Politics and domestic space*
Only after the currency reform in 1948 did domestic life begin to differ
substantially among groups or between Occupation Zones. The nearly
universal chaos in the Berlin of the late forties began slowly to take on
distinctive East and West patterns, reflecting the interaction between
people's daily lives and the different policies of the Allied Occupation
Forces. In their narrations, East Berlin men and women of Generation I
tended to end their household history by 1950, thereafter going on to
other themes. The domestic histories of workers after 1950 were
periodized with reference to non-domestic events: the Wall, work and
travel privileges, city renovations such as the Berlin Program. Within a
year of the founding of the state, domestic experience took its narrative
form from politics, everyday life took its periodizations from the state.
    During the 1950s and 1960s, the GDR experienced neither a *Wirt-
schaftswunder*, economic miracle, nor a *Freßwelle*, gorging frenzy, as
did West Germany. Even within the public working world, workers

experienced few improvements in material life until the late sixties. Building the Wall in 1961 stabilized the economy, allowing for more reliable economic planning and steadier growth, but it did not lead to an immediate change in social policy. The *Aufbau*, construction period, aimed to develop heavy industry, a focus that changed only after head of party and state Walter Ulbricht was forced to resign in 1971–1972. After 1972, family policy and housing renovation/construction became essential aspects of the new Honecker-era political strategy. Yet, personal wealth and income did not show any dramatic growth for the masses until the late 1970s, at which time the coherent social policy aimed at increasing individual living standards began to show results. Yet these policies privileged Berlin substantially, creating resentment in other parts of the republic. Additionally, these improvements were always evaluated by the population with respect to television images from the Federal Republic, where, as we shall see, citizens were enjoying an incredible economic boom that trivialized the growth in the GDR. East Berliners, given their proximity to West Berlin, were most aware of the differences.

In March 1976, Honecker announced a new Berlin Program giving preference in housing policy to Berlin, aimed at solving the housing shortage, at least in the capital city, by the year 1990 (Keiderling 1987: 704). The situation had been severely neglected from 1949 to 1975 for two major reasons: first, the government's emphasis on heavy industry had left little money for social policy; second, people who owned their own houses and apartments were reluctant or unable to maintain them, and those who rented from the state took little or no initiative in improving or maintaining their own buildings. Of the 472,000 East Berlin apartments in 1975, only some 60 percent had a shower or bath, 81 percent a toilet in the building, and 15 percent central heating (Keiderling 1987: 688). By the early seventies, however, the structure of domestic groups had already been substantially recast, influenced equally by interrelated social, political, and economic factors. Moreover, the Honecker-era pro-natal and housing policies ultimately had minimal effect on increasing the size of families. In fact, better housing in Berlin has coincided with a decline in the size of domestic groups. As of 1981, 33 percent of all households were single-person and 53 percent of all multi-person households were childless.

Berlin has always been a renter's city; less than 10 percent of the residents at any time in its history have owned their own homes. In this respect, both Berlins have a much higher percentage of renters as against home owners than do other German cities. After the war the prewar Berlin apartment structure of a front house connected to one or more back houses assumed new meaning. Apartments in the front houses traditionally signified higher social standing; living conditions (size of apartment, amount of light, state of repair) worsened in the back houses. After 1945, these units lost much of their old social class character; living spaces were redistributed according to criteria other than wealth, and social classes were themselves reorganized. Contrary to policy in the West, returning "anti-fascists," "victims of fascism," Spanish Civil War veterans who had fought on the side of the Republicans, and members of resistance movements received priority in apartment allocation, meaning better apartments in better locations. While these groups were symbolically significant, their numbers were relatively small. Those people with Nazi ties often lost their apartments, especially if it could be proved that the residence had been obtained by expropriation from Jews or others sent to concentration camps during the war. The Allied occupiers were also under pressure from the massive migration out of the eastern territories, a refugee population that totaled almost 9 million, or approximately 20 percent of postwar residents in the East and West Occupied Zones. In Berlin, the percentage of refugees, or *Umsiedler*, as they were initially labelled by the Allies and are still called in the East, was even greater, numbering approximately 25 percent. The Allies often forced reluctant residents to share their apartments with these strangers.

Two principles of socialist housing policy in East Berlin that remained constant over time were that rent prices remain low and stable, and that apartments be distributed in a way so as to include and integrate different social strata, defined occupationally (Aßmann and Winkler 1987: 112). In the prewar period, the Social Democratic Party (SPD) had concentrated their political organizing in the neighborhoods, whereas the Communist Party (KPD) had organized in the workplace. After the Communist Party forced the larger Social Democratic Party to merge with them into the Socialist Unity Party (SED) in 1946, the prejudices and policy preferences of the KPD took precedence, and SPD-organized support bases, such as those in neighborhoods, were viewed with suspicion. In the early fifties, the state initiated programs to integrate households into politically active housing complexes, *Hausgemeinschaften*. These programs, didactically formulated and at times carried out with crude political methods, were met with equally firm resistance during the High-Stalinist period.

In their reconstructions of experiences living in *Hausgemeinschaften*, people of Generation I did not heroize their resistance to policy, even though it was considerable; instead they emphasized their victimization. They talked about fear of denunciation, always placing the time of denunciations in the past. That period apparently reached its summit several years after Stalin's death in 1953, lasting until the mid sixties. In life constructions, one example of such policy often comes to the fore. The new state set up a structure where a resident in each house, *Hausgemeinschaftsleiter*, HGL, was responsible for registering all visits. This reminded many people of the Nazi *Blockwart* program, which maintained a system of *Gestapo* informants in residential areas. In 1987, there were 85,000 such registers turned in to East Berlin authorities from the HGL (*Neues Deutschland*, October 13, 1988, p. 8). From the reports I heard, the vigor with which each HGL carried out his/her task varied greatly, some not performing the function at all, others performing it zealously.

Many people also stressed that state attempts to have a *Stasi*, state security agent in each apartment complex did not encourage a friendly, socially engaged atmosphere in the units, and that the HGL's work was often conflated with the spying done by *Stasi*. Most people suspected that they had been spied upon at some time, and this certainly influenced their present behavior, even though they thought they were no longer under suspicion by the state. Yet the observable behaviour of Generation I was still marked by these past experiences: most feared speaking too loudly when the topic concerned politics, and in extreme cases, some even indicated a fear of being denounced for "inappropriate behaviour." One type of behavior in which all people, regardless of age, remained truly cautious was their telephone conversations. Everyone suspected that either their phone or the phone of the person they called was being tapped; they adapted by lowering their voices and censoring their speech.

In the 1980s, the fear of denunciation considerably lessened, as did the willingness on the part of authorities to tolerate a "live and let live" attitude – so long as it did not question the power of the ruling SED. This tolerance was certainly more marked in Berlin than elsewhere in the GDR, and more apparent among younger government employees than older ones. Many Berliners also reported that having *Stasi* agents in their apartment buildings no longer bothered them; the state would know what it wanted to know, they said, so why not just ignore it and live?

Apartment complexes in the late eighties remained highly integrated units, with different social groups represented within each building. Older residents, mostly widowed or divorced, benefited from the mixed composition of cohabitants in these complexes, for some socially minded younger members of the *Hausgemeinschaft* committees were usually on hand to share responsibility for special needs of the elderly. From approximately 1970 to 1989, rents in the GDR averaged only 3 percent of the average household's disposable income, although this could reach 10 percent of a single person's income. Rents for old apartments were fixed at their 1936 rate, and rents for new or renovated apartments were heavily subsidized by the state (*Materialien zum Bericht* 1987: 534–540). Furthermore, rental laws were written so strongly in favor of the renter that they practically excluded the possibility of evicting someone from their apartment, even in cases where rent hadn't been paid or where the individual was an object of political harassment. The typical contemporary housing complex in Berlin includes three apartment units (one front house containing over 50 percent of the apartments and two rear/side houses), all sharing a common entrance but with individual side entrances from the inner courtyard. This complex is then divided into forty to eighty residential units, the average number per house being twenty-two, of which more than a third are single-person households (Aßmann and Winkler 1987: 119).

Because the crowded housing situation did not substantially change until fifteen to twenty years after the war's end, more than half of all Generation I households during the 1950s included either extended kin (uncles, aunts, cousins) or non-kin. Not until the late 1960s did an increasing number of residential units become coterminous with the nuclear family, but one constructed by their children. By that time many members of Generation I had either lost a spouse, been divorced, or "lost" children to marriage or to emigration. Aging parents, normally the mother's mother, either never left the household of one of their children or, if they did leave, they were at times reincorporated into those households in the 1960s. A steady movement of retired widows (both Generation I and their mothers) in the 1970s and early 1980s to the West, overwhelmingly to West Berlin, alleviated the apartment crunch for some domestic units. The approximately 3:2 ratio of women to men in Berlin is more pronounced among the elderly, not only because of the number of men who died during the war, but also because women outlive men on the average by six years.

**Families: partnership and childcare**
*The disappearance of the couple and redefinition of family*
The bonding patterns of the war years, distinguished above all by the nearly total absence of the father, did not change substantially with the return of the men from the POW camps. The missing father for the child signified in turn the missing husband for the wife. Much as the father had disappeared during this period, so did the couple. Partnership had been reduced to a memory, becoming a fixed symbol without practical referents and without an experiential history. The absence of partners and fathers, did not, however, remove or lessen their significance as kin. Rather, as partnership and fatherhood lost their role in practice, they received exaggerated treatment in the imagination. Rilke had prophesied the Modern as an attempt to reveal a *Tun ohne Bild*, an act without a picture. The picture of the German father and the "(in)complete family" inverted the axiom of modernity. Father and complete family became a picture without an act, *Bild ohne Tun*.

"It took over a half year," reported Anna Falk, "before my son got used to the fact that now a man belonged to the family, and that his picture or this word, *Vati,* papa, was a person who would be staying with us" (Meyer and Schulze 1985: 144). Anna Falk was one of those mothers in Generation I who repeatedly showed a picture of *Vati* to her children, imprinting a memory of an absence. The return of the father and not his absence was perhaps the most traumatic psychological experience of Generation II children. In fact, for most of them, he never replaced their imaginary father. Fathers for them became taboo items, and even today, many members of Generation II, especially the men, do not or can not talk about their fathers. Dora Brandenburg reported about the return of her husband:

Rolf, the youngest, completely refused to recognize his father. He didn't know what a father was. We didn't have a single adult man among our friends [during the war]. So the child just couldn't accept him: "Mommy, is that the gentleman to whom I must say father?"
Our youngest would always come in the morning and lie by me in my bed. Suddenly my husband was there, and he sat up on the bed and said to the child, "Get out, get out, don't you see that the place is already taken here?" And another time, my husband had said something to Rolf, something that made Rolf very angry. And I can still see him, standing there with his fists clenched, and his face filling with rage. He walked around the table and walked up to his father and said, "You, you, you have absolutely no say here." . . . The oldest said to me once, "Mommy, it was a lot better when father wasn't here."

*(Meyer and Schulze 1985: 145–146)*

In the absence of "the man of the household," a new power configuration arose, where son and mother, or even daughter and mother, often shared responsibilities and authority. The reappearance of the husband and father challenged this egalitarian relationship, threatening to replace it with a patriarchal model. Dora Brandenburg, like the majority of women, stayed with her partner, hoping that things would get better. Other women divorced.

The hope that the return of the man would make childcare and domestic life easier for the mother quickly revealed itself as illusory. Husbands, feeling threatened by the newly found independence and strength of their wives and the close mother–child bond that had developed in their absence, reacted by alternately withdrawing and increasing authoritative demands on the women in their households. "My husband started drinking immediately after his return from the POW camp," commented Martha M. "Not just drink, but *saufen*, really get loaded. Then he'd pick a fight with the children, whom he didn't know, since he'd been gone for almost six years. My youngest child, five years at the time, refused to recognize him. And I'd always be put in the middle, between the children and my husband."

Men of Generation I, in talking about their lives, did not tell this particular story, except to say it was "difficult" for them to readjust to domestic life after the war. They preferred to focus on their work, if interesting to them; they avoided mention of their kin relations. When the topic of kin did come up, they referred only to their mother, wife, and children. Women of Generation I, on the other hand, quite frequently used the term "family" to refer to a domestic unit that does not include an adult man. Elsa Köhler, for example, defined family as her children, sisters, and her mother. When she referred to her own father, she absorbed him into the term "parent."

I was only happy that I had my *family* in this period. My parents were both still living, around the corner. And both my sisters were also still there . . . My mother offered me and my children a lot of support. When something went wrong, she stayed with the children. And my sisters often picked up things for me or did other chores. I never felt myself alone, thank God. Life must somehow go on.                         *(Meyer and Schulze 1985: 22–23)*

For Elsa, the family was no longer couple-centered; it had been redefined to include siblings, parents, and children, but no husband or father.

Klara L. shared a postwar household with her father, sister, cousin, and cousin's husband. Her own husband had been killed during the war; her younger sister and father were both initially sick with typhus. For several years, she had worked in the household of a Soviet family, part of the Occupation forces in the Karlshorst section of Berlin. She defined her family in the following context: "In sum, I was never once sent home from Karlshorst without also having been given something [food and coal] to take along with me. That's because they also knew that I had a *family*" (Herzberg 1987: 253).

The sisters Erna and Frieda Eschenburg shared an apartment with Erna's son and with their mother and grandmother in the postwar period. Erna's husband had been killed during the war. Frieda described the situation:

Okay, it was not always easy with such an elderly grandmother. No, definitely not. I mean, she came out of a totally different world. So, we already had two dependents to carry through the period, our grandmother and our little Hans. And mother was also no longer so young. So, I believe that these chores and responsibilities themselves gave to us the strength and the impetus we needed to carry on. But perhaps we can explain it this way: that we women were then somehow ourselves, yes, an intact *family*.          *(Meyer and Schulze 1984: 86)*

The two sisters raised Erna's son together and today continue to share a household with each other.

In the case where the man reentered a household as husband and father, he almost invariably generated conflict. The women were then forced to function as arbiters between their children and husbands. But relationships with the children were not the only source of dispute between partners. Women of Generation I also fought with their adult male kin to retain their newly found autonomy and independence. During the war, women had taken over household budgeting, and except where there were large inheritances at stake (a factor for very few Berliners), they maintained this role after the return of their male kin. This new exercise of power by the woman directly challenged the authority conceptions of the man, conceptions which had crystallized before the war. More often than not, he contested her authority whenever possible.

The major site for this contestation over authority within partnerships in the immediate postwar period was over control of the food supply. "During the war the food supply [in Berlin] was really quite sufficient," explained Martha M. "But as soon as the Soviet army marched in, the delivery system fell apart."[5] The situation worsened overnight with the end of the war and the collapse of German administrative structures. Critical shortages in foodstuffs and in coal for heating turned the household into a highly charged political unit. In July 1945, the death rate among newly born infants was 66 percent (Keiderling 1987: 109). Between October 1945 and March 1946, 60,000 Berliners died, many if not most from causes relating to hunger and cold. During the winter months of 1946–1947, an additional 40,000 Berliners died, of whom 285 froze to death and 67 died after amputation of frozen limbs, more than 53,300 patients were treated by doctors for frostbite, with 1,376 suffering from exposure admitted to hospitals. In December 1946 alone, the tuberculosis-related death rate rose 15.6 percent (Heimann 1985: 118).

Hunger strained relations within domestic groups, especially those between husband and wife. Anna Wilke, a West Berlin woman, explained:

My husband had difficulty understanding that I was so active and that I had in fact supported us. The food supply was short despite my efforts. Then at every opportunity he would complain that there wasn't enough to eat. He was a big man, six feet tall, and correspondingly needed more food. But where should it come from? He always thought we weren't giving him his share, and then he argued with me, having no idea of how unjust and immoderate his accusations were. I often had to keep changing the rations, redividing them, to stretch one meal into two. He didn't want to understand that. Once he slugged our daughter, because he thought she'd snuck a piece of bread. But I had given it to her. He didn't think it was right.

Then there was a scene when I had bought two new burners for the stove. He was astonished that I would buy two new burners without his permission. But then I stood up and said to him, "Haven't you yet heard about the equality of women before the law, *Schlüsselgewalt der Frau*? In this case, I am totally in the right. I run around the whole day doing things for the family. I am quite able to decide such little things myself."    *(Meyer and Schulze 1985: 119–120)*

In her conflicts with her husband, Anna's final appeal was to equality, to the *Schlüsselgewalt der Frau*, a trope congruent with formal goals of the regime in the GDR but absent in the FRG. Women in the East who told this kind of story found official state approval. The legitimation of Anna's story in the West, as we shall see, was much more complicated.

Most married partnerships of Generation I stayed "intact," including the younger mothers who remained bonded primarily to their own mothers and children. Most men of this generation reentered their families as a symbolic presence, an ideal figure that was to make whole an embattled, seemingly leaderless unit. Few managed to reintegrate in practice. As practicing fathers, brothers, uncles, or sons, these men were both everywhere and nowhere; that is, everywhere in the imagination and nowhere in practical male kin roles. Most married partners continued to share a household despite the fact that the relationship with their children became the casualty of their staying together. The children of these couples became simultaneously the *raison d'être* for and the victims of the marriages of Generation I.

Some women refused to remain in these marriages, and, in fact, the number of divorces in Berlin as a whole reached a peak of 24,998 in 1946. (For the entire GDR, divorces peaked in 1948.) The divorce rate in Berlin remained relatively stable for several years, increased dramatically again in 1949, and thereafter slowly declined during the fifties. Marriages, on the other hand, steadily increased until 1966, then stabilized until the mid 1980s. The proportion of divorces to marriages did not again surpass the 1946 number until 1984, at which time we are dealing with the divorces of their children and grandchildren. Hildegard L. offered an example of one of these patterns:

We got married in 1940, a so-called war marriage, and I had my first child a year later. When my husband came back in 1947, he refused to do anything, to help with anything. I was fully exhausted, working in the ruins and living with another family in the apartment. I finally said I'd had it – that was in 1948.

Hildegard talked about her divorce proceedings as relatively unproblematic.

Other women encountered resistance both from their men and from the legal system. Johanna J., born in 1912, returned with her six children in May 1945 to Berlin. During the next four years, she rebuilt her partly destroyed home and supported her children without aid from her husband. New social welfare measures for large families in the Soviet Zone provided her with the basic food and provisions necessary for survival. "Large families have always received extra support," commented Johanna. "At that time there was state support for a child of school age." In 1949, she said, "I asked for a divorce. And then the lawyer said, 'You should give it another try. Stay together. Think of your six children. You shouldn't make a rash decision.'"

Johanna first began working outside the home in 1950 at the age of thirty-nine, and at that time tried again to divorce. She had not been living together with her husband, nor did she have regular contact with him. In three scheduled appointments before the court, her husband failed to show up all three times. Then he wrote her that he would not agree to a divorce. The court suggested that he return home to his family, which he did in the fall of 1951. She finally divorced in 1953, reasoning, "I had become more self-reliant, thoroughly autonomous." In the divorce settlement, her husband was awarded their house outside Berlin, which they had originally built together but which she had restored after the war. She was awarded an apartment. The experience embittered her about men: "I have not tried to meet anyone again. I fear . . . that it could again be someone who drinks. No, that's not for me" (Herzberg 1987: 36–46). Two tropes, both of which are largely dependent on the state for realization, dominate Johanna's story: her autonomy and equality with respect to all others, and her integration into the society. Her narrative of belonging, like that of many other GDR women of her generation, was both framed by and legitimated the story of the state.

*Partnership, romance, and sex*
The relationship of state to sexual practices in the GDR was an indirect one insofar as the state had no discourse on sexuality until the mid sixties. When the state did begin talking about sex, its message was directed to Generation II. For the most part, members of Generation I practiced sex without naming what they were doing. Hence men and women of Generation I rarely discussed their sexuality in terms of the contemporary categories of hetero-, homo-, and bi-sexual. Rather, they talked about relations with particular individuals that may have become sexualized without ever relating these practices back to an identity focused around them. The coherence they gave to their sexual practices existed only in retrospect, and it was a coherence that did not revolve around their sexuality. What they did tend to focus upon in recon-structions was their productiveness and reproductiveness. Sexual prac-tices were always placed in the context of other desires, practices, and institutions.

Most members of this generation were too young for the wild experimentation of the twenties,[6] and had their first sexual experiences under the Nazis. The Nazis did not so much repress sexuality as try to control it for reproductive purposes. (Their policies regulating sex among "non-Germans" was an entirely different matter.) This does not mean that sex under the Nazis was practiced in radically different ways than it was under Weimar or in the GDR; rather, it means the Nazis merely selected particular aspects of sexual practices (procreative ones) to sanction positively and others (nonprocreative forms of sexual pleasure) to sanction negatively. Homosexuality, in particular, was used by the Nazis as a category to eliminate homosexual practices (by exterminating men and imprisoning women who engaged in same-sex practices) and to discredit political opponents.[7] East German authorities after 1949, while intent on encouraging reproduction, did not focus on sexual practices to do this, but on motherhood.

Likewise, both men and women talked about sexual practices as part of a larger complex that pertained less to sexuality *per se* than to "family" and "marriage." In my interviews with men of Generation I, two aspects of marital relationships repeatedly came to the fore: romance and sex. In my interviews with women, work, autonomy, sacrifices and suffering, and kin were the themes; love and romance were minor subjects, sex was avoided. The title of Meyer and Schulze's book (1985) of women's protocols from this generation, *Nobody Spoke of Love Back Then*, remained a personal leitmotif for East and West Berlin women. This was not so for their male counterparts.

What unites the narratives of women and men of Generation I most when they discussed postwar sexual life is a sense that it was unpleasant. Women, in particular, commented on how returning soldiers stank, how they were sick and emaciated. Already by the late forties, the divorce rate had tripled from its 1939 level. As many women discovered that their husbands would not return (or could not discover when or whether they would return), they entered a form of partnership without marriage, now called *Lebensgemeinschaften*. It is impossible to determine the statistical distribution of this partnership form, especially since there was no word for it until Generation II began widely practicing it in several different forms in the late sixties. In 1988, many of the widows and widowers of this generation chose to live together without getting married; often it was their second or third such partnership. Since issues of inheritance and level of pension were normally not at stake, the need for state or social recognition of the partnership was minimal. The motivations for this later life partnership ranged from loneliness to convenience to love; regular sex played a major role for some men – rarely were property or social status relevant to the partners.

A wide range of individuals in the GDR across generations practiced forms of domestic partnership that did not have a legal correlative. For Generation I in the GDR, this represented a dramatic shift over the last thirty years in their attitudes about partnership, marriage, and sex. "I have been married for thirty years," said Karl, the boss of a company, "and we have four children. Marriage, yes. But whether one should marry right away? Back then when we got married, that was normal. But today, I think you can live together better if you are not married to each other" (Eckart 1984: 112). In a separate interview, his wife Ilse, the chairperson of a production company, GPG, commented,

"And then, I wanted to be an illustrator. I visited a school for that in Berlin. But because of the bombing attacks I couldn't travel there anymore, it was too dangerous. I also didn't want to marry. I just wanted to live freely and work. In the early period [after my marriage], I just wasn't able to get around to the drawing anymore. Whether I could succeed today, to start up again?"

*(Eckart 1984: 132).*

Ilse reflected regretfully back upon talents that she gave up when she married, and doubted whether she would be able to develop them again now that she was nearing retirement age.

Men of Generation I who did remain in marital units, much like their female counterparts, did not reflect back upon the past as a time of marital bliss. Their statements differed from those of women in that they were less detailed and referred to other aspects of conflict. Ernst, a gardener born in 1919, reflected:

I regret two things in my life: [First], that I didn't study, as I already said. [He was encouraged to qualify further in his field during the early fifties, but rejected the opportunity.] Just because of that, I'd like to be younger once more. And [second], that I did not divorce my wife. My daughter even shakes her head: You torture each other so! And mother doesn't even need a man! Once I was ready to do it. Erika, my friend, had decided she was going to divorce her man, leave him for me. And I went to my wife to tell her I was also leaving. Then I saw her sitting there and crying like a baby. I asked: Why are you crying? You know, she said, I cry because that's what I am like. Why am I like that? She hurt me there, for the first time. I noticed, she isn't only dissatisfied with her place in the world, but also, she isn't satisfied with herself, she hasn't made peace with herself. And then I couldn't say [it] to her. The tormenting of each other continued. Instead of marrying Erika, I ended our relationship and wrote a poem. I have it memorized.

Ernst later related how sex for his wife was something she merely put up with "because she wanted children," that she always had excuses. It is apparent that he construed the aspects of sex, love, and romance as closely intertwined, while his wife thought of them separately.

Many married women, on the other hand, tended to portray their husbands as insensitive, sexual insatiables and themselves as victims. They contextualized the sex act by relativizing it *vis-à-vis* other acts;

their husbands singularized the sex act in terms of bodily and emotional needs. Johanna J., born in 1912, explained:

When my husband would come home from work, and then not speak a single word to me – I couldn't take it, I couldn't go on like that. Then he would look at me: Aha, then you're ripe for bed again, something like that. But that wasn't the case. He just wouldn't leave me alone. I couldn't take it, that pouting, the sulking was something horrible for me. I would have spoken out about it much sooner, but my husband wouldn't allow that.    *(Herzberg 1987: 28)*

Johanna suggestively shifted the theme three times: initially, her husband refused to talk and she "couldn't take it" – she tried to make him talk. Then, his insistence on sex was met by her (unsuccessful) resistance of sex – she was not "ripe for bed." Finally, her solution was to repress her desire "to speak out about it" but her husband "wouldn't allow that." Apparently, she wished that he would follow up on her solution and respond to her wishes by repressing his desire for sex. In Johanna's world, talk was both her weapon (something she inflicted on her husband) and her pleasure (something she sought from her husband), while for her husband, sex was both his weapon and his pleasure. This pattern was common among heterosexual partners of this generation: the women fought with words, the men with sex.

### Relations in retirement

During my fieldwork, about half of the living members of Generation I were retired, the minimum age being sixty for women, sixty-five for men. Leaving the world of work reshapes an individual's relationship to other people as well as to the state. In order to qualify for GDR pensions, individuals must have performed fifteen years of socially recognized work. Special allowances were given to coalminers, women with five or more children, individuals who fought against the Nazis ("anti-fascists"), and "victims of fascism." For women who had borne or raised more than two children, and for the third and every additional child, every four years of care were counted as a full year of public work. This provision also held true when a woman was not able to work because she was responsible for the continual care of *Angehörige*, the next of kin, not able to care for themselves. Legal recognition of women's nurturing role provided some compensation and recognition to women who sacrificed career for family.

Pensions in the GDR also varied according to occupation group, number of years employed, and income. On the whole, they were extremely low, especially when compared to those in West Germany; in 1988, pensions totaled approximately 30 percent of the average income of a full-time worker (*Materialien zum Bericht* 1987: 573–580; *DDR Handbuch* 1985: 1,117). Yet retirees I met did not complain as much about their low pensions as about restrictions on their travel to the West, past injustices attributed to state ineptitude or malice, and what they perceived to be a decline in societal standard of living compared to the West (dilapidated housing, collapsing transportation system, deteriorating quality of public services, nonavailability of fruit and vegetables). This personal narrative of decline and fall directly contradicted official silence about such matters.

The most common household forms of members of Generation I in 1988 included living with a married partner, in *Lebensgemeinschaften*, or alone. In Berlin, few of the elderly lived with their children (or if they did, it was for a short period of time), and few lived in separate homes for the elderly. Household decisions in such elderly partnerships were usually made by the woman. *Volkssolidarität*, solidarity with the people, the organization set up to aid members of the society who needed extra care, played a major role in enabling many elderly to remain in their homes and not be institutionalized. I asked two young men I know who worked for *Volkssolidarität* to observe the power relations between the couples for whom they cared. Altogether, they cared for twenty elderly couples between one and three times a week; the care included shopping, preparing meals, and cleaning the apartment. The woman alone paid the bills and made financial decisions in sixteen of the twenty pairs; in these cases, she also appeared to make the decisions about time scheduling, vacations or visiting relatives and friends in West Berlin, and domestic routines. In the other four, the woman deferred to the man in decisions concerning time or resource allocation and the man appeared to have the domestic authority. In none of the pairs did it seem to the caretakers that the decisions were shared by both partners equally. In eighteen of the pairs, the woman seemed to have more frequent contact with her own children and with her female friends than did her male partner.

My own encounters with retired partners confirmed the general patterns described in these two reports. Whereas the man of Generation I rarely had anything to replace the loss of his occupational identity that accompanied his retirement, the woman continued to have her area of competence and activity in organizing domestic life. In addition, several retired women with non-blue-collar jobs reported to me that they maintained contact with their former work colleagues, often doing voluntary work one day a week. These relations between workers over time took on ersatz kinship meanings, especially important for those individuals who lost family members over the years to West Germany. Many work units made efforts to honor former colleagues by inviting them to ritual events, mainly work parties and holiday festivals. These invitations played an important role as integrative mechanisms for the elderly, especially as many were without children and close siblings.

Ritual events related to work were often used in narratives to periodize the retirement years. Hence blue-collar workers might have obtained part of their yearly rhythm from their former workplace, which in turn was dependent on the state for its directives.[8] Among blue-collar workers, patterns varied greatly from company to company. Those without siblings, children, or close work colleagues were relatively isolated after retirement. For white-collar and professional men, on the other hand, retirement most often meant a withdrawal from the work domain, as offices and bureaucracies were not conducive settings for creating strong cohesion between coworkers. Yet the social isolation of the elderly in all groups was often delimited by a combination of contacts through *Volkssolidarität, Hausgemeinschaften*, and the former work units.

### Grandparenting and kin

A final transformation in the lifecourse of this generation concerned the role of grandparents, Oma and Opa. As in other Western countries, women in the GDR tended to outlive men, in 1952 by 4.1 years, in 1982 by approximately six years (*Demographische Prozesse* 1984: 48). This meant that from the perspective of Generation III (the grandchildren), the Oma was a part of the kinship unit for a considerably longer period of time than the Opa. Given the fact that men of Generation I had such estranged relations with their own children, it is also understandable why, in most cases, they also often failed to play a significant role as grandparents.

Grandmothers often continued to play a vital role in childcare, especially in Berlin, where some 48 percent of all first-born children were given birth by single women. Since over 90 percent of the women of Generation II were working full-time, and since new mothers in the GDR tended to be very young, and simultaneously involved either in *Ausbildung* or in establishing themselves in a career, the great-grandmother, still called Oma, was frequently involved in childcare. In talking about their relationship to grandchildren, Omas and Opas often claimed that they had very little, if any, influence on them. One 56-year-old woman said about her grandchildren, "The first years of childhood are very important; I took them very seriously with my children. I now have, unfortunately, no influence on my grandchildren" (Eckart 1984: 132). This personal assessment of powerlessness in influencing future generations was based in part on the assumption that the grandchildren would be influenced most by state-run childcare institutions. In addition, a large number of grandmothers were still young enough to be fully employed and therefore did not have much time for grandchildren. Yet many Omas, despite negative assessments of their own influence, performed vital, regular childcare for their daughters.          .

For members of Generation I, partnership and childcare remained the integral and interrelated action domains of kinship. In their life reconstructions, they tended to avoid mention of their friends in the context of a discussion about kin unless directly asked. Yet, when asked to talk about their daily or yearly routines, the women often mentioned important female friends or schoolmates from the Weimar period, or friends and former housemates from the immediate postwar period. When they visited these friends, many of whom now lived in the West, the trip was usually combined with a visit to their kin. They often claimed that they had more in common with these friends than with their relatives, and not seldom enjoyed the stay with friends more than the obligatory stop by relatives.

### Travel to the West

Closely connected to retirement and grandparenting was the right to (and role of) travel to the West. From 1961, the time of the building of the Wall, to 1964, the possibility for travel to West Berlin or West Germany was extremely restricted, if not totally impossible. As of September 9, 1964, retired persons were allowed to visit West Berlin or West Germany once a year. This immediately elevated the status of "being retired" for two reasons: first, retired people were now responsible for maintaining contact between kin in East and West. Second, retired people were now able either to obtain information on, to purchase, or to transport Western status goods for their kin in the East. Not until 1971 did this situation change, when rules for reciprocal visits were relaxed and regularized: West Berliners or West Germans could with an official invitation now visit their East relatives more than once a year, and East Germans, other than retired persons, could visit the

West in cases of *dringenden Familienangelegenheiten*, extreme family emergencies. Possible grounds for visits because of family emergencies included births, marriages, life-threatening sicknesses, deaths of grand-parents, parents, siblings, and children; all requests were and are by no means automatically approved. In sum, after 1961, the state took over kinship categories and used them as emplotment forms regulating the distribution of privileges. For elderly GDR citizens, the relations with and meaning of kin were in part shaped by the definition of their respective political membership. To this we must add the international dimension: approximately two-thirds of all East Germans had kin in the West, but only one-third of all West Germans had kin in the East. This quantitative asymmetry increased the relative dependence of East Ger-mans on kin in the West, since in yet another respect the West was more significant to them than they were to the West.

Once in the West, East Germans received greeting money, *Begrüßungsgeld*, out of which they bought small gifts, mostly for their grandchildren. In 1987, *Begrüßungsgeld* totaled 290 million D-Mark ($145 million). The greeting money was never enough to fulfill the wishes of the grandchildren, but then the Omas often asked their West kin to buy the desired goods for them. West Germans sent on average 26 million gift packages yearly to East Germans; 9 million packages were sent in the opposite direction. It is estimated that such gifts together with money given directly to East Germans totaled 2,200 million D-Mark ($1,100 million) yearly (*Materialien zum Bericht* 1987: 633–634). West Berliners or West Germans could deduct from their income tax much of the cost of gifts to their East German relatives. With money from these contacts, Omas in the eighties often obtained the desired new pair of jeans, jeans jacket, Sony Walkman, a Swiss-made Swatch, or pop-music records. If Oma eventually moved to the West, she remained equally important, if not more, as her pension was usually large enough for her to afford more gifts than she could on the mere once-a-year greeting money.

Since the early eighties, disposal income for consumer goods in East Berlin increased greatly, so that grandmothers were often given D-Mark from the East German kin themselves (exchanged on the black market) to purchase Western goods. Before 1986, the total number of East travelers not yet in retirement age who traveled to the West did not exceed 60,000 per year. In anticipation of Honecker's 1987 visit to Bonn, West Germany and of the expected *de facto* West German recognition of the East German state, the GDR relaxed travel restrictions for its citizens in 1986. Thereafter the number of visits by citizens below the age of retirement allowed to visit the West jumped more than ninefold, to 573,000. In 1987, this number again more than doubled, to approximately 1.2 million visits. The number of visits of retired people during this period remained constant, if not showing signs of decline, from 1.7 million in 1985 to a high of 1.9 million in 1986, with a decline back to 1.7 million in 1987.[9] The majority of these visits were to West Berlin.[10]

This freer travel of non-retired people again changed the role of grandparents, both taking away their special travel status and removing some of the material incentives in their relationship with children and grandchildren. New legal ordinances that took effect in July 1989 (discussed in chapter 8) defining which kin could visit Western relatives again relativized the role of grandparents. For some families in East Germany, retired people were still the only ones with guaranteed access to the West. Without access to West Berlin at the four levels of gifts, greeting money, personal visiting, and purchasing, the standard of living of many East Berliners (measured by their criteria) drastically decreased.

For GDR citizens of Generation I, travel to the West often increased their general dissatisfaction, at least for the immediate period following their return. This was expressed to me in two ways: by a general hostility to the way the regime presented itself and by an extremely critical, dismissive view with respect to their own personal past. Men and women gave similar accounts of visits to what was enviously called "the Golden West." They uniformly criticized the "hectic" life in the West: its fast pace, the advertising, loud youths, and the overabundance of stimulating signs. Likewise, they often praised the slower pace and more predictable course of events in the East, as well as its friendlier atmosphere and general lack of pretentiousness. Yet trips to the West generally unsettled more than fulfilled. People of Generation I were especially impressed with the *Sauberkeit und Ordnung*, cleanliness and order, of the West, traditional German values that reinforced in them a feeling of inferiority relative to their West German peers.

After a long tirade against "the corrupt political regime we have here" and of the difficulties of everyday life in the East, Elke S. told me following her return from a five-day trip to West Berlin: "You know, after you hear how they talk over there, always going on about how free and good it is there, you begin to resent how they put us down all the time. After a while I began to think, maybe we don't have it so bad here after all, and I even started to defend our life over here!" She explained how her friends in the West never worked like she did, how they never acquired any skills, though they now feel justified in saying that they, too, had created the *Wirtschaftswunder*. After her visits to the West, Elke felt caught between total abnegation of her postwar life, envy for the wealth and comfort (undeserved, she would say) of her peers in the West, and pride over her own accomplishments. Always dependent on the goodwill of her West friends during her visits, she felt particularly humiliated by her inability to reciprocate *in kind* for the ostentatious displays she experienced in the West. Limited travel to the West may have made the elderly more personally compliant and passive with regard to the regime in the short run, but it also decreased their self-esteem and sharpened the comparison of material life between East and West, a comparison which always ended up devaluing "made in the GDR."

## Work and domestic restructuring
### Black-market activity

*Hamstern, organisieren, kohlenklauen, ranschaffen, geschäftstüchtig sein* – gathering, organizing/stealing, pilfering coal, coming upon things, and being entrepreneurial, the domestic unit in the early postwar period created a special vocabulary to describe daily work habits, routines that involved all of its members. Unofficial, often illegal work and domestic life were not easily separable domains. Whatever their differences, they were connected to each other by an overall ethos of production. The buzzwords of the time illustrate the fine gradations of necessity, the illegal activities that made it possible to carry on, work, and produce under adverse circumstances. In 1947, approximately 85 percent of the Greater-Berlin population was involved in black-market activity (Meyer and Schulze 1984: 102–103). Female-organized trading networks were not restricted to inner-city exchange, but involved contacts with other cities, such as Leipzig–Berlin and Hamburg–Berlin rings which were described to me during my fieldwork. The activity quickly became normalized, and many women and children took pride in how well they worked the black market. Police would raid now and then, often catching a "little fish," but they rarely got hold of the big dealers. In any case, most people resisted the attempt by officials, supported by Soviet authorities, to organize the labor market and plan the economy. This resistance was directed against the new state after 1949.

To *hamstern* meant to gather and collect items which one might need either immediately or, more likely, in the future. People would then hoard them until the time arrived when they could trade for other goods that were needed. Gathering quickly became habitual, routinized activity. "We went *hamstern* every weekend," explained Martina S. "Potatoes were not always easy to come by because everybody in the country wanted them. We ended up trading furniture or jewelry for potatoes or beetroots, whichever was cheaper." *Organisieren* was simply stealing by another name. Klaus Staek described the activity: "The magicians' formula was then called *organisieren*. At that time we were delivered from our everyday life of war and transported into a peace permeated with poverty. You didn't steal, you organized. It sounded less severe, and the organizer could even get a certain recognition from it, the better he understood how to organize" (Böll 1985: 91). *Ranschaffen* referred to the activity of coming up with things on the black market that were difficult to find. *Kohlenklauen* meant to steal coal from public supplies, mostly from train stations and mostly in the evening when authorities were sleeping. *Geschäftstüchtig* meant business-wise, literally, but referred to being good at trading on the black market.

This whole genre of entrepreneurial activity was initially a domain dominated by adult women and their children. With the West German Currency Reform in 1948, most black-market activity in West Berlin dried up. In the East, because the Currency Reform itself created additional disparities in the value of their currency, the black market continued but with new dealers. It was immediately taken over by adult male traders upon their return from POW camps and continued to thrive through the fifties, often in the form of East–West exchange. The majority of GDR court proceedings in the fifties dealt with property crimes, often involving black-market activities, and only the building of the Wall actually put a halt to many forms of illegal trade (Aue 1976: 20–21). Major black-market exchanges of foodstuffs continued until the regime eliminated the food-coupon system in 1957. Shortages in goods (primarily in building materials), forbidden items (such as pornography or some Western publications), and Western-produced consumer products continued to generate a restricted domain of black-market activity in the GDR in the 1980s.

The restructuring of domestic/public boundaries in the late forties created, in turn, new relationships and tensions among kin and between the sexes. A common response of men to their exclusion from the domestic unit was to indulge in non household-related work, to rebuild a public domain distinct from and untainted by domestic life. Adult men found it relatively easy to reassimilate themselves into the hierarchical work patterns common to all-male work domains, and those men who could not adjust to socialist forms of collective work habits had few problems throughout the 1950s moving to the West. But the majority of women were also working during the 1950s, some in traditionally male-only occupations.[11] These working women posed psychological problems for men, particularly since industrial leaders (mostly men) were under pressure from the new political leadership to support women's advancement in the workplace.

Helmut K. clarified the man's perspective:

It was not so easy to work with the women back then . . . Earlier, there was work only for men. The women really shouldn't have worked, because there wasn't enough work for both men and women. Women who were single – they could also work . . . I once had a problem with my nerves for 14 weeks. Nobody has to watch over production workers in order to get them to work. But with office workers – this is true overall – when you check in on them, when you aren't there steadily, they'll simply not work diligently. When one of the women buys a wig *drüben* [from the West], then if I wouldn't be there, they'd all stop by to try it on. Or when one has bought a new pair of shoes *drüben*, then they'd all try them on. They do all that during work time.

*(Herzberg 1987: 191–223)*

Despite the resistance of men to working women, the 1950s and 1960s were the decades when women in the GDR enjoyed the widest range of occupational choices.

Until the signing of a basic agreement in 1972 between the GDR and the West German government, West German policy was to isolate and bankrupt the East German government, planning to incorporate the "Soviet Zone," as it was called in the West, into the West German state. GDR officials named this *Ausblutung*, bleeding-dry policy. It functioned more effectively in the East/West Berlin relationship than elsewhere. Helmut K., who worked in West Berlin until the early fifties while living in the East, described the attitude of his fellow workers at that time in the West:

"They would say, 'Now is the right time, now we'll be able to exchange some on the black market.' And for us then, there'd be nothing left to buy. When we'd come home from work, the stores would be empty. I left my job [in the West] at that time. It went like this: I was supposed to work in the West, but got only East money for my work. And then my fellow workers would say to us, 'You Communists and Reds.' I finally said, 'I've had enough. This is nonsense what they're giving you. Let them do their own work.' So I began to work for the lightbulb company [here in the East].    *(Herzberg 1987: 210)*[12]

By the early fifties many members of Generation I in the GDR had begun to look to the state to protect them from the more powerful, richer market in the West. Even in the area of black-market activity, their West German/West Berlin friends and kin were getting the better end of the deal. The structured, regularized, and secure work relations that the East German state began to offer seemed a superior alternative to the irregular, capricious rewards to be found on the black market.

*Women and work*

The number of women of this generation involved in an outside-the-home job or training, either part or full time, increased steadily, from 44.9 percent in 1949 to 76.2 percent in 1976 to 87.6 percent in 1978 (Gysi and Speigner 1983: 33). Women of Generation I evaluated their occupational practice either as important to their self-esteem or as an ambivalent involvement that deprived them of precious time with their children. In reconstructions of their work experiences, they often simultaneously complained about having to work like the men during the *Aufbau* period and reflected back upon the work outside the home as a positive and essential aspect of their autonomy- and consciousness-building. "The fifties were for me a turning point," reported Johanna J., a mother of six who divorced in 1953:

My life just began then, but it had not yet crystallized. You have to try things. It wasn't easy to be alone, to have to make all the decisions, to stick to a budget that would cover all the costs. And the divorce, that wasn't all that pleasant. But I wanted to find myself, to develop my own person. That was also naturally a struggle. Life had to go on, and the children also wanted to have something.

Work became for her an activity in which she could positively realize herself, where she experienced equality and group affirmation.

Johanna became incredibly enthused about her bookkeeping and inventory for a lightbulb company. Previously she had never imagined that she was capable of performing a job with responsibilities. Though unskilled and inexperienced, she enjoyed the same rights and responsibilities as her fellow, better-qualified workers. "It was as if my life had now just begun. It was simply wonderful, and I did it!" She retired in 1972, but has retained contact with her former colleagues, seeing herself as "a kind of mother" to them. "There I learned for the first time what a collective was" (Herzberg 1987: 48, 49).

Frieda S., a single woman, reported a similar experience: "I also helped in Magdeburg. It is true that I sacrificed my personal free time for the *Aufbau*, but I saw that it was appreciated and valued" (Herzberg 1987: 133). Single women, with and without children, were given political and ideological support in East Berlin in helping them to integrate into the workforce. Marital status was consistently downplayed. In 1949, authorities removed the legal stigmas attached to children born out of wedlock, and pressured the population to accept and utilize the contributions of all those capable of working. Labor shortages played a role in forcing fellow workers to integrate into their work units colleagues who they under other circumstances might have rejected. Single mothers and older unskilled women were major beneficiaries of this policy.

Since few women were granted access to *Ausbildung*, education/training, before 1945, most also failed on the whole to develop expectations tied to fulfillment in an occupation. An additional factor that should not be underestimated is that the initial occupational experience for many women of this generation was the menial labor they were forced to perform during the last years of the Third Reich. Many of these women remained unskilled and hence continued to work in unskilled, poorly paid, and personally unrewarding jobs after the war. Consequently, females continued to dominate some of the more poorly paid, less highly skilled industries, and subsequently never attained parity in pay or status with comparable industries that were male dominated. This is not to say that Frieda S. and Johanna J. were alone in their positive reconstructions. Yet their positive narratives represent more the exception than the rule to the experiences of women of their generation in the GDR. Experiences of this sort were, however, even more exceptional in West Berlin, where after the war upwardly mobile career trajectories for adult women were nearly non-existent.

The effects on the domestic unit of the integration of women into the labor force were often class specific. Professional women or women who in some sense were further qualifying or advancing did not have as much time to invest directly in domestic units as those women who remained aloof from their occupations. Although many expressed some guilt over not having given their children enough time, others insisted that their child(ren), especially the girls, learned to be more self-reliant by seeing their mothers with an identity outside the home. On the other hand, women who retreated to a domestic life (a steadily decreasing percentage) were also retreating from playing an active role in the *Aufbau*. These women, who worked part-time or remained occupied at home as housewives, tended to concentrate in their reconstructions on how bad the GDR and socialism were. They asserted that they were victims of a series of bad events outside their control, and certainly hadn't experienced the *Aufbau* as something positive. During the course of my fieldwork, several of these women, one of whom was still a member of the SED, told their sons several times to warn me about representing the GDR and socialism too positively in my work.

### Men, work, and domestic exclusion

Working-class men excluded from the domestic domain, either as a result of their own unwillingness to reintegrate or inability to reenter the nuclear unit, had two emotional responses. The first response was to withdraw into what has become known as "inner immigration," to restrict life to immediate, pragmatic needs. In many ways the regime encouraged the development of a "niche society," a term coined by Günter Gaus (1981), through an expansion of the weekend garden houses outside the cities and in the country. Not all members of Generation I were sympathetic to this development, which they saw as encouraging *Kleinbürgertum*, petty bourgeois culture. One retired painter told me the cabins resembled "pig stalls, where one looks at the ass of the next." The houses were uniformly regulated with regard to exterior features, especially size and color, and therefore look identical to an outsider. Yet many people invested more in the weekend houses than in their own apartments, and utilized literally every square meter of space to design their *Wochenendhaus* or *Datcha* to the specifications of their dream. Men who partook in this pattern thought not in terms of the quality of kin relationships, but in a model of a privatized material world where membership was restricted to a narrow group of kin. The second emotional response for men excluded from the domestic domain was to frequent the neighborhood tavern after work or on weekend evenings. Here many men developed *Kumpel* (buddy) relationships.

The *Kumpel* (derived from Latin *companio*) was a term initially used by coalminers to refer to their relationships of total interdependency – working, eating, sleeping, and drinking together with their fellow workers. It began to circulate widely at the turn of the century among male industrial workers, and after World War II it achieved wide usage among other nonprofessional men. This usage was much more common in the GDR than in West Berlin or West Germany, which may have had much to do with the idealized model of proletarian behavior appropriated by the political leadership of the GDR. Additionally, in West

Berlin, other more material-based processes limited the appropriation of the *Kumpel* model, including, e.g., fragmentation of life-styles and increased differentiation among classes, the mobilization and standardization of private lives in the expansion of markets, intensification and rationalization in the workplace.

Gustav R., born in 1902, described his *Kumpel* relationships in the coal mines: "In my time there were no transport machines; we still used horses. The horses, they were our most loyal *Kumpel*. We always said: *Kumpel* with long ears." In his teens Gustav shared a room with three or four fellow workers, "who all worked different shifts. One would work early and sleep in the afternoon. Another would work nightshift and have already slept during the day, and be ready to get up when the others came from work. We would all sleep in the same bed." After retirement, Gustav maintained contact with his *Kumpel*. "I still meet them after the work. We don't go out to get smashed, we just meet each other, with my old *Kumpel* from earlier, who are also no longer working, and retired. Then we enjoy conversations with each other. But there are already many who have died" (Herzberg 1987: 68, 71, 94).

Workers often had a special *Kumpel*, but the pattern was not romantic, not based on idealization. Helmut K., born 1910, described such a special relationship during his childhood:

That was truly the most fantastic, when we were bathing together. We would dig around together in the hot sand. We had no worries. We were two *Kumpel*, two youths, who were tried-and-true friends. That meant we were forever indivisible. We often ate together. He shared my philosophy, which was a working-class philosophy. When we had anything, we would share with each other. We had understood each other's interests.    *(Herzberg 1987: 187)*

These friendships arose out of concrete personal circumstances and increased in intensity through shared experiences over time, often lasting through a lifetime.

Interactions in a *Kumpel* relationship were taken for granted and rarely verbalized. This nonverbalization had two consequences: first, it was more difficult for women to appropriate because of its reliance on nonverbal communication; second, it was distinctly working class in origin, and thus less positively valorized by classes with higher rank. This also explains why the *Kumpel* has not been well researched, and why intellectuals (people reliant on words) find the relationship difficult to understand. Yet, like all kin terms, it has a history, and has become more important and widespread as a source of male bonding patterns in Generation II.[13]

## Conclusion

The kinship practices of Generation I in the GDR grew out of pragmatic considerations that often had quite tenuous relationships to the strategies of the East German state. Having lived through the politicized Weimar years and the heavy indoctrination of the Nazis, most people considered all forms of politics somewhat suspect. Furthermore, many of the laws and state strategies enacted in the fifties had a delayed impact (e.g., school reform, full incorporation of women into the workplace, childcare reform), influencing the lives of Generation I belatedly, if at all. The strategies of the GDR state, if we remember, were generally future oriented, with the children and youth considered the raw material out of which a new socialist nation was to be crafted. Changes in divorce and inheritance law, as well as work organization, dramatically changed the lifecourse design of many members of Generation I; but others lived through these significant state reforms as if they hadn't occurred. After the switch in state policy in the mid sixties to a sentimentalization of kinship, a refocusing that politically neutralized many individuals, problems encountered with radical re-construction during the *Aufbau* period seemed, in retrospect, no longer so significant.

Of even more importance, though, is the Cold War context in which Generation I constructed their identities. The West German state confronted them with a counter-plot that over time proved itself overwhelmingly superior in the production of material goods and images, as well as the means to achieve prosperity – the promise of both republics. By the mid eighties, members of Generation I, many by then in retirement, had resigned themselves to living out their final years without much ado. At that point in their lives, they were unable to articulate a coherent narrative other than victimization. This inability substantially to confirm the strategies of the state ended up delegitimating their own experience along with the state they lived in, presenting an absent legacy to future generations of children born in the GDR.

Moreover, the radical transformation in kinship practices of members of Generation I, particularly concerning partnership and childcare, was not accompanied by an equal transformation in their ideology of kin – as if they could not trust their own experience. The official definition of kin formulated in the BGB, the Civil Code from 1896, wherein conceptions of lineage (primarily patrilateral inheritance) replaced conceptions of kin through a shared dwelling, *Hausgemeinschaften*, was substantially changed over time. The Nazis further refined this definition in their race laws to a concept of *Blutsverwandschaft*, blood relative. Generation I grew up with this ideological heritage – the categories of kin and non-kin based on shared blood – and although their practice subsequently deviated from it, and their state legalized and legitimated other forms of joining and belonging to the group, they remained ideologically true to the heritage of their old categorizations.[14]

# 6

# Sentimentalization, fear, and alternate domestic form in East Berlin: Generation II

Members of Generation II, born between approximately 1940 and 1955, were the intended targets of the most significant postwar legislation affecting the lifecourse of citizens in the two German states, the *prima materia* out of which, the topos on which, the future nation(s) were to be fashioned. East and West German statesmen and policymakers knew that the future, the long-term legitimacy of their states, depended on ultimately securing the approval of their youths and children. Yet the two states went about obtaining this agreement with oppositional strategies and substantially different means to implement them.

As we have seen in the last section, the GDR, motivated by a utopian, future-oriented narrative, encountered substantial resistance from the generation of adults it inherited from the Weimar and Nazi eras. Aimed at radically changing gender significations at home and in the workplace, taking away vested male privileges, redistributing property for the benefit of the working class, and reducing parental control over children, its policies were met with considerable skepticism by members of Generation I. Their children, however, did not initially share this skepticism, and for good reason: the state placed their interests at the center of policy, often ignoring or opposing the wishes of their parents. Later, when these children became adults, their relation to the state, and this state's relation to them, again changed, becoming more antagonistic.

This chapter will concern itself with how Generation II in the GDR came to rely on a set of experimental tropes quite different from those of their parents, and how these tropes took on meaning in interaction with state narrative strategies of construction (1949–1965) and sentimentalization (1965–1989) along with state emplotments of romance, integration, and equality. Let us begin then with the Allied bombing, the collapse of the Third Reich, the Russian occupation, and the *Aufbau*. How were they experienced by children and youths? Generation II shared some of the same turbulent political history as their parents, but they did not see it through adult eyes.

### Childhood, youth, and domestic anarchy
*Liminality, inversion, and the end of the war*
Klaus Staek, seven years old at the end of the war, described how he perceived the bombing raids in Bitterfeld, a town 120 kilometers south of Berlin:

> Because the city was in an airplane corridor, I spent nights during the last years of the war mostly in the basement. That sounds worse than it really was. From as long as I can remember I hated going to bed at night. Therefore I rejoiced every time during the night when the sirens howled. I would always already have made a date for the coming evening to meet my playground mates.    *(Böll 1985: 88)*

Hannelore König, born in 1934, on the cusp of the two generations, explained:

> It was like this. For us children then, in 1942, it was still like a small sport, experienced with joy. When there was an alarm after midnight, you didn't have to go to school the next day. Imagine that! We children loved it. The alarms would go off in any case, so we looked forward to the ones that went off after midnight. Then we wouldn't have to go to school on the next day.

Hannelore and her mother left Berlin after their house had been destroyed by a bomb in 1943, but returned early in 1945. She experienced both the evacuation and return to Berlin as an adventure, with new travel mates and unusual games to play. Unlike the adults, she did not feel herself victimized by the Soviet occupation:

> When the Russians came in May, they suddenly needed drinks and food and butter and bread. We should have celebrated. Berlin had been invaded. And, we were liberated. We didn't believe that for a moment. We were, you know, when all's said and done, Germans. And as Germans we naturally hoped that we would win. That's logical, isn't it? That was all clearly nonsense. I can't say that I believed in it, that I was liberated, or that I believed that the Russians were good guys. No, absolutely not. What was important to me was that we had a garden, that we could go into and play in it without being bothered.
>
> Then, the Russians looted like the devil, and we heartily joined in and helped. For example, one time we went to a marmalade factory. And we took a fairly large quantity of strawberries and marmalade jars, really big jars, and then we ate it up. I had never before been able to get so many strawberries from my grandmother's garden . . . We children "organized" that. It wasn't right, we

knew that, but we also knew that everything had just come to an end. Why should we deprive ourselves of eating strawberries? [Hannelore also had no problem convincing the Russian soldiers to give her bread and butter.] We would whine and say, "But we are alone, our mother is working in the airport and has not returned." Then we would cry crocodile tears and he'd give us some bread. I was ashblond. They called me Blondinka, and Blondinka always got something. I would always return home cheerily with something. Either some bread or a piece of bacon, even a bag of millet seeds.

*(Meyer and Schulze 1984: 117–121)*


Klaus Staek also told a story about stealing preserves: "I experienced the end of the war more like a banal event. The so-called order appeared to have already disintegrated before the Americans arrived. For two days something like German anarchy reigned. That means, each person tried so much as it was possible to prepare for the coming insecurity, which we expected to last a long time." The people in his neighborhood stole a wagonload of cheese conserves from army supplies, and then divided the goods among themselves. "That was the only action of a group character that I can remember from my early childhood," he concluded. "Because we were frugal in using the cheese, it lasted us for almost three years" (Böll 1985: 89).

Children's experiences during this period differed according to quite arbitrary criteria: sometimes age was a factor, sometimes parental wealth, sometimes parental fear. But what they shared in common was a liminal experience of the everyday, where the usual rules ordering reality were suspended, authority figures suddenly lost their control, and suspicious strangers now controlled the administration of power. For many children, the world was like a carnival, threatening and thrilling, full of intrigue and mystery. Reversal and inversion marked their relations. They experienced a new sense of membership in a leaderless group, a kind of *communitas* without the ritual elders, quite different from the rigidly controlled *Volk* community the Nazis had propagated. Unlike their parents, they made no distinction between private and public space, between domestic life and public life, between the home and the working world. Their playground was the street where their mothers cleaned up rubble, their bedroom often a kitchen.

The end of the war was not met with joy marked by silence, as in the case of their elders, but with joy over the tumultuousness, the unruliness of the moment. As Victor Turner remarks of such events, there tends "to develop an intense comradeship and egalitarianism. Secular distinctions of rank and status disappear or are homogenized" (1969: 95).

Children, who were inferior in status, "in marginality," according to Turner, experienced the events at the end of the war as transgression, a suspension of kinship obligations and of the norms that govern structured and institutionalized relationships. The loss of the war resulted in a levelling, if not inversion, of authority patterns – and, mostly, to their advantage.

### The pleasure of theft and the affirmation of pleasure

Domestic anarchy had actually begun several years before the end of the war and continued until approximately 1950. This was the period officially labelled in the GDR the *antifaschistisch-demokratische Umwälzung*, anti-fascist, democratic renewal. Although official history claimed that a new period began in 1949 with the founding of the state, the renewal, largely under the direction of the Soviets, continued much longer before the new state assumed more sovereignty. As described above, most children and youths experienced this initial anarchy with abandon and exhilaration. The economic role of Generation II in supporting their kin – in *organisieren, ranschaffen, kohlenklauen*, and *hamstern* – provided them with a measure of autonomy that defied their categorization as "children" or "youths." While parents bemoaned the fact that their babies were skipping childhood, young people revelled in their early independence and in the absence of parental control. Children neither played in the crowded apartments nor in distinct "children's playgrounds." Preferred playsites were ruins, either in street rubble or in abandoned houses and basements. Many of the elderly youths oriented themselves to lives of adventure and were attracted to dangerous occupations, such as international spying and smuggling (Heimann 1985: 109; Sträter 1985).

Mothers who had initially employed their children in various forms of stealing were soon trying to rein them in. Frau Fischer, a single mother who'd worked in the Treptow district of East Berlin after 1945, described the competing moral claims from her perspective:

I was never able to really fill up my children with the food we got from ration cards. We were always hungry. Because they couldn't get enough to eat at home, they began to steal. Then we had problems with the police. A few years ago I began to think about how I could have done it differently. Friends of mine have told me how they used to travel out to the country and pick things up: potatoes and everything that they could find. And they would trade this for that. They would steal some goods and pick up other things elsewhere. Then I said to myself, "Yes, you should have also gone *hamstern* and shouldn't have begun immediately to work." But my opinion was that the Nazis had torn everything so dreadfully apart, now we have to rebuild. When I would look at the building on our street, the rubbish and ruins! You could count on one hand the houses which were still standing. I always said, "We want to rebuild." And to do that you have to have a respectable job. I had to go to work because I didn't have any money. But today I look at it differently. Organizing and *hamstern* would have been more useful for my children and myself than all that working for money, *die ganze Arbeiterei*. I still can't get over it. If my children had really been full, they wouldn't have to steal, and we wouldn't have had so much trouble with the law.

*(Meyer and Schulze 1984: 99)*

Stealing had become a routinized, everyday activity; for the parents, it was a source of guilt, for the children, it was neither work nor play, but pleasure. Children stole and traded not merely out of hunger or dire necessity, as in Frau Fischer's portrayal (cf. Heimann 1985: 122). Their economic activity led to increased autonomy and self-esteem. Adult attempts to discipline the children with a now-discredited moral authority, enforced by local civilian police or foreign occupation troops, were unlikely to have much success. As early as the fall of 1945, youth gangs comprised partly of former Hitler Youth "child soldiers," those who had fanatically defended the city during the last months of fighting, began to gather in Alexander Platz, the old city center in East Berlin.

The most well-known of these gangs were the *Gladow-Bande*, whose membership (at the time of their trial in 1949) numbered fifty-six, and the *Fliegenpastetenbande*, whose membership numbered twenty-three. The *Fliegenpastetenbande*, a group of boys in the north part of the Soviet Sector of Berlin, engaged mostly in disturbing dances and fighting with nonmembers. The more infamous *Gladow-Bande* was named after Werner Gladow, the "Al Capone of Prenzlauer Berg." A protocol of a Court Doctor described Gladow: "He can be characterized as having a psychopathological drive for freedom and unboundedness, which was already apparent in his early childhood, and since then has vastly increased; this can be traced to his development as a youth, when his parents did not in the least provide any barriers to his behavior." Another evaluation of Gladow reads:

His courage, his attitudes about an invulnerable villa in Dahlem that is reinforced with steel, his dreams about cool bankrobbing, his wish for a gunshot-proof auto; these are things he has simply taken out of American books about gangsters and criminals, and without being critical, he has adopted them to fit other kinds of relationships here in Berlin. And in his endless fantasies, he has built all this up in a really grotesque fashion.     *(Heimann 1985: 108, 109)*

Gladow testified during the trial that his life was quite normal until his father entered the military in 1940. Thereafter, he was constantly shuttled in and out of Berlin and felt forced to steal potatoes to have enough to eat. His father was released from a POW camp in 1946, and upon returning to Berlin he tried to reassert his authority over his son and his wife, often beating both of them. Gladow more or less left the family and hung out with his former school friends, engaging in crimes in all parts of the city. In April 1950, he was condemned to death by an East Berlin court for murder, attempted murder, robbery with a weapon, theft of weapons, and carrying a weapon. In line with the draconian penalties often given to members of youth gangs by the Allied authorities, Gladow was executed in Frankfurt an der Oder on December 10, 1950 (*Landesarchiv Berlin*, Rep. 13, Acc. 1052). In both East and West the problem of youth crime took on the label of *Notkriminalität*, crime of necessity. Allied Occupation forces and local German authorities became so distracted by youth problems that the crimes of former adult Nazis – now quite well-behaved and eager to carry out Allied commands – soon paled by comparison.

Older girls also engaged in crimes of necessity, but were rarely accepted into youth gangs. Since police concentrated on male-dominated gangs and youth groups, girls were arrested and imprisoned in far smaller numbers than their male peers. The form of young female behavior which most outraged the authorities was not stealing, however, but the more traditional offense of prostitution. Venereal disease increased exponentially during the time of Allied Occupation, as older girls and young women consorted with the Allied soldiers. A report of the *Berliner Jugendfürsorge* from 1947 contended that girls were staying at home rather than working "because their lovers make their life easier for them, or because they can earn the kind of money on the black market not so easy to come by in regular work. It is especially easy to earn money if they are able to get cigarettes or chocolate from their soldier friends and then sell part."

Already in 1947 it was apparent that some members of Generation II had rejected their parental model of value based on production, and were replacing it with a consumption model based on the affirmation of pleasurable desires. A report of the Evangelical church from the same year talked of "unrestrained voluptuousness as a typical postwar phenomenon that has led to epidemic rates of venereal disease." Hilde Thurnwald, in her 1947 Berlin study, attributed this sexual "lack of restraint" to a *Lebenshunger*, hunger for life, due to *erschütterte Daseinsbedingungen*, violently shaken conditions of life (cited in Heimann 1985: 125–126).

Official youth crime peaked in 1949, thereafter declining in both parts of Berlin. Thus the two states, with the help of the Allies, did have a quantitative effect on the way in which the lifecourse of its youth was to be tracked, putting them to work, in prison, or in school. Yet the effect of the state qualitatively measured was not immediately apparent, for children and youths had already experienced a model quite different from the one that motivated their parents. It took both states slightly longer – for they encountered resistance along the way – to standardize their model of order, creating a clean, disciplined, productive German, alert to the moral authority of officials. Members of Generation II, regardless of whether they were part of a gang, remembered and narrativized this pre-state period – despite the hunger and hardships endured – as one of the most exciting and formative times of their lives.

Younger members of Generation II did not directly experience either the war or this early anarchy. Their childhood and youth were in the late fifties and sixties, during the construction period and at a time when all institutions had become arenas of the Cold War. Dreams of adventure played hardly any role for these children. Ruth B., born in 1953, commented, "I think of my childhood like a street with signs saying that you cannot do this or you must do that, absolutely no free room to maneuver, where you cannot deviate even a little without having a bad conscience. School [for me] was a torture chamber" (Wander 1978: 75). The "psychopathological drive for freedom and unboundedness" of Werner Gladow and the "lack of restraint" among Berlin children reported by Hilde Thurnwald were no longer so observable by the mid fifties, as the institutions of state along with those acting on behalf of the state began substantially reshaping German youth. The building of the Wall, in particular, had a tremendous effect on East German youths, containing them within an officially demarcated and inscribed space with no independent access – outside of television – to their other half.

### Schooling and the domestic group
*Youth politics: parents against the state*
Following the war, parents who found it impossible to control their children looked to public authorities and schools to perform a disciplining function. Both states eagerly stepped into this role, but employed different strategies. For the East German state, communist ideology,

centered around the importance of labor, played a central motivating role in policymaking. Guaranteeing employment was considered basic to the regime's political legitimacy; hence the state created massive public work projects with itself as employer. Although the number of unemployed in East Berlin doubled between 1946 and 1952, older youths were often given job preference and rather quickly incorporated into the labor force. (This was not the case in West Berlin, where the number of unemployed tripled between 1946 and 1950, and where youth unemployment remained exceptionally high throughout the fifties.) Mainly because of economic opportunism and fears of communism, people continued throughout the fifties to move to the West, which created an ongoing labor shortage in the GDR, much to the immediate benefit of women and younger workers. As a result, between 1952 and 1955 unemployment in the East was more than halved, then by 1960 reduced to a negligible amount. In West Berlin, substantial progress was also made in reducing general unemployment in the 1950s, but the number of unemployed began rising again by the late 1960s (see table 6 in chapter 3).

Intent on making its youth into ideologically fervent socialists, the East German proto-state founded the FDJ, Free German Youth (from ages fourteen to twenty-four), in March 1946, and it created the Young Pioneers, a separate club for children (from ages six to thirteen), in December 1948. Many if not most parents initially viewed those associations with great skepticism, worried that the state would not only discipline their children, but also usurp some of the authority parents traditionally exercised over their children. Parental appeals to traditional authority, now somewhat delegitimated by the Nazi past, competed with authority claims of East German educators, and, after 1949, state authorities were quite explicit in their appeals to Marxist principles – thought to be fundamentally secular and scientific – regarding the function of education. The fact that this contest between state agents and parents was fought openly helped to demystify the intentions of both, making the conflict into one over instrumental control of education in its broadest sense, and thus of acknowledged power plays on both sides. Yet the state's final appeal for authority was not in terms of *Zweckrationalität*, but to an ultimate value: its utopian future. Thereby the state placed itself in a schizophrenic position. On the one hand, it justified its policies with appeals to their scientifically determined, instrumental value; on the other hand, it appealed to a mystical, romantic ideal – socialism – as its final goal and the ultimate value of policy. Parents were in a much weaker position, however, for they had no ultimate values to appeal to for their authority, nor could they claim their knowledge was scientifically based – hence they were reduced to acts of resistance in order to assert their tradition-based authority.

Despite this conflict, membership in the state-run organizations quickly expanded, and over time became as routinely accepted in the lives of young people as were the schools. In 1961, FDJ members totaled 50.3 percent of all youth; by 1978 they totaled 69.9 percent. In 1985, nearly all youths between fourteen and eighteen were members; the membership total began to decrease after the age of eighteen, although 5 percent of the membership was still older than the maximum age of twenty-four. Youths in career tracks considered important to the state tended to remain in the FDJ for a longer period of time, and their percentage also increased over time. In 1950, for example, 53 percent of all students at Humboldt University in Berlin were FDJ members, in 1988 they numbered more than 95 percent (Keiderling 1987: 423; *DDR Handbuch* 1985: 453).

Since its founding in 1948, the Young Pioneers was a less contested organization. It reached a 76 percent participation rate by 1960, a 99 percent rate by 1970 (Keiderling 1987: 493; *Statistisches Jahrbuch der DDR* 1985: 404). Yet, in the early fifties, many parents resisted their children's membership, placing themselves in direct conflict with the schools and the regime. "I remember never being able to understand why my father tried to prevent me from joining the Pioneers," explained Edith N., who entered the first-grade class in 1950. "My mother didn't say much about it, but father wanted to keep me out of the organization, even though all my friends were already members." Parental opposition to the schools and youth organizations was interpreted in the Western press as evidence of the "Pankow regime's" attempt to create a totalitarian state, and this portrayal was embraced by parents in East Berlin, always eager to cast themselves in the role of victims.

The theory of "totalitarianism" – of complete state regimentation of everyday life – put forward by observers living in capitalist countries[1] as a comprehensive description of their communist counterparts is inadequate to account for the complexity of experience in the GDR. It may accurately describe the aims and goals of the regimes ruling Soviet-bloc countries, but it falls short in depicting the effects of their policies. It omits the intricate tactics of resistance and evasion, complicity and secrecy that characterized (in uneasy combinations and alternations) the everyday life of the people.

It is true that throughout the fifties and sixties children inadvertently informed on their parents to school authorities, relating activities (such as watching West German television or meeting with West German kin) that were interpreted as resistance to socialism or lack of compliance to official authorities. However, parents would usually not learn of these slips of the tongue until long after the telling, and the consequences to them and their children, while creating some initial turmoil and suffering, were rarely in any sense decisive or final factors in career or lifecourse development. A more important consequence for the parents was the sense that they could not control the activities of their children in the same way as their parents had controlled their activities a generation earlier. They resented this undermining of their authority, and often blamed the new state for their feeling of powerlessness.

Yet, at least in East Germany, totalitarianism never existed. To confuse the theory of totalitarianism with the practice of everyday life is to mistake an ideal type for an empirical reality, a fundamental confusion of the scientific model with the phenomenon it seeks to describe. Yet it served the interests of the ruling elite within the GDR, as much as the elites in the capitalist West, to propound theories of total control. What better mechanism of control than to convince the people that, from cradle to grave, Big Brother's electric eye was upon them?

Perhaps the best example of how parents and the state struggled for the control of children and youths is the *Jugendweihe*, a state confirmation ceremony for fourteen-year-old youths, modeled after the Christian confirmation ceremony. When the GDR introduced *Jugendweihe* in 1954, parents often took this as conclusive proof that they were losing control of their children to the state (Jeremias 1956: 15–23). Children and youths, however, experienced the group-organized activities not as inimical ideology, but as forms of play, involvement, and commitment, of belonging to a group which doted on them. The conflict between parents and their children was played out as one between parents and the state. Parents immediately found an ally in the church, and the dispute over the confirmation ceremony quickly took on larger dimensions. The Protestant and Catholic churches initially opposed the ceremony, with the Catholic church even forbidding its youth to take part. The state confronted the church head-on by scheduling its confirmation during the same weekends in the spring as the church and by denying university study to youths who took part in church activities.

Youth participation increased despite parental and church opposition. In Berlin, participation increased from 20.7 percent in 1955, to 42.8 percent in 1958, to 73 percent in 1959, to 92.3 percent in 1965. In 1986, the participation in Berlin totaled 98 percent. Eventually parents turned the *Jugendweihe* into a kinship festival, connected to the event but privately celebrated, where parents and friends gave coming-of-age youths quite expensive gifts. (I was told of several people receiving cars.) This particular transformation of the *Jugendweihe* took place in the late seventies, thus affecting Generation II as parents rather than as youths (Winkelmann 1986: 185–193; 1983: 15). By the 1980s the confirmation ceremony had become a symbiosis, where neither the state nor parents got exactly what they wanted, but both participated, though in a discordant rhythm, in a mutually advantageous partnership.

*Education reform*
Equally important as the children and youth organizations, and closely tied to them, were the schools. All authorities in Greater-Berlin agreed on the centrality of education to the new politics of the postwar period. The Communist Party (KPD) and Social Democratic Party (SPD) together called for a "democratic school reform" on October 18, 1945. This was followed by the first pedagogical congress in 1946 in Leipzig and by an East German "antifascist-democratic school reform" within the same year.[2] The traditional, hierarchical German structure of *Volks-, Real-,* and *Oberschule* was replaced by a horizontally structured, uniform school system, including eight years of compulsory primary school, two years of middle school, and four years of high school. In 1959, the compulsory primary school period was extended to ten years. School classes have been coeducational since 1945, reversing the traditional German system of separating the sexes and denying women access to higher education. Over time, this policy gradually improved the competence and educational level of members of Generation II and those that followed. In 1962, 57 percent of all students went beyond the eighth grade; that increased to 72 percent in 1967, to 91 percent in 1970; by the eighties nearly the same number of men and women were entering professions and seeking higher education (though still differing in the choice of professions, with the men choosing more prestigious ones) (Keiderling 1987: 609).

An ambitious Soviet denazification program included the dismissal of all Nazi judges and most Nazi bureaucrats and schoolteachers. But since the Nazi state had integrated most occupations into its administration, there were few professionals in 1945, including teachers, without some sort of tie to the Nazi Party. This meant, for example, that while 11,000 self-confessed Nazi Party members in the Soviet Zone were fired within the first six months of occupation, 15,000 remained in their posts (Weber 1986: 107–108). Changes in education personnel continued throughout the fifties, although firings tailed off in number, and after 1949 were seldom related to former Nazi activity. Empty teaching slots were filled from primarily two sources: newly trained teachers and POWs who had returned. Although conditions varied greatly between cities and between school districts, a strenuous denazification of the schools was no doubt more uniformly practiced in Berlin than elsewhere. Allied authorities in Berlin also monitored each other's compliance with the Potsdam Accords until the Berlin Blockade in 1948. Furthermore, local Berlin education authorities from all four Zones worked together on panels and exchanged information regarding school-reform proposals even after the political division of the city, up until approximately 1952 (see chapter 8; see also Füssl and Kubina 1981).

A second high-school reform in 1951 was directly aimed at economic class privileges, and set up quota systems to guarantee underprivileged children access to higher education. The number of children of working-class origin in advanced and technical schools increased from 50.3 to 58.4 percent between 1951 and 1960. After 1963, officials stressed performance criteria alongside political ideology and class origin, resulting in a drop in the percentage of working-class children, who did not perform as well as children from the middle and upper classes, to 38.2 percent in 1967. (In West Germany at that time, working-class children comprised 5.7 percent of the total in advanced and technical schools.) Children of the intelligentsia in 1967 made up 20.4 percent of this elite group, despite being only 6.8 percent of the population (Rytlewski 1972: 734–742; Bathke 1985). In their life reconstructions, members of Generation II from working-class families tended to acknowledge that they benefited in their life trajectories from these affirmative action – or, minimally, class-neutral – programs. Without the official programs, they said, they would never have had access to higher education. Children from the intelligentsia whom I know often remarked about feeling they had to overcome discrimination, and always attributed their own success to individual initiative.

Education policy in East Germany was never limited in scope to the reform of schools for children and youths, but, as indicated above, was also concerned with adult education and political reeducation. For example, educational authorities in the East, unlike those in the West, thought that part of the solution to youth crimes entailed changing the social conditions that produced it. Hence parents as well as their unruly children were objects of policy. Authorities hoped to incorporate the parents into the educational system as well as the children into the family. Much of the early political reeducation work (denazification) in the GDR was handled by the Democratic Women of Germany (DFD), founded in March 1947. These women organized public seminars and discussion groups in all geographical areas of the Soviet Zone to discuss a wide range of topics, including the meaning of Nazism, the role of property, the position of women, and the goals of socialism (Ansorg 1986).

Parental seminars, *Elternseminare*, and parental advisory committees, *Elternbeiräte*, were legally established in 1951 to provide more direct communication between parents, schools, and the mass societal organizations that were sponsored and approved by the state. Run by the DFD, parental seminars were to engage in pedagogy and enlightenment, to convince the parents to raise their children "in the spirit of peace and democracy." The parental advisory committees, still active in 1988, were established to strengthen the relationship of education in the schools to education in the family. Already in 1951, more than 1,000 parental seminars had been organized by the DFD, consisting of, for example, a course over ten evenings (Obertreis 1985: 90–92). Seminar themes included questions of general and political education, avoiding corporal punishment as a means of discipline, creating more democratic schools, understanding new laws concerning youths and women and their relationship to children, working with the children and youth groups (Ansorg 1986; Walther 1986).

The practical work of parental advisory committees concerned quite mundane activities: setting up and realizing a school lunch, working with the Pioneer Organization, corresponding with West German parental committees, or visiting the homes of parents. Although set up to mediate between parents and school authorities, the committees often became objects of scorn as education was increasingly taken over by the state. Members were elected every two years in a parental gathering at the school and, according to one source, the Ministry of Education wanted absolutely loyal members on the committees. Other social groups would at times organize to elect their own members to the committees; for example, the clergy would run a minister as opposition candidate. Initially teachers in the classrooms were also not always cooperative, above all resisting "the education to patriotism" by refusing to give credit to the Party where it claimed credit, by not showing enthusiasm for the school policy of the regime, and by avoiding political discussions (Obertreis 1985: 95; Lange 1954: 233–234).

*Effects of attempted standardization of education*
Rarely does the everyday experience of policy present as coherent a picture as the policy itself, and such was the case with schooling in Berlin. The extreme chaos of the early Allied Occupation in Berlin made it difficult to standardize educational praxis, even within a particular zone. Many schools were initially used to house refugees. Many children and/or parents were missing: in Mecklenburg, just outside of Berlin, there were 16,000 homeless children, among whom 4,000 did not even know their names (Weiß 1976; 1986). Greater-Berlin schools reopened in the fall of 1945, but under quite different conditions from before the war. A citywide total of 124 schools had been destroyed and 11 severely damaged. Of the 292 remaining schoolbuildings, only 1,300 of the 3,000 rooms were usable during winter 1945. The extremely cold winter of 1945–1946 forced local administrators to cancel school, as classrooms could not be adequately heated. "There was no instruction [during that winter]," reported Hannelore Könnig, "which we of course very much praised. That's the way it is with children. Our opinion was that they could also burn the school down if they liked" (Meyer and Schulze 1984: 124). By summer 1946, the number of functioning schools had increased to 331, but the number of students had also increased by 384,000 (Heimann 1985: 120). In any case, Berlin children in the late forties most often denigrated school authorities, regardless of size or state of repair of the schoolroom. This situation changed when German parents and the Allies began working together to break up youth gangs and discipline the children.

Hans G., who entered the fourth grade in the fall of 1945, reported that his teachers in the Soviet Zone were initially of two kinds: very old women and young girls and boys who had been quickly trained for the profession:

Everything was new. Naturally, the younger people began with much enthusiasm. But they lacked knowledge about how to teach and they lacked information about the topics. They didn't know what they were teaching, and we made fun of them whenever we could. We were tough kids then. And it wasn't easy for the older ones either, but some of them were very good teachers. I mean, they knew how to teach, to get us to listen.

Hans' description of the schools followed an East-specific ordering: he began with a statement about "enthusiasm" or idealism, followed by a critique based on the assumption that teaching correct information is more important than teaching how to think. Although the GDR was not able to uniformize the perspectives of their citizens, they succeeded in providing a standardized form for speaking about things. The romantic goals of the regime provided an orientation from and against which people measured their own experiences.

In 1947–1948, many returning POWs moved into teaching. Hans said that many of these ex-soldiers were politically minded. "They never avoided talking about the war, about Fascism. And they were more or less left alone to handle the classes as they saw fit. I remember a lot of discussion. Actually it was fun. The curriculum is much more controlled today than it was for us. My parents were both unskilled. Neither one had an education." Hans estimated that of his teachers in the early fifties, approximately 60 percent were women and 40 percent men. This slowly changed, as women moved into the teaching profession at the lower levels.

Hans' educational experiences were not unique. I repeatedly asked people about two aspects of their education experience: what happened to the Nazi teachers in their schools, and how did the students appraise the quality of their education? Apparently, many former Nazi Party members were reincorporated into East Berlin schools in the early fifties. When this occurred, students observed some open conflict between committed communists, now SED members, and the new teachers, who were accused of being opportunists. Yet all new teachers represented themselves as anti-fascists and adherents of the new regime.

As part of denazification, or "reeducation" (as officials in the East called it), schools regularly showed documentary films about Nazi war crimes, with footage of concentration camps and mass executions. These films were simultaneously supposed to demarcate present life (and GDR policy) from Nazi life, and contribute to constructing a new East German socialist, anti-fascist identity. "We saw films showing mountains of corpses piled up outside of concentration camps," said Anne W., "but eventually I think that was counterproductive. The first time I saw it, in 1953, I think, I was about nine, it had an impact. I was unbelievably terrified. I went home and tried to discuss it with my parents without success. But then I saw the same footage, again and again, of the corpses and all those bones, and I think I became immune. It became like propaganda." Anne then confronted her parents with the pictures in these films. Her mother responded that she had been helpless back then, that any resistance would have led to arrest. Her father, who had worked in the civilian bureaucracy during the war, replied that Hitler had changed the whole climate against the Jews, that he had poisoned the relationship of "Germans to their Jews." Anne reported that in the schools she learned to think about Nazism as a total system, and not as her father had explained it, the result of a single man, Hitler. Partly as a result of this continuing confrontation with her parents, they lost much of their luster of authority. Through the showing of such films and the emphasis on anti-fascism, the regime had a tremendous influence on the way in which members of Generation II dealt with the past of their parents, and hence how they related to them in the present. Yet, as Anne stated, the actual effect of policy was quite different from the intended one.

*'Abgrenzung' and ideological rigidification*
Although the most intense period of Stalinism in the GDR with regard to state politics was approximately from 1949 to 1954, it was not until several years after Stalin's death (in 1953) that children and youths of Generation II began to experience Stalinism as an everyday phenomenon. Stalin had been portrayed in the media as the best friend of the GDR, as being the great anti-fascist who defeated Hitler and ended the war. Many people experienced his death with fear and mourning. Several Berliners of Generation II told me that they observed their mothers crying after Stalin's death. One man said that his mother, an elementary school teacher, cried at the evening meal on the day she had heard of Stalin's death. Yet Stalin's German followers did not have immediate success in setting up a totalitarian model in the Berlin schools. Tightening up of authority in local schools and universities was a gradual process, facilitated both by retirement and by movement of people to the West. Students reported that teachers would inexplicably disappear. The number of sudden absences increased higher up in the educational ladder. Certainly, in the fifties a greater proportion of university teachers moved to the West than did elementary school teachers. This teacher exodus ended and a new stage of ideological control began after the building of the Wall in 1961, which prevented sudden emigration at all levels in the society.

Ideological rigidification, part of *Abgrenzungspolitik*, narrowed the spectrum of legitimate opinions, although this too varied from school to school. Dissident voices could either shut up or move West (until 1961, with ease, and thereafter with difficulty) – and they did both. In retrospect the late fifties appeared to people as a period of ideological fanaticism, as the regime struggled with international isolation and with an economy that could not keep up with West German standards. From 1949 to 1963, only twelve other states, all socialist republics, recognized the GDR as a state. Up to 1972, West Germany had tried to isolate the GDR fully, claiming that recognition of East Germany by any capitalist state would be treated as an act hostile to the FRG. In 1972, West Germany finally established partial diplomatic relations with its eastern counterpart, and other states immediately followed in breaking with the policy of isolation. By the end of 1973, 99 states had recognized the GDR; by the end of 1983, 132 states. In retrospect, the diplomatic recognition came too late, however, for by 1972 GDR investment in heavy industry and complete centralization of economic planning made it difficult to establish a wide range of economic relations with capitalist countries in the fastest-growing and least-controlled sectors of their economies: service and information industries.

In their reconstructions, members of Generation II mentioned predominately three ideological symbols of the late fifties/early sixties. Walter Ulbricht's famous slogan with reference to the West German economy from the late fifties, *überholen ohne einzuholen* (to overtake without catching up), caught the desperate, twisted verse of official discourse at that time. A second slogan that reappears in the period of *Aufbau* was *Chemie gibt uns Brot, Wohlstand und Schönheit* (chemicals will give us bread, prosperity, and beauty). Again, the slogan addressed itself to the poor economic standard of socialism at that time, but denied its reality by projecting the future onto a simple miracle product, the chemical industry, which would finally bring about the socialist economic victory. A third symbol is the "Ten Commandments of Socialist Morality," promulgated by Ulbricht in 1958 (see chapter 4). Schoolchildren in the sixties were required to memorize these commandments. Until the building of the Wall, the regime had, in effect, little else but ideology to offer its citizens to convince them to stay.

By 1988, these three symbols took on added meaning because of bitter disappointment at the undelivered emotional payload. The regime used Marxism and its utopian promises much like messianic leaders manipulate cargo cults.[3] Marxism's wider appeal,[4] much like that of the messianic cults of Christianity and Islam, lay in the stress on eschatological notions of a morally evaluative after-life – meaning, of course, after *Aufbau*. The moral order to which the East German leadership initially appealed was sustained not primarily by prosperity and happiness in the present, but more significantly by the conferment of these rewards under the socialism of the future. This was the basis for the belief in *Aufbau*, the source of its ability to give meaning to individual experience.

Yet as the economic policies of the regime, its administrative socialism, proved increasingly impotent with respect to the cargo produced by its West German counterpart, the central messianic revelation of its moral teaching, embodied in these three symbols, lost its appeal. The regime, aided by its intellectuals in romanticizing a link between the state and the *Volk*, then tried to save itself through a sentimentalization of *Aufbau*, making the accomplishments of the fifties into an origin myth. It became increasingly clear, however, that not only had socialism not overtaken capitalism, but also it had not produced the superior moral community it had promised. And since children and youths of Generation II often naively appropriated the slogans as orientations, firmly embedded as they were in a moral order, a Marxian religion taught in the schools and youth organizations that distinguished good from bad and right from wrong, their disillusionment over unrealizability only heightened with reflection and the dawning understanding that they were purposely misled.

Official *Abgrenzung* was increasingly perceived not as protection from an enemy as much as limitation on personal freedom. Its demands on young people's behavior, asking them to demarcate the GDR by divorcing themselves totally from contacts with the "imperialist West," often appeared as absurd and contrived. The rather frenzied attempt to delineate all aspects of life in the GDR as uniquely its own (namely, socialist work and production, socialist law, socialist family, and socialist personality) often led to bizarre official denunciations of all that was strange or new. Wolfgang K., an engineer who attended an advanced high school in the late fifties, reported:

When I was in high school, I was taught by a Professor S., who was well-connected at every level and had a lot of influence through these contacts. In a discussion I attended between [SED] Party Kader, he said that I was inconsequential because I had a religious attitude toward people. He asked me, for example, "Would you be prepared to shoot your brother-in-law (who lives in Cologne, West Germany) on the border?" That came so quickly, without preparation. And then during the discussion, it came up that I was Chair of the Revisions Commission of the Labor Union. He [the Professor] grinned evilly and said, "That sounds like you're a Revisionist!" Then his Party Secretary even had to ask him to stop. Those are people who are able to destroy a great deal.

*(Eckart 1984: 53)*

This obligation to proclaim and prove one's loyalty through signs of devotion and sacrifice – and the resistance to this pressure – was a recurrent theme in the life histories of Generation II.

### From construction to sentiment

Helga R., who lived in a boarding house/school from the ages of fourteen to eighteen, from 1958 to 1962, described the everyday aspect of demarcation politics on youth in the Sixties:

I was horribly naive, actually naive until I was 18 . . . I wanted to study, and that [my relations with men] was not important to me . . . I had the feeling that I had to do something, and that I was doing something right . . . And I did it, I really did something. Not like it is today, when [the students] only talk; no, we really did what we could, as well as we were able to . . . Today, even studying is no longer so important. Only money counts today. But it was not so with us. I would have never asked, for example, "What will I earn when I finish my studies?" I know that is naive and stupid. But I would have never asked myself that. The questions would have been too insolent, too primitive . . . We [in the school] had begun to discuss earnestly and to read seriously and to confront ourselves with our lives and the problems around us.

Helga then related how in 1962 in the school she received her first lesson in disillusionment. It concerned the way in which officialdom in the GDR rejected everything Western – whether ideas, people, or goods – as inherently evil and threatening. This anti-West, anti-American strategy had found a great deal of resonance among members of Generation I, who had been raised with the motto: "The true culture is the culture of the heart." Hence America, the Reich of materialism, represented the antithesis of the "heartfelt culture" of the Slavs. East versus West then was understood as what is inside (truth) versus what is outside (untruth).[5]

A group of students organized a *Fasching* evening in the youth house for the other 150 students at the boarding school, "only in order to make the other students happy. That was by far the most important thing." Although they had no money and hardly any props to work with, they set up a milk bar and elaborately decorated the school. A sign behind the milk bar, playing on Marx's famous slogan, read, "Milkbars of the World, Unite!" And they created a still-life scene with a water pistol and a red-painted bottle, marked "Thieves' Blood." That evening, the district leadership of the FDJ checked up on the local gathering. Helga continued:

and all hell broke loose. [The idea for] that could only have come out of West literature. And I have to tell you that we were so naive and tried so hard to do something original, to produce something ourselves. Yes, I suffered my very first, real, authentic shock. The director of the school spoke with us, and I then realised that we couldn't understand each other anymore, that he spoke a totally different language. They accused us of things that they knew weren't true, but nobody would believe us. And that was actually my first, authentic experience, where I realized that as soon as one enters this functionary apparatus, this catch twenty-two, you're lost.

I fought like a lion, I spoke with my teachers, and they were also naive . . . they consciously didn't want to understand us. They knew us all, and they believed us. But they had to be loyal to the institution and pay attention to what happens there . . . That's the worst of it. The director wanted to keep his position, and therefore couldn't fight for us, and therefore had to disappoint us. With his refusal [to help] we were finished. I still find it right, and in a situation like that today I would react the same way. He earned nothing but our scorn . . . Above all, that he could so disappoint the youth, people in that age who are so naive, and that he did it in front of everyone at our expense. You have to understand that the room was huge, like a ballroom . . . The result of this event was to make me keenly aware, to protect me from such things in the future. That's something that happens so often among the youth here: you really want to do something, and then you're shocked, and then you drop everything like a hot potato.

The meaning of this experience for Helga was clearly no longer shaped by the construction strategy of the state, as were experiences in the fifties. Rather, the state had already sentimentalized that period, and Helga was simply being asked to enact a drama already written. Unlike Wolfgang K., who was asked to enter into a dialogue with the state's policy, however coercively that exchange was structured, Helga was presented with a plot that asked her not to respond and engage, but merely to execute.

Although official discourse focused on demarcation before the fifties, it wasn't until after the building of the Wall and the consequent total physical separation from the West that youths and children experienced clear, one-sided control attempts on their imagination. If relatives had moved to the West, students and workers in certain occupations were asked yearly to sign an agreement to avoid all contact with people from capitalist countries. The Helsinki Accord, signed by the GDR in 1975, forbade, among other things, this restriction on movement – but its provisions were only incrementally implemented. By the mid eighties, the state required only those in national-security-related positions to sign an official statement. Since the GDR, like all states, reserved for itself the right to define national security, a wide range of occupations remained strategic enough to warrant restrictions on contact with Westerners, including, for example, some hotel receptionists and all elementary school teachers. While the regime over time narrowed the range of occupations formerly considered part of national security, school-teaching remained a sensitive point. For example, a kindergarten teacher in Berlin reported to me in 1986 that one of her co-teachers had applied to leave the country. Within a week, the other teachers were called into a meeting by the director, and informed that they should isolate and avoid all personal contact with this particular woman. Since there was a general shortage of personnel in kindergartens, so-called national security needs in this case were in direct conflict with the needs of the kindergarten center. The most significant result of the state's attempt to ostracize this kindergarten teacher was an increase in tension between employees and thus a less cohesive workplace – all unintended effects antithetical to the state's larger goal of an integrated community of equals.

Until the signing of a Church–State Accord in 1977, children of Generation II with Christian parents suffered continuing discrimination in the education system. As already mentioned, throughout the fifties, sixties, and seventies, the state and the church, especially the Catholic church, directly confronted each other, with youth and education policy the major contested sites. Despite the official policy of preferring non-Christian children in higher-education positions, a surprisingly large number of Christian parents managed to secure study places for their children. Those who could not obtain university admittance for their children tended to send them to the West, often West Berlin, until the building of the Wall stopped that. Many members of Generation II who completed their education in the late fifties in West Berlin reported that nearly half of their classmates were former schoolmates from the GDR. The shared sense of discrimination among Christian believers intensified ties between family members, as well as the emotional and economic dependence of Christian children on their parents – exactly the opposite of the intention of the state. Christian parents were then, in response to this policy, even more active in pursuing the interests of their children. To counteract the exodus of people with talents, educational authorities since the sixties were more flexible in admissions policies than their education dogma, such as official representations in texts, would lead us to believe.

Increased flexibility in admissions did not, however, result in a more liberal atmosphere in the schools themselves. Youths in the sixties and seventies emphasized quite different aspects in recounting their education than students from the late forties and early fifties. A tendency toward ideological discipline and study specialization were the two characteristics most frequently mentioned. "The standing at attention in the school, this external, senseless discipline, flagwaving, look left, look right. What does that have to do with socialism?" asked Rosi S. in 1975. "It totally rubbed me the wrong way. I felt as if I had been raped" (Wander 1978: 59). A student in the early seventies, Gudrun R., reported about her teachers: "Their only interest is in their stuff, and they can't see beyond their subject area. And we, we're simply directed to consuming knowledge. Earlier the main things were grades; today it is only the stuff" (Wander 1978: 85). By the time of my fieldwork, this control in the schools seemed all pervasive. A logical consequence of the ideological tightening-up by the regime was a retreat by teachers to narrow reliance on the "facts" and a refusal to examine subjects beyond their area of specialization. Students tended to perceive this as a lack of interest or enthusiasm in the subject matter, or as reluctance to deal openly with conflicting points-of-view.

### State paranoia, increased 'Angst', and the reintroduction of silence

A final periodization made by members of Generation II in their reconstructions related to their experience of increased fear during the growth of the State Security (Stasi) apparatus in the seventies. In Western history books, this period is officially called "détente," in the GDR it was "peaceful coexistence." At that time, West German Chancellor Willy Brandt ushered in a warming of relations with the GDR, including a partial recognition of their political status and increased trade, which made the previous mirror-imaging through *Abgrenzung* seem less relevant, if not absurd. This opening with the West generated commerce, in its broadest sense, increasing the exposure of East German citizens to West German goods and ideas. The comparison of West with East consequently seems to have increased citizen dissatisfaction, at the same time increasing the paranoia of the regime, which then resorted to an Orwellian expansion of all control mechanisms. Silencing proved to be the major technique of the expansive apparatus.

The February 8, 1950 law that created the Stasi did not specify its tasks or size, and put no limits on the domains of its authority. Indeed, it lent itself to misuse. Officially the Stasi was to "prevent surprises from the *Gegner* [adversary/opponent]," and to "prevent subversion." Army general Erich Mielke took over control of the security system in 1957, and expanded it greatly in the seventies and eighties. By the time of my fieldwork, every post office had its own rooms for intercepting mail; nearly all phones were wiretapped, and millions of apartments were bugged; virtually every public or private assembly of any sort (Jehovah's Witness meetings, university seminars, gay bars, gardening clubs) had a Stasi agent in attendance to report on what was said – often to provoke, then later denounce. Wherever two or three were gathered in anybody's name, the Stasi was there also. By 1989, it employed 85,000 full-time workers and 109,000 "unofficial workers." They had a huge stockpile of rifles, panzers, hand grenades, and machine guns; owned 2,037 buildings, apartments, and country houses, with 652 in East Berlin alone; had 24 vacation spas with 2,058 beds as well as exclusive hospitals and sport facilities for Stasi workers only; and had a yearly budget of 3.6 billion Marks ($2 billion calculated at internal GDR value). The central Stasi headquarters in Berlin-Lichtenberg encompassed 3,000 rooms.

At the heart of Stasi operations was Division XX, responsible for dissidents. The *Gegner* within was always the obsessive object of their attention. Internal dissent ebbed as the Stasi extended its sway, and by the early eighties the state appeared to have eliminated most of its adversaries, either by shipping them to West Germany or by silencing them. The next few years, however, saw a revival of opposition groups who in various fashions developed localized counter-discourses. Ecological and human rights groups, especially organized within the churches, were a focal point of dissent. As the SED regime became increasingly paranoid about the general negative mood in the country, it tightened control within the Stasi itself, militarizing the entire apparatus and setting up new spy units so that Stasi agents could surveil each other (see *Spiegel* 1/1990; Mitter and Wolle 1990).

Thus, during a period of sentimentalization of kinship policy, and of "peaceful coexistence" in foreign policy (according to the official parole regarding the state's external enemies), the state built a vast machine of *Angst* that ultimately amassed files on one-third of all citizens. In other words, the state shifted from demarcating itself from an external enemy to identification of internal opponents – a move, as we shall see in the next chapter, mirror-imaged, though in much milder form, by the West German state. Members of Generation I, if we remember, complained about the lack of political freedom, but did not trope as part of their narrative the construction of a regime of fear; they pushed this fact to the side, making taboo their own silence. Members of Generation II most directly experienced the period when the state built this massive control machinery; they were, in fact, the primary objects of that state, which by the early seventies had quit romanticizing its youth in a future-oriented narrative. The state goal had by then become pure sentiment, a nostalgic clinging to past images that were to be reenacted by new generations in the present and future.

In their life stories, members of Generation II dealt with this atmosphere of fear and techniques of silencing indirectly. Rather than railing at fear generally, people tended to select out particular institutions taken over by the state where the lack of freedom reigned. They expressed the influence of the Stasi most often by what they were denied and what they lacked – freedoms to express themselves, publicly assemble, participate in politics, travel to the West, buy whatever goods they wanted, pursue careers of their choice – rather than by talking about actual encounters with the security apparatus. Yet that apparatus was ubiquitous in their lives, and every person came to some personal decision about what tactics to pursue in dealing with it, ranging from total compliance to outright defiance. In only one case, in 1986, did someone initially refuse to meet me because she was involved with the Stasi. By 1989, even this person was talking to me, in violation of her written oath with her place of employment not to do so. In sum, the Stasi and regime of fear operated as meta-master narratives for most people in the GDR, only rarely directly designing their lifecourse, but always presenting constraints within which public expression, public space, and social life in general could take place. If the Stasi did enter the lifecourse directly, it either ended up recruiting someone's services (and then rarely let them exit out of the security force), or it harassed the individuals concerned into submission or provoked them into defiance. The latter response usually meant that those people would eventually resettle to West Germany.

**Households and the domestic group**

The *Aufbau* period from 1945 to 1961, while politically characterized by a process of centralization of power at all levels, was at the same time domestically characterized by an anarchy of forms. Multiform horizontal links between individuals existed alongside a newly erected infrastructure of extended vertical links between individuals and societal, public institutions. *Stunde Null* in 1945 was literally a zero point, the hour in which old routines lost their authority and were replaced by non-routinized, pragmatic actions – with the effect of increasing the variety of patterns and routines. Attempts by the Allies, and after 1949 by the two states, to bring this anarchy of forms into a regularizable order were met most frequently by surface compliance, making invisible the many acts of deception, evasion, and resistance. Political regularization did not produce domestic uniformity.

Adults who did not leave for the West before 1961 lived under a regime that responded to lack of local and international support by centralizing its power. Shortages of workers and raw materials kept the economy reeling from crisis to crisis. The absurdity of the situation was such that the state had to subsidize most industries, often paying workers to produce at a loss. For those who stayed in East Germany, the situation put great demands on personal investment in the work unit and time allocation. Little time remained for constructing an autonomous realm of kin relations, and little time was left for children. This was true equally for women and men, and was contingent neither on occupational status nor age. Crowded housing conditions, a problem for the vast majority of households well into the late seventies, mandated flexible and unconventional sleeping, eating, and leisure-time patterns. Consequently, every imaginable household and kin combination was improvised out of the exigencies of the moment: they were planned neither from the top down nor from the bottom up.

In the first part of this chapter I outlined the range of household structures in the postwar period for both Generation I as adults and Generation II as children and youths. This section will take up narratives about the residence patterns for members of Generation II from the time they entered training/education programs to 1989. Partnership and childcare patterns, two central aspects of the domestic group, will be dealt with separately in the next sections.

Household groupings – coresidents within a particular dwelling – take on meaning as they are brought into combination with native concepts of the domestic group – who is kin? Until well into the fifties, both the structure of Berlin households and meanings attached to membership in a domestic group were in constant flux. Furthermore, the relationship of household structure to domestic group for Generation II did not simply repeat the transformations of the previous generation. Only in the folk ideology of the fifties and early sixties was there a typical model of the relationship of home to family, a model that assumed children would grow up with two parents of opposite sexes then marry and simultaneously establish their own residence, followed by the production of children or "family founding," and finally retirement. This model was assumed to be cyclical, meaning that each generation would repeat it: birth, marriage, children, death. Only birth and death, two of the four lifecycle elements, can be said to be ritually demarcated in a similar way for Generations I and II. Some members of Generation II never married, others married and divorced several times; and few of the men played a role in rearing children, while nearly all of the women did. Simply stated: marriage and childcare were no longer the central structuring institutions for kin and residence patterns of Generation II.

Yet laws directed to marriage and childcare were, in fact, two of the major instruments used by the GDR to bring anarchic domestic patterns under control. A third policy tool took on increased importance during the seventies: housing construction and residential allocation. Interacting with this policy, two experiential factors, one pertaining to household structure and one pertaining to the internal dynamics of the domestic unit, most significantly shaped the relationship of household to domestic group for Generation II. Instability in household structure from 1945 to 1961 can be traced to three sources: loss of adult men due to the war, incorporation of refugees from the Eastern territories, and continuous emigration of people to the West. With respect to the internal dynamics of domestic groups, the full incorporation of adult women into the workforce, a major political–economic goal of the regime, forced a restructuring of the domestic group. Before describing the changes in the domestic unit, let us focus first on residence patterns.

### Why they stayed in East Berlin

Because Berlin was divided into two opposed occupied zones/states, where the West German Zone/state was most often considered superior to the East, it may be useful to ask what factors led individuals to set up households in the "inferior" Soviet Occupied Zone after 1945. Why did they stay? Near the end of the war, many domestic groups began returning to Berlin because they had a house or apartment there, or at least thought they did. "My mother and I were in Thuringia [in 1944], and everything was so undecided. Nobody knew what was going to happen. She [mother] couldn't get along with the farmers who were housing us, so we took the train back to Berlin. She had an apartment there, so that's where we returned and where we ended up staying," commented Gabi L. The three-room apartment suffered very little damage during the war. Gabi and her mother shared it for three years, 1945–1948, with her paternal grandparents and with a neighborwoman. Gabi's father died in the Allied invasion of Normandy, something her mother first discovered in 1952 from an agency in Hamburg, West Germany. Maternal kin were never part of the domestic group: the mother's parents were already dead, two of her mother's brothers had died in the war, one escaped in 1942 to Argentina, and one sister-in-law lived in Hamburg. In 1964, Gabi married, and her husband moved into the residence with her and her mother. In 1967, Gabi and her husband found their own apartment. Her mother retired to West Berlin in 1980, and Gabi's two daughters, then aged sixteen and fourteen, took over the apartment.

For the vast majority of Berliners in the Soviet Zone, initial postwar residence had little to do with political orientation. Like Gabi's mother, if they found a place to live or had some relatives or friends with accommodation, they initially disregarded the political orientation of the occupying force. While it was possible for Generation I to make a conscious choice to live in a particular political system, Generation II inherited the choices of its parents. Because countless men never returned or simply abandoned their wives in the East and moved to the West, women of Generation I often developed strong emotional ties to their children and their home. Consequently, the decision for older members of Generation II to remain in the East was frequently related to a refusal to "abandon" their mothers.

The decision to stay in the East, then, was closely tied to feelings of membership in familiar domestic patterns. The decision to leave the domestic unit in East Berlin, however, most often had little to do with family reunification, though that was the best legal justification and thus most frequently offered reason for leaving. When individuals moved to the West (very few moved from West to East), they effectively divided the blood–kinship network. For many members of Generation II, the Cold War division of Berlin into a dual organization forced them to demarcate themselves simultaneously in terms of membership in a kinship system and in a political–economic system. Over the lifecourse, however, membership in both kinship and political–economic systems changes; the demarcations do not remain constant. In order to grasp more fully the range and historical specificity of these changing demarcations, I shall describe the relationship of the lifecourse to the changing structure of domestic groups for three particular individuals.

Throughout the 1950s, many women in the GDR were presented with the promise of a political–economic situation much more favorable than the one available to their sex in West Germany. The decision to stay tracked their lives in ways differentiating them from their cohorts in West Germany. Siegrid M., born in 1941, reported that all her relatives except for her mother had moved to the West by 1958. During the fifties, she would visit them regularly, and they encouraged her to join them in the West. The offer was tempting, she reported, because they were wealthy and could obtain for her entrance into any occupation she desired. Yet she ultimately remained in East Berlin for one reason: the men of her age in West Germany thought of her only in terms of sex and as a prospective wife, whereas the men in East Germany took her political opinions and career hopes seriously. In 1961, she freely broke off contact with her West German relatives, married a Party functionary, and had two children while practicing an occupation as journalist. After divorcing in 1980, she lived alone and enjoyed a wide circle of friends.

In their life reconstructions, most members of Generation II explained that they stayed in the East because at the crucial point in their lives when their futures were open, they never thought of leaving. Rarely was the decision to stay or leave so conscious as it was with Siegrid. As Generation II reached adulthood in the 1960s, friendships played a larger role in their kin networks than did extended blood relatives, such as cousins, uncles, and aunts; having grown up in the GDR, that was where most if not all of their significant friends and kin resided. When blood relatives remained important, it was more often because of concrete aspects of the relationship than because of the ties of shared blood. Jörg B., born in 1944, reported that he was an ideologically enthused youth throughout the period of his army service and his early career. Not until 1973 did one of his close friends leave for the West. A wave of his friends left in 1977–1978, others left slowly throughout the eighties. He explained that three whole groups of friends left *en masse* in the last fifteen years. Each time, he established a new circle of friends. The major reason for his remaining, he offered, was his refusal to abandon his foster mother (who is an aunt by blood). This relationship was not based on deep, nurturing emotional ties, he explained, but on a sense of obligation. As his birth-mother was caught in the line of fire and shot by a Russian soldier in 1945, his aunt Else (now adoptive mother) in the East Zone took him in rather than giving him up to a foster home. His father deserted the family and moved directly to Bavaria after being released from a POW camp. For this reason, he still feels that he has a lifelong obligation to his aunt/ adoptive mother. At the same time, however, he had developed other roots and a sense of belonging in a society he valued; he did not find equally attractive the offer of a better material life in West Germany.

Given his decision to stay (and that of many of his friends to leave), Jörg's residence patterns as they relate to his domestic group underwent a series of disjunctive transformations. In 1947, his grandparents asked his aunt to move to Chemnitz to take over an empty house in the country and help on the farm. He lived with his aunt and her husband (Else married a soldier in 1956, who then divorced her in 1975) until he was fourteen, before moving into a boarding school for four years. Several months before the Wall was built, when Jörg was sixteen years old, his aunt and her husband adopted him, changing his family name. His boarding-school years were followed by two years in the military, and one year doing occupational training in the textile industry, this time living in student housing. Thus, for his first fourteen years, household was coterminous with domestic group, which was defined as married couple with foster child. For the seven-year period between ages fourteen and twenty-one, his three different households lodged age-segregated (one also sex-segregated), non-kin groups.

At age twenty-two, Jörg moved to Berlin to study at the university, and lived in a one-room student apartment with a male lover for three years. During these three years, his lover's two children (the lover had never married) visited them on weekends. At age twenty-eight, in 1972, he married, sensing that the SED – he had since joined the party – preferred their *Kader* in a marital relationship, for married people were assumed to be more stable and loyal. He moved into a two-room apartment with his wife; the basis of the relationship was friendship, sex was secondary, love wasn't mentioned. After two years, he took on a male lover living in West Berlin, who visited three times a week over the next two years. In 1975, a new male lover, from Cuba, moved into the household with him and his wife. Jörg divorced in 1976, but continued in the same household arrangement with his ex-wife until 1979, when his wife moved to West Berlin. In 1983, Jörg's lover returned to Cuba, and Jörg has since resided alone. In sum, Jörg lived in three basic household structures, one where the household was organized around a marital unit (initially his foster parents, later his own), one where the household was organized around a common work/study unit, and one where he lived alone. The domestic unit during his adult life was organized around changing partnerships, not around a familial unit with children, and in only one instance around a secondary relationship to marriage.

A somewhat more conventional set of kin and household transformations characterize the life of Rosemarie S., born in 1942 near Dresden. She lived alone in an apartment with her father and mother, the only relatives she had ever known, both white-collar workers, until the age of eighteen. Then she moved to Bulgaria for two years to study medicine: so many doctors had left for the West that the other socialist countries began training doctors for the GDR. She became pregnant in her second year of medical school, married the father (at the time of pregnancy, an acquaintance of two months), and returned to Dresden to complete her studies. She moved into student housing, but there was no accommodation for married couples or children. Therefore the son resided with her parents and she visited him nearly daily; her husband resided in another town where he had obtained a job, and they saw each other at weekends. In 1965, she obtained an apartment for her husband and herself, but it had no kitchen or bath, so she still could not keep the child, now three years old. The following year, she obtained an advanced training position in Berlin, and a year later brought the child, against his wishes (he wanted to remain with the grandparents), to live with her. In 1970, eight years after her marriage, she finally obtained an apartment and her husband obtained a position, where they could live together in Berlin. In 1977, she filed for divorce, which her husband (without success) resisted. Her husband, after a year alone in a tiny apartment, remarried and moved into the residence of his new wife. A schoolmate of her son asked to move into the apartment in 1979, because she could not get along with her parents – Rosemarie agreed to the new resident. The initial romance between the son and his girlfriend ended within a year, but the girl remained another year. Rosemarie continued to share the same apartment with her son. Her mother also lived approximately a third of the year with her. In sum, Rosemarie lived in three kinds of households/domestic groups, two organized around marriages (with her parents and with her husband), three organized around educational institutions, and one organized around a three-generation grandmother–mother–son relationship. For Rosemarie, as for Jörg, marriage was seldom coterminous with household – for only seven of her fifteen married years. In addition, childcare was not part of a stable domestic unit, but practiced in three different household structures.

*Alternative households: single mother, single person, domestic partners*
Due to the destruction of residential space during the war, true not only
for Berlin but for most of East Germany, many people were forced to
live in small, improvised spaces. Reductions in residential space along
with changes in the perceived needs of individuals have led to the
creation of alternative households. In 1976, when the East German
government finally initiated the Berlin Program, a substantial renovation and new building program, the substance of buildings had so
deteriorated that the government consciously sacrificed the size of
residences in order to create more, often dividing one former apartment
into two. The resulting small size of apartments placed physical limits on
the size of a kin gathering, thus limiting the possible development of
extended kin residences. Moreover, public space for "family reunions"
was not readily available. Since only a limited number of restaurants
was available where one could seat a large number of people, and since
those needed to be booked well in advance, such gatherings tended to
be infrequent, small, and intimate.

The right to a residence, like the right to a job, was constitutionally
guaranteed in the GDR. This basic guarantee, while quite important in
and of itself, did not solve the problem of finding social criteria by which
to evaluate competing preferences: where will one reside, under what
conditions, and with whom? For the state and for a majority of its
citizens, the *kleinbürgerliche* family was the norm, the center around
which legal regulations and domestic practices defined themselves. Yet
this norm coexisted empirically with a vast array of alternative forms,
which the government, in turn, was constantly seeking to define and
regulate. As far as I could determine, based on interviews with housing
officials and discussions with hundreds of citizens about how they
obtained their residence, the official allocation scheme for apartment
allocation in East Berlin was roughly as follows: apartments were
allocated first to mothers of large families, followed by single mothers,
then married mothers, then married couples, and finally singles.

In the case of married couples who divorced, the woman nearly
always obtained the apartment, as was the case with Rosemarie.
Prioritizing women for apartment allocation, provided that they were
mothers, gave women of Generation II freedom of choice which their
mothers did not have. Since over 92 percent of all women of this
generation had at least one child, this power displacement was experienced by nearly all women (Speigner 1987: 26). The consequence for
men, certainly an unintended consequence for the regime, more often

than not was to make them dependent on women for accommodation. It was quite common for divorced men to remarry quickly, as Rosemarie's husband did, and then to move into the residence of their new wives, whereas divorced women remained in their old residence and remarried less often. As a matter of fact, the rate of remarriage for women in 1984 was 45.6 percent less frequent than that for men. Moreover, if women did remarry, they tended to do so after a longer delay (6.5 years) than their male counterparts (3.6 years) (see chapter 3).

Another reason why households tended to be controlled by women was that women also obtained the custody of children in 93 percent of all divorce cases (Stolpe 1986). Though the law stated that custody should not be denied to one parent in preference to the second, judges rarely enforced a shared parental arrangement, and even more rarely decided for the man alone. Monika T.'s houshold changes followed such a pattern. She was born in 1950 in Dresden. Her father, a refugee from East Prussia, was a doctor, in his second marriage, with two children from his first marriage. Her mother was twenty years younger than her father and worked as a nurse. Monika lived to the age of eighteen with her parents and step-siblings, in an apartment obtained from a Russian officer. As a child, she always had a live-in maid to do cooking and cleaning. She became pregnant in her second year of medical school in Greifswald while living in an apartment with a friend. She married against her parent's wishes, she said, transferred to medical school in Berlin and moved into a new residence with her husband and another couple. Within a year, she and her husband obtained their own apartment, and she stayed home for a year taking care of the baby. After fifteen years of marriage, she filed for divorce, to the complete surprise of her husband who resisted the divorce and fought for child custody. She obtained both the child and the apartment, and three months after the divorce, her husband moved into his own flat. Unusual in the case of Monika T. was that she never lived in a household organized around education, as did Jörg and Rosemarie. For most of her life, she lived in households organized around both marriage and childcare. That situation would soon change. At age forty-one, her marriage was already a factor in the past, and her daughter was also unlikely to remain in her household much longer.

The trend toward single-person households (for East Berlin, 34 percent in 1971; 33 percent in 1981) is a clear indication that, for a significant portion of the adult population, the household had been practically divorced from marriage, partnership form, and childcare patterns. This separation was precisely the opposite of policy goals, namely, a desire for complete overlap between marriage, partnership form, and childcare. The number of singles as a group in the entire GDR, given a stable population base, increased by 42.7 percent between 1964 and 1983. Singles, divorced, and widowed persons together made up 36 percent of the total GDR population (as of 1984), also slightly higher in Berlin than elsewhere. Angelika B., born in 1949 outside of Berlin, offered an example of household changes for a single woman. Her father died when she was three years old, and she had two married siblings, all raised by her mother sharing a residence with her grandparents. After leaving her grandparent's residence, Angelika lived in various student-type housing arrangements for four years. Since 1978, she has had two successive apartments, each consisting of a single room with kitchen and bath. She obtained the second one by trading the first.

In another significant household pattern, partners used marriage to obtain a Berlin residence. Lothar B. and Marian S., a doctor and elementary school teacher, respectively, had a three-year-old child and were living together unmarried in Rostock. This use of the marriage law was in direct conflict with its intent: marriage, with all its material benefits, was supposed to be the reward for heterosexual love; it was not supposed to be motivated by property procurement. Such an arrangement was sometimes called *Lebensgemeinschaft*, domestic partnership. While both Lothar and Marie could obtain jobs in Berlin, they could not be put on a priority list for an apartment unless they were married. They promptly wed, and within three months moved to Berlin and began their new work. After three years in a Prenzlauer Berg-Berlin flat, they were forced to move while city authorities renovated the building. The city gave them a choice between a new apartment in another section of the city or a two-to-three-year wait in a small, run-down flat, after which they could move back into their old residence. Rather than waiting the three years, they agreed to move to another district of Berlin. They reasoned that in the future they could always trade with other people if they so disliked their new living space.

Only three alternative residence patterns – single-mother households, retired-person (single, widowed, or divorced) households, and *Lebensgemeinschaften* (domestic partnerships) – showed some continuity from the fifties to the eighties. Single mothers, for example, were consistently supported and legitimated by the state as childcare units, despite the fact that they did not correspond to either the legally preferred household or family form. The number of illegitimate births went up dramatically in the sixties as women began to realize that state support, though minimal, was still sufficient to permit them to become mothers without dependence on a stable partnership with a man. This support was initially only in the form of a secure residence and food, and protection from work discrimination. Many women told me that they had initially decided together with a man to have a child. When the relationship fell apart before the baby was born, they carried through with the pregnancy anyway. Nearly all women I talked to about this matter assumed it was their right and privilege "as women" to have children. Through the continuous practice of this form of childcare over the last two to four generations, the single mother and child(ren) unit had, in effect, become viewed as fulfilling three functions: those of a childcare unit, a household, and a family or domestic unit. Single mothers were close to becoming the norm: by 1986, approximately 48 percent of all first-born children in East Berlin were born to single mothers, and approximately 34 percent of all children were being raised by single parents, 93 percent of whom were women.

**Partnership, friendship, and the redefinition of kin**
In addition to the limitations placed on domestic group composition by residential space, consciousness about disparities between imagined relations and actual ones also brought about a reconceptualization of kin among Generation II. Relationship models have important descriptive and normative components alike; they contain both models of reality (how people do relate) and models for reality (how people should relate). Both practices and the fantasies about them change over the course of a lifetime. For Generation I, there was often minimal correspondence between their model of and model for kinship; objective circumstances forced them to live under unforeseen conditions that were not within their repertoire of possibilities, conditions for which their models could not account. Partnership was often not practiced within a marriage, marriages often ended in divorce, women became wage-earners outside the home as were their men (when they had men), and children did not readily submit to parental authority – all empirical conditions outside their mental repertoire of possibilities. Given this set of life circumstances, it was hardly surprising that silence played a major role in their life reconstructions.

Silence also entered the reconstructions of Generation II, but only in reconstructions of their adulthood. Indeed their postwar life began in a turbulent uproar, with an experience of adventure and a desire to affirm this experience through its articulation. They often saw their parents' silence as hypocrisy regarding the disparity between kin fantasies and kin practices. "My mother always gave moral lectures, [namely,] that one may not live together without being married because God would not approve. And I never could understand," said Erika D., born in 1934, "why she then [lived that way] herself despite [her own moral injunction against it]. I must say, I hated her so much sometimes that I just left the room, because there were absolutely no points of agreement. Actually, I despised what she did, and I held what she preached to me for the Gospel truth" (Wander 1978: 90). Erika's reaction to her mother's hypocrisy was to internalize unwittingly her mother's moral norms, her "model-for" kin, while simultaneously practicing kin in a quite different fashion. For members of Generation II, working through the contradictions between what their parents preached and how they lived was a major structuring element in their own lives, and often resulted in a conscious redefinition of kinship. Central to this redefinition were their own experiences of partnership and friendship.

### Women and the redefinition of kin

By the time members of Generation II began constructing their own kin relations, kinship had been legally recoded, formalized in the Family Law Book in 1965. Three of the codes substantially altered their situation compared to that of their parents: first, marriages and divorces were now nearly costless and no longer connected to principles of male inheritance and prerogative, nor to sexual fidelity in the marriage; second, women of Generation II were qualified workers and guaranteed a job, which in turn provided them economic independence from their husbands; third, childcare was now largely supported by the state and not financially or otherwise dependent on marital status. While these laws changed the objective status of relationships, their efficacy depended in large part on their appropriation by individuals in everyday situations. This appropriation was neither automatic nor immediate; it required a redefinition of subjectivity, a new model of an ideal self.

"I was raised with strong sexual taboos," explained Monika T., a doctor, born in 1952. "My first husband, you know him, had something solid, fatherly about him. But we had nothing in common. Now I seek a man for totally different reasons." Monika had initially sought out a husband who would support her. She was sexually involved with a single man her age who for the last ten years had been living with another woman in a marriage-like situation. To be sure, the degree of Monika's independence was connected to her occupation. Yet the practice of divorce and self-reliance was not something limited to upper-class women in the GDR.

The women of Generation II, not the men, took the first steps toward freeing themselves from "bourgeois morals," as they were called, which to them meant more than freedom from sexual taboos. "In my family [two girls, one boy], the girls had to do all the housework, the cleaning, my brother had free time for his sport and his friends," explained Kathe K., an elementary-school teacher now in her second marriage. Kathe claimed that although many of her patterns with her current husband conformed to the sex-stereotypes, she still tried to get her husband to be more active in fulfilling domestic duties. She was quite conscious of the discrepancy between what she thought a partnership should be and what she had. Her own emancipation, she said, was not independent of her husband's, but limited by the fact that her husband had not changed to the same extent. Similarly, Rosi S., born in 1941, asked, "Is it useful to a woman to try to emancipate herself from her partner?" (Wander 1978: 61).

The fact is that many women had done precisely this: after first trying and failing in a heterosexual marriage, they emancipated themselves from a partner. "I tried a marriage for eight years," said Christina A., a divorced mother of two, born in 1948, "and I won't enter another one now, at least not on the same terms as before. After the divorce I really tried to keep my sons in contact with him, because I thought they should know their father. But he got increasingly abusive, so, finally, the boys themselves said they had had enough." Christina explained how proud she was of her sons, that they were different from the men of her generation, more sensitive to others and more respectful of women. She still had relations with men, but she did not intend to marry; instead she prioritized her relations with friends and her sons. An increasing number of women in this generation consciously decided to live either without a man or in a non-domestic, non-committed partnership. Unlike their mothers, few said they were forced into single life by a lack of available men.

For many of the men and women of Generation II, the heterosexual model of partnerships had not lived up to its promise. Since 1964, the total number of divorces more than doubled, and 40 percent of these involved marriages of less than five years (Heyl 1986: 19). The city of

Berlin, moreover, had the highest divorce rate in 1986 in the GDR: 4.3 divorces per 1,000 people (significantly higher than the next closest city, Rostock, with 3.7 per 1,000); but also one of the highest rates of marriage: 8.6 per 1,000 people (*Statistisches Jahrbuch der DDR* 1987: 360). The rate of breakup was significantly higher for *Lebensgemeinschaften,* domestic partnerships without a marriage certificate. Heterosexual partnerships did not prove to be a fortress or private retreat from public life, the secure place free of political and social conflict that their mothers and fathers claimed existed before the war. Domestic life, when centered around a heterosexual marriage, was precisely an arena filled with great expectations and politicized desires.

If the majority of the population still experienced a traditional marriage and family, it lasted only for a small segment of their lives. Social scientists in the GDR were beginning to recognize the empirical plurality of partnership forms. "We have to acknowledge that in the future we will be living with a permanent, possibly even increasing number of people who marry several times, live in domestic partnerships and in incomplete families," concluded family specialist Jutta Gysi. "There will be a multiplicity of life-forms, which in their totality will play a role in constructing our lifeways" (cited in Ziegenhagen 1987: 8). This recognition did not, however, lead to a change in the law.

Equally important for this new perspective on life-long heterosexual partnerships among Generation II was a socially engineered experience, namely, the opening of the public world to women. As children and youths, the women and men of Generation II shared the same access to public institutions, e.g., kindergartens, schools, apprenticeships and work units, governmental agencies. Whereas the domestic education and life of Generation II had many traditional, sex-specific dimensions, the non-domestic world was often not divided primarily along sex lines. While the GDR did develop some sex-specific occupations at both the upper and lower levels of their social hierarchies, men and women of Generation II, from early on, were provided with the opportunity for contact and experiences with the opposite sex in a wide spectrum of relationships not based on a heterosexual partnership model. These experiences provided the basis upon which men and women could relativize their model for domestic life, that is, relativize their domestic fantasies. Their fantasies opened up new practices, in turn, including the possibility for emotional investment in other relationships, redefining the meaning of partnership, friendship, and kin.

The relativization of heterosexual partnerships, an integral experience for many members of both sexes, however, had more of a direct effect on the lifecourse of women than men. For women of Generation II, same- and cross-sex friendships now play an integral role in emotional fulfillment. These friendships took on increased importance after a divorce, although for some women they were also important during the first marriage. Since women tended to be responsible for planning the details of kin gatherings – writing letters, sending invitations, telephoning – they were also seen as the ones who attached more importance to the maintenance of relationships. The building of friendships both raised the expectations of a partnership by providing a comparison, and took the pressure off by providing other emotional bonds and outlets. Whatever influence friendships ultimately had on partnerships, many women of Generation I insisted that they could not survive without the daily or weekly interaction and support of female friends.[6] Older men of Generation II often reported that they had shared the same friends with their wives during the marriage, but severed contact after the divorce; the only friends that stood by them, if any did, were often work colleagues. This pattern is not so true of the younger men of Generation II, who maintain a wider range of male friendships outside the marriage.

*Men and the redefinition of kin*

Since the end of the war, men's ability to control the domestic sphere, and thus influence the lifecourse of their wives and children, has been severely curtailed. Men experienced a diminution of the significance of being a father, exemplified by a decline in the use of inheritance as a leverage for fathers and by a growing asymmetry between the parental rights of the father compared to those of the mother. Additionally, his role as husband was no longer anchored in law and economics, for most adult women, who now got training and jobs much like men, were capable of a large degree of economic independence. The father and husband had, in effect, been reduced to a merely symbolic status, devoid of former positive and negative sanctioning devices. As a result, the relations of men of Generation II to their wives tended to be based solely on emotional dependence. Relations to their own children, including those that were maintained during and after divorce, tended to revolve around a non-obligatory friendship or *Kumpel* model.

The major new element in the male practice of kinship, then, was the expansion of the importance of non-obligatory friends. Let us outline what these practices meant. Experiences of men of this generation were in no way uniform, and they disagreed among themselves as to what

*Kumpel* meant.[7] Yet, based on the discussions I had with men, the *Kumpel* model for Generation II had two primary variants: first, it replaced the authoritarian father–son model with *Kumpel–Kumpel*; second, it eroticized same-sex male relationships, opening them up for possible emotional attachments. Udo G., whose father was born in 1940, related that his father was "more of a *Kumpel*. He never played a father role." His mother divorced when Udo was fourteen, because of his father's alcoholism and sexual affairs with other women. The father relocated away from his kin to Rostock, but not being self-sufficient enough to care for himself, sank deeper into alcoholism. "At the time I supported her [mother] in the decision," commented Udo, "although it was hard on me, a difficult time . . . She did not ask me before she made the decision, no. But I think and thought back then that it would have been worse had they remained together." For Udo, the relationship with his father was a voluntary one, "like a *Kumpel*," he said, a special kind of friend. When the father left his kin, it did not harm the domestic unit financially, nor did it drastically change the nature of domestic authority, for the father already had been acting more on an equal basis, like a *Kumpel*.

The *Kumpel* model was also applied in relations between those friendships where life-long trust and loyalty were assumed. Often these relationships took place in all-male settings – sporting events and bars were the two most frequent – and there they were subject to periodic eroticization. In these settings, the *Kumpel* relationship can provide a legitimate cover for socially prohibited homosexual behavior. Even though such friendships rarely resulted in a homosexual identity, the fact that men could engage in same-sex physical and emotional bonding opened their horizon of experiences and made them less emotionally dependent on their wives and female kin. In the all-male settings, *Kumpel*s made ritual displays of their fondness for each other with a kind of public openness that they rarely if ever showed to their female partners.

In general, working-class men in Berlin still tended to have the strongest *Kumpel* ties. Compulsory military service was a period of between one and three years when men experienced hierarchy and particular forms of all-male bonding. This army experience remained totally outside the realm of female understanding, since women had no access to it and most men refused to talk about it. People responsible for occupational training of youths told me that after army service men changed in ways that made them more radically different from women

than before. Thereafter men were more willing to discipline themselves and accept authority, and often sought a quick marriage or
stable relationship. Women in their late-teens and early twenties were
still experimental and inquisitive; they, in turn, underwent a major
transformation after they had a baby, mostly between the ages of
twenty and twenty-four.

### Kin of choice versus nuclear family

Although Generation II practiced a wide spectrum of relationship
forms, often called *Wahlverwandtschaften*, relatives or kin of choice,
the majority of citizens, including East Berliners, were still ideologically committed to a nuclear-family model. Herr M., age forty,
described his friendship and kin circle:

> Friends? We don't think too much about them. I had a friend earlier, and
> then you know a few from the army and from the school. But that's gone
> now. My wife couldn't stand them, and the friends of my wife – they weren't
> anything special either. We have our work, the children, the boat, and we
> meet others when we go sailing. We visit the family, and you don't have time
> for any more. During the short weekend we're either in the country or at her
> mother's. Whether I miss that? I don't know.

The sociologist Irene Runge concludes from this passage, "Each
person outside the nuclear unit is classified here as a disturbance"
(1985: 79). The only kin attached to Herr M.'s marital unit outside of
the children was the mother's mother. There appear to be two
competing models of kin operating, that of an exclusive nuclear unit
and that of kin of choice. The former was based on categories of
consanguinity and affinity, the latter on shared time and space.

Among more critical Berliners, the name given to the type of
person whose identity is organized around a narrow, stereotypical
definition of belonging to a nuclear family was *Stino*, meaning "stink
normal." The term originated in East Berlin (few West Berliners
know what it means), and was used widely among people living in
alternative kinds of relationships. Many East Berlin heterosexuals
associated themselves, embarrassedly, with the term, assuming that it
meant the opposite of homosexual. Yet I repeatedly heard *Stino* used
in a variety of ways, even referring to homosexual pairs who led lives
modelled after the stereotype of normality. The word referred to a
cluster of meanings, which only in some kind of combination lead to
the label. Included among the most-frequent characteristics I heard

were: married, living like one is married, narrow-minded, and sexually non-experimental.

### Childcare, work, and domesticity

The entry of the women of Generation I on such a large scale into the labor force (by the sixties, 50 percent of all workers were women) changed, above all, the routines of domestic life. But it did not immediately change the way in which individuals conceptualized work. In my discussions with women and men of Generation I, they reconstructed their lives in categories based on those of the late nineteenth century: they often described "work" and "family" as antithetical activities; family became the domain of the woman, work became a domain of both men and women. Women and men of Generation II figured their narratives by using experiences made meaningful through reference to these two categorical domains, but they rejected the meanings given to them by their parents. Women, for example, no longer considered work and childcare to be separate private and public domains; for both men and women, partnership was often divorced from family and childcare. While reconstructing action domains continued to be gender-specific, the most significant factors creating a specific generational identity held true for both men and women: the gradual redefinition of parenting and childcare, the separation of partnership from marriage and childcare; and loss of the centrality of work.

### *The meaning of parenting and childcare*

Although laws aimed directly at changing the position of women – legitimizing children born out of wedlock, supporting single mothers, and enforcing equal rights for women in work outside the home – date back to the early days of the Soviet occupation, they only gradually influenced the meaning of childcare, occupation, and domestic life as it was practiced. In their reconstructions, members of Generation I who were mothers of children born out of wedlock tended to deny that they experienced social discrimination on account of their non-marital status. On the other hand, their "illegitimate" children often remembered acutely moments of harassment by their peers. "I was born in 1944," related Stefan F.:

My mother, she never did tell me how she got pregnant, or who it was. I was like a duty for her; she gave me no affection. Nor to anyone else, either; we were very isolated. Anytime she wanted me to shut up, she'd just hit me. Like that [alongside the head]. She never really had any time either, working full time . . . And there were a number of other kids in my classes who also only had mothers. We'd have to say in front of the class: father: occupation; mother: occupation. It was clear to the others who didn't have a father.

Although the GDR in 1950 changed the law to free children of the social stigma attached to illegitimacy, social attitudes and domestic authority structures resisted immediate change. Many members of Generation II experienced this stigma, both as children and then as mothers of children born out of wedlock. It took one additional generation, until the seventies, before this stigma disappeared.

Stefan F.'s account was also revealing in how he portrayed his relation with his mother. Working full-time during the *Aufbau* period, she had neither the time nor energy to offer him much emotional support. This changed minimally for women of Generation II as they became mothers, which 92 percent did, in the sixties and seventies. Rosemarie S. and Monika T., who described their households in this chapter, both had unplanned pregnancies in the sixties. Like many of their peers, they described the pregnancy as an embarrassment and something shameful. Monika said that her parents even tried to persuade her to abort illegally. Although both women married shortly after the pregnancy, and did so at that time only because they wanted to avoid the stigma of being single mothers, they received little childcare support from their husbands. This, they explained, was solely because their husbands were also in the middle of career training and had neither time nor financial resources. Although the legal structure protected them from formal discrimination, and political measures enabled them to pursue career training and simultaneously act as parents, the social institutions were structured in ways that did not take into account their special status. Social practices did not fully catch up to the legal reform that addressed them until after the mid to late seventies.

Helga explained in more detail the milieu of the sixties. She had a baby in 1966:

Study, child, and career. Now it's no problem, but then it was unthinkable. I couldn't get a room alone. Those went only to boys. I had to quit my study, I had no choice. It has totally changed today, I know that.

She had been in training in an all-male occupation. In her third month of pregnancy, she quit her study to earn some money and began working in a gas station. (Students received financial support, but it was only minimal.)

It was a great disappointment for my school director that I was pregnant and that I had to quit my study. My fiancé's mother was so shocked. She asked me what was I doing to him, to her son. It was no problem for her that I had to give up my career. She herself had four children and no husband. I began working eight months after the birth, got a place in the day-care center, as a single mother, and I finished my study then three years later. [I suffered] unbelievable isolation [for those first three years].

There were no others around to help her, although a neighborwoman stopped by now and then. She had no contact with other single mothers, and said she never even considered it.

I couldn't imagine that. At 6:30 I left the house to work, at 7:00 at night I came back with the baby. At that time, also living in my building was a girl who had a child fathered by an African. The baby suffocated [one night]. Then I feared I might lose my own.

Helga therefore never left the child alone for the first three to four years, even for a single evening.

I was so poor then. I couldn't even afford a cup of coffee. I wasn't hungry-poor, but we had nothing back then. I borrowed money from my mother at the beginning of the month and at the end of the month I would pay it back to her.

In 1969 she married the father of her child. She explained:

He wanted to begin his work as a married man [after he finished his education]. He wanted order from the beginning. He wanted to change his name initially to mine, because his name sounded dumb in German. But his mother said, "No, you are no longer my son when you do that." I took his name then, but I really had no choice. It was important for him but unimportant to me, so I did it.

The experience of Helga was characteristic of women of Generation II. The laws now seemed to establish equal rights and presented her with new opportunities. After marriage, she could even have kept her maiden name, and her husband could have taken hers. But no. She was unable to realize most of these choices. It took another generation before they began to take effect and substantively change the lifecourse.

Yet Helga does signal one significant change that took place within her generation: motherhood, work, and domestic life were no longer separable domains. She experienced childcare not as a distinct domain of action but as an activity immediately impinged upon, supported, or thwarted by other practices and institutions.

Working women of her generation began to enjoy the state support for childcare through the institutions of preschool care and after-school care. Helga described childcare in the context of decisions about occupation, marriage, and name change. Significantly, she strays from the narrative of Generation I in that, in her discussion, she neither brings partnership to the fore, nor retreats to motherhood as a refuge from the stress of public life.[8] She did not enter into a marriage to legitimate her partnership before the state, but for purely social reasons. In contrast to the description of women of Generation I, the complex meaning-cluster "marriage, children, and family" was deconstructed. Generation I had already left out the "love" code in their descriptions of this complex. Generation II not only omitted love, but categorized partnership with other relationships of choice, and childcare with relationships of obligation.

Men of Generation II did not usually mention childcare in their narratives. Fathers with positions well-connected to the political structure used them to secure educational access for their children, but these men were few in number, at most 30 percent of the population. Private capital accumulation on a socially significant scale began only in the last decade, hence inheritance among Generation II also played a minimal role. This pattern may have been changing, as disposable income and private wealth increased quite markedly in the eighties, but on the other hand, children's material wealth was after a certain point more contingent on West German contacts than on East German family ties.

### Men and domesticity

In their narratives, men of Generation II stressed, much more than women, dependence on partnership. Domesticity, or *Häuslichkeit*, was something about which men paradoxically seemed much more concerned than women. The explanation for this is rather simple. At the time of my research most of the men of Generation II were either married or divorced. Apartments in the GDR were hard to come by, and in the case of divorce, especially if children were at home, the women nearly always kept the apartment. Divorced men and women told me of living with their spouses for several tense years after the divorce because they had to wait for another apartment. Often a man found another apartment only by finding another partner first, in other words, a woman with an apartment. Thus the tendency was for men to move into female-run households, rarely vice versa. In addition, most mothers in the early postwar period did not teach their sons how to take care of households; thus cooking, cleaning, and domestic abilities needed to be learned as adults – not an impossible task, but something only a small (but increasing) number of the men managed.

## From work to free time

Finally, the introduction of the concept "free time," to be counterposed to "work," played a significantly greater structuring role for Generation II than for Generation I. Because this division was much better articulated and taken more to an extreme among Generation II in West Berlin, I shall here discuss only how this related to the specifics of identity and work in East Berlin. Because of the egalitarian wage policy of the regime, wage differentials were not great, and work hierarchies were based more on power concentration (the most important reason being party membership) than on income or status differentials. Thus for the majority, the incentives to invest heavily in the work domain were few (the money wasn't that much more and the political control of the person was greater).

For those who simply held positions (there was virtually no unemployment) without investing their *selves* heavily into them, the concept "free time" was clustered together with an expanded version of domesticity, of creating a home-like atmosphere. Free time became an opportunity to retreat from the grey world of work to the garden house in the country or, for others, to cultural events in the city. Unlike Generation I, there was a much wider range of possible retreats, often involving traveling to other socialist countries, and often involving activities with close friends. The idea of retreating to the nuclear family was but one among many models of free-time use employed and, in my experience, people turned to it only when a more expanded network of kin (including but not limited to those related by blood and marriage) was unavailable.

## Conclusion

When the state singled out family law as a discrete area of concern in 1965 and focused on the family as the "smallest cell of society," it was proposing to regulate, support, and legitimate the folk model of kinship from the fifties: a nuclear, *kleinbürgerliche* family. By inscribing in law a sentimentalization of policy, it signaled the end of the strategy of construction. The state specified that marriage, particularly the "marriage of love," remained the legal instrument through which heterosexual partnerships could become objects of state policy. Alternate household and domestic arrangements that in the fifties were practiced without being named (e.g., communes, apartment cooperatives, and multi-generation households) had by the mid sixties practically withered away. Nonetheless, people created other alternate domestic forms centered around the single person. Residential construction dimensions of family policy further reinforced either nuclear-family parenting units (the legal norm) or single-person households by setting up structural constraints and incentives. Building small apartments, or in the case of renovation policy, cutting large apartments in half, for example, reduced the possibility for creative, collective use of space to structure living units, while encouraging single persons, single parents, and nuclear couples.

The small size of apartments also placed physical limits on the size of a kin gathering, and public space for "family reunions" was not readily available. Furthermore, only a few restaurants were available where one could seat a large number of people, and these needed to be booked well in advance. Hence all gatherings tended to be small and intimate. Large family reunions were now, if experienced at all, mostly limited to *Jugendweihe*, the state ceremony demarcating passage from childhood into youth. Marriages, births, and funerals only rarely served the ritual function of bringing extended generations of relatives together. Apartment complexes themselves, inhabited by separate, distinct family units with no particular common feature, were rarely places where one could construct extended kin networks.

Yet the state's conscious attempt to reproduce a specific family form did not uniformize so much as narrow the range of possibilities; it did not eliminate the range in household structures so much as reduce the scale of experimentation. Competing social policy goals often fostered contradictory forms of praxis. On the one hand, the state's interests in socialist collectives, most vigorously pursued during the period of construction, encouraged people to think in units larger than the individual. On the other hand, the state's interests in reducing the individual to a loyal *Kleinbürger* dependent on the state for goods and services, financially secure from cradle to grave, and hesitant to use his/her own initiative, encouraged the citizen to withdraw into privatized and isolated niches. In praxis, this state policy dried up public space by colonizing it, encouraging a duplicitous person who in public defined him/herself in terms the state desired, in private experimented with alternate forms of belonging, variously defined. Only in the domain of work did the state encourage participation, of men and women equally. Many women of Generation II identified with the state precisely on that account. But as we have seen, free time, and the state's restrictions on its enjoyment, increased in importance, while identification with work actually declined.

Intensification of fear through the development of an ubiquitous police apparatus followed the building of the Wall, and this coincided with a sentimentalization of kinship policy by the state. Members of Generation II experienced this stage of *Abgrenzungspolitik* in early adulthood, at a time in the lifecourse when an expansive horizon of expectations, strongly encouraged during their childhood by the state's future-oriented master narrative of construction, was most important to them. Hence Generation II experienced the seventies and eighties, in contrast to the two decades preceding them, as periods of contraction and limit. In comparing their lifecourse with those of West German peers, for whom material prosperity was a constant (despite whatever other problems were encountered), they developed a sense of themselves as weaker and poorer, "lacking" something ineffable.

Generational specificities become more apparent only by examining the generations in relation to one another. Women of Generation I invested most of their emotional capital in their roles as mothers, many initially resisted investing themselves in work, even though the majority were continuously employed after the war. Men of Generation I played, on the whole, a minimally active role in kinship, although as fantasy figures they often took on increased importance as counterparts to the overinvestment of the mothers. This affected their daughters and sons, that is members of Generation II, quite differently. The form of love offered by mothers of Generation I to their daughters encouraged their independence. Mother–daughter ties after childhood were then strengthened through the role of Oma in the childcare of Generation II. The relation of Generation I mothers to their sons had a quite different effect and purpose. Few of these women had more than one son, many only one child. They often sought a surrogate husband in their favorite son, and thus worked to increase the emotional dependence of their sons on them. The reaction of these sons varied greatly, but, in general, Generation II male ambivalence to emotional dependence on women was an important legacy of relations with mothers that reentered into relations with female lovers and wives.

# 7

## *Hausfrauenehe* and kinship restoration in West Berlin: Generation I

Silence plagued the postwar life of Generation I in West Berlin much as it did the lives in the East. The silencing of this generation, born approximately between 1910 and 1935, limited its competence in articulating present needs as well as its ability to confront the role of the past in ongoing lives. While this unfilled, erased space enervated the individual, it proved enabling for the two nascent states. In both East and West, this silence was filled in by the state: for those in the East through work programs connected with the *Aufbau*, for those in the West by creating conditions for the *Wirtschaftswunder*. Both economic plans were state-inspired visions of the future, master narratives of prosperity that would please the *Bürger* and legitimate the governing system.

This mirror-imaging in economic categorization, socialist *Aufbau* versus capitalist *Wirtschaftswunder*, was not sustained, however, by a comparable periodization. The *Aufbau*, as economic period and category of experience, lasted until approximately 1961, whereas the *Wirtschaftswunder*, at least for Generation I, is continuing today. Hence East Berliners, who in the fifties began finding their voice in the state's master narrative of construction, felt themselves stymied into a nostalgia trip by the mid sixties, a reminiscence increasingly blind to or bitter about a failing economic plan, augmented by a selective memory that either created new silences or new dissatisfactions. West Berliners, on the other hand, found themselves truly at home with their attained voice of prosperity, which enabled them to periodize their lives, along with the history of their state, as linear progress. Compared to their East Berlin comrades, their narrative of the past was nearly seamless, a plot waiting to be found, and then told with neither hesitation nor discomfort. The confidence and durability of their voice authorized them to bask in the mirror-imaging process, for by the eighties it was clear that they, together with their state, had written a dominant narrative and established an asymmetry in imagery that would last. The dual organization worked to their benefit.

This chapter concerns itself with how Generation I found its voice in interaction with the strategies of the state. I minimize repetition of patterns that hold true for both sides, already described in the previous chapter, and instead emphasize the distinctiveness of West Berlin stories. Hence the account here should be read as a sequel to chapter 5. Before presenting the life constructions of West Berliners, let us again review the general framework in which their personal narrative is constructed. In chapter 4, I summarized the narrative strategies of the West German state (see table 15 on page 77). In this chapter we will be dealing first and foremost with the narrative strategy of restoration, and only in chapter 8 will we address desentimentalization. The former more directly influenced the experience of Generation I, the latter that of Generation II. As we shall see in the following pages, the modes of emplotment provided by the state fit well the overall strategy aimed at the restoration of tradition; they enabled an assimilation of Generation I into the Germanness of the *Bundesbürger*, into a hierarchically ordered, prosperous community held together by aesthetic appeals to a superior (traditional) authority.

### Households, the domestic group, and foreigners
*Reterritorializing Berlin (West)*
The Allied bombing and occupation of Berlin dramatically changed its geography, permitting and requiring a new territorialization of Germans into households, domestic groups, and political alliances. Let us first briefly describe this new territory in which households and domestic life took shape. Between 1945 and 1948, variance in individual living standards in Greater Berlin was more dependent on personal luck and inheritance than on official Occupation policy. People who still had residences standing after the war were clearly in a more secure and stable position than those who had lost theirs, though other forms of property ownership did not automatically translate into a higher standard of living. The fact that the Americans occupied some of the wealthiest zones (Zehlendorf and Steglitz), and the French two of the poorest (Wedding and Reinickendorf), provides a partial explanation. Yet, any generalized attribution of differences in living standards to the peculiarities of Occupation policies alone is suspect, since there was also

much movement between sectors, including the Soviet one, so that life at that time was not primarily determined by conditions in the place of residence. Moreover, isolated differences in administrative policy between the sectors (with respect to factors such as size of family and food rations, treatment of women head-of-households and working women, and enforcement of the Potsdam Accords) affected individuals in ways that are not easily generalizable.

Only with the surprise currency reform in June 1948, a demarcation policy forced on the West Germans by the Americans, did domestic life in Berlin begin to vary significantly between the Occupied Zones. At that time, Cold War demarcation strategies were still being mapped out, both cognitively and territorially; thus the Allies agreed on a "double-currency" system for the two Berlins. This attempt to keep East Berlin somehow tied to its western half, while appearing to benefit both sides, cost the East Germans much more than the West Berliners, because it allowed for and stimulated a black market, effectively increasing the asymmetry between the sides. Black-market exchange rates immediately emerged, ranging from 1:4 to 1:7 East Mark/(West) D-Mark, bringing about a tremendous economic advantage for individuals who worked in West Berlin and bought subsidized goods in East Berlin.

In March 1949, the authorities in the western zones, realizing that they had a trump card to play, refused to recognize further the currency in the Soviet Zone. This reduced most exchanges between the zones to officially tolerated and sometimes encouraged black-market transactions. Up to the building of the Wall, many people continued to buy the subsidized goods in the East and work in the West. In their reconstructions, members of Generation I in West Berlin often referred to how they managed to make ends meet only by buying in East Berlin, but they avoided using the East German name for this practice, *Ausblutung*, bleeding dry. For West Berliners, the Other had become the eastern half of their city, and exploitation of this Other – enabled by misrecognition of them as non-kin – was an officially encouraged survival strategy. Hence by the time of the founding of the West German state in 1949, the postwar geography of Berlin (West) had already taken on sharp contours: with the return of adult men from POW camps, social contacts and networks of the war and prewar years recrystallized and their associated privileges and hierarchies quickly reasserted themselves; with the help of the Currency Reform, a latent, unofficial system of exploitation of the Other in the East became official and institutionalized.[1]

*Households and refugees from the East*

Those citizens in the worst economic and social positions were the refugees from former East Prussia, of whom approximately 25,000 to 30,000 were arriving daily in August 1945 in Greater-Berlin. Without networks of friends and relatives to whom they could turn when in need, they were totally reliant on local residents and authorities (Müller 1953). Whereas these people were officially welcomed in the GDR to shore up a depleted labor force, the official West German/West Berlin response was more ambivalent: public-works programs were limited in scope and it was assumed that "the market" would eventually absorb them. Native West Berliners report in their reconstructions that they initially resented the increased competition from refugees for living space, food, and clothing.

Furthermore, the resettlement of Eastern refugees – a total of 9.1 million to all of the Occupied Zones by the end of 1950 – was of more direct consequence and for a longer duration to West Berliners than to West Germans.[2] After 1949, the majority of refugees stayed initially in West Berlin before moving to the Federal Republic. For example, on November 29, 1952, 200,000 refugees left the GDR, of whom 150,000 went to West Berlin. Between 1949 and 1953, a total of 617,000 individuals left the GDR, of whom 335,100 went on to West Germany. Helmut Schelsky estimated that between 1.5 and 2.5 million of the initial East refugees were highly qualified *Beamte* (civil servants), career soldiers, and Nazi Party members, who had worked well with Nazis and lost their positions after the German defeat; another 2.5 million were war widows and orphans; 1.5 million were seriously disabled through injury; 2 million returned late to their former homes, and 4.5 to 6 million had lost their homes through bombing and were residing in destroyed or damaged places (Schelsky 1951). The entire group of refugees is considered, in retrospect, an essential factor in creating the *Wirtschaftswunder* in West Germany – a skilled, mobile, highly qualified laborforce, with Prussian work habits, eager to serve and sacrifice (Welzk 1987: 16–17).

Nearly all members of Generation I in their reconstructions mentioned the instability and chaos of the early postwar years. Few Berliners lived in nuclear-family households before the mid fifties, and thereafter the numbers increased but incrementally over time. In her 1946 study of Berlin, Hilde Thurnwald concluded that more than half of all domestic units (she used the word "families") housed relatives or friends in their apartments. She estimated that the average residence included two persons per room, and that 81 percent of the people were undernourished (Thurnwald 1948: 40). The situation of refugees was assuredly even worse. A 1947 study of housing in Hessen, West Germany estimated that for refugees the number of persons per room averaged 2.8; for non-refugees the average was 1.8 (Edding 1952: 316). Since the percentage of refugees in Berlin was greater than in Hessen, the differential between refugee and non-refugee crowding was no doubt even greater in Berlin. One can safely assume that, until the mid fifties, Berlin residences were of tremendously varied shapes and sizes, often including basements, warehouses, and subway stations. The content of the household was also fluid, with changing members and consequently, changing uses of space. Private and public space divisions were a matter of constant negotiation. In sum, massive migration with large numbers of refugees, frequent illnesses, lost children, and missing adult men were the major factors adding to the instability of the household and domestic group.

*Households and 'Gastarbeiter' from the Mediterranean*
The building of the Wall in August 1961 abruptly ended the easy resettlement to the Federal Republic and West Berlin of "Germans from the East," or *Flüchtlinge*, refugees, from the *Ostgebiete des Deutschen Reiches* as it was called up to 1973 in the FRG *Statistisches Jahrbuch*. Immigration to West Berlin declined correspondingly, from 233,500 in the first half of 1961, to 15,000 in 1962. For the Federal Republic as a whole, 6.2 million refugees crossed the border between 1949 and 1961; of these 3.5 million were citizens of the GDR. During this same period, West Germany lost 3.55 million citizens, most to the United States and Canada (Korte 1985: 18). (The Federal Republic had, by contrast with the GDR, 3.6 times more people.)

With the migration from the GDR closed off, the Federal Republic, and particularly West Berlin, began by 1963 to experience labor shortages. Unable to rely on labor from the *Ostgebiete*, West Berlin/ West German authorities responded by recruiting and importing southern European workers to compensate for labor shortages. Initially called *Fremdarbeiter*, foreign workers, in a carry-over from the forced laborers imported during the Third Reich, they were quickly rechristened *Gastarbeiter*, guestworkers. All Germans believed that these guests, who were considered *Ausländer*, foreigners, would eventually return to countries in which they were *zu Hause*, at home. The composition of the guestworkers has also changed over time: in the early sixties, primarily Spanish and Greek, followed by Italian and Yugoslavian, and after 1968, predominantly Turkish. Their numbers increased tenfold between 1965 and 1970. Since 1972, every sixth to eighth child born in the Federal Republic, depending on the year, was born to foreign nationals (Korte 1985: 21). The labor shortage turned into a labor glut by the early eighties, and West Germany then tightened its laws concerning immigrant and refugee rights.[3] Ambivalence about, even hostility to, integrating the guestworkers and their children, many now permanent residents, into the Berlin economy and culture plays a major role in neighborhood and housing politics in contemporary West Berlin (see Mandel 1988).

*'Abgrenzung' and housing policy*
By the early fifties, housing policy in West Berlin, as in the East, was the captive of well-defined political interests, with *Abgrenzungspolitik* a central concern. The Adenauer regime stressed the building of *Eigenheim*, one's own home, which was contrasted with the "eastern collectivism" of the GDR. This ideology set the national tone for housing, even if never realized. A new residential building law in 1956, *Wohnungsbau und Familienheimgesetz*, apartment building and family home law, intended to "eliminate the shortage of residences and . . . create a broad group of the population with widely disseminated property." This would, in the words of Building Minister Paul Lücke, make "consciously responsible citizens out of propertyless proletariat" (Brunhöber 1985: 187). The political intentions of the law could not have been more transparent: keep the population quiet by supporting the nuclear family in private homes.

In West Berlin, however, this federal policy had more rhetorical effect than actual influence on housing practice, for several reasons. First, housing in Berlin has traditionally been structured around rental units that are in some fashion subsidized by the state. West Berlin has the highest ratio of rental households in the FRG: 92 percent, with only 8 percent of the people owning their own homes (one-third of the number in Munich or Hamburg). Second, there was simply little private money for housing in West Berlin while its political status remained in doubt. Hence in 1985, over 50 percent of all existing apartments had been built before 1945, with somewhat less than 20 percent of those built in the nineteenth century. And third, until 1981, West Berlin was for the most part ruled by coalitions led by the opposition Social Democratic Party, which favored social housing over single family homes.[4] Until the mid fifties, Berliners continued to use the phrase *Notwohnung*, meaning temporary housing, and also called housing "not constructed for living use over time." In a society that valued durability and permanence, such language use highlights the unsettled, unstable situation of West Berlin.

Housing construction with direct symbolic intentions began in 1952, with an international competition for a housing project in the Hansa Viertel near Tiergarten. This marked a continuation of the use of Berlin as a showplace for the will and resolve of the West as it demarcated itself from the "totalitarian East Bloc." For such staged dramas, certain sections of the city were selected for resurfacing, and then put on display as a mirror-image to the East. Known as Interbau '57,[5] this competition drew architects from fourteen countries, showing *Verbundenheit mit den Völkern der freien Welt*, Unity with the people of the Free World. The project was initially provoked by the building of Stalin-Allee (now renamed Frankfurter-Allee) in East Berlin, for which building began in earnest in 1953. The new housing in the Hansa Viertel was to showcase the latest in Western architectural design, thus giving evidence of the integration of West Berlin/West Germany into "the West." Building for this *Stadt von Morgen*, city of tomorrow, as it was called, began in 1955, and intensified from 1957 to 1959. Initially thought of as an open competition with several projects in the East, by completion it had lost some of the glamour of competition. Knowing it would lose the competition, and struggling with financial difficulties, East Berlin dropped out of the competition in 1957; hence the initial plan to make the Hansa Viertel a model for all of West Berlin was also subsequently scrapped. Today, these apartment complexes, a combination of sky-scrapers and two-to-four-story units with well-planned green spaces on all sides, remain highly coveted living spaces.

Another showcase housing project was planned in connection with the 250th birthday celebration of the Charlottenburg district of Berlin in 1955. Built from 1953 to 1960, these units were all block apartments six to nine stories high, of the style now internationally looked upon as archetypical fifties. Also in the mid fifties, authorities began building new apartment complexes of four to five stories outside the city; they accelerated this development in the sixties.

By the early sixties, new apartment buildings were increasing in number, growing taller, and destroying the integrity of neighborhoods. Berlin housing authorities, regardless of political orientation, seemed intent on erasing the past rather than building on it. In everyday speech

Table 17. *FRG apartments with bath and toilet, 1950–1978*

| Year | % of total |
|------|------------|
| 1950 | 20 |
| 1960 | 43 |
| 1972 | 82 |
| 1978 | 90 |

Table 18. *FRG apartments with bath, toilet, and central heating, 1960–1982*

| Year | % of total |
|------|------------|
| 1960 | 10 |
| 1965 | 30 |
| 1972 | 41 |
| 1982 | 66 |

*Source:* Vaskovics 1988: 37

West Germans oftentimes use the word *die Vergangenheit*, which means the past, to refer specifically to the Nazi period. The well-known *Sprengprojekt*, demolition project, in the Luisenstadt section of Berlin-Kreuzberg in 1960 so totally destroyed the character of the neighborhood that it was completely unrecognizable to former residents, many of whom, despite the bombed-out nature of the city, had returned to Berlin after the war precisely because of their familiarity with local neighborhoods. High-rise projects outside the city in Reinickendorf, Marienfelde, Tempelhof, and Neukölln took up most public-housing money from 1963 to 1977. This movement became known as the "new brutalism" in architecture because it totally demolished the old and replaced it with new, sterile complexes.

In life reconstructions, sixties architecture was symbolized by three complexes: Gropiusstadt, Falkenhagener Feld, and Märkisches Viertel. Märkisches Viertel in Berlin-Reinickendorf, for example, was completed betewen 1963 and 1974. It contains 16,943 apartments for 45,000 people. These complexes make radical spatial distinctions between private and public space, essentially creating privatized spaces for small nuclear units without providing comparable spaces for public activities. People living in them remain rather isolated from one another, nearly the opposite of the old inner-city Berlin apartment structure, where contact between occupational and class groups was unavoidable, and public and private spaces were in close proximity to one another. In the older, inner-city structures, work and living spaces were often shared by front and back houses of the same complex, and free time could be enjoyed at *Eckkneipen*, local "corner" bars (largely for men), and culture houses near the home within the same district. These high-rise apartments were increasingly populated by the very old and by young adults.

Within the Federal Republic as a whole, the number of apartments more than doubled between 1950 and 1970. The average size of apartments also increased, from 57 square meters in 1950 to 82 square meters in 1981. This growth in the size of apartments was true for all households except those with three or more children, who all along enjoyed considerably less proportional room per person. Not until the late sixties and seventies did the interior of apartments substantially change, with interior toilets, central heating, more flexible use of hobbyrooms, separate kitchens, and separate bedrooms for the children. Tables 17 and 18 illustrate the progressive change for bath, toilets, and central heating. Because West Berlin lags considerably behind the Federal Republic in housing/renovation policy, all these percentages can be assumed to be lower for West Berlin. But the important comparison is always GDR/FRG, East and West. Such comparisons were published regularly in newspapers and periodicals, reminding the West German citizen how much better they have it than their East counterparts. They also become fancier and more elaborate over time. The *Bundesministerium für innerdeutsche Beziehungen* put out a yearly book, *Zahlenspiegel: Ein Vergleich*, for example, where the two Germanies were compared using colored graphics, in, e.g. education systems, preschool care, pensions, military capability, economic power, foreign relations, population size and territory, automobiles, household appliances, free time, and churches.

Although there was steady improvement in living conditions for nearly all parts of the population after 1949, especially of apartment furnishings and household goods, the major boom in new apartment building and renovation did not begin until the seventies – for West Berlin, in the late seventies/early eighties. Despite its tremendous superiority over the GDR in wealth, not until the mid seventies did West Germany as a whole catch up to the apartments-per-person ratio of the GDR. In 1977, the GDR still had 8 percent more apartments per

1,000 residents than did the Federal Republic. The explanation is twofold: the West German territories suffered greater war damage to residential areas, and they absorbed a larger influx of refugees and resettlers from the Eastern territories, and from the GDR itself (Bartholmai and Melzer 1987: 186). And there is a third reason for renovation delay in West Berlin: the insecure political status before 1961 resulted in a capital drain – including skilled labor, industries, and capital for investment – from West Berlin (true also for the entire GDR) to West Germany.

Despite the cheaper cost of renovation in comparison to new construction, city planners together with construction concerns were initially able to carry through expensive, inflation-prone new building projects. Housing policy up to the 1980s was characterized by bulldozing away the past, resulting in the deterioration of the inner city, destruction of the integrity of local neighborhoods, and the creation of new, alienated spaces in skyscrapers outside the city. In 1980, for example, over 10,000 apartments earmarked for demolition stood empty while speculators capitalized on federal financing schemes, and used these "Berlin-Help" programs for tax-write-off purposes. Dissatisfaction with the political response to the shortages in available living spaces culminated in civil protests in the form of a civil rights and squatter's movement, which will be discussed in chapter 8. By 1981, young people were squatting illegally in over 150 houses, much to the horror of most members of Generation I.[6]

Already at the end of the seventies, some politicians in the Federal Republic/West Berlin began to support renovation as a more popular and cheaper housing solution than demolition of the old and the building of new, high-rise complexes. This sentiment eventually made itself felt in policy. Approximately 130,000 renovation and *Sanierung*, sanitation projects (cleaning up the building and "upgrading" or gentrifying the populace), were completed between 1963 and 1977; after 1978, renovations more than doubled in number, with no fewer than 20,000 projects completed in any single year. This increase in renovation paralleled the decrease in new construction; in 1970 for the entire FRG, one-fourth of all new apartments were created through renovation, by the end of the seventies, one-third, by 1985, 40 percent (Bartholmai and Melzer 1987: 185).

The new emphasis on maintaining continuity by renovating old buildings was well suited for postmodern architects. From 1981 to 1989, the Christian-Democrat-controlled government in Berlin concentrated on building a few select new apartments designed by international architects that subsequently won international acclaim for Berlin. This policy did more to showcase Berlin to the outside world than to solve chronic housing shortages. Policy buzzwords included *Nebeneinander*, mixing together the old and the new, with pluralism in form and expression now considered important, *Stadtreparatur und behutsame Stadterneuerung*, repair and careful renewal of the city. The new architecture crystallized around the IBA '87 project, 1987 being the date picked because it coincided with the 750th birthday celebration of Berlin, again a competitive celebration on both sides of the Wall.[7]

The first of the new postmodern housing projects was a pilot study done by Rob Krier in the south Friedrichstraße area of Kreuzberg. Building began in 1978 and as the project area kept expanding, the entire complex was completed in 1988. In addition to many new projects throughout the city, old complexes from the twenties, still considered some of the most attractive, cost-efficient designs available, have been or were being renovated. My own probe by checking names on mailboxes was that one-fifth to a quarter of the residents in the new projects were of non-German origin, one-fifth had hyphenated names, indicating probable Yuppie German "married" couples, and approximately half were German middle- to upper-class couples. There were few single names on most of the mailboxes – which does not foreclose the apartments being registered as single-person households. Today, housing in Berlin is comprised of a dizzying variety of property forms, all in one way or another federally subsidized, ranging from complicated city-supported apartments for unemployed or poor people to city-subsidized renovation for industry or groups of individuals as well as for private building and private housing.

Rental arrangements are still the predominant form of housing in Berlin, although forms of private ownership, supported by the policy initially formulated under Adenauer, are growing slowly. In 1978 in West Berlin, 91.8 percent of all residences were rental apartments (compared to 63.3 percent for the FRG), and 8.2 percent privately owned apartments (36.8 percent for the FRG). This ratio changed by 1988 to 88.8 percent rental/11 percent private in West Berlin (59.9 percent rental/40.1 percent private in the FRG). In terms of age of buildings, conditions of repair, and size of apartments, residences in West Berlin are substantially worse than those in any other part of West Germany. For example, 46.6 percent of all West Berlin apartments are under $60m^2$, the smallest of three official size categories, but only 18 percent in West Germany; 55 percent of all West Berlin apartments were built before 1948 but only 36.7 percent in West Germany; 20.6 percent of all West Berlin apartments were built between 1948 and 1978, but 28.3 percent in West Germany (*Vierter Familienbericht* 1986: 118–119).

Complete state regulation of the rental market continued through the late seventies, when some forms of control were lifted. Most of these controls are supposed to be removed by the early nineties. In 1985, rents averaged 10 to 20 percent of net income for the Federal Republic as a whole, not including water and heat. The tendency, though, was for the percentage of income going to rent to increase rather drastically, from 1972 to 1982, those individuals paying 10 percent or less of their net income for rent decreased by half; those individuals paying 25 percent or more of their net income for rent increased by half *(Materialien zum Bericht* 1987: 537). The elderly I knew complained bitterly about rental increases, though they feared most the anticipated increases after controls are lifted.

**Domestic authority: partnership and childcare**
*Social science enters the discourse on Germanness*
In the early postwar period, domestic authority patterns for members of Generation I were nearly identical in both Berlins. Periodic illness, mostly resulting from war injuries, inadequate food and heating, as well as stress, greatly exacerbated already strained relations within households. By 1950, one out of every eight West Berliners had applied for welfare assistance on the grounds that they were "war victims" – that included, e.g., the disabled and handicapped, widows and widowers, orphans, and indigent parents. By 1952, the number of such victims totaled 199,388, with nearly 70 percent being widows (Albrecht 1986: 202–221). Germans in the West who had cooperated with the Nazis, either actively or passively, often found a refuge for their bruised and battered selves in their own suffering; they garnered a great deal of authority from public recognition that they were also victims of the war, that they, too, had been wronged.

In East Germany the state recognized only official "victims of fascism"; individuals in need were not given special status or care because their neediness derived from war experience alone. In West Germany, authorities concentrated on a small number of "persecuted by the Nazi regime" (which generally replaced the "victims of fascism" label some time before 1952), and then created a much larger category of "victims of war." Whereas the East German regime went about convincing its citizens that the Germans, albeit capitalist-driven ones, were the perpetrators of the war, the West German regime quickly shifted its discourse away from guilt to one of victimization, a labelling that fitted much better the actual circumstances under which most Germans were living at the end of the war, and also did much to assuage actual feelings of guilt; thus it had widespread public resonance that in turn legitimated the regime.

Entering into this official, state-sanctioned discourse on victimization and authority were social scientists and historians.[8] At the end of the war the state of the family and its relation to Nazism were of special concern to West German social scientists and to American occupiers as they debated how to go about denazifying Germany. West German family specialists and politicians were quite aware of the variety of actual kinship practices, but rather than acknowledging this plurality of forms as a creative response to different and difficult circumstances, they chose to evaluate it as something dangerous to the child, and therefore focused on how to bring these living arrangements back into line with familialism (see Rosenbaum 1978). Hence most analyses posited the centrality of the "complete family," and sought to explain how "non-complete families" might become more whole and healthy.

The "emergency situation" of the postwar period, as it was called at the time, was subject to different evaluations by social scientists, which, in turn, fed back into people's conceptions of what they were experiencing. All accounts were influenced by sociologist René König's concept of "family disintegration and disorganization," although people used his findings to support opposite conclusions. In his 1946 study, König claimed that "disintegration" marked the family's relation to the total society; the family had lost functions, shifting from a production to a consumption unit, and lost its security functions to the school and state. Furthermore, the family had now been reduced to its smallest possible size, the nuclear unit (married pair–child relationship). Family "disorganization" referred to effects of the war: the large number of widows, POWs, deserters, the increase in divorce. König warned against *überlebten Patriarchalismus*, outlived patriarchy, on the one hand, and *mütterliche Überorganisation*, motherly over-organization, on the other, as threats to family stability.

Other accounts were less differentiated than König's. Hilde Thurnwald (1948) saw the emergency situation as threatening to the family *per se*, and she was pessimistic about how to overcome it. Helmut Schelsky

(1954: 63),[9] perhaps the most influential postwar family sociologist, and Gerhard Wurzbacher (1954) saw the family as being strengthened through this disorganization, for it was forced to take on significant functions as a reaction to social disorganization, which then brought family members closer together. Schelsky was correct in observing a retreat from public life (what I would more generally call a self-flight) among members of Generation I, but the retreat did not, as he maintained, strengthen domestic ties. Although the ideology of familialism remained dominant until the late sixties/early seventies, people found it difficult to realize this model for any length of time.

In reaction to these social-science descriptions of familial disorganization, the West German state and church, in particular, felt themselves confirmed in their prescriptions, motivated by a fantasy of the *Hausfrauenehe*, a stagnant, unchanging family-love unit that would recreate order and prosperity, and restore morality to the Germans. This official discourse was directed primarily to controlling the behavior of women and children, much as it was in the East, but with one major exception: the intention was not to create a new family form but to reassert traditional authority patterns – return women to the home and reduce child and youth behavior to a model more closely corresponding to expected behavior for their chronological age. These political and social scientific judgements influenced domestic life not by describing a reality and reflecting it back to the public, but by evaluating the variety of forms in such a way as to condemn practices that didn't conform to the preferred model. This model – the *Hausfrauenehe* – was then propagated in the media and remained for members of Generation I the litmus test by which they measured their own practices.[10]

According to the official logic of the early fifties, generally shared by social scientists and statesmen, the Cold War struggle required a healthy, normal individual to resist the sirens of communist ideology, variously called "Bolshevism" and "Sovietization." Family life in the West was considered a representation of the state's model, a negative image of family life in the East. In the words of Helmut Schelsky, "the isolated individual [would become] partner and foundation for the shape of the society, especially for the state and political life" (cited in Ruhl 1988: 134). Unlike East German authorities, who initially politicized and resignified the public domain, West German authorities politicized private life as it served the interests of public representations.[11] In both states, everyday life was asked to yield to the dictates of the Cold War. Of course, the costs of these dictates were much greater in the poorer and weaker GDR.

Pedagogue William Tebbe, in a book about the intellectual and character development of schoolchildren published in 1950, spells this out more concretely:

> With the founding of a family a parallel is created with the law of the state. This is a necessary development to support; its mandate must be followed if one does not want to harm oneself and others . . . The relationship of the state to the people asks for serving submission and selfless achievement – but one finds no deepening of this relationship in this age group [12–13 years old]. Rather, one can see a regressive development, in which the child often looks at the state as if he should be served by it.                                    *(cited in Baumert 1952: 778)*

There is a great deal of continuity between Tebbe's prescriptions and those of Nazi authorities.[12] Tebbe was no doubt correct in noticing a skepticism of the youth *vis-à-vis* founding a family and serving the state; but he immediately evaluates that development as "regressive," and pleads that in the tenth grade (children of age sixteen) the founding of nuclear families should be encouraged so that the authority model appropriate for a healthy state–citizen relationship will have been learned. Gerhard Baumert, in his 1950 study of youths in Darmstadt, West Germany, cites the Tebbe research, and concludes that Tebbe's proposed authority model is, in fact, one of several found among teachers in his study. For Baumert, a student of Adorno and critic of the official line, the most important factors in the development of a child are the education in the family and the school, and the kind of relationship between the two institutions (1952: 778).

Americans as occupiers were also busy interpreting the changes in German sources of allegiance, primarily in their political activities and family practices. Studies of the internal structure of German families shortly after the war by two American scholars reached what seem to be diametrically opposite conclusions. David Rodnick writes in 1948: "The father's role, during the early formative years of childhood, is secondary to that of the mother, who occupies an extremely high position within German Protestant culture. In all classes, the education of the young, the training in cultural behavior, and the implanting of goals are more within the domain of the mother than of the father" (1948: 27). Reaching exactly opposite conclusions, Bertram Schaffner writes in 1949: "Family life revolves around the figure of the father. He is omnipotent, omniscient and omnipresent, as far as this is possible for a human being. He is the source of all the authority, all the security, and all the wisdom that his children expect to receive. Every other member of the family has lower status and lesser rights than his" (1949: 15).

The two American accounts can be reconciled if we distinguish between ideology and practice, the role of the father in the imaginary world and of the mother in practice. Schaffner projects stereotypes of the patriarchal German family type from the late nineteenth century onto present patterns. Rodnick measures German *practices* according to the regnant nuclear family model in the United States; he generalizes from childcare patterns to personality structure without also taking into account the role of family ideology and actual household/residential patterns. Schaffner describes a family *ideology*, at that time in direct conflict with actual practices, without also looking at actual patterns of partnership, childcare, and residence.

Baumert clarifies the discrepancy between the two American studies as follows. First, the patriarchal family type exists only for certain families, and not for the majority. Second, the authority of the father may remain decisive and omnipresent, even when the father isn't actually present, because the mother exercises her authority only as the representative of the father. She does this by threatening in his name, "I'll tell your father if you aren't good!" (1952: 79). He concludes that in Darmstadt, the mother dominates in childcare and in caring about education; the father exercises the most influence in the training/ occupational choice of the child. He makes another distinction between lower-class children and those of the upper and middle classes: the former are raised to be dependent on the parents for a longer period of time; the latter are raised to be more independent. Another difference: in the former the mother tends to give the corporal punishment, in the latter it is the father that disciplines (1952: 83, 85). But Baumert's voice, however insightful it sounds in retrospect, was not widely heard; it did not have much influence on the official social-scientific discourse on the state of being German and the policy of the state.

*Household, marriage, sex, and the domestic group*
Although similar factors were at play in families during the postwar period, the configuration of the domestic group in East and West Berlin took quite different gestalts, primarily due to the different master narratives of the state. For West Germans, in opposition to their East German counterparts, it was a process of restoration rather than construction, and an hierarchical assimilation rather than an egalitarian

integration. Of the kinship groups that survived the war intact, the upper classes and the more conservative, reactionary groups in the population were over-represented compared to the liberal-progressive or revolutionary groups. "The upperclass, overwhelmingly conservative and anti-progressive in their actual opinions and values, is the most strongly represented," comments Gerhardt Baumert in his 1954 study. "That means, the elements who have the will to socially improve and who through their development have a revolutionizing effect are in the [West] German postwar society relatively poorly represented" (1954: 40). These factors are quite different in East Germany, where land reform initiated by the Soviets in 1945 and carried out in the subsequent years drove many politically conservative groups to West Berlin/FRG. The large number of refugee families also experienced different fates in the two Berlins: although generally suffering a downgrading in their status, in the East they were desperately needed as labor; in the West, they were often slowly assimilated, for they had to wait until the labor market expanded enough to absorb them.

The changing relationship of residential form to the domestic group affected relations between kin and non-kin and between household form and marital status. The life history of Klara, a former *Trümmer-frau* born in 1927, provides one illustration of how these complex interactions change over a lifecourse. She was the younger of two children, raised by a "hysterical, unloving mother" and a father who was a Nazi Party member, in a "good bourgeois family" in Berlin. Shortly after the Soviet occupation of Berlin, she left her family (living in the Eastern half of the city) out of fear that she would be sent to a Russian forced-labor camp, and fled to West Berlin. Her mother, still living in the East, then denounced her father as a Nazi to the Russians, who sent him to the former concentration camp Buchenwald, just north of Berlin. In West Berlin, Klara immediately "fell in love" with an Irish soldier, a member of the British occupation force, moved into an apartment with him and had his child. After three years, the soldier was sent back to Ireland. Klara was to follow him, but suddenly discovered that he was married with four children. She then had no option but to remain in Germany.

In order to "find a father for the child," something that remained important in West Berlin through the mid seventies, she immediately found a German man to marry. The family – mother, child, and stepfather – moved in the early fifties to a small town in West Germany "to get a new start." As her new husband could find no work, he moved to a larger city, Hamburg, and secured loans to open up a gas station, leaving Klara with old debts and her child. She moved into a shelter for homeless people and shortly thereafter found her own housing. In the late seventies, she married a second time, to a widower with a daughter. This husband died ten years later, whereafter Klara continued to raise her stepdaughter – her own child was long gone from her household. The stepdaughter left Klara's household around 1984. Thereafter, Klara began suffering from "psychosomatic disturbances," and joined the Grey Panthers, who, she said, were helping her find new direction (Unruh 1987: 32).

In the course of her life, Klara had lived with her parents and a sibling for seventeen years, then in a public shelter, then in a series of apartments alternately as a mistress, a married wife with husband, and a divorced mother. She had lived in three heterosexual partnerships (also sexual unions) in three cities, and had been married to two of the men (one out of loneliness, the second in order to legitimate her child). The one man whom she loved and with whom she had shared a residence was a foreign national already married to someone else. It would be exaggerated, though not incorrect, to characterize Klara's postwar motivations as a desire to retreat *from* public life, but it is, in fact, quite incorrect to claim that she retreated *to* a domestic life with strong nuclear familial patterns, as Schelsky, along with other West German social scientists, has argued.

The approximately 3:2 ratio of women to men among Generation I certainly influenced their partnership patterns, but even more important in West Germany was the role of the *Hausfrauenehe*. The expectation of men and women that they would find fulfillment in a state-sanctioned marriage, even though this idea was often at odds with their experience, resulted in a peculiar kind of psychological dependence of Generation I women on men. "The important thing for our mothers was to have a man – any man will do, so long as he's a man," explained Dorine T., a West Berlin woman of Generation II. For many of the women of Generation I, this man no longer needed to be around much, nor need he even be living, in order for them to approximate their ideal selves. Maintaining dead/missing husband marriages, which I discuss in chapter 9, and divorcee statuses (as opposed to being a "single woman") were quite common responses to this situation. Despite the high divorce rate in the early fifties, most of the men from these divorces found new wives if they wanted them. Most of the women did not – there weren't enough men to go round. And unlike their East German counterparts, they encountered many more obstacles in integrating themselves into the workplace. Several married women told me how they always had to watch over their men in the presence of other women, for there were so few men that even unattractive types were considered valuable.

One of the responses of women was to raise their sons to take the place of the husband in a kind of marriage-without-sex relationship. Dorine continued, "The sex probably wouldn't work out between them anyway [if women in their 70s found a husband their age], and the sons don't make those kind of sexual demands on their mother – and they're more faithful than would be the husbands." Mothers with this kind of partnership ideal used two kinds of strategies to keep their sons tied to them: they made them feel guilty and they spoiled them. One man in his forties, for example, now divorced with a twenty-year-old daughter, found an apartment three minutes from his mother. She cooked for him three times a day, took care of him when sick, listened to him without ever contradicting him. Another friend of mine reported that his mother always chided him for not visiting her enough, even though he saw her at least once a week. He said he won't invite her to his apartment anymore because she complains too much about how dirty it is.

Daughters of members of Generation I had a quite different set of ties to their mothers and fathers. Usually their fathers were now dead, and when not, they rarely mentioned them. They visited their mothers regularly – they said out of obligation and not choice – and their mothers expected care and comfort from them. Several women of Generation II reported to me that their mothers often took the side of the son-in-law over the daughter, admonishing their daughters, "Consider yourself lucky to have a man."

To be sure, not all women succumbed to the pressure to desire housewifery. Another prevalent pattern in response to the lack of men was simply to adjust to males as secondary and non-stable kin. Frau Friedrich, born in 1923, lived with her brother and mother in the postwar years, and never herself married. She explained,

That's right, the lack of men was naturally a condition then, but I never really worried about it, for I couldn't do anything about it anyway. Actually, I had a friend now and then, but when you live with your mother and little brother together, then you cannot bring a friend home with you into a two-room apartment. When you need a man, you don't have to marry him right away. You don't have to buy a cow right away, when you want to drink a little milk.

*(Meyer and Schulze 1984: 169–170)*

Frau Freidrich illustrates an interesting pattern in that she was independent of a husband, but still able to maintain fulfilling relations, including sexual ones, with men.

### Inheritance and intergenerational contact

Much as in the East, the role of inheritance changed drastically after the end of the war, diminishing in its significance for holding the generations together. Perhaps the major factor in this was the postwar change in the nature of property, whereby education and access to education for youth became "property" equal in value, in many cases, to what could be inherited from parents. Hence "success" was no longer contingent primarily on parental status and support. A second factor was that the war had destroyed so much property that new forms of wealth accumulation competed with more traditional prewar patterns. Yet in West Berlin/West Germany prewar inheritance patterns that privileged the son over the daughter within families continued to play a role, if primarily an ideological one, in structuring domestic authority.

With regard to parental expectations of sons in complete families, Baumert explains, "A dissimilar, more important role is played by the son in the attitudes of the parents. He is the *Stammhalter*, the heir of the property and tradition; he embodies the future to the parents, the status climbing or downgrading of the family" (1952: 109). What Baumert noticed in the fifties is no longer commented upon in the eighties. In those intervening thirty years the relationship between the generations changed drastically, as we shall see in chapter 8. Why this is so has much to do with the way in which the two generations differed in dealing with the Nazi past. Arne W. of Generation I described his relationship to his son in these terms:

He has his own life. I don't always approve of it. It was so easy for him to accuse me of being a Nazi and of all the things that happened back then. As if I did it all . . . I don't have much inheritance, the family lost everything in the war, but I gave him a better education than I myself had. That he decided not to make much of it – couldn't keep his wife, no steady job – well, that's his life.

It was apparent from Arne's statement that he did not have the amount of control or influence over his son he would like, which he in part attributed to the small inheritance he had to leave his son. Yet, as we shall see in chapter 8 many members of Generation II still very much calculated inheritance and other forms of direct financial aid from their parents into their lifecourse plans, though they were no longer dependent on them for life chances.

While the significance of inheritance in partnership patterns and intergenerational contacts did not develop as Baumert described it in the early fifties, it continued to play an important, though no longer dominant, role in determining a lifecourse or shaping relations between Generation I, their children, and grandchildren. Approximately 5 percent of all parents gave financial help to their children who no longer lived with them. A 1967 study found that the aid was much greater to single or divorced mothers – 30 percent of these daughters received aid for two to five years, 17 percent for more than five years. As for inheritance after death, from 1960 to 1981, 8.5 percent of all households in the FRG had an inheritance to leave for their children; the average actually left was 1,000 DM ($500). This inheritance was heavily concentrated among the wealthy, however, with 20 percent of the people inheriting 73 percent of the total amount (cited in *Vierter Familienbericht* 1986: 84–85). Because of West Berlin's physical separation from the mainland, and its weaker financial base, it is likely that the above-quoted percentages for Berlin are smaller. In East Berlin, policy oriented to eliminate the controlling role of property radically diminished the ability of men and women of Generation I to control their children through inheritance; it was thus rarely mentioned as a factor in their reconstructions.

Contact between the generations in West Berlin was also fostered through grandparent–grandchild relations. Due to the lack of adequate daycare in West Berlin (though still far superior to that in the Federal Republic), especially for the middle and lower classes, Generation I in West Berlin continued to play a significant role in directly shaping the lifecourse of their children and grandchildren, a proportionately greater material role than for their counterparts in East Berlin. Grandmothers did this through household help and the care of grandchildren (public childcare was not as well developed as in the GDR). A federal study in the mid seventies found that 46 percent of all children under three whose mothers worked were cared for by the grandparents – only 4 percent were in daycare centers. A 1980 federal study found that 23 percent of all women aged between the ages of forty-five and sixty (born between 1920 and 1945) regularly took care of their grandchildren. There is evidence that this percentage increased for older women (between the ages of sixty-five and eighty). Grandmothers also performed a great deal of housework for their daughters – anywhere from

10 to 50 percent (depending on the study) of all grandmothers aided in their daughters' housework (*Vierter Familienbericht* 1986: 84–85). Hence intergenerational contact, however strained at times, continued primarily through the medium of a third generation, even though inheritance and the emotional bonds formerly tied to this form of property exchange no longer had the significance they once did.

**Domestic life as political history: events, work, and prosperity**
Within two years of the German defeat, the early discourse on victimization was supplemented by what were to become even more important experiential tropes: prosperity within the community and aggressive demarcation from the (increasingly nonprosperous) East.[13] With the warming of the Cold War, the Allies in the Western Zones relaxed their enforcement of the Potsdam Accords (democratization, demilitarization, denazification, land reform), and shifted efforts from the restructuring of an authoritarian society to the cultivation of a Cold War mentality and economic development in the form of Marshall Plan aid (see Tent 1982; Niethammer 1988b). This shift in policy locus, from domestic affairs to the domain of work and international demarcation, did not leave the family untouched, but rather thrust it into a different set of contexts. We will review here the way in which a series of international events – the Currency Reform of 1948, the Blockade and the Airlift of 1948–1949, and the Wall of 1961 – became mythologized in the narratives of West Berlin citizens. These events of state were the periods of domestic life for Generation I.

*The Currency Reform of 1948: anti-communism and the restructuring of employment*
Before the return of adult men from the POW camps, women were primarily responsible for care of the domestic unit and for *Trümmer-arbeit* – the necessary clearing away of the debris from the war. The extreme self-reliance of women of Generation I in this period was counterbalanced by two dependency patterns formally encouraged by West German authorities. First, women assumed an in-waiting attitude: they believed their activity to be temporary – or so they told their children and themselves; the return of their adult men would allow them to concentrate on the home and on "women's work." The satiric state facilitated this behavior by propagating the *Hausfrauenehe*, a nostalgic cultivation of a past ideal that strongly contrasted with postwar practice. Children of those women who did work outside the home were

mythologized as *Schlüsselkinder* (children wearing a key around their necks), pitiful creatures who carried a key to open the house door when they returned from school, for nobody was waiting to let them in – the working mother often returned home later than her children. They were especially pitied because they had to cook for themselves (at that time mothers were to cook for children in Germany), and thus were assumed to be undernourished. Second, women were particularly dependent on their half-grown children, notably the eldest son (when they had one), for help with black-market activity necessary for support of the domestic group.

"My son was only eleven years old at that time, but he could trade," commented Gerda Hoffmann. "I couldn't use the black market, I was just too dumb. But I could rely on my son. [Somehow he would find the necessary exchange goods.] I was no great racketeer, but I was a learned *Hamsterer* [dealer/gatherer]. In this way in the end we had more provisions than we could get from our Berlin ration cards" (Meyer and Schulze 1985: 101). Gerda's comments were typically self-deprecating: she could only cope because of her son's capabilities; she herself had none. She was living for and through him. These women engaged reluctantly in the black market, many considering it shameful and degrading.

In 1947, approximately 85 percent of the Berlin population were involved in black-market activity (Meyer and Schulze 1984: 102). The key words of the time, we recall, were gathering, organizing, coming upon things, being entrepreneurial, and pilfering coal. The female-organized trading networks were inner- and intra-city businesses. The activity soon became normalized, and many women began to take pride in how well they worked the black market. From the perspective of the government and the majority of citizens, the provision of basic necessities in West Germany and West Berlin was not improving noticeably enough. The black markets themselves were undermining the value of the official currency. Four out of five West Germans were considered officially undernourished – and the rate was higher in West Berlin. Worker strikes in West Berlin and West Germany, due to dissatisfaction with the food supply, worried government officials and the Western Allies. The American response was to force the cautious Adenauer regime into a surprise Currency Reform, for which it then took total credit (see Friedrich 1988). Citizens woke up on the morning of June 17, 1948, to stores full of goods, and each person received 50 DM from the state with which to buy something.

While the Currency Reform eliminated major shortages and effectively dried up most black-market activity, it did not make the goods equally available to all – the majority of people still hadn't enough money to buy them. Unlike in the East, where egalitarian distribution linked to a productivist metaphor was a major form of policy legitimation, in the West self-initiative and productivity were linked; distribution remained a secondary theme. (The later emphasis on a "social-[oriented], market economy" did indeed lead to the construction of a massive welfare state, but the goal was to eliminate the extremes of poverty, and not to achieve an egalitarian, classless society.) Thus, many women and children, especially those with large families, continued to rely on black-market activities to supplement their official food rations. Medicines for sick relatives, for example, were rarely available except through goods or money obtained on the black market. For West Berliners this meant going to East Berlin or the GDR to buy subsidized goods, the sales of which were still regulated by a quota system for their own citizens. Scarce goods were readily and cheaply available *drüben*, over there, for the valued D-Mark. Furthermore, many Berliners tended small gardens for vegetables and potatoes to supplement their official quotas. Because of poverty, unemployment, and housing shortages, youth, remained in domestic units with their parents and postponed planned marriages for several years, putting extra pressure on the partnerships of their parents.

In both Berlins, the vast majority of all fathers eventually returned to their families, at least for a brief period. From the perspective of returning men, reintegration into home and society was complicated by the fight for jobs and the loss of authority, due partly to the humiliation of defeat in the war and partly to the autonomy of action their wives had attained in their absence. The major difference between East and West men's narratives was in how they spoke about this change in authority. Men in the East problematized their loss of authority much more than did those in the West. I suspect this is because more men in the West benefited from the kinship and employment policies that later restored their authority. In their reconstructions, West Berlin men tended to report an end to their struggles as their labor slowly created the economic miracle and prosperity.

### The Blockade and the Airlift of 1948 to 1949

Here we must backtrack slightly and contextualize the citizen's narrative, for several significant events, obliquely mentioned in their stories, precipitated the Currency Reform. In response to the Western Allied decision on February 23, 1948, in the London Six-Power Conference to integrate West Germany economically into Western Europe, the Soviets began a small-scale blockade on April 1. The limited blockade ended any remaining goodwill between the Allies, hardening the differences between the American-dominated West and Soviet East. The civilian populations continued to have contact with each other across the sectors, but the blockade also reinforced all the anti-communist political rhetoric in the West. West Berliners felt strengthened in their image of themselves as victims, and of the East Zone as Bolshevik controlled.

The Marshall Plan, announced on April 16, 1948, followed by the Western Currency Reform on June 18 to 21, 1948, raised the stakes and left the Soviets with no alternatives other than acquiescence or continued use of force. On the positive side for West Berliners, however, the Soviet Blockade essentially completed the job of drying up black marketing for the West Berlin authorities, for it resulted in increased military control between the sectors. These two events – the Currency Reform and the "small" Soviet Blockade – resulted in an immediate decline in the standard-of-living for households primarily dependent on black-market activities (mostly poor, unskilled, female-headed), and a more gradual worsening of the situation for some others. A small number of households benefited immediately from both events. The Soviets escalated the conflict in what Germans call the *Großblockade*, the Great Blockade, on June 23 and 24. In their reconstructions, members of Generation I periodized their narratives without mentioning the "Small Blockade": they used the sequence: Currency Reform, Great Blockade, Airlift – the founding of the state was omitted.

Western Allies responded to the Blockade with an Airlift, concentrating on basic necessities: a steady supply of milkpowder for children, dried potatoes, and, as Berliners were quick to mention, "a cup of coffee every ten days." The Airlift, immediately mythologized as *die Luftbrücke*, cemented a positive relationship between West Berliners of Generation I and the Western Allies – a trusting, deferent relationship that still plays a role in this generation's attitudes. Conversely, the event embittered Berliners even more against the Soviets, convincing them that the fight against the Soviets in World War II had not been in vain. The Russians were still the enemy, threatening German *Lebensraum*, room for living. West Berlin interview partners of Generation I turned to the Currency Reform as a point of internal (German–German) demarcation, to the Blockade as a point of external (German–Russia) demarcation.

The Blockade lasted from June 1948 to May 1949. Insecurity concerning the status of West Berlin led many firms to move to West Germany, increasing the number of unemployed from 47,000 to 137,000 in less than a year. The majority of those to lose their jobs were the unskilled and the least experienced – above all, women. Unlike policy in the Soviet Zone, Western Allies did not pass an equal protection clause for women. Returning war veterans were, in fact, officially favored for jobs. This combination of events – the Currency Reform, Blockade, and return of POWs – forced many women to take lower-paying jobs in order to remain employed. Single women and single mothers were especially hard hit by the preference for and priority given to men in the workforce. Immediately after the war, it was quite common for women to work in formerly male-only occupations, such as in construction or public transportation. In 1946, for example, 49,711 West Berlin women were employed as construction workers or aids; by the end of 1950 the number had dropped to 11,146 (Meyer and Schulze 1984: 138). Within five years of the end of the war, sex-specific public-employment policies in West Berlin/West Germany had already begun to track the lifecourse of women and men differently. In reaction to the vacillation in public policy, between incorporating women as equals into the workforce and overtly discriminating against them, neither private employers nor families made clear decisions regarding the role women were to play in public life. Unlike their East German counterparts, most West German women of Generation I began at this time to consider their life goals in terms of the vagaries of labor-market policies and to subordinate their active participation in public life to that of male relatives. The lifecourse of these women in West Berlin began already in 1948 to differ clearly from that of women of Generation I in East Berlin.

Lifting the Blockade slowed down the exodus of West Berlin firms to West Germany, and extreme shortages in foodstuffs quickly disappeared. Elimination of food-rationing coupons on March 1, 1950, marked the official end of black-market trading within West Berlin and between West Berlin and West Germany. (Food rationing continued in East Germany for another five years.) Thereafter, only continued shortages in the East and disparities between East and West currency evaluations created the conditions for smuggling and other forms of illegal trading. Illegal trading after the Currency Reform was, however, no longer an activity for women and children, but primarily controlled by adult males. Throughout the 1950s, the GDR – in its need for "hard" currency (D-Mark) – encouraged West Berliners to buy East-produced goods, thus legalizing many kinds of exchange, but at the same time the West Berlin Senat tried to discourage people from buying in East Berlin, for this buying, in turn, dried up demand for goods and services in West Berlin. The situation was quite destabilizing for both economies, though ultimately working to the benefit of individual West Berliners. Such West Berlin buying practices continued through the eighties, two of the favorites being haircuts and subsidized children's toys in East Berlin.

A final event used to categorize this period was the *Freßwelle*, gorging frenzy, which most people experienced first in the mid fifties.[14] A hunger trope is elaborated in this display of conspicuous eating, but food as a symbol had additional figurative uses in the narratives of women and men. In the early fifties, many women obtained food from the Allies in exchange for sexual and other services. (And one should not forget the humiliating work before 1950 as *Trümmerfrau*). The *Freßwelle* comes later, and marks a clean break with this kind of hunger, in that people now could gorge themselves ritually on what they had earned though *anständige Arbeit*, respectable work. It marked the conjuncture of work and prosperity, two postwar identity tropes of West Berliners. Both food and prosperity took on qualities partaking of the sacred, with a significance that transcended the context in which they were experienced.

Germans called the *Freßwelle* a *Nachholbedarf*, catching up on a need. For both men and women, red meat was perhaps the most important thing to *fressen*, and descriptions of such gatherings where everyone gorged themselves invariably centred around diverse and plentiful supplies of pork, sausages, and beef, in that order. Those who experienced the *Freßwelle* in the fifties, whether of Generation I or II, continued to find it difficult to throw away leftovers from a meal, or to leave the table without cleaning their plate. Following upon the heels of the Blockade and Airlift, the eating orgy was in a sense a cultural response to the historical fear of the Germans of being surrounded and blocked. West Berliners experienced the Blockade as an incredible trauma, and the oral orgy following it is often jokingly acknowledged as a reward for having survived.

*The Wall and the economic miracle: gendered work and differential prosperity for all*

The West German *Wirtschaftswunder* of the fifties did not significantly affect the domestic lives of most West Berliners until at least a decade later. Only with the building of the Wall by the GDR in 1961 did the defection of businesses from West Berlin to West Germany slow down. At that time West Berlin finally had the chance to become a stable political and economic entity, within which rational, long-term economic planning could take place. For most West Berliners, the availability of goods through the capitalist market system in the fifties had a symbolic meaning of differentiating themselves as a group from the East Germans. But only after most people could afford to purchase the goods did prosperity also become a trope which identified them and with which they identified. The significance of these two aspects of identity – demarcation from the East and prosperity – should not be underestimated. They were central to the sense of self, to the Germanness, of this generation of West Germans since the end of the war. The Wall, much like the *Freßwelle*, was for them a central marker in their postwar identity construction. In constructing a sense of belonging, the Wall periodized their lives by exclusion, the *Freßwelle* categorized them by inclusion.

Not seldom, the substantial fruits of the *Wirtschaftswunder* began to trickle down first in the seventies. "It was still always tight until 1960," reported Charlotte Wagner, "although it [my work] provided a little security for me, my son, and my mother. That the prosperity had suddenly broken loose, erupted, as they say – we had to wait until 1970 to experience that." In the immediate postwar years, Charlotte began working in the construction industry, finally acquiring knowledge and skills to perform at the level of engineer.

I found it difficult. But then I became quite occupied by the fact that women had always earned less then men. I had performed the same work as my colleague – no, not the same, even better work. But he had earned more. He was a man. I found that uniquely unfair and I told that to my boss. First nothing happened, no reaction. It took a while before it got under my collar. Then I erupted. I threw a fit because it was so unfair. I went to the top, and then finally got what I deserved. Then I was placed approximately in the same position as my colleagues. I had [during this time] a child to raise and my aging mother to take care of. *(Meyer and Schulze 1984: 55, 56)*

After telling us about her fight for comparable worth in the workplace, Charlotte immediately reverted back to a description of her activities in the household, care for her mother and child. To her, domestic life remained the central core around which other activities took on meaning.

Status in the workplace during the fifties and sixties was the major field in which hierarchical assimilation of Generation I took place. From

1950 to 1960, employment in West Berlin/West Germany grew phenomenally, at nearly the same rate both in the public and the private sector, with official unemployment totaling less than 1 percent by 1960. Yet these numbers hide the sex-specific aspects of employment policies, and the part-time and low-skilled nature of most female employment. One indication of this is that the public sector, which employed a much higher percentage of highly educated workers than the private sector (in 1980, 62 percent of all highly educated persons worked in the public sector), also employed 13 percent fewer women than men (Schmidt and Rose 1985: 126–162). Unlike in East Germany, women of Generation I in West Berlin had little or no opportunity for education or training after the war. Of West German women born in 1901, 70 percent remained unskilled; of women born in 1925, 49 percent remained unskilled. Thus there was considerable educational improvement among the younger members of Generation I. Yet only 13 percent of women born in 1901 reached middle and upper-educational levels, and a modest 18 percent of the 1925 cohort did so. The increase at the middle and upper levels was merely 5 percent. Until the late sixties, most West Berlin women remained concentrated in sales and secretarial work (for those who acquired skills) and house cleaning for those who did not. In 1989, the pensions of women in the FRG were much lower than those of their male counterparts, in large part due precisely to their lower earning power after the war (*Vierter Familienbericht* 1986: 41–43). Moreover, those who did have steady employment often stressed guilt feelings for neglecting their *Schlüsselkinder* rather than pride over their own labor accomplishments.

Consequently men narrated their major lifecourse transformations from soldier to POW to unemployed male to employed male. Women, on the other hand, stressed the transformation from daughter to mother, with alternating combinations of wife, unmarried or divorced woman, and worker creating secondary roles and marginal statuses. From 1945 to 1989, employment policy in West Berlin was characterized by a consistent hierarchy ranked by prestige accorded to sex, age, and marital statuses: married adult men, single or divorced adult men, young unmarried men, divorced mothers, single women, married women.

While work remained central to the identities of men of Generation I, women in their narratives never reported the same kind of investment in work outside the home. Although the concept of work should be analytically broadened to include other types of activity necessary for support, such as *hamstern* in the early postwar period, women themselves did not evaluate this activity as on a par with regular public employment. Baumert's 1952 study found that in over 50 percent of all households all of the income was used for life support, and "the mother controls the money in the household" (1952: 64). Throughout the postwar years, women were in fact making important contributions to "family income," and did not always relinquish control over the household budget. However, not until 1977 did women in West Germany begin to enjoy legal rights in the workplace comparable to those of their East German peers. Consequently, it is to be expected that a significantly higher percentage of East Berlin women, supported by the state, invested more of themselves in public work. West Berlin women, on the other hand, had fewer positive experiences outside the home, with an ambivalent if not actively antagonistic state negatively emplotting their work experience.

*Symbols of Germanness (West):* **Persilschein,** *automobiles, consumer goods, and free time/vacation*
In narrating their lives, men and women of Generation I made use of four symbols, which, in the context of a life construction, are subsumed under the general tropes of anti-communism and prosperity. Categories with material or ideological referents, these items included: the *Persilschein*, automobile, consumer goods, and free time/vacation. Not only did they serve to categorize and name experience, but also they periodized the lifecourse, helping to create a common generational narrative out of very disparate lives. To the extent that this generational narrative coheres, it speaks to the political legitimacy of the group. Let us deal with each symbol and trope separately.

Primarily limited to Nazi Party members, the process of denazification in West Berlin was not experienced in any standard way. Yet ideally each member of Generation I who went through this process defined themselves with reference to a coveted *Persilschein* (a comparable American euphemism would be a Tide certificate). The Allies didn't actually give out such certificates, but they did assert whether individuals had been denazified, after which Germans themselves referred to their "being clean" and having obtained a *Persilschein*. This period of denazification lasted, for the most part, until May 11, 1951. On that date, the "131 Law" passed by the West German parliament took effect, granting all former Nazi Party members an amnesty. Whether or not the "131 Law" directly applied to oneself, its effect was to demarcate officially the end of the *Naziriecherei* (search for the smell of Nazis) as Chancellor Adenauer once dubbed it, and the beginning of a new, postwar sense of being German. Then in 1954, with the West German victory in the World Soccer Championship, the slogan *Wir sind wieder wer* – we're somebody again – took on the status of a kind of proof to many Germans (West) that they also were good and worthy – and the "the past" was behind them.

Individuals began enjoying the fruits of the *Wirtschaftswunder* by buying consumer goods, which were now used to periodize the life-course retrospectively. Women's and men's narratives differed only in which consumer goods were named, with the women more often referring to household appliances and the men nearly always to automobiles. Sometimes the radio was mentioned in the 1950s; the purchase of a television was nearly always an important date in the 1960s or 1970s. While over half of all West German households had no television until 1965, 95 percent owned one by 1978 (Maase 1985: 220–221). West Berliners used material goods much more frequently to periodize the lifecourse than did their peers in East Berlin. The use of consumer items to periodize an autobiography illustrates the success of the particular type of politicization – integration into West consumer culture – desired by postwar West German governments. It categorized everyday life in terms of economic categories the parameters of which were set by the state. To remember personal history in terms of categories and periods created by the *Wirtschaftswunder* legitimated the narrative of the West German state. West Berliners of Generation I tended to omit from their narratives any mention of political participation not choreographed by the state. In other words, even elements of dissatisfaction with work, former strikes, the mass demonstrations in the fifties against rearmament and for a more effective reunification policy, were not part of life histories, most likely because those actions were not legitimated by subsequent History, that is, the history of the state's official narrative (see Schöll 1985: 82–91).

The significance of the automobile (a West German brand, of course) lay in its allegorical qualities for the postwar West German self; it demarcated West from East and it displayed Germanness as perceived in the West. In nearly all the accounts of domestic life related to me, the purchase of the first automobile (usually Volkswagen) along with reference to other well-made West German models (especially Mercedes and BMW), most of which were initially available only for the well-to-do, was an important rhetorical device. In East Germany, the

Table 19. *Private automobiles per household in the FRG 1950–1985*

| Year | % of households |
|------|-----------------|
| 1950 | 1 |
| 1955 | 5 |
| 1959 | 20 |
| 1965 | 36 |
| 1969 | 50 |
| 1978 | 62 |
| 1985 | 83 |

*Source:* Maase 1985: 220; *Zahlenspiegel* 1988: 9; Engelmann 1981: 56–57)

most widely produced and owned car was the small, heavy-polluting, state-produced, two-cylinder Trabant, made purely for domestic consumption. It was banned in most European countries because it did not fulfill safety or environmental standards, making it expensive if not impossible for GDR citizens to travel abroad (see Borneman 1992). Private-car ownership in West Germany increased steadily since the war. Of all households, as can be seen in table 19, 1 percent had a private car in 1950, 20 percent in 1959, 50 percent in 1969, and 83 percent in 1985. By comparison, in 1985 only 48 percent of all East German households owned private cars as opposed to the 83 percent in the FRG (*Zahlenspiegel* 1988: 79).

In the sixties and seventies the auto took on an additional meaning for the masses, one which it already had for the well-to-do in the fifties, as a symbol of escape beyond Berlin and West Germany, of being able to flee Germany (and in a sense, flee the German self).[15] As has often been noted about tourists from all Western countries, Germans being no exception, having fled their home context seemingly to "get away," they often display themselves even more aggressively once abroad. For the Germans of Generation I, by the early seventies, the *Urlaub*, vacation, preferably in a foreign land – symbol of the new general level of material wealth, of freedom from work, and of territorial movement (*raus*: to get out) – became a yearly ritual of significance to definitions of self. The car, in particular, functioned as *Abgrenzungssymbol*, differentiating symbol, since GDR citizens could at most travel to Czechoslovakia and Romania (and Poland, the USSR and Hungary with restrictions), never to the far reaches of the former German empire

Table 20. *Length of vacation in the FRG, 1975 and 1985*

| Weeks | 1975 (%) | 1985 (%) |
|---|---|---|
| Under 4 | 15 | 0 |
| 4–5 | 55 | 3 |
| 5–6 | 30 | 25 |
| 6 or more | 0 | 72 |

*Source:* Süßmuth 1988: 225

– meaning Austria and Italy, the two favored vacation lands for West Germans. It is also important to note that West Germany remained the only country in Europe without a speed limit on its freeways.

Notions of free time among Generation I were directly related to the centrality of work in their identity. Free time was associated with vacation and thought of as meaningful in opposition to work. In contrast to American concepts of time-effectiveness, West Germans of Generation I thought of time in terms of function. Thus time off was associated with free or non-work time (where one need not function properly), and work time was associated with strict conformance to particular pre-given behavioral rules. The shortening of one time domain meant the lengthening of the other, so that fights between labor and management, for example, center around labor demands to shorten the work week and increase free time, not around pay and increased benefits, as in the United States. In 1950, the average work week was 48 hours; by 1985 it was shortened to 39.6 hours (Süßmuth 1988: 225).

As free time increased, so did vacation time. By the end of the fifties, vacation time averaged three weeks a year (not legally mandated until 1963), and between 1953 and 1956, one-third of all West Germans (including West Berliners) traveled during their vacation. In 1954, 5 percent traveled outside Germany; by 1956, that rose to 8 percent. By 1972, more than half of these vacations were spent traveling, and half of those in a foreign country. By the early eighties, 58 percent of all Germans traveled on their vacation, 67 percent of those to a foreign country – that included 35 percent of the total population (Maase 1985: 214–219). In the late eighties traveling on vacations became extremely stressful because the highways were blocked, making it difficult and time-consuming to get to the foreign place to recover.

To West Germans of both Generations I and II, the significance of free time and time away from work was the ability to recover from work (*Erholung*: recovery) in order to be able to return later and function again. Since 1960, free time was invested in extending the length of the yearly vacation, by 1985 reaching more than six weeks on the average. As table 20 illustrates, between 1975 and 1985, the great majority of the population had earned six or more weeks of vacation, with 97 percent taking at least five weeks.

During a vacation, Germans were known – in a pattern not unlike many other Europeans – to take their culture, especially their cuisine (e.g., *Sauerbraten*, *Wurst*, and *Sahnetorte*) with them, rather than experiment with the lifeways of the natives they were visiting. After a vacation, West Berliners almost always organized photo and slide shows for their friends. Hence even before leaving on vacation, the desire to document the trip in anticipation of the return home was strong, so one could remember and reminisce with friends. One of the major discussion topics at such gatherings was where they would take their next vacation, pointing to the way vacations and free time ritually demarcated the year, *the* event to look forward to. This photo-show meant much more than an exchange of travelogues with friends and neighbors. It was part of the display of self, showing not really a cosmopolitan German, *Weltbürger*, but one who nonetheless knew the world well through traveling, and had the money to see it, a reaffirmation of Germanness as constituted at this point in time.

### Conclusion

Out of the experiences of war and defeat Generation I generated a story, shared by Berliners in both city-halves, of postwar victimization. In the East, the state was unable to reemplot these experiences into its own romantic, future-oriented narrative. In the West, the state's lapsarian appeal to tradition, virtue, and assimilation into a prosperous community of Germans, served for most West Berliners precisely as an antidote for their sense of victimization. Consequently, West German citizens have been quite eager to use and identify themselves with the state's periods. Because their belonging and loyalty were inscribed at a time when the state's master narrative was restoration, they essentially ignored the desentimentalization of kin policy that occurred after 1968. By that time their lifecourse had already unfolded according to anticipated design, and this new policy orientation had little influence on their own practices and orientations.

Work and prosperity were the central organizing tropes of their life constructions. They saw virtue in work, and pensions and free time were understood as rights earned in exchange for labor. Prosperity forms the integument of West German identity, enabling them to erase their pasts, both in memory and physically, and to allay their fears of disorder and dirt, both of which were largely absent in pre-unity West Berlin/ West Germany. They also saw this prosperity as compensation for their victimization, and linked its gradual achievement to the periods and categories of state: most importantly, the currency reform and consumer goods obtained through the *Wirtschaftswunder*.

Members of Generation I remained loyal to *Deutschstämmigkeit*, categories of blood and kin, consanguinity and affinity, which were understood to be *Ur-deutsch* and natural. A relativization of these categories was feared because it would open up the possibility for a definition of Germanness as multicultural, hence an inclusion of the guestworkers who had been brought to West Germany to sustain the *Wirtschaftswunder*. The kin model of the *Hausfrauenehe*, while serving men well, did not always serve the interests of women of Generation I. Why didn't they complain more? Some in fact did. But the large majority of citizens benefited to some extent from the general prosperity; and certainly the standard of living was far better than that of their East comrades, which was, after all, the comparison that counted. Women of Generation I, whose self-confidence was never that great and whose participation was never encouraged, tacitly participated in the postwar deal, much as they did in the bargains that sustained the Third Reich – although, as we shall see in the following chapter, their daughters were now talking up and speaking out.

# 8

# Politicized kinship in West Berlin: Generation II

We now turn to the life reconstructions of one final group: West Berlin Generation II, born approximately between 1940 and 1955. My interview partners from this generation showed considerably more diversity in their lifecourse trajectories and kinship practices than did members of the other generations examined in this study, but a diversity more apparent in the problems encountered than in the solutions to them. Reasons for this are twofold. First, unlike their parents, they experienced as adults no "total event," such as war or famine; and unlike their GDR counterparts, who grew up in a social and state context that was relatively uniform from district to district, they experienced their childhoods in different *Bundesländer* governed by a decentralized state. Second, most of my acquaintances in West Berlin were not native to the city, as was the case in East Berlin also. The foreign-born nature of Berliners has always been one of the city's peculiarities. In 1905, 40 percent of its residents were foreign born; in 1946, the last census to be carried out in the entire city, the number increased to 48 percent (Berlin 1988: 7), and since then has certainly increased. The majority of people I knew had initially moved there to study, others to enjoy some aspect of Berlin's anomaly status (to avoid army service, join progressive social movements, take advantage of business opportunities or tax breaks) – a range of conditions, when considered as a whole, unique to West Berlin. Hence West Berliners of this generation were a highly selected population, a group more dynamic personally and politically than one might find in the Federal Republic.

Yet, once in West Berlin, members of Generation II began to formulate, to a surprising degree, common responses to their collective problems, a striking uniformity that, regardless of the nuances regarding their own forms of societal participation, can be seen in their self narratives of the late eighties. They articulate this generational *collective conscience* with regard to several mass movements: e.g., a working-class mass pop movement in the late fifties (the Halbstarken), a student rebellion, initially including some young workers, in 1968 (the *Achtundsechziger*), and a successful political party (the Alternative Liste, known outside West Berlin as the Greens) in the late seventies – all firsts in postwar German history. These social movements not only created generational unity, but also served and continued to serve to demarcate this group from the generation of their parents and the one that follows them. While Generation I very consciously pursued demarcation from the lifecourse of East Berliners, Generation II inherited and internalized this demarcation without purposefully constructing it, as we shall see. Because the process of generational identity-building in West Berlin had been, on the whole, a very conscious affair, "generational coherence" was perhaps the most salient characteristic of West Berliners of Generation II.

In narrating their lifecourse, members of Generation II relied primarily on their own participation in or *identification* with social movements in periodizing their histories. This periodization was quite different from that of their parents, who tended to appropriate the periods of the state and further define them in terms of corresponding consumption items of a personal – not collective – nature. The categories of Generation II, however, were formulated in close interaction with and *reaction* to the normalization techniques of their elders and the state. The lapsarian state strategy of the FRG – "It's all in the Basic Law!" – and the refusal by the state to experiment in the fifties and sixties, to imagine a new future, made many if not most of Generation II (including those who had formerly lived in the GDR) suspect as subversives. Moreover, the assimilative strategy of the state, its attempt to incorporate Generation II automatically into an already established hierarchy, regarding them as of the same substance (*deutschstämmig*) as their elders, produced a counter-reaction among Generation II, who wanted both to see themselves as different and to constitute democratically a new basis for group membership. Hence the narrative of Generation I and its state, both of whom read themselves as virtuous, with an authority anchored in tradition, was set on a collision course with their offspring, bent, as they were, on autonomy, anarchy, and experimentation.

Generational conflict at the end of the war began with negative definitions of youth gangs by elders and by representatives of the proto-state; it later crystalized in the three successive movements mentioned above. For Generation II the 1950s were not categorized primarily in terms of prosperity, but rather as a period of domestication. By the mid sixties the domestic group itself was a politically contested category, and by the seventies so were the *Wirtschaftswunder*, work, and what had been dubbed the *Konsumgesellschaft*, the consensus categories key to the identity of members of Generation I. This confrontation slowly lost its edge as the state began pursuing a policy of desentimentalization, and members of Generation II began assuming positions within the state machinery. At the end of the seventies, the major points of ideological opposition between Generations I and II tended to revolve around a set of categories omitted in the allegorized versions of Germanness narrated by Generation I: Nazism and class structure (or hierarchy). Generation II forced these two categories into public discourse. Their particular domestic history, which itself structured much of the political history after the mid sixties, redefined the key categories of marriage, kin, friends and lovers, work and free time, and consequently, what it meant to be German.

**Youth domestication**

From the end of the war up to approximately 1950, children and youths experienced a similar anarchy and freedom from everyday routine in both East and West. Many of the oldest members of Generation II lost one or both of their parents during the war. Except for some people in the upper classes who often managed to avoid military service, most Berliners lost kin during or after the war. Illness, death, and migration restructured the domestic unit. Instability and flux at home, along with a general loss of authority accompanying the German defeat and the Allied occupation, contributed to a breakdown in hierarchy and a perception by children and youths that the rules and conventions of traditional authority no longer had to be respected.

The "emergency situation" of the postwar period, as it was called at the time, was subject to different evaluations by social scientists, which, in turn, fed back into people's conceptions of what they were experiencing. This I discussed in chapter 7. What should be emphasized here, however, is that most scientific accounts, while condemning Nazism and at least certain aspects of the patriarchal family, nonetheless supported the model of the *Hausfrauenehe*, with its prescribed roles for housewife-mother, working father, and children, as an official version of the lifecourse. Men and women of Generation II appropriated this model neither as an ideal nor as a description of reality corresponding to their natal units. Rather than modelling their lifecourse around the legal institution of marriage, West Berliners of Generation II in their reconstructions tended to narrate their lives in terms of confrontations with legitimate order and the pursuit of pleasure. The household and domestic group were thus secondary categories that were organized with respect to conceptions of legitimate order and pleasure.

Questions about what constituted legitimate order entered public discourse, framed as a generational problem, even before the end of the war, in what came to be known as "youth criminality." Often encouraged by mothers, fathers away fighting the war (and later in POW camps), nearly all youths in Berlin engaged in property or petty theft, illegal activities involving mostly lifesupply provisions and heating materials. After the war, the Allies tried to crack down on these youths, and in particular were suspicious of former Hitler youth members involved in such activities. These police actions provoked protests by youths against parents who had often encouraged them to join the Nazis, and, after the war, to steal provisions for the family. The Allies elicited parental support, for without their cooperation control of the children would be impossible. The fight over domestication of the youth crystalized in school reorganization, which was also supposed to be part of the denazification mandated by the Potsdam Accords.

*Education reform*

A major difference between the education systems in the East and West as they developed and were experienced by Generation II lay in the perception of their role within power hierarchies in the two systems. In East Berlin, the family was integrated into the school system run by the state, and the children were told they were responsible for the future. Thus the parents in the East, much more than the children, resented the state and the schools for usurping their authority. In West Berlin, the school was regarded as an instrument of the parents, aided by the state, to integrate the child into an orderly family.[1] Thus the children in the West, not the parents, resented the state and the schools. These different initial alliances resulted in specific configurations and alignments that became more regularized and institutionalized over time.

Progressive school reformers in West Berlin were both greater in number and under more political pressure for *Abgrenzung* from the East than in West Germany. Suspected of placating communists and radical reformers on the one hand, and forced to reassure conservative elements of the population on the other, West Berlin school reformers were continually forced to compromise on their goals. Between 1945 and 1947, a joint, comprehensive school reform was planned for the entire city of Berlin. Increasing enmity between the Allies in 1948 prevented the enactment of these reforms in West Berlin. Thereafter, liberal school reformers in the West were on the defensive; progressive school reform became hostage to the Cold War, and the restorative, authoritarian function of the schools again came to the fore.

Hannelore König commented on how she experienced this early period:

I should say that [during the last years of the war] we had become more autonomous, but then [we] were again oppressed. Namely, that was in the school. You had to again obey orders, yes, you had to again knuckle under. Corporal punishment was done away with, but you still had to be submissive. You were again oppressed. Anyway, our generation was.

*(Meyer and Schulze 1984: 127)*

Despite the pressure from the Cold War, West Berlin authorities managed to carry school reforms further than did the other West German *Bundesländer*, increasing the length of mandatory schooling for all and removing some obstacles to access by disadvantaged children. Education authorities enacted a scaled-down version of the proposed *Einheitsschule*, uniform school system, between 1948 and 1950, and constructed a special "Berlin school" between 1951 and 1954. Thereafter reform attempts were unsuccessful until 1972, when more pragmatic and piece-meal reform began to open up university education to women and to children from poor and working-class backgrounds.

Initial debate over school reform centered on the education of talented children and admittance to the *wissenschaftliche Oberschule*, scientific high school. In a radio speech from 1949, a Berlin education expert summarized the debate: "The problem of selection of talented children is as lively disputed as is the concept of talent itself. Certainly, nearly all parents maintain that they have prematurely talented children." Parents did not want their talented children mixing with working-class kids, fearing that "my talented child will be held back in his development by the masses of untalented children" (Füssl and Kubina 1982: 45–46, 48). In this period, the crucial concern of the schools was to reestablish hierarchy; that concern took the form of a debate over the nuturing of talent – a substance ascribed from birth and not learned. Schools with an open learning atmosphere, where different social classes mix, it was feared, might actually taint and spoil the inherited talent.

Even before the founding of the state in 1949, debate over education reform was held hostage to the political needs of *Abgrenzungspolitik*, infecting all discussion and preventing attempts at reform. In a letter to city Mayor Walter May in January 1948, Wilhelm Blume expressed the sentiment of many parents: "Are you unaware, your honored Mayor, that the Berlin *Einheitsschulsystem* resembles to a threatening degree the East school system? And that it increasingly deviates from the school system in other *Bundesländer?*" (cited in Füssl and Kubina 1982: 79). The official line was that "resemblance" with the East in any respect was "threatening" to the establishment of a distinct West German identity. In their reconstructions, members of Generation II frequently commented on three aspects of their education: its hierarchical nature, the pressure to be anti-communist, and the authoritarian nature of their teachers.

Astrid, six years old at the time of the schools' reopening in Berlin and now a psychologist, explained from the experiental side of the education system in Berlin:

I never went to school willingly, never. I never enjoyed it. The boys and girls were divided. And I'm sure the girls were treated more severely. We had to do the same drills in the school recesses as we had to do in the Nazi period, mainly, run around the middle of the courtyard in an orderly line. The smaller ones couldn't keep up; they were punished afterward; there was lots of punishment – corporal punishment hadn't yet been abolished in the schools. I remember some parents asking the teachers to be especially hard on their children, to discipline them more severely. There was one teacher who was definitely an old Nazi, so authoritarian. All of my teachers were authoritarian teachers, in fact. Nearly all were women, many quite old women. But I hardly remember. And curriculum? I had to do sewing, cooking, learn to be a housewife. The men, on the other hand, had to learn either auto mechanics or a practical skill.

Astrid emphasized aspects of gender division and authoritarianism in her education. Much like many of her peers with whom I spoke, she did not mention anti-communism and the *Abgrenzungspolitik* of the time. This aspect of experience was recovered only when I asked about it. During the fifties and sixties, the policy of demarcation from the East was often expressed through avoidance: no mention was made of the GDR (it was called the *Ostzone*), and until the seventies maps continued to show the boundaries of the Reich from 1937.

Yet, while Astrid and her generation learned to avoid the GDR as a geographical, cultural, and political unit, their education took place within a context of official confrontation with it. Before speaking out on issues, educators were required to distance themselves from policy in the East in a manner similar to how East German educators were required to begin every speech with citations from Marx and Engels. In a text addressing proposed reforms, written in March 1960 by Berlin educator Carl-Heinz Evers, the "Bolshevik ideology" in the East that aimed to educate for the *Kollektiv* was contrasted with the "autonomy of the personality" in the West. Evers defended a "pluralistic education" and a Martin Buber-inspired "I–thou" dialogue model of understanding (cited in Füssl and Kubina 1982: 104–106). Certainly until the late sixties, educators avoided images of the collective and aspects of collective education, but in the Cold War atmosphere policymakers were better equipped at avoiding through demarcating than at attaining new goals. Progressive West Berlin pedagogues could not attain the stated goals of pluralism, dialogue, and discussion. West Berliners of Generation II, like Astrid, related experiencing the opposite: control, discipline, and repression.

When I asked several members of this generation about why they omitted the debate on *Abgrenzung* from their reconstructions, they explained that nobody questioned the portrayal of the evil East, and that they absorbed these values as taken for granted. For them, demarcation was *doxa*, part of the "self-evident and natural order which goes without saying and therefore goes unquestioned" (Bourdieu 1977: 166). Many explained that they had no means of articulating a critique: the language simply failed them. One woman commented that only in the late sixties did some of her university classmates have tools necessary for a critical analysis, and more often than not, that critique was initiated by former GDR students who had been exposed to readings from Marx and Engels. Not until the late sixties did Marxist discourse reenter West German academic life, and some students began to articulate a critique of the role of the academy in reproducing hierarchy.

### The limits of domestication: the Halbstarken

In the early fifties, parents, local authorities, and Western Allies worked together to discipline and domesticate adventurous children and youths, a scenario that was quite different from what the youths experienced in the East. The reasons for this difference are several. First, particularly troublesome or dissatisfied youths in the East moved West, depriving the East of its most critical voices and thus of a necessary social impetus in the long run. But in the short run, this exodus of unruly youths eliminated a police problem for the East – and created a problem for West German authorities, who had nowhere to exile their critics. Second, youths in the East were immediately absorbed from the education system into the labor market. Youth unemployment in West Berlin remained exceptionally high through the fifties. Not until 1959 did West Germany enter a period of nearly full employment (lasting until 1973); West Berlin, in fact, did not substantially reduce its youth unemployment until the early sixties (Lampert 1988: 17). Third, in East Germany, the state made an early alliance with the youths (often against the will of their parents) organising youth activities and extending educational opportunities, offering social incorporation and advancement to both sexes and to children of all social classes, often through affirmative-action type programs. The state-identified authorities in West Berlin, as described above, allied themselves with the parents against the rebellious children. Generation I wanted, above all, normalcy: that meant silencing unruly youths and assimilating them into a community that looked to the past, to tradition, to elders, for its authority. Accustomed to the anarchy of their childhood and excluded from political activity, by the mid sixties West German youths became increasingly conscious of the way in which they were being normalized and marginalized.

In less than three decades, social movements comprised of different members of this generation arose successively out of reaction and resistance to these normalization pressures. The first such movement was working class in origin, the Halbstarken, half strong, and, as with the other social movements that followed it, organized in terms of domestic categories. Unlike the movements that came later, however, it did not spread to other social classes and it did not articulate political goals.

The Halbstarken appeared first in early 1955 in West Berlin when groups of up to twenty youths on motorcycles began gathering in doorways and orderly public places to *randalieren*, make a stink. Comprised of nearly all working-class boys (although girls were not totally excluded), they gathered on street corners, at playgrounds, or in local bars, dressed in black leather jackets if they could find them, "especially harrass(ing) young girls with words or even with actions." The goal, according to accounts of participants, was merely "thrill and excitement" (Bondy 1957: 9).

Alienated by the contradiction between their own unemployment in the late fifties – true especially for the working class – and the growing economy and visible improvement in living standards for others, many usually compliant youths began to rebel. Coupled with this abysmal work situation was the political–domestic attempt to restore the authority of the father, even if he wasn't there, and to return to "respectable authority relationships" (Bondy 1957: 62). Although, in its heyday from 1955 to 1960, only approximately one-fifth of all youths were involved in the Halbstarken, the movement became an identification symbol for those bored or disaffected by the "No Experiment" political motto of the conservative Adenauer regime. From April to October 1956 in Berlin, 445 youths took part in *Krawalle*, rabble-rousing, among whom only 17 were girls. Girls made up 2 to 5 percent of those identified with the movement, and numbered approximately 5 to 12 percent of those involved in rabble-rousing incidents (Bondy 1957: 53).

Models for the Halbstarken came from the United States. Although the West German regime officially welcomed all things coming from the United States having to do with the *political model*, they frowned on aspects of American *pop culture*, often introduced by the Occupation troops. Several members of Generation II told me that their first exposure to Americans was to black GIs, and some even had their first sexual experience with American black men. Having been told by their parents that the Americans were their friends (unlike the Russians, from whom they were to run), they were shocked when their parents used racist grounds to forbid them from having contact with Americans. Many members of Generation I pointed to how their parents had praised and identified with the *Amis*, but yet held race categories to be more important than national ones.

Indeed the pop culture that so captivated the youth came from American black culture, especially jazz, rock and roll, and new forms of dance. Yet the pop cultural icons most salient in bringing black culture into public discourse were still primarily white Americans. The music of Elvis Presley, who himself served as an occupying soldier in West Germany, and the films of James Dean and Marlon Brando functioned as super-models for a whole generation. Rock-and-roll music became the rage – with its aggressive, sexual themes and its loud, driving rhythms, so very different from traditional German musical forms expressed in low and high culture: the popular middle-class *Schlager*, the polka and waltz, classical music and opera. With its boundary-breaking gender conventions, new clothing and moving styles, and challenge to racial categories, the Halbstarken served simultaneously as a proud generational demarcator for the young and disenchanted and a provocation and threat to the established order.

Mass media and the social-scientific community immediately condemned the movement, trying effectively to denigrate it but thereby ironically giving it publicity and making it into something more glamorous and adventurous than it in fact was. Even the Council on Europe in a 1960 report passed judgment on the movement, which was not limited to West Germany, concluding that the goal of the Halbstarken was "to destroy family life" (Fischer-Kowalski 1983: 58).

In reconstructions of former activists, they emphasized the importance of rebellion against the everyday. One woman remembered, "And our concept, which we and other people always used, was *spießig* [small, narrow-mindedness]. Not simply *Spießer* [someone who fits those characteristics], but to be *spießig*! That was the key word. For us, it was important to have a jazz basement and not to have fun in some nice bourgeois thing. We acted against our parents, against *Spießertum* [the act of being *spießig*], that meant breaking out." (Dietz 1985: 36). And break out, indeed, they did.

**The politicization of domesticity**

"1968" is a magical year for Generation II, many of whom call themselves *Achtundsechziger*, sixty-eighters, for that was the year when a critique narrowed to the politics of domestic life broadened into a political critique of the West German state. The formal politicization and reemplotment of domestic experience might even be precisely dated to 1969, when the so-called *hedonistische Linke*, hedonistic Left, split off from the *Politgenossen*, political comrades. To understand "1968" one must go back to the international relations of the fifties, specifically to the relationship of Germans to Americans, which were nowhere in Europe so intimate and multidimensional as in Berlin. As just described above, many West Germans of Generation II, not only the Halbstarken, modeled themselves on the American "beat generation" of the fifties. In doing so, they developed nonconventional styles in dress and tastes in music repellent to their parents, who also, as it was, identified with the Americans, but decidedly not with American youth culture.[2] Through the cultivation of a taste for jazz and rock and a new aesthetic of appearance, German youth embraced a new semiotic: visual images and sounds that inverted the everyday categories of their elders. They disputed the meaning of neatness, cleanliness, discipline, order – values that embodied the very essence of Germanness at that time.

The reaction of Generation I and the state to this behavioral and sartorial assault was anything but measured. In the words of Chancellor Ludwig Erhard, the Christian Democratic leader who had replaced Konrad Adenauer in the early sixties, "So long as I govern, I'll do everything I can to destroy this nuisance" (Aust 1989: 38). Aggressive metaphors of attack, destruction, and war characterized the discourse of both the state and their opponents within Generation II. Yet the beatniks and their followers, who were students and non-students alike, did not initially formulate political demands and attack the state. Instead, their critique was cultural, expressed in a gestic of signs subverting domestic life; it preceded by several years the development of a political critique, articulated verbally by another sub-group of Generation II, mostly students. These two groups did not begin to interact with one another until after the visit of the Shah of Iran and his West German-born wife to West Berlin in 1967, an event that radicalized Generation II in its self-conception. What the Halbstarken initiated in challenging sartorial and behavioral convention, the sixty-eighters continued to develop, supplementing it with what Adorno and Horkheimer of the Frankfurt School called *Ideologiekritik*, an explanation of the sources of the dominant ideology. This critical theory was oriented to a holistic critique of society, *Gesellschaftskritik*, and saw the state as integrated into, not apart from, the society.

### *"Wohngemeinschaften" and otherness in household structure*

Postwar households in West Berlin were in a constant state of flux largely because the city itself was being continually reterritorialized with new peoples, buildings, and spaces. Until the building of the Wall, people of all ages tended to leave West Berlin for the Federal Republic. Many were well-to-do residents and left behind large apartments that were then available for cheap rent. This movement from Berlin to West Germany reversed itself after 1961, when young people leaving their natal homes in the FRG began moving to West Berlin. As mentioned earlier, most of my discussion partners in the West as well as in the East were not born in Berlin. Reasons for coming to Berlin tended to be fourfold: first, the desire to get away from parents; second, to study; third, to enjoy Berlin's social and night life; and fourth, among young men, to escape military service. Because of West Berlin's special status under the Potsdam Accords, young men with a permanent residence in

West Berlin could not be forced to serve in the military or to perform alternate service, that was, unless they again moved from Berlin to live in West Germany.[3] Whatever the reason for the move to Berlin, people made it consciously; rarely did members of Generation II say they were in Berlin by fate or accident.

By the end of the sixties, many young people in Belin were living in *Wohngemeinschaften* (WGs), large apartments formerly inhabited by the wealthy. These unconventional living arrangements were initially unique to Berlin where the rent for such large spaces was very low by West German standards. Some of these WGs developed into communes, the first of which, *Kommune I*, was founded at the end of 1967. Their goal was "to revolutionize the bourgeois individual" and to develop their sexual needs unfettered by societal norms (Brügge 1988: 78–96). With the transformation of some WGs into communes, household structures, which up to that point had been determined by marriage and residence needs, were suddenly also organized around sexual interests and friendship needs.

*Wohngemeinschaften*, communes, and collectives never became the mean household form in West Berlin, although it is likely that every member of Generation II experienced them, if only as party guests. They did, however, increase dramatically, by 277 percent for the whole FRG between 1972 and 1982, with perhaps two or three times that number in West Berlin (Nave-Herz 1988: 64). The household form that grew the most numerically, though, was the single person; the one that declined the most was the nuclear pair with children. Both the increase in single-person and decline in nuclear-family households was centrally related to experience with the WGs. The interrelationship of these different living arrangements is best illustrated by presenting six prototypical examples, indicating the range and historical specificity of how West Berliners of Generation II experienced changing household forms.

Hans-Peter, born in 1948, moved with his parents to West Berlin from West Germany in 1950. His parents divorced in 1952, whereafter he gradually lost contact with his father. His mother remarried in 1958, but he never developed a significant relationship with his mother's second husband who, in any case, divorced her in 1968. At the age of nineteen Hans-Peter moved into an apartment with two male school friends; two years later they moved into a WG with one other man and two women. All six were students at the Free University. The WG changed its members and the form of their relationships over time. Most changes in membership, said Hans-Peter, were provoked by heterosexual couples who wanted to move into private apartments. They were always replaced by singles, mostly students. The WG was large enough to offer a room to visiting guests, many of whom were from the United States. Sexual partners, both male and female, were brought into the WG and members often had sex with each other, either in the context of an intensified relationship or in an orgy. In 1979, Hans-Peter moved into the apartment of his girlfriend, with whom he still lives. Since 1988, he has had another woman friend he visits several times a week and with whom he occasionally vacations. He continues to visit his former WG, now inhabited by two male lovers.

Helene, born in 1947, moved from East Berlin to Prague in 1967, from Prague to Vienna in 1968, from Vienna to West Berlin in 1972. She lived with her mother and father in a small East German town until 1963, moved to East Berlin to go to school in 1967, married a Czech citizen six months later in order to join her (female) lover in Prague. Her husband promptly left Czechoslovakia to seek asylum in West Germany. She then married an Austrian and moved there with her lover until 1972. She and her lover then moved to West Berlin.

Anne-Marie, born in 1939 in East Prussia, was raised by married parents until her father joined the war effort in 1943. In 1944, she fled with her mother, grandmother, younger sister, and four other women to parts of what became East Germany, moving from farmhouse to farmhouse for nearly two years. They finally settled in a refugee camp in Bavaria, where she lived with the all-women group until 1950, when her father returned from a POW camp. She lived together in a small town with her father, mother, and younger sister until 1961. Shortly after the Wall went up, she moved to Berlin "in search of excitement" – she also went to the university there. She lived in a boarding house for her first three years in Berlin, then met her future husband, also a student at the Free University. They moved into an apartment together in 1965, married the following year, and then lived together in communal apartments until their son was born in 1968, after which time they moved into a private apartment. In 1982, they bought the floor of the house they were living in.

Gerhard, born in 1951 near Cologne, lived with his mother, father, and younger brother until he passed the *Abitur* in 1970. He then moved to West Berlin to avoid military service and to study film. Between 1970 and 1976, he lived in three WGs, each with a different mix of men and women, the largest group numbering seven. In 1977, he and another male friend, Frank, started their own WG in a four-bedroom apartment; in 1981, they moved to a seven-bedroom apartment, which they shared with three women. One of the rooms was used as a guest room, in which I was also once a guest. Two of the women had regular visiting (male) friends with whom they had nearly monogamous sexual relations; Gerhard and Frank both had girlfriends who visited them occasionally, with whom they also had sexual relationships. Gerhard reported that he and Frank had a sexual relationship with each other for short periods several times in the past. They both viewed the current WG structure as a permanent arrangement.

Barbara, born in 1941, was raised by her mother in a small town in the middle of West Germany. She married in early 1961 and moved six months later to Berlin, where her husband had obtained employment. After two years in an apartment, they bought a house in a Berlin suburb. She had a son in 1965. Her husband left the household in 1974, whereafter they lived in separate households. They both explained that they never divorced because "we just never bothered to." Her son found an apartment of his own in 1988.

Petra, born in 1953 in East Germany, moved with her mother to Hamburg, FRG, in 1956. She moved to Berlin in 1970, and found an apartment for herself. In 1973, she entered the university and has since studied part-time and "jobbed." Between 1978 and 1980, she shared an apartment with a female friend, but then decided to live alone in the apartment. In 1984, she decided to have a baby. She has raised it alone, though she often relies on her female friends.

It may be impossible to isolate any single variable that organized the transformations in household structure of this generation. If, however, any motivating principle stands out, it is the drive for autonomy, which led to self-fulfillment and heterogeneous patterns. Heterogeneity itself might be considered a generative category, an over-arching trope, producing the following structural changes: first, participation in many different living arrangements, including the WG movement, marked the lifecourse of nearly every Berliner; second, the inter-generational household had all but disappeared, at most two generations shared a home for limited periods of time; third, marriage no longer organized household structure, but was itself organized by other factors, such as childcare, the fluidity of sexual practices and love, and the extension of kin to categories not related to affinity and consanguinity. We will return to a discussion of these factors later in this chapter.

*The surfacing of the past in the political context of 1968*
In what context did these household patterns unfold? How did the experiences of kinship relate to politics and the political context of

1968? The politicization of Generation II grew out of a critique of the lack of an anti-fascist policy by the conservative and popular Christian Democratic governments in the fifties and early sixties. Not only did the Adenauer and Erhard regimes, with American support, ignore major provisions of the Potsdam Accords, but they also promoted former Nazis to leading positions in government administration and industry (Engelmann 1981; Niethammer 1988a). In the early fifties in the FRG the term anti-fascist, when used at all, came to mean anti-communist. Authorities usually justified their decisions based on appeals to tradition, the authority of the father, or the constitution (Basic Law). Consequently, when the FDJ, Free German Youth organization, was declared illegal in June 1951, when the Communist Party was banned in 1957 (after years of harassment), and when pacifists (in the fifties), anti-war (in the sixties), and anti-nuclear (in the seventies and eighties) groups were spied upon by West German secret police, the official justifications were always the same, *verfassungsfeindlich*, enemies of the constitution.[4] This reasoning gave the opponents to authority a very easy target: the state and its representatives.

The Social Democratic Party (SPD) followed the Christian Democratic leadership on these issues, so that by the early sixties they increasingly alienated their own youth movement, the SDS (Socialist Students of Germany). Conflict between the SPD and their youth group crystalized around the SDS demand that West Germany stop supporting American involvement in Vietnam. Yet the decisive issue which caused the Social Democrats to kick the SDS group out of the party was their demand that the West German government hold direct parliamentary talks with East Germany. Minimally since the crushing of the East German worker uprising in 1953, the "GDR" had been an issue around which West Germans united, a trope that immediately produced consensus. Now it was being used by the SDS as a critical wedge to divide and differentiate. The more pacified youth organization that the Social Democrats founded shortly thereafter recruited its supporters from among the youngest members of Generation II and the generation that followed them. Attempts to formulate political critiques, a general *Ideologiekritik*, were centered around a magazine out of Hamburg called *konkret*, whose chief editor in the early sixties, Ulrike Meinhof, would later become one of the leaders of a radical West German urban guerilla group, the Red Army Faction (RAF).

The event most often referred to in reconstructions as responsible for creating generational consensus and unity on political issues was the 1967 visit of the Iranian Shah to Berlin. Police brutally repressed student demonstrations protesting West German governmental compliance and support for the Shah's dictatorial policies. During one rally, police opened fire on the crowd, killing Benno Ohnesorg, a pacifist student and member of the Evangelical student organization participating in his first demonstration. Shortly thereafter, in a meeting at the SDS headquarters in Berlin, Gudrun Ensslin, a minister's daughter and soon to become one of the leaders in the RAF, touched a raw nerve of Generation II with her statement: "This fascist state is organized to kill us all. We must organize resistance. Violence can only be answered with violence. They are the generation of Auschwitz – you can't argue with them" (Aust 1989: 54). In the eyes of many in Generation II, their elders, most often including their parents, were to be held accountable for the concentration camps such as Auschwitz, an issue about which their parents had remained silent.

Silence regarding personal participation in the Third Reich thus became a major source of conflict between the generations. Anger was most often specifically directed against the father. In reconstructions, nearly all members of Generation II made reference to how their attempts to discuss the Nazi period with their parents was met with silence, and to how their parents tried to cleanse themselves of the past, symbolically and administratively, through the *Persilschein*. When newspapers in the fifties printed pictures of concentration camps, parents would often say, "Don't let the paper fall in the hands of the children." For Generation II, the concentration camps, particularly Auschwitz, became a key symbol around which guilt, Germanness, and the identity of Generation I cohered (see Ortner 1973).

Official silence concerning this issue and the complicity of the Christian Democratic government in its suppression were then linked to the policies of the Federal Republic. Silent parents, especially the fathers, became metaphorical equivalents for the state; both state and father being synecdochic for *die Vergangenheit*, meaning the Nazi past. Auguste Kühn, born in 1936, wrote about how she experienced this symbolic configuration within her family. Her father had returned from the war in the fall of 1945 and her Aunt Friedel, who had spent time in a concentration camp, visited them on several occasions: "[She was] so gaunt that I was initially afraid of her bony appearance. When she began to talk about what she had gone through in those years, I would be sent out of the room and told to play. 'That's not for children.

You'll not be able to sleep because you'll have bad dreams'" (Böll 1985: 126). By the sixties, members of Generation II increasingly broke the taboo concerning discussion of the role of their parents in the Third Reich. Gudrun Ensslin's statement, "They are the generation of Auschwitz – you can't argue with them," became the rallying cry around which a generation united.

In their reconstructions, those West German members of Generation II who experienced any of the events surrounding "1968" tended to be quite unforgiving and critical of their fathers. Even when the father was absent as they grew up, he took on contours over time, and by 1968 he was a real person to be confronted, in particular regarding his Nazi past. Günther Seuren, born in 1932 and therefore several years older than members of Generation II, nonetheless explained forcefully a sentiment regarding fathers that I often heard: "After the war I thought that perhaps my father still lives, somewhere, and he would still be returning home. Perhaps later. As an old man, he would stand before the door and maintain that he is my father." Seuren made it clear that despite the fact his father was dead, he must confront him, if only in an imagined scene, for daddy lived on in his fantasy. "I did not want him to return home," – the meeting was being forced on him – "what for? So that I could shake his hand, now empty, the hand with which he used to shoot?" Father's hand, which was to greet him, belonged to a trigger-happy marksman. "I did not want the usual coming home, so that he could one day travel with me abroad. I did not want to look on as he pointed to me with his finger into some area and said: 'My occupation base.'" He did not want to travel with his father through *die Vergangenheit.*

"Later, I answered the troublesome question about what happened to him by assuming that perhaps he was resting somewhere in a *Kameradengrab*, grave with his comrades. His people" – Seuren distinguished his generation from that of his father's – "would be most happy with his hospitable terminology: everything best accords to the rules in a *Kameradengrab*. I did not want that he would receive *Gnadenbrot*, clemency bread, from us." No forgiving! "Our fatherland is not a table at which one can cosily sit with well-soaped hands" – perhaps made *sauber* by Persil – "and marvel about the wonder that has come out of the ashes. The Nazis all look much like they speak: 'Truthfully, respectably, and comradely to members sharing their own blood'" (Böll 1985: 57).

Seuren made it clear that he rejects not only all association with Nazi crimes, but also with the blood ties, *Blut und Boden*, which inspired and informed Nazi policies. In this short statement he brought together his fundamental opposition to a consensus category of Generation I: a definition of kin or Germanness based on shared blood.

### *"1968"*

Violence between the police and students escalated after the shooting of Benno Ohnesorg in 1967. As students became politicized about the Vietnam War, they increasingly took to the streets in mass protests. The right-wing press used the student demonstrations to mobilize the rest of the population against the student *Krawalle*. For Generation II, Springer publishing house, with its gilded headquarters in a skyscraper built facing the Wall in the Kreuzberg section of Berlin, became a symbol of the conservative forces. Many people told me they were convinced that people at Springer wanted to incite the general population to lynch radical students.

This polemic by the right-wing press did contribute to a near-successful assassination attempt on the student leader Rudi Dutschke. The headlines, covering the entire front page, of the Springer-owned daily *Bild* on February 2, 1968, read, for example, "Stop the terror of the young reds now!" (Chaussy 1985: 54). Shortly thereafter, the *Deutsche Nationalzeitung* wrote "Stop Dutschke now. The alternative will be civil war. The order of the day: Stop the left-radical revolution now. Otherwise Germany will become the mecca of all the dissatisfied people of the world." Under the article they published five photos of Dutschke, representing him from various angles as do the police in their most-wanted lists (Aust 1989: 63). Dutschke was indeed stopped, and never recovered from his bullet wounds, eventually seeking refuge in Denmark.

### *Social protest as terrorism: the Red Army Faction and reaction to the state*

The relatively ineffectual student demonstrations led to a splintering of a now-politicized generation into a multitude of factions, with bitter fighting about tactics between the groups, whose memberships and sympathizer bases were extremely fluid and relatively small. The most salient division, in reconstructions, was that between the anarchist groups (e.g., Second of June, Spontis) and the Marxist-Leninist/Maoist groups (*K-Gruppen*). Berlin was known as the *Hochburg der K-Gruppen*, and has maintained this reputation, with the amorphous *Autonome*, which grew out of the late seventies squatters' movement, carrying on the tradition of random violence and resistance to all forms of authority derived from *Anständigkeit*, respectability.[5]

Urban terrorism was one of the products of the more Leninist and Maoist of the *K-Gruppen*, culminating in the murder of a hostage in what has since become known as the "German Autumn" of 1977. Public bombings, and later kidnappings, galvanized West German, and to some extent Western European, public opinion against these activities. While active terrorists were few in number, their activities – and the counter-reactions of the state – set the context in which people in Germany lived in the seventies. For members of Generation II, the phenomenon of terrorism, including the reaction of the state to it, was a trope that periodized and figured their narrative of the seventies, giving form to disparate experiences.

In March 1968, Andreas Baader, a member of the culture scene in Berlin, and Gudrun Ensslin, a student, decided to hit capitalism at the heart of one of its symbols. They put bombs in two Frankfurt shopping centers, *Kaufhause Schneider* and *Kaufhof*. Here, for the first time, a political critique was consciously brought together with a cultural one, and expressed in public action. The way to undermine the political structure, it was thought, was not to attack directly agents of the state, but rather the structures which produced them and which they represented and defended. Accordingly, at the heart of the capitalist culture of the Federal Republic lay consumption, with the large shopping centers as central symbols. Baader, Ensslin, Ulrike Meinhof, and several others formulated a "Concept City Guerilla" manifesto. They called themselves the RAF, *Rote Armee Fraktion*, playing off the romantic association with Mao's guerilla movement and the dislike of the British Royal Air Force. The British RAF had bombed German cities from without; now a Maoist-type RAF was going to bomb the cities from within the culture.

Throughout its stages of protest, the RAF displayed remarkable continuity in cultural form. They continually relied on symbols significant to German culture, and transformed these symbols in a sequence of acts that followed other sequences within German history. The initial act of Baader and Ensslin was to set a fire to a large shopping center. In Christian symbology, fire is a sign of overcoming, a possible transformation into a new period. Shopping centers, on the other hand, were symbols of *Konsum* to which members of both Generations I and II were attracted and at the same time by which they were repulsed. During the twenties, nearly all large shopping centers were owned by wealthy Jews, which the Nazis then used as symbols to rally middle- and lower-middle-class support for their cause. In many ways, the resort to violence against the symbols of consumption by the terrorists of the seventies was a return to the tactics of the generation that preceded theirs – though, of course, they conceived of themsleves as fighting for the exact opposite cause, and their appeals were no longer linked with anti-Semitism. When members of the RAF later turned to bombs instead of fire, they had effectively broken with the society, no longer intent on warning or transforming, but rather with the single goal of destruction in mind.

The state responded to its perceived threat in a way that eventually made real the worst Orwellian nightmare the RAF could have imagined. In building a massive police apparatus to monitor "enemies of the state," the West German state paralleled East Germany at the time. It also carried forth the logic of dual organization, from a concentration on *Abgrenzung* and the enemy without to a focus on the enemy within. This period in the seventies thus marks a turning point in the strategies of the Federal Republic. In the mid sixties, the state began substituting a *Realpolitik* and desentimentalization for its former strategy of restoration, policies that affected practices first in the seventies. The state pursued a Janus-faced strategy of progressive domestic reforms aimed at assimilating Generation II along with a closing of the ranks involving a redefinition of the Other. For a mirror-image and public enemy number one, the West German state no longer looked primarily to the GDR (which it had by then "defeated" economically), but to its own radical youth. With this new alter-ego in mind, the state marshaled its resources and expanded its arsenals, all in the name of *Verfassungsschutz*, protecting the constitution.

What was nearly unanimously perceived by West Berliners of Generation II as the first direct assault on them as a group was the ordinance "Principles to the Question concerning Enemies of the Constitution in the Public Service," passed on January 28, 1972, under the leadership of Social Democratic Chancellor Willy Brandt. Commonly known as the *Radikalenerlaß* (decree about radicals), the decree was actually a *Berufsverbot*, black list, to prevent those in the student movement who were politically engaged (on the "wrong" side) from entering into public service. Because of this decree, up to 1982, according to official statistics, the government investigated over 1.4 million applicants for public service. In 25,000 cases, authorities already had information about the applicants; in 16,000 cases, the information was forwarded to the potential employer. In minimally 1,102 cases, the information caused a rejection of the applicant (Chaussy 1985: 55). Given the large number of jobs connected with the public sector, members of Generation II, even when not personally affected by the *Radikalenerlaß*, took offense at this ordinance as an example of institutionalized mistrust of them by the state.

As the West German state became increasingly apprehensive about its radical youth, it increased appropriations and positions for criminal police. In 1969, the BKA, Federal Ministry of Crime, had a budget of 24.8 million D-Marks, with 934 civil servants. By 1970 the budget was 36.8 million D-Marks; by 1971: 54.8 million D-Marks; by 1981: 290 million D-Marks. Furthermore, the number of positions appropriated to the BKA doubled between 1969 and 1971, with another 70 percent increase between 1971 and 1981 (see Aust 1989: 155; Katzenstein 1990; CILIP 1981).

By 1981, the BKA had even filled more positions than had been officially appointed to it. This is all the more remarkable in that, by the end of 1974, the RAF existed only in prison. Even though all RAF members had already been arrested, the state continued arming for the battle. And the battle, indeed, presented itself: a whole new group without personal contacts to the first RAF paralleled and *followed* the growth of the Federal Ministry of Crime. In 1977, the state and terrorists had reached a total impasse in negotiations about releasing hostages (held by the terrorists) for prisoners (held by the state). The Federal Republic, under the leadership of Social Democratic Chancellor Helmut Schmidt, decided to sacrifice the well-known industrialist (also former Nazi), Hans-Martin Schleyer, rather than negotiate with the new group of terrorists who had kidnapped him.

What were the terrorists actually demanding? While in prison in 1975, Ulrike Meinhof formulated the goal of the RAF as follows: "Terrorism is the destruction of life support systems, of dikes, wells, hospitals, energy plants. Everything that the American bombing attacks systematically targeted in their fight against North Vietnam since 1965. Terrorism operates because of fear by the masses. The City Guerillas, contrariwise, carry this fear into the Apparatus." These goals found widespread sympathy among her peers. In 1977, Federal Minister of the Interior Maihofer, using different terminology, nonetheless explicitly clarified the civil war or inner-familial nature of the conflict with the RAF: "There are no capitalists – now don't be shocked by what I am about to say – who do not have terrorists among their closest relatives or friends" (cited in Aust 1989: 350, 453). And by this, Maihofer did not mean kin in the GDR. People were to look at their own domestic group within the FRG and identify the enemy.

The battle to eliminate the RAF quickly took on a tragic quality whose meaning transcended the people directly involved. Ironically, both the state and members of the RAF pictured themselves as tragic heroes struggling against extraordinary odds to save society; and, from the perspective of each, they were both right. What the RAF perceived as a *Totentanz* came to signify, for Generations I and II, a generational conflict and control over *die Vergangenheit*, identified by Generation II as the state and society that had incorporated Nazi functionaires into its privileged structures. Social Democratic leaders of the government defended their fight against terrorism as necessary to protect the constitution, legitimating this struggle in the name of the office, employing the police force established for this job. Yet it had been clear since the early fifties that enemies of the constitution were nearly always defined as those on the left and not on the right. Not only the Baader-Meinhof group but also the whole generation of which they were a part shared a paranoia and fear of constantly being overwatched by the police. And the state reproduced this paranoia with regard to its fears of Generation II. Neither group lacked evidence for its thesis. Some of the early bombs used by the RAF were constructed by secret agents working for the *Verfassungsschutz*, the Office of Constitutional Protection; prison conversations between members of the RAF and their lawyers were bugged (in violation of the constitution) by police working for the *Verfassungsschutz*; and the RAF had, after all, explicitly stated its intention to destroy the state.

Despite disagreement with many of their methods and tactics, members of Generation II initially had great sympathy for some of the goals of the RAF, defined in many circles as a "war against a neo-fascist state." When the so-called "Baader-Meinhof Gang" went underground in the late sixties/early seventies, they had enough sympathizers throughout the FRG to give them refuge despite not knowing them personally and despite misgivings about the methods they employed. One man testified after he'd been arrested for giving members of the RAF refuge: "Basically, I did it because I'm good natured. In any case, people who are chased by the police are still closer to me than are the cops." An early member who was also imprisoned, the lawyer Horst Mahler, explained the conflict in terms of class interests: "Class conflict is not a civil servant career with expectations of a pension at the end" (cited in Aust 1989: 142, 223). He disagreed personally with some of the goals of the RAF, but still used the same language as they did, rejecting the lifecourse of Generation I as a particular bourgeois version of everyday life. The roots of the movement can be seen in causes identical to those of the Halbstarken – a reaction to the normalization techniques of the West German state – though its followers were better educated and more consciously political.

The period from 1968 to approximately 1981, then, an extremely formative one for the identity of Generation II, was full of paradox and reversals. By 1972, the Vietnam War had ended and the Social Democrats proposed a thorough education reform. By 1977, the state had enacted major, radical reforms in education and kinship law. The demands for cultural reform of the generational movement had successfully fused with political ones and provoked a change in the discourse of the state. The reaction of the state,[6] however, was twofold: on the one hand it incorporated as many members of Generation II as possible into the various institutions, including into government as *Beamte* (as civil servants), and on the other hand it excluded those members too radical and threatening – or not assimilated enough in their Germanness – for the state.

The emergence of a new group of radicals in the mid seventies who used violent tactics – including murder, hijacking airplanes, and kidnapping of civilians – caught the Federal Republic by surprise. The initial RAF had, in fact, rejected such tactics for itself. Seven years after publication of *Konzept Stadtguerilla* by the RAF, where they described their goal as "to destroy the myth of the everydayness of the system and its invulnerability" (Aust 1989: 581), they had ironically succeeded. But in the meantime, the apparatus of constitutional protection had become larger and more grotesque than its opponents' fantasies. New repressive laws allowing suspension of civil liberties, armed courtrooms, new security prisons, massive increases in money for and number of police and internal security agents, and random citizen controls, had by the late seventies become part of the everyday. This turn to force and construction of a huge apparatus was, moreover, more a sign of the state's vulnerability than its strength.

During this period, members of Generation II, nearly without exception, experienced domestic and political life as fused; a large group even came to an understanding of how the two were linked. Not only did political conflicts reach into the domestic sphere in the form of political fights with their parents, but domestic conflicts quickly became politicized. A squatters' movement and extra-parliamentary movement (APO) grew out of this new understanding.

### Squatters and the Alternative Liste

The squatters' movement in West Berlin began near the end of 1979, concentrated in the Kreuzberg district. In the sixties, partly because of links between realty interests and politicians and because of a planned freeway through Kreuzberg, housing policy, especially in this district, focused on the demolition of old apartment buildings, resulting in the destruction of the integrity of residential neighborhoods. At the same time, the demography of Berlin, and in particular of Kreuzberg, was changing quickly, as many middle-class residents moved to other sections of the city (if not to West Germany) and many foreign *Gastarbeiter* moved in. By 1980, approximately half of all Kreuzberg residents under eighteen were Turkish; 27 percent of the total number of Kreuzberg residents were non-German. (In 1987, the number of non-Germans in West Berlin as a whole totaled 11.1 percent.) "Section 36" (*SO 36*), became famous for its "Kreuzberger Mischung," a mixed community of Turks, the elderly, and the Left *Szene* people – unique for a German city.

The first squatted building was the Bethanien Hospital, a large complex forming an architectural unity that had survived the war relatively undamaged. Now displayed as an architectural icon attesting to the political effectiveness of squatters' movements, Bethanien had been scheduled to be torn down. After citizen appeals to housing authorities failed to bring about a reconsideration of policy, people just moved in and squatted. The movement spread quickly, increasing the number of occupied buildings between 1980 and 1981 from 18 to 150. Lack of adequate housing, along with environmental and peace issues, brought together a coalition of groups that found themselves not represented by political parties already sitting in parliament. The movement was consciously APO, outside-of-parliament organization, and it led in 1979 to the founding of the Alternative Liste (AL) in West Berlin (later to ally with the West German Green Party). In May 1981, the AL won over 5 percent of the Berlin vote, thus achieving the right to representation in the Berlin Senat and the West German and European parliaments.

By 1980, approximately 1,000 buildings, containing anywhere from 12,000 to 20,000 apartments, were owned by real-estate speculators who left them either empty or partly empty. At its height, the squatters numbered from 2,000 to 3,000 people and occupied 150 buildings, though the movement included enough sympathizers to total 10,000 to 15,000 at each demonstration or police confrontation. From the start, the movement was considered an affront to private property laws and opposed by civil authorities and the police. Given the 22,000-strong Berlin police force, with approximately 15,000 involved in daily patrols, the numbers of police were nearly double those of squatters and their sympathizers. In the *Szene* the police were referred to as *Bulle im Kampfanzug*, cop/bull in fighting suit, or as "civilian in the costume of his scene."

Increased confrontations and forced evictions of squatters by the police escalated the conflict. An encounter on December 12, 1980, for example, a demonstration on Kurfürstendamm in the center of West Berlin, resulted in 36 arrests and 200 wounded. Confrontations over the next several days resulted in an additional 73 arrests. Security experts, local politicians, and the press continuously speculated about the "terrorist orientation" of the squatters. Many people I talked with who had not sympathized with terrorist goals in the seventies suddenly found themselves lumped in this same category merely for engaging in legal civil protest to fight a wasteful and inept housing policy. Subsidies to buy houses in West Berlin had coaxed many West German businessmen to do just that – but only as tax refuges. They would then slowly evict all the tenants, and leave the building empty. Such buildings were more profitable as tax write-offs than as rentals, and the subsidies permitted speculators to wait for the day when rent controls would be lifted. Rent controls in Berlin in the late eighties were slowly being lifted, and many speculators held empty but usable buildings waiting for the moment when controls would be lifted. I met two such speculators myself, who admitted privately that it was not difficult to manipulate the regulations as long as one had no tenants. By 1984, the local Christian Democratic government policy toward the squatters in publicly owned buildings granted long-term leases or often sold buildings to the occupants, encouraging them to assume part of the renovation costs. (All statistics taken from *CILIP* 9/10, 1981: 2–5, 25–47, 72–86.)

The AL grew directly out of this confrontation, but was continually accused by the media of having created the *Krawalle*, demos and confrontation. Rather than raising suspicions about the goals of the AL, this accusation actually increased the support of Generation II for their political actions by confirming their opposition to official culture and the state. The description of the AL as an incoherent political-interest group also helped to constitute it in the minds of Germans. It became a coherent extra-parliamentary political party, representing itself as a coalition of disparate, heterogeneous interests and practices, primarily environmental and humanistic, many of which were specific to Generation II. In the January 1989 election, they achieved 12 percent of the total vote and entered into a coalition with the Social Democratic Party to rule West Berlin, effectively changing their political status from outsider to insider.

### Sexuality and partnership

The meaning of the politicized household growing out of the '68 Movement is now being openly disputed in a well-publicized media debate by participants and other interested parties alike. Its presumed consequences and results, intended and inadvertent successes and failures, were integral to the identity of Generation II, making up the categories (in various configurations) of their narrative of belonging. Their Germanness was quite differently constructed from that of their parents, organized around other sets of experiences and lifecourse transformations. In particular, marriage and the *Hausfrauenehe*, both state-sanctioned institutions, lost their centrality in structuring the lifecourse of Generation II in West Berlin, being replaced largely by a new meaning cluster shaped by the centrality of sexuality, partnerships, and free time. To explain how this new meaning cluster took shape is the purpose of this section.

The media debate about the meaning of the sixties, which began during the very time that the sixties were being created, forced Generation II to be hyper-articulate about their practices, often to justify what they thought they were doing before they actually did anything. Additionally, the changed political-economic situation of the early and mid 1980s (e.g., a conservative Christian Democrat/Free Democrat government, rising unemployment, and a worsening economy for some) forced members of Generation II into a defensive position, shortening the time-lag between doing and reevaluating the past.

### Disaggregating kinship

In their reconstructions, most West Berlin members of Generation II made it clear that they have tried to disaggregate kinship: that means to distinguish being in a partnership from both being a married partner and being a specific type of legal object for state policy. We can better clarify the distinctions they made if we apply Foucault's three analytical techniques discussed in chapter 1. Members of Generation II delineated (1) relationship aspects of partnership (communication techniques such as being in a *Zweierbeziehung*, an exclusive two some, or a *Beziehungskiste*, a boxed-in, problematic relationship, or simply having a *Freund/in*, with whom one may or not be involved sexually) from (2) the self-aspects (self-techniques such as playing the role of "husband" and "wife"), and from (3) being objects defined by the state (signification techniques used by the state to define the subject, such as married, divorced, widowed, single). By disaggregating this complex of meanings defining partnership, all tied centrally to the institution of marriage, members of Generation II opened up the space for new practices, with new significations, and ultimately new selves.

Let me offer an example. Hans-Peter, in his conversations with me, distinguished between his *Freundin*, whom he visited several times a week, his *Frau*, with whom he had lived for ten years, and his status as a single man, *ledig* or single. He delineated being a partner from what it meant for his definition of personhood, thus denying the state a direct role in defining his relationship and making him a particular object of policy. I am arguing here only that most of Hans-Peter's peers made distinctions between sets of practices (which can be isolated into different analytical techniques), and not that they made the same distinctions. Rather, the distinctions they made grew out of their model self, which, I have been arguing, saw itself in opposition to their parents, to the past, and to the state. To the extent they defined themselves positively, it was based on an agreement about the heterogeneity of practices, experimentation, and a discontinuous lifecourse.

Having already examined the fluidity of household patterns and their politicization in the socio-economic context of the last twenty-five years, we can now discuss partnership and childcare, two essential aspects of kinship. Before proceeding, it is important to emphasize that partners did not always live together, and that those who did live together were not always cohabiting. Partnership, household, and cohabitation were often not coterminous. For example, that 52 percent of all West Berlin households were defined as "singles" reflected only on marital status; it did not address coupling patterns. Many singles lived with others, in fact, but maintained their own, second household; it is unlikely that most were celibate. For members of Generation II in West Berlin, not only had the range of possible partnership patterns increased, but so had the social legitimacy (and in some respects legal legitimacy) of practicing this range. Increased legitimacy opened up space for individuals to change the form and meaning of their partnership patterns, not only in contrast to their elders but also with respect to their own pasts. A single lifecourse could, then, follow several careers, reverse trajectories, and assume discontinuous patterns. This "discontinuous lifecourse" was, in fact, a characteristic that demarcated Generation II in West Berlin from its predecessors and, more than likely, will demarcate them from the next generation.

### Berlin's postmodernism

The increased spectrum of possibilities did not appear spontaneously, however. Certain individuals, and the WG as a household form, in particular, were instrumental in creating alternative, experimental models that opened up the range of partnership and childcare patterns. The practice of these alternatives, which prior to 1968 were subversive significations, became conventionalized in a mere twenty years. *Die Szene* in Berlin and alternative lifestyles were now as essential to the topography of West Berlin as was KaDeWe, the *Kaufhaus des Westens*, the Wall, and World War II widows. Tourist brochures from the Berliner Senat metonymously incorporated the *Szene*, along with historical buildings, the Wall, East Berlin, the Turks, KuDamm, and the visit of John F. Kennedy in 1962, as part of the essential Berlin (what one must see and know). What in the early sixties had been heresy, a "nuisance" that Chancellor Erhard would "do everything I can to destroy," was now part of the permanent, official display of West Berlin.

In official pictures of Berlin, the city was represented not in terms of a set of model or typical things but as the range of its objects. Even the ruling Christian Democrats of the early eighties sought to represent Berlin in postmodern colors: as heterogeneous and polysemic. This new state strategy dates to former Christian Democrat Richard von Wei-zäcker, who was mayor from 1981 to 1984, and tended to emphasize hierarchical incorporation over assimilation and exclusion. It character-ized policy in the eighties generally, and was applied more fully in West Berlin and the province Baden-Württemberg than elsewhere in the Federal Republic.

This new metonymy of late-capitalist West Berlin, partly a marketing strategy to prevent it from losing its status as a metropolis, originated in contests around definitions of sexuality in the mid sixties, specifically in challenges to the hegemony of the *Hausfrauenehe* model, to which we must now briefly return. If we remember our analysis of West German policy, the model of the housewife marriage, while not literally written into the Basic Law of 1949, was nonetheless read into it as the center of kin policy in the fifties. By focusing state policies and legal discourse around a procreative, productivist model, the Ministry of the Family, along with other social institutions, sought to construct a *habitus* with a narrow range of family forms, and thus standardize the production of married couples who would reproduce. These couples were best stabilized if tied to a specific model of capitalist property ownership: the single family home. Generation I did not often practice this kinship configuration, and the state was never able to realize this model in all its policies (least of all in Berlin,where Social Democrats at times propagated oppositional policies). Yet until the late sixties resistance to it remained private and certainly was rarely articulated as a challenge in the domain of sexuality.

*Transformations in sexuality and gender*
A general liberalization of sex practices began in the late sixties, but did not become part of mass youth culture (and then initially only of students) until the early seventies. As late as 1966, one survey revealed that 66 percent of all female students were virgins. "To sleep together was taboo," wrote Ingrid Schmidt-Harzbach, who was born in 1941. "Petting was the magic word then, and for that there were also unwritten rules – down to the bellybutton, then you had to quit, then began 'Forbidden Territory,' as we called it . . . Faithfulness and such things also played an important role" (1985: 39). During the sixties, most young people still lived with their parents, who forbade any sex before marriage; those who studied away from the parental home normally encountered housemasters who demanded a clause in the rent contract forbidding visits by the opposite sex. Even though the pill was by then legal, unmarried women reported that they had no alternative but to go to a doctor known for treating prostitutes, who, one woman told me, "handled us accordingly."

Yet, even as social authorities tried to restrict the sexual practices of Generation II, to hold what people heralded as the "sexual revolution" in check, a sex wave hit the press, especially the right-wing, conservative tabloids. Popular illustrated magazines such as *Bild* and *Stern* began at this time to show nude women on their covers. A specific capitalist form of pornography-based sexuality, based on the public sale of women's sexual services, quickly established itself in the middle and upper-middle classes of large cities, epitomized in the ubiquitous "Sex

Shop" to be found in every business or non-residential area of West Berlin. In other words, for certain kinds of sexual practices, the market principle established itself, exploiting unfulfilled heterosexual desires already there and creating new desires that could be satisfied without threatening marriage and other institutions basic to the sexual and political order. Meanwhile, the liberalized practice of sexual expression – e.g., sex between unmarrieds and homosexual practices – remained socially taboo, although over time, as housing became less crowded and legal penalties went unenforced, there were fewer negative sanctions that could be brought to bear on such practices. Under the general label "homosexuality," a number of practices remained illegal until 1972, and thereafter legal only for consenting adults practicing them in certain spaces (depending on a number of factors having nothing to do with homosexuality *per se*, such as, e.g., the biological age or social class of sodomy or fellatio partners, the time of day in which the sex was practiced – public spaces after dark preferable to any space in daylight, and the nature of the public facility).

By the late sixties, the demands of those in the movement, according to one of the participants, the writer and sex theorist Ulrike Heider, included sexual equality, the overcoming of bourgeois (double) morality, and the right to refuse to marry and found a family (1989: 129–130). Note the trajectory of these demands: from the specifics of sexual practices, to domestic life more generally, to the legal and political. Whereas some writers argue in the press today that women in the '68 Movement were sexually oppressed and repressed, other women in their reconstructions remembered it differently. Heider sides with the latter group, recalling that women shared their sex experiences with each other and prized men who showed affection and sensitivity. Women, writes Heider, were neither primarily operating under an *Orgasmuszwang*, compulsion to have orgasm, nor required "to be sexually available" to all men, although there were, of course, those types of men and women also (1989: 129–130).

Raising all this to a conscious level and creating a discourse concerning the range of possibilities regarding coupling and sexuality, a task many members of Generation II took to be their mission, changed the nature of practices, both continuously generating new practices and increasing the pressure within small groups to conform to the latest rage. An *Alternative* avant-garde growing out of the *Szene* and the student movement became the vanguard for the movement. The situation was quite unlike that in East Berlin, where, for example, the

*Kumpel* relationship, with its origins in working-class, male behavior, was slowly appropriated by both sexes in other classes. Since few students in West Berlin/FRG came from working-class families, working-class culture played a minimal role in producing behavioral models for partnership or sexual behavior in West Berlin. Male students often had their first sexual experience with working-class girls, since it was well known that working-class boys and girls had sex earlier than the German bourgeoisie. But until the early seventies, sex remained taboo for most female students, in accord with the behavioral mores of their social class. The models for the West Germans of Generation II came from the *Adel*, upper-bourgeois culture, and from America, neither of which sought to challenge dominant norms.[7]

Feminist challenges to gender significations also contributed to transforming both the overall significance of sexuality and the way it is practiced. Mostly students from white-collar families who obtained access to higher eduction following university reforms after "1968," these women reacted to the bourgeois model of the proper. Bourgeois families differed most from working-class families in that working-class women always labored as much as the men, whereas in the adapted *Adel* model, taken from German nobility, a cultivated housewife and mother was prized. Working against this bourgeois tradition, avoiding any association with GDR initiatives having to do with the reorganization of labor (East Germans were dismissed generally as inferior and politically backward), West German feminists in the early seventies challenged the significations of gender, reproduction, and sexuality.

Although women of Generation I experienced most directly the elevation of *Hausfrauenehe* to a social norm in the fifties and sixties, their daughters of Generation II first brought this model into consciousness, politicizing it as a socially imposed *male* institution. This reaction introduced a quite different dynamic for men and women of Generation II regarding the practice of sexuality and gender. If women defined their own sexual identities in opposition to a gender signification, to being male ("patriarchal" was the word most often employed), men defined their sexual identities in opposition to the sexual practices of the generation that preceded them. In other words, women sought to resignify gender; men sought to resignify sexuality. Admittedly, changing one signification would influence the other, but the point is that women and men moved out of different assumptions about what was central. This difference in approach explains many of the subsequent conflicts and antagonisms between women and men of Generation II in their political agendas.

Early feminists objected to the way in which capitalist market mechanisms, which they associated with the *Wirtschaftswunder*, had fetishized them as heterosexual sexual objects for the purpose of selling goods, ranging from cigarettes to cars, and of course, selling themselves. This was, they maintained, a system for the benefit of men, including also their male partners. The fact that German men, even those in the movement, rarely took this critique seriously increased tension between the sexes. On the other hand, men of Generation II concentrated their own critique on sexual represssion *per se*, their goal being to liberate desire and the possibilities for its practice generally (by which they usually meant heterosexual desire and practice), and not to resignify the gender system that constructed this desire in a particular way.

Many women reacted to the ideological configuration inherited from the Adenauer and Erhard era by rejecting sexually encoded partnerships with men. This model, we remember, situated the housewife at home in a heterosexual marriage and gave her a marginal position in the labor force. Feminists in West Berlin reconstructed a series of campaigns that, while never fully participated in by a majority of women, nonetheless referenced points alluded to by nonparticipants also. These campaigns highlighted the tensions surrounding contested sexual meanings in nearly all relationships of the mid to late seventies. The campaign against the *Schwanzfick* (literally, fucking-with-the-cock) encouraged women to have sex with men only on the condition that there be no penetration of the vagina. In the late seventies, a popular slogan was, "Feminism is the theory, lesbian is the practice." By the early eighties, this had been parodied by some women, who coined the term *Berufsles-ben*, occupational lesbians, to refer to their friends who did not limit the practice of homosexuality to sexual life, but radically extended it into an entire lifestyle that avoided all contact with males. One of the major influences or legacies of these "movements" was that the number of women of Generation II who experienced forms of love and sex with other women, or at least those who spoke about and affirmed such experiences, far outnumbered their counterparts in East Berlin, and most certainly it was an experience few of their mothers had. This sensitized them to issues relating to their identity as women, creating a specific (and larger) set of shared lifecourse transformations that made their generational unity gender-specific.

Because of the way in which this identity had been constructed – opposed to the masculine gender and opposed to the state apparatus aimed at restoration of patriarchy – West Berlin women differed considerably from their East German counterparts, who did not face the same kinds of male- or state-constructed obstacles, and thus did not see themselves in such stark opposition to males. Additionally, the contintuity between generations was stronger in the East. While East German women of Generation II could draw on the positive accomplishments of their mothers in establishing an autonomous identity outside the home, West German women were often required to break with their mothers and forge a new way. Only with the student movement in 1968 did women begin developing a positive attitude toward work and public life, overcoming myths such as that of the wicked working mother and the *Schlüsselkind* – the mother whose child must wear a key around his/her neck to open the house door upon returning home, for mother is at work. And not until the eighties did a majority of West German women begin thinking in terms of "their own life" and not "being there for others" (Sommerkorn 1988: 136).

Men of Generation II did not articulate as coherent a narrative concerning sexual practices in their relation to partnerships as did their women counterparts. Largely, this was because so many aspects of gender and sexuality were taken for granted by men, assumed to be "natural" and therefore not questioned. Unlike in East Germany, where certain working-class-based models had been appropriated in wider circles of public life, in West Berlin sexuality and gender patterns remained more class-specific.

Men in the traditional working class of West Berlin, much like their East Berlin counterparts, tended to avoid discussions of sexual identity. In their life reconstructions, men of the middle and upper classes tended to begin with declarations of whether they were homo or hetero, in other words, they identified a sexual object choice as either male or female, and then out of this choice deduced a sexual identity. Often the first sexual experience had little to do with current sexual identity, since first experiences, for both men and women of Generation II, were often with older male family members or neighbors. Not until the sixties did most youths have their own bedrooms. It was not uncommon that young boys who slept with older siblings or relatives would often be introduced to sexual activity by them. Many men told me such stories, portraying them as sexual adventures. Women who told me of sexual experiences with relatives tended to reconstruct them as experiences of rape.

The experiences of men in all social classes exhibited a much broader range of practices than did their self-definitions (or silences). Men who identified themselves as heterosexual tended to exile experiences that contradicted this concept of self to the distant past. Those who had lived in communes or WGs often reported nostalgically about the "free-sex" days, of the ability to change partners and partnership form fairly easily, and of having had some group sex experience. The several men and women still living in large WGs or communes whom I befriended, all of whom identify themselves as heterosexual, claimed that they no longer partook in sexual experimentation. Most had steady partners with whom they had sex; few of them tended to live with their partners.

Since the early seventies, the *Schwulenszene*, gay scene, in Berlin again achieved something of the notoriety it enjoyed in the twenties, and gay men from all over Germany (as well as from the United States and other European countries) tended to gather in West Berlin because of its tolerant atmosphere, as well as, of course, to escape military service. It was centered around bars, discos, and cafés, had its own museum, monthly magazine, and political organizations, and since the advent of AIDS education campaigns by the Federal Ministry of Health and the Family, achieved a kind of unity it hasn't had since before the war. Gay organizations were well integrated into the Alternative Liste – several of whose delegates were gay or lesbian – so that gay culture in Berlin was incorporated into alternative-oriented groups and thus formed an integral part of Generation II. Because of the many political or social integrative mechanisms in West Berlin, gays were not as autonomously organized as in e.g., England, France, or the United States.

As the gay and lesbian movements grew, they changed the lifecourse trajectories not only of the men or women who took on such identities, but also of others in West Berlin who frequented their bars and clubs. "Mixed" places, as they were called, where homos and heteros mixed, were now often places where sex and sexual identity played a secondary role to aspects of self-allegorization such as rejection of normality, experimentation, and leftist political orientation – dimensions central to the Germanness of Generation II. Men who frequented these places exhibited an extremely wide range of behaviors that, while signifying sexuality and gender, generally, were quite ambiguous in what they specifically expressed. Purely hetero bars and discos, some specializing in the singles scene, were also quite common in Berlin, but these tended to be more strictly class-segregated than the mixed or homo bars. In four visits to working-class hetero bars in Wedding, I noticed remarkable uniformity of clothing and style, and heard mostly Berliner dialect.

In many visits to middle- or upper-class hetero bars, I heard many more dialects, indicating that most of the people came from parts of Germany outside of Berlin, and I observed a wide range of fashion and etiquette. This excursion into sexual meanings cannot do justice to the intricacies of practices, movements, and identities, for they fit no neat typology, and their range was greater than I am capable of describing here. Nonetheless, this discussion indicates how a cluster of meanings appropriated by Generation I, radically organized around the *Hausfrauenehe*, was displaced by one organized around sexualities and gender. This sexuality- and gender-centered identity displaced the meaning of having children, when that was at all part of the lifecourse for members of Generation II, by placing childbirth and childcare in a new meaning cluster, attached not to status accrued from marriage but to free time and work. Let us lastly examine that particular reconfiguration and its significance for the lifecourse transformations of Generation II.

**Children, work, free time, and friends**
Germanness for Generation II was a set of lifecourse transformations that took them through a number of social movements, generally directed against sources of traditional authority (their parents and the state), to a point, in the late eighties, where they had largely been incorporated into the structures of everyday life (highly subsidized and often choreographed by the state) that characterized West Berlin. At the time of my study, members of this group were anywhere between the ages of thirty-three and forty-eight, and had already settled into patterns of work, relationships, and time allocation unlikely to change radically for the rest of their lives. In this section, I would like to focus on the meaning of childcare and free time, and explain how these two activities have come to structure the space formerly occupied by marriage for the generation of their parents.

*Why marry?*
Changes in the interrelation of domesticity and politics, including new forms of households, partnerships, gender significations, and political participation, radically decentered the legal institution of marriage for Generation II. Niklas Luhmann (1982) has noted that sometime during the seventies marriage lost its monopoly on fulfilling emotional needs. This loss of centrality was largely due to the gradual conventionalization of alternate forms of *Lebensgemeinschaften*, living-together arrangements, and childcare patterns. Changes in household structure coincided

with the appearance of new partnership forms, which, in turn, created a new context for posing the question, "why marry?"

Unlike in East Berlin, where women and men tended to marry primarily for partnership considerations, marriages among West German women were intimately linked with the expectation or wish for children. This did not mean that all West Berlin women who had children married (21 percent did not), but simply that, of those who did marry, the most common reason was that they were having a child. Rosemarie Nave-Hertz calls this phenomenon "child-centered marital grounds" (1988: 67). The question that follows is why women who expected to become mothers decided also to become wives.

In many conversations, women confirmed to me that they either married or stayed married when (or after) they had children, because they realized their standard of living would fall drastically should their male partners leave them. Despite many subsidies by the West German state to mothers, the absence of a second income made raising a child extremely difficult. Single mothers reported feeling socially marginalized and being unable to participate in public life. Baby-sitters were quite expensive, and taking children into the public sphere, something accepted in certain circles in East Berlin, was frowned upon in West Berlin. Married women said that being a mother and wife was better than just being a mother, because they were financially better off than they would have been as single mothers.

It is quite seductive to draw a causal link between legal incentives for marriage and the differing personal motivations in East and West Berlin. The major motivation for marriage in the East was legitimation of partnership, which also happened to be the official strategy of the legal institution; in the West it was the legitimation of children, which also corresponded to the strategy of the law there. But a causal inference, that the intent of marital law was read into, and thus caused its (proper) reception, would be an oversimplification. Many social processes, not the law alone, were involved in supporting or severing the link between coupling (through marriage) and having children. We will discuss these below.

My own ethnographic data in West Berlin indicates that pregnant women married not to legitimate the relationship of child to father, as the law intended, but to secure the status of mother within the set of social and state-defined supports and incentives tied to being a "married woman." In other words, marriage in West Germany strengthened the state–society support system for the signification "wife/mother." It made it difficult for a woman to be a mother without also performing the role of a wife. A mother in West Berlin, I was often told, had few recourses to state support and suffered from social isolation if she had no husband – a pattern that did not hold true to the same degree for a single mother in East Berlin. Hence the best security in raising a child for a West Berlin woman was to have herself defined as married.[8] The relationship with the partner was rather secondary to being in a marital state that legitimated the parental relationship to the child, and bestowed it with statuses, financial rewards, and social opportunities not available to a single parent.

This discussion has focused on why women married, which still leaves us with the question of why men did. When I asked men this question directly, they usually answered, "for love." Yet, from their reconstructions, I know that some preferred not to marry, and did so only after being pressured by their partner. Many men admitted that the decision to marry rested more on their girlfriend's wishes than their own. For men of Generation II, "being married" or "having a wife" did not carry the same social status as it did for their fathers. If anything, marriage had a negative connotation, of being *spießig* and of asking the state for legitimation of a personal relationship. They would have preferred to keep the state out of their lives. (In fact, the number of men opting out of marriage was greater than the number of women who did so, while the total number of marrieds had also consistently declined since 1964.) Hence, among my acquaintances who were married, most would have preferred to remain unmarried, but in a more-or-less permanent partnership. Having a child, according to these men, was a mutual decision, although ultimately they felt they were dependent on the wishes of their partner.

*Parenting and partners*

As marital partnerships became more child-centered, they lost a great deal of their emotional intensity, even to the point of no longer having much independent meaning. Parents now reported having little time for each other, and children tended to see parents separately and not with each other together. Parents proclaimed that they wanted to raise their child to be self reliant, but they rarely left the child unattended and alone (Schütze 1988: 111). The emotional dependence between parents and children had therefore increased over time, and it went both ways: as a major 1985 study concludes, "[Children function] as ersatz partners and parents cannot break away from their oldest children" (Jugendwerk der Deutschen Shell 1981: 252). This held true for both men and women, who increasingly shared in parenting.

The contemporary parent–child relationship was now more idiosyncratically styled and negotiable than in former times. Members of Generation II as parents sought to eliminate the authority aspects of their role; hence they often did not teach their children to address them by the titles "mother" and "father." It was now convention to have their children address them by their own personal names and not by the generic name for the role. Since partnership could be practiced outside of marriage, marriage was increasingly reduced to legitimating this procreative relationship, again increasing pressure for meaning on the parent–child relation to hold together the couple.

Having a baby reduced free time and shrank the circle of friends. Many parents moved to the place in West Berlin considered outside the center or outside the *Szene*, in districts such as Wedding or Reinickendorf, where the rent was cheaper and there were more "green spaces," considered an important part of a child's environment. This movement out of the center made it more difficult for friends to gather, hence further isolating couples with children. Researchers have noted a general trend in the Federal Republic (I assume this holds true for both Berlins and East Germany also) for the nuclear-family type to unite at the home around television (Lukesch 1988: 173–197), and to restrict their familial network to blood relatives; in one study, half of those interviewed had no friends at all (Lüschen 1988: 145–172). Because of the transient nature of much of the Berlin community, as noted in chapter 4, the option of a family larger than the nuclear unit comprised of only blood relatives did not even exist for many young parents. This lack of blood kin "forced" West Berliners to experiment more with the definition of family, and it was my impression that they practiced a far greater range of kin and childcare patterns not defined by affinal or consanguinal ties than did people in the Federal Republic.

### The new meaning of children

The child, no longer an object for the social climbing or security of the parents (as in the fifties), instead became extremely valuable as an emotional dependent. This meant that as a child aged, and perhaps became less dependent, it lost in value. Members of what will be Generation III were not expected to play a productive role as individuals in supporting aging parents, since the state's pension and elderly care system was extensive. The child was thus increasingly valued in and for itself, as a non-adult who consumed items rather than produced them. Children in the late eighties consumed more of parents' money and for a much longer period of time than did Generation II, and given the gloomier economic outlook for them compared to their parents, they were not expected to pay anything back. The most frequently used word in reconstructions to describe these children was *satt*, full or sated. Many members of Generation III even used it, albeit somewhat ironically, to describe themselves.

In the eighties, the role of father gained in prominence, and an increasing number of men saw fatherhood as a neglected aspect of their lifecourse. This was due both to the large numbers of single and divorced mothers in West Berlin – still less than in the East – and also to the necessity for mothers to find others to help in childcare. Thus many women sought out fathers for their children. The lack of state support for working mothers, meaning lack of both monetary and institutional support, forced many West Berlin women to rely on husbands, ex-husbands, ex-lovers, and male and female friends to assist in parenting. For men, in turn, this meant that fatherhood was no longer always attached to being a husband. This trend was not true for men with either very high- or low-status jobs, who were, on the whole, socially discouraged or even penalized by their employers for making parenting a priority. Yet West Berlin, with its large and quite visible alternative scene, may have been the one West German city in which nonconventional forms of parenting were so widespread that the "normal" housewife/mother and working father/husband was more the exception than the rule.

Children were only part of the story of Generation II, and a declining part, as an increasing number of West Berlin women and men chose not to become mothers and fathers. From 1965 to 1980, the number of births per 1,000 women in the Federal Republic as a whole decreased from 17.7 to 10.1 (Nave-Herz 1988: 73). This decline is not attributable to an increase in abortions, as they were first legalized in 1979, well after the birth rate had declined. For an increasing number of women and men, the decision not to become a parent was a conscious and *positive* part of identity. East Berlin women, contrariwise, nearly unanimously included becoming a mother as an essential transformation of their lifecourse; they did not view it as one among other alternative options. State policy was intimately related to these two identity constructs. In the East, the vigorously pronatal policy so strongly supported mothers that the state ended up encouraging motherhood to be regarded as one essential component of personhood along with others, such as public employment and civic-mindedness. In the West, motherhood was also singled out by the state as a primordial role, but it existed in an ambivalent relation to other significations of personhood, such as public employment, status, and wealth. Most mothers of Generation II whom I knew claimed that motherhood and childcare involved a trade-off with other activities important to them, such as careers, political involvement, and relations with friends. Consequently, many women in West Berlin were opting against motherhood.

*Childcare*

By the end of the seventies, several formal aspects of childcare had restructured its content. First, playgrounds increased in number and decreased in size. Whereas in the early fifties, children in Berlin played in streets and old buildings without being watched by their parents, by the mid seventies the traffic was too heavy to leave children alone in the streets, and special children's playgrounds had been built. Furthermore, the number of children in kindergartens increased from 40 to 80 percent between 1970 and 1980, meaning that within a ten-year period twice as many children entered public care units for at least part of the day. This institutional shift is significant in that the state began to share more of the burden of parenting, much as in the East, though for fewer people and fifteen to twenty years later. From the perspective of the child, s/he was being constantly supervised by an adult: at home, at daycare, and at play.[9] The experience of anarchy so important to Generation II was totally lacking from the lives of their children.

A second formal aspect changing the nature of parenting was the modernization of apartments, with time-saving technical accoutrements, which has made it technically easier for parents to care for children. For example, for the FRG as a whole, from 1950 to 1982, the number of apartments doubled and the size increased from 57 to 82–95 square meters, and the number of apartments with toilets, bath, and central heating increased from 30 percent in 1965 to 66 percent in 1982 (Vaskovics 1988: 37). The advent of television as ersatz baby-sitter, as mentioned above, also somewhat alleviated parental-care responsibilities, while perhaps creating other problems to be encountered later.

In their reconstructions, many women complained that the lack of public childcare support systems forced mothers to withdraw from participation in public life. Their situation was, however, less dramatic in West Berlin than in other *Bundesländer*, because West Berlin had always been, by comparison, a model of support systems for children and mothers. For example, although only every fifth child in West Berlin attended the *Kinderkrippen* (preschools, from eight weeks to the end of the third year), West Berlin itself had half of all preschool enrollment of the entire FRG. The situation in West Berlin might not have been as extensive as in East Germany, but it was much better than in West Germany. Single mothers or fathers were the most seriously disadvantaged by this lack of public support. Nearly all children between the ages of three to six were enrolled in *Kindergarten* (because these were considered educational preparation). For working parents whose time schedule did not match that of the schools, there were the *Horten* for children ages six to nine, and 38 percent of all children participated in these. The total participation for children in *Horten* ages one to three was 28 percent, ages three to five was 69 percent, ages five to six was 52 percent (*Familienbericht* 1987: 36–39). In East Berlin, where many kinds of public support were readily available, people complained about the quality of their care; in West Berlin, they complained about the difficulty in obtaining care.

### Free time and work

Finally, we should note changes in the relation of free time to work, and then relate this work/free time complex to children, especially as it pertained to women. We can show how this new meaning cluster influenced the redefinition of kin and friendship. Among members of Generation II with whom I spoke, the domain of work did not function as the central defining feature of identity. In this sense, they differed radically from their parents. This did not mean, however, that work was unimportant, but rather that the organization of free time was always juxtaposed to and given priority over work responsibilities.

Unlike their parents, members of Generation II had not experienced anxiety concerning employment, for most assumed positions during the greatest period of economic expansion, or they collected welfare benefits that did not lower their status or change their yearly routines substantially. Women of this generation had also done much better than their mothers, although their incorporation into the labor force still did not parallel that of women in the East. In terms of education, this generation had also done well. Still, proportionately fewer German women had qualifications appropriate to the higher administrative grades, meaning that fewer women percentage-wise occupied white-collar jobs in the public sector.

The government employed an increasingly large percentage of people in upper-level white-collar jobs. It was an impersonal employer, giving positions out on the basis of formal qualifications and not patronage or spoils. Only with the exception of political criteria used in the *Radikalenerlaß* had the government strayed from this principle. The number of public employees lacking intermediate educational qualifications dropped from 43.8 percent to 26.3 percent, while those with such education increased from 5.7 percent to 11.1 percent, with most of the educated newcomers belonging to Generation II. Between 1950 and 1980, public (state) employment doubled, with the largest relative increase, 18 percent, from 1970 to 1975. By 1980, 50.6 percent of all primary incomes received by West Germans (largely pensioners and unemployed persons) came from the government, compared with 34.6 percent in 1960 (Schmidt and Rose 1985: 126–162).

Although work continued to play an important role in the lives of Generation II, it was now tied to the expectation of self-fulfillment (either pleasurable in and of itself or the means to procure pleasure). Nearly all members of Generation II whom I knew either expected fulfillment in their work, or they worked at jobs just to get by, *vorübergehende Arbeit*. They lacked the investment and commitment to work that characterized the postwar identity of their parents.[10] If either the "jobs to get by" or their normal work (*ordentliche Arbeit*) for which they were trained: (*mit Ausbildung*) did not fulfill the individuals, they became *faul* (lazy, uncooperative) and performed their work functions demonstratively displaying extreme displeasure. *Beamte*, civil servants, were exemplars of this kind of behavior. It seemed as if they tried to humiliate and dominate customers when they were forced to serve them – which was, of course, their job. Since civil servants had for-life tenures, it was nearly impossible to fire them. Many members of Generation II who did not hold *Beamte* positions nonetheless took from them their behavioral model. The extreme autonomy needs of Generation II thus often translated into romanticized versions of work free of control or domination, or into self-realization as free time: freedom from work and institutional control.

The *Urlaub* was the paradigm of free time, as intimated in the section on Generation I in chapter 7. It became a nearly sacred affair for Generation II as adults. Over half of my acquaintances took at least two vacations a year. Even those who were unemployed still managed to organize their own birthday party and take at least one vacation to a sun spot. Anything less than a month was considered more a break than a vacation. Long trips were usually made with one or several friends, most of whom had known each other for a lengthy time. Married and unmarried couples with children tended to travel without friends. Married people without children, however, often took separate vacations, traveling with a friend or friends of the same sex.

Much as their parents, members of Generation II considered vacations a time for *Erholung*, relaxation and recovery from work. Vacations were the key event that periodized the year, divided it into a before and after, meaning before and after work. For Generation I, pleasure was often attached to *nachholen*, making up for time lost due to the war. This concept was no longer significant for Generation II, who sought instead self-fulfillment in pleasurable forms of *Erholung*. Really to recover from work meant to them, even more than for their parents, to travel to a foreign country, away from Germany and other Germans, preferably to a place in the sun. Many people tended to want to see the whole world rather than repeat vacations, to seek new adventures in places not yet explored. Planning the vacation was extremely important, and often began while on the present one. This pronounced value given to free time was, they felt, due reward for the high productivity of the West German worker within the present economic–political system, though this was a *statistical* artifact of the West German economy, rarely a reference to their own productivity.

This free-market framework, dubbed by the Christian Democrats in the fifties "the social-market economy," allowed for groups with critical relations to the center to create their own cultural milieux, relatively unfettered by state ideology. Women in West Berlin reaped some unexpected benefits from their free space independent of state control, much as other less powerful groups did. Since the mid seventies, the establishment of women's bars, cafés, and bookstores, serves as a unique testament to this generation of German women. Along with the expanded role for women in the Alternative Liste (which also contributed to an opening of political roles for women in the other political parties), these efforts enabled women to consolidate an autonomous identity both as women and as a specific generation of women. Even women who did not frequent these avant-garde institutions were affected by them, for they served to politicize issues normally thought of as domestic, and therefore often not acknowledged in public discourse. This relationship between women, at various times involving shared households, children, sex, or political actions, provided a counterbalance or alternative source of self-signification to the "mother", "wife," and "worker" provided in the state's account. In their reconstructions, even those women of Generation II not active in this institutionalized, gendered activity who continued to follow the lifecourse transformation of a "traditional" German woman and did not themselves utilize the larger repertoire of significations, identified with many of the goals of the women's movement, and appropriated its language for their own purposes.

Men of Generation II, while certainly affected by the women's movement, did not use it to categorize their life constructions. In fact, many men on both sides of the political spectrum spoke quite derisively of women, and felt that women's attempts to attain autonomy had been at their expense. Fatherhood and childcare, as mentioned above, was considered a new male activity, and more men took an active part in childcare in West Berlin than in the East, though this activity was only rarely used to periodize the lifecourse. More important was the vacation and free-time activities. West Berlin offered an incredible panoply of forums in which one could enjoy free time and meet friends. Most free-time activities centered around going to the *Kneipe* or the Café, but many men also attended concerts, movies, plays, and other neighborhood cultural activities. Men mentioned forms of male bonding that had developed around activities and institutions such as living-together arrangements in WGs, vacationing together (or, for blue-collar workers, weekly sport groups) as peculiarities in their histories that made their lives unique.

Much like their fathers, these men figured their life story more centrally with reference to categories primarily drawn from politics and economic life; they simply used a different periodization, often drawn from social movements rather than official politics. The various movements of Generation II increased the range of possible lifecourse transformations for West Berlin men in ways that differed from the choices available to their East Berlin peers, and they politicized domestic life as well as mobilized men of Generation II for political activities, unlike their fathers.

Consumer goods did not play the same role as they did for their fathers in periodizing the lifecourse. Although automobiles played an equally central symbolic function, they were neither primarily extensions of family status nor vehicles for flight, but rather, served solely as private consumption items and forms of self or ego-assertion. Most men of this generation of my acquaintance defended quite vehemently the lack of a speed limit on the West German freeways, and drove fast and aggressively whenever given the chance, even though in other respects they were much more sensitive to others as well as more secure of themselves than their fathers.

Both men and women of Generation II tended to celebrate one ritual, their birthday, usually attended by people of one's own generation, and narrowed to closest friends or would-be friends (meaning no *Bekannte*, acquaintance, or *Verwandtschaft*, relative, unless they were also friends). The ceremony attached to birthdays was somewhat frowned upon in the late sixties, but since the late seventies, birthdays again reestablished themselves as central ritual events. The person whose birthday it was must organize and pay for it. I found little variance in these activities by sex or class. All guests were expected to bring a gift, but little hoopla was made about them. Birthday celebrations were the one festival that I found nearly identical for Generation II in East and West Berlin. Given their personal significance to members of Generation II, along with the vacation, they should be taken seriously as rituals that both constituted and displayed categories of belonging. They brought together the important categories of free time, friends, and self-realization (hosted by oneself at one's own convenience) that made up the Germanness of Generation II.

## Conclusion

Members of Generation II were children of the German defeat and the politics of the Cold War. Reared by parents with limited means in an anarchic childhood, predisposed to rebellion against authorities severely undermined by the defeat in World War II, the majority of West Berliners of Generation II, nonetheless, reached adulthood as relatively assimilated and comfortable Germans. Much like their parents, they experienced a discontinuous lifecourse. But for them, this discontinuity was planned, a result not of imposed depression, war, and dictatorship, but of their own experimentation and striving for agency against the control instruments of social and state structures. However, this lifecourse obtained coherence not merely with reference to an internal social dynamic, but also as an integral part of a dual organization, constructed in contradistinction, as mirror-image, to the lifecourse in East Berlin.

Issues of morality demarcate Generation II most significantly from their parents: the role of the past, *die Vergangenheit*, as a protest for generational conflict, experimentation with new forms of sexual expression and household structure, challenges to property relations and social class, and renewal of the basis of political authority. Each issue, in turn, took on the importance of a moral imperative, and in each case it seems as if, in retrospect, Generation II prevailed, provoking radical changes in kinship law and enlarging the discourse of politics. This story of unfolding progress is not, however, the way they would see their own history.

They saw the use of a succession of social movements to periodize history as a direct challenge to the official version of history in a continuing contestation of nationness. And they saw the significance of free time and vacations as tropes that subverted what they perceived as an obsession with work and production on the part of their parents. Yet the transformation of anarchic form into recognizable resistance was most often less a displacement of what it meant to be (West) German than a movement out of *doxa* to heterodoxy. Thus it was relatively easy for Generation II to define themselves against the hegemonic definitions of their parents but at the same time risk very little by moving within those definitions. Try as they might, they were not able to jump out of their culture. Consumerism, though in different form than for their parents, brought them back into the fold.

The shift in state narrative strategy in the sixties and seventies, from restoration to desentimentalization, enabled an assimilation of Generation II into the structures of Germanness. Many squatters became property owners, the APO (extra-parliamentary movement) now sat in parliament (as the Alternative Liste and Greens), and many members of Generation II became dependent on the state for employment or welfare payments of one form or another. For them the state's master narrative of prosperity functioned as an all-purpose aphrodisiac, an elixir of pleasurable things that made digestible otherwise distasteful social and state controls. It pacified many would-be rebels, breeding what the East Germans regarded as an arrogance and confidence that Generation II shared with its parents, making them all the more recognizably West German, and demarcating them from their East German counterparts. This was the work and the legacy of *Abgrenzungspolitik*. The demarcated lifecourse entailed an internalization and routinization of everyday behavioral patterns and operative norms that function like common sense, difficult to articulate with precision, yet forming a social glue that, despite variations by class, gender, and region, bound all West Germans to the Federal Republic.

What Generation II shared with their counterparts in the East, and what most demarcates them from Generation I in both Berlin halves, was a rejection of kinship inscribed in blood and mud, a refusal to grant biology a primordial role in kin formation and thus a centrality in the definition of the nation. For them, much more than for their East Berlin counterparts, the tropes of experimentation and heterogeneity lived on, especially in constructing kin networks. Their relativization of the state's narrative on ascribed, inherited belonging brought about the possibility for transformation of Germanness to a multicultural or cosmopolitan sense of self.

When the state decentered the *Hausfrauenehe*, which had been the symbolic focus of kinship law, it was not abnegating its control over marriage and family, but attempting to assimilate heterodox household, partnership, and childcare forms of legal codes without yielding control and influence over them. This shift in strategy was provoked by the tactics of Generation II, specifically of women who challenged the authority of old forms. Unlike their counterparts in the East, West Berlin women had a more antagonistic relationship to the state's version of their lifecourse. Thus the larger strategy of the Federal Republic since the late sixties was to legitimate selectively heterodox forms by legalizing them, emplotting experiential tropes into its larger master narrative that sought assimilation into hierarchy. The law, in this sense, was quite plastic, increasing its range of influence over forms while yielding on the control of content. For both the state and members of Generation II, this involved a trade-off: the law encompassed more action by dispersing its control, the citizen was given the means to articulate him/herself in a dialogue with the state in many different action domains. A final summary explaining how this dialogue feeds into the narrative about Germanness will be the purpose of the following chapter.

# 9

# Marriage, family, nation

> Unpolitical attempts to break out of the bourgeois family usually lead only to a deeper entanglement in it, and sometimes seem as if the fatal germ-cell of society, the family, were at the same time the nurturing germ-cell of uncompromising pursuit of another.
>
> Theodor Adorno, *Minima Moralia*, 1951

## Introduction

In the long conversation that marks the course of a life or the building of a nation, the individual encounters many different societal instances, be they religious, medical, or scientific institutions, media accounts, myths, or industrial organizations. Societal instances all have something to say to us about how we should orient ourselves and act, about who we are and to whom we belong, but their commentaries are not all equally significant. In this book, we have focused on encounters with one such instance, the state and its proto-forms, not because it exerts the only such influence on life constructions, but because of the power attached to its commentary.

From an experiential perspective, the state in the industrialized West, despite its range of competitors and accomplices, exerts perhaps the most significant contemporary influence on the organization of lifecourses – that means, on the organization of nationness – more than all other social institutions. Herein lies the key to its legitimacy and its longevity. Although many scientists have followed Max Weber in his succinct definition of the modern state as a unit having a monopoly on the use of violence within a particular territorially circumscribed space, the modern state as we approach the twenty-first century seems far from having a monopoly – witness the power of drug lords over governments in south Asia and the Americas, the flow of transnational capital, the disintegrating Soviet and Indian states, as well as the longstanding disputes over territoriality in South Africa, Ireland, and Israel, to name but a few of the most salient examples. Far more important for the state today, I would argue, is its ability to make people into nations.[1]

That the two German states never succeeded in completely standardizing their commentary about what the individual should be is less indicative of lack of power or effort than of the difficulty inherent in uniformizing heterogeneous desires and aspirations within a group living within world historical time. Try as they may – to reduce women to mothers or homemakers (in the FRG), to mass-produce the ideal nuclear family (at different times in both states), or to sire children true to the state (to name but three of their many goals) – states have in some way to reckon with their raw material: the people they actually have at hand, their nationals. These individuals themselves construct lives, using a logic that knows but one rule: to thyself be true. This "self" – always an allegory of the person and never merely a fact – not only gets in the way of the state but also of individuals who themselves no longer wish to be true to it, or desire to avoid or escape from its signification or communication techniques. Hence individual and state narrative constructions are dynamic and dialogic affairs, which neither participating side can arrest except through suicide or annihilation. Like the factitious dichotomy between nature and nurture, the individual and state allegorize themselves in a symbiotic process in which it is illusory to think we can isolate the point where one begins and the other ends.

While states lack the means – available to Thai forest monks, as Tambiah (1984: 81–131) has shown, or to Western asylums or prisons as Goffman (1961) and Foucault (1979) illustrate – necessary to totalize experience and fix the essence of the nation, they are nonetheless able to set, through their powerful legal and political commentary, the aesthetic and ideational framework in which experiences are categorized and periodized, in which memory selectively recalls the past as legitimate history. Following this logic, I have looked at the matrix of power which is the state less in terms of its self-representation as eliciting opinion and enacting laws, or, as Clifford Geertz writes, "postulating forces and measuring them" (1980: 178), than in terms of its control over how everyday symbols were manufactured, consumed, and made part of German subjectivity. Hence I examine how laws are read rather than written, understood rather than explained, how policy is actively appropriated rather than submissively received, and how states produce process and pattern rather than things. In order to frame the generative principles of state policy together with generational experience, I have engaged in linguistic analysis of legal texts and life histories, using tools primarily borrowed from the study of narrative, and I have interpreted these two discourses in their national and international contexts.

Table 21. *Narrative strategies of the East and West German states, 1949–1989*

|  | East Germany (GDR) | West Germany (FRG) |
|---|---|---|
| Strategy |  |  |
| 1949–1965/68 | Construction | Restoration |
| 1965–1989 | Sentimentalization | Desentimentalization |
| Emplotment |  |  |
| Aesthetic | Romantic | Satiric-lapsarian |
| Ideational | Integrational | Assimilational |
| Teleological | Egalitarian | Hierarchical |

Table 22. *Narrative tactics of Generation I in East and West Berlin*

|  | Women | Men |
|---|---|---|
| *East Berlin* |  |  |
| Tropes | Hunger, shared blood, *Aufbau*/work, victimization, self-realization, "lack" | POW camp, shared blood, *Aufbau*/work/family, victimization, "lack" |
| *West Berlin* |  |  |
| Tropes | *Persilschein*, consumer goods, free time/vacation, shared blood, *Hausfrauenehe*, *Wirtschaftswunder*/ prosperity, anti-communism, victimization | *Persilschein*, automobile, work, free time/vacation, shared blood, *Hausfrauenehe*, *Wirtschaftswunder*/ prosperity, anti-communism, hierarchy |

This chapter will proceed in five steps: first, I summarize the efforts of German nation-building by comparing life constructions in the two Berlins with the two states' accounts; second, I examine marriage as a case study for the interaction between individual tactics and state strategies; third, I show how marriage relates to external demarcation; fourth, I place this process of nation-building in the context of Berlin–Berlin exchange; fifth, I relate this analysis to the city of Berlin.

**Nation-building**

Throughout this study, I have proceeded on the assumption that in the modern world system, states, of which the two postwar German states are but single examples, are organized according to the principle that they have a nation (or several nations) they can call their own. Making a

Table 23. *Narrative tactics of Generation II in East and West Berlin*

|  | Women | Men |
| --- | --- | --- |
| *East Berlin*<br>Tropes | Domestic anarchy, work,<br>self-realization,<br>heterogeneity, free time/<br>vacation, fear, "lack" | Domestic anarchy, political<br>resignation, heterogeneity,<br>free time/vacation, fear,<br>"lack" |
| *West Berlin*<br>Tropes | Domestic anarchy,<br>heterogeneity,<br>experimentation, critique,<br>autonomy, social protest,<br>gender, free time/vacation | Domestic anarchy,<br>heterogeneity,<br>experimentation, critique,<br>autonomy, social protest,<br>sexuality, free time/vacation |

nation involves the (re)creation of belonging patterns that form the basis for feeling *zu Hause*, at home, in one place and not another. Being at home is essentially being among kin, experiencing a particular set of lifecourse meanings that enable the individual to belong to a group demarcated from other groups. The state is successful in its nation-building only when it can legitimize itself as having (re)created this unique group, whose members will, in turn, reciprocate by retelling their histories in terms – categories and periods – congruent with those that the state uses in its accounts.

Let us review, then, the categories and periods of the two German states and two generations of their citizens in Berlin. Tables 21 to 23 can serve as an orientation for discussion.

Like all tables, these oversimplify the range of tactics and strategies employed during the last forty years. Furthermore, the boundaries between generations were more fluid than such tables allow. For comparative purposes, I am overdrawing the lines. Nonetheless, let us attempt one final summation of the relation of state narratives to autobiographical accounts.

The major difference between East and West Berliners of Generation I lies in the fact that the *Wirtschaftswunder* is translated into prosperity by West Berliners, whereas the *Aufbau* is translated into work by East Berliners. Of course all Berliners worked equally hard in the fifties and sixties to rebuild their war-torn city halves, but the pay-off, in emotional, cognitive, and physical terms, was much greater for West Berliners. In troping their stories, East Berliners remained tied to a past and present sense of victimization and an experience of "lack" when compared to the West. Only some East Berlin women escaped these tropes, and instead countered with their own work experience as one of self-realization. Contrariwise, West Berlin women relativized their own victimization with a sense of satisfaction at being anti-communist and identification with the prosperity obtained through the *Wirtschaftswunder*.

Thus East Berlin women and men of Generation I did not resort to the master narratives of the state to connect their experiences to the same extent as their West counterparts. In fact, they often appealed to no master narrative at all, and their life histories took on more the character of a chronicle than a narrative. The particular master narrative offered by the state to emplot their experiences (romantic, integrative, egalitarian) rarely sufficed as a connecting thread to lend the individual tropes coherence. Indeed construction of life histories in the two Berlins always took place in the context of the dramatic asymmetry between East and West, hence the plot offered in the West derived added coherence from its superiority in ordering contexts and emplotting experiences according to design. Therefore, West Berliners, regardless of sex and class, told history in terms of the state's narrative categories (satiric, assimilative, hierarchical).

Both states played an even more determinate role in emplotting the life constructions of Generation II, whose members reached adulthood under the new regimes. During childhood and youth, East Berliners benefited from the utopian, egalitarian, and integrative master narrative of the state, whereas West Berliners faced a relatively antagonistic state, focused on restoration of hierarchy. By the late sixties–early seventies, the two states in effect reversed their postures, with the GDR tightening control in creating an atmosphere of fear and restricting the political expression of its young adults, while the FRG, though with reluctance, turned to a more reconciliatory, integrative policy as the country became more prosperous. East Berliners of this generation experienced this about-face of their state with disappointment and resignation; West Berliners sensed that their own agency, in the form of social protest movements, had forced some change. Women of Generation II did not experience these changes exactly like their male peers; unlike in West Berlin, East Berliners did not have to struggle for employment (indeed most of their mothers were already employed by the state); in West Berlin, a grass-roots feminist movement politicized gender differences, problematizing old tensions and creating new opportunities.

Heterogeneity, articulated both publicly and privately in West Berlin and only privately in the East, became a value for many members of Generation II, shifting the basis for kinship membership away from a reliance on shared blood, hence closer to the GDR model and in opposition to the model of the FRG. In effect Berliners in both city halves ended up effacing much of the distinction between politics and domestic life. The West German state's early resistance to change and its satiric-lapsarian aesthetic often represented Generation II itself as an ultimate source of decline. Many members of this generation reacted by rejecting the assimilative and restorative aspects of the state's narrative, instead stressing either private pleasures (free time and self-fulfillment) or experimentation, both of which run formally counter to the satiric-lapsarian emplotment of the FRG, yet are made possible only because of the prosperity already reached by their parents and the state.

In general, we might ask why the satiric-aesthetic emplotment has been much more effective than the romantic in providing an idiom in which to emplot experiences. Walter Benjamin offers us a clue, calling satire "the only legitimate form of regional art" (1978: 260). It is precisely the parochialism of satire, its roots in the local, that makes it so appropriate for nation-building. Because it is tied to the concrete, satire must first recognize difference before undermining it. Romance, on the other hand, tied to an idealization of the other that is often merely a projection of the self, ignores difference altogether; it represents itself as open to change but is actually rigid in form. Satire worked especially well in the German and Berlin context because it could both present itself as representing the transcendental and unchanging good, while also adapting to changing local circumstances and times. Perhaps only with such an emplotment, lodged in the mentality of a nation tied to the provincial, and in the wisdom of the Basic Law, could the Federal Republic satirically undermine its opponent to the East as well as its internal adversaries – the communists, pacifists, recalcitrant youth, Halbstarken '68ers, *Baader-Meinhof Gruppe* – while siding with a delegitimated traditional authority, seamlessly incorporating into its leadership former Nazis who had since obtained *Persilschein*. More-over, the FRG could not exile its dissidents as could the GDR; it had no choice but to "eat" them, or as Benjamin dubs it, "the devouring of the adversary" (1978: 260). Under the rubric of a virtuous critique, the state incorporated all differences into its very apparatus, assimilating the opposition ostensibly against its will. It is clear that this strategy of the particular, the morally superior, the restorative and lapsarian, made the adjustment to a new state and to a new conception of the group effortless for the majority of Generation I, who had reached adulthood before the end of World War II.

A romantic emplotment works by opposite means. Idealization is sustainable only with illusion, which is difficult to maintain over time, expecially when one is forced to confront, and distance oneself from, past ideals. And when identity is constructed through mirror-imaging, the self is mirrored back too often to remain in love with its image. Instead, the tendency is to note that something is lacking – usually whatever it is that the Other has. Integrative, universalistic, and future-oriented, romanticism denies the moral superiority of the past – a rather treacherous position for a state, which usually relies on the construction of a glorious history to justify its present. Even when, after 1965, the GDR began to sentimentalize marriage and the family, it did not idealize a past version but romanticized what it had already reached, culminating in its present. Proclaiming that the golden age had arrived only increased citizen dissatisfaction with the regime. Contrariwise, when the FRG began infrastructural change after 1968 and moved away from its model of the housewife marriage, reforming family law and incorporating women into the educational system and labor force, it did so under a coalition government (Christian and Social Democrats) with no admission of a break from its high moral grounds, effortlessly assimilating the new into the old.

Neither state strategy worked well in interaction with Generation II, though a rejection of state narratives did not necessarily indicate an escape from them. This rejection has been more pronounced in West Berlin largely because of the alignment between the state and parents of Generation I. However, with the gradual assimiliation of Generation II into the different sectors of public life, their opposition has been muted. Since the parental narrative in East Berlin was never fully in accord with the state's account, and since the state romantically curried the favor of Generation II, divisions between the generations and between Generation II and the state in the East were never framed as oppositionally as in the West.

It should be clear from the above discussion that state narrative strategies are not incidental aspects of life constructions, but very much integral parts of them. Narrative strategies and tactics interact to emplot the experiences of groups, to weld disparate contents into a common form, creating a processual political economy of meaning in which the semantics of Germanness are defined. In West Germany, satire presupposed a stable society with homogeneous moral standards, one that took itself seriously, was quick to ridicule vice or folly, yet unable to commit itself to a present. In East Germany, romance presupposed a utopian society with future-oriented moral standards; it never subjected itself to reality tests, was quick to dream, slow to act. These strategies permeate the ways in which younger generations of Germans from various class and regional backgrounds allegorized themselves, and hence played a constitutive role in the creation of meaningful subjects in Berlin.

**Marriage and nation-building**
In this section, I will use the specific case of East/West German marriages as an exemplary instance of the interaction between individual tactics and state strategies, as a privileged field of kin meanings in which the state and individual contest and cooperate over the meaning of the nation. During my fieldwork, I encountered in everyday speech and official texts the following twenty marriage types:

1 *Hausfrauenehe* (housewife marriage): a legally recognized man–woman unit based on the woman taking care of the home and the man working to support it; the central generative model for FRG law in the fifties;

2 *Liebesheirat* (love marriage): a marriage where the motivation for the union was initially love; in the GDR, this type is reached officially only at the stage of socialist production where women are no longer economically dependent on men and the system of class exploitation has been overcome; in the FRG, this marriage type has not achieved centrality, either in law or in everyday life;

3 *normale Ehe* (normal marriage): a heterosexual dyad that adheres to standard legal and social conventions;

4 *eheliche Gemeinschaft* (marital partnership): a legal concept from the Civil Law Book of 1896, distinguished from 7 and 8, where the marriage is sexually consummated and the partners share a household;

5 *Onkelehe* (uncle marriage): an unmarried man–woman unit that functions like a marriage but is not legally legitimated; a precursor of the *Lebensgemeinschaft* of the seventies and common among Generation I in the immediate postwar years in both Berlins; the actual husband often was missing or in a

POW camp, and the new man and woman were paramours (often including shared residence), but the man in the relationship was called "uncle" and not "father" by the woman's children;

6 *kinderlose Ehe* (childless marriage): a normal marriage without children practiced in both Berlins;

7 *Kriegsehe* (war marriage): a marriage that was consummated and legally legitimated during the war years, but the couple usually did not have a chance to cohabit because the man was most often a soldier;

8 *Namensehe* (marriage in name only): an illegal marriage because engaged in for purposes not recognized by the state; §19 of the Marriage Law passed in 1933, eliminated in 1946 in the East, in 1976 in West Germany, to prevent individuals (mostly Jews) from marrying in order to change their name and thus hide what was called their "racial heritage";

9 *Zweckehe* (instrumental marriage): a legal marriage that does not meet the criteria of an *eheliche Gemeinschaft*, namely, love as the motivation, shared sex, shared residence, and children; most often applied to foreigners who marry Germans primarily to obtain residency permits in the FRG;

10 *Scheinehe* (sham marriage): primarily a West German legal marriage where the couple only appears (*Schein*) to be married as opposed to practicing the being (*Sein*) of marriage; often implies that the man–woman pair are not sharing sex;

11 *hinkende Scheinehe* (limping sham marriage): a West German bureaucratic refinement of definition 10 applied to a German/non German marriage, where the German woman loves the foreigner but the foreign man does not love her (see IAF 1985: 24);

12 *Besuchsehe* (visiting marriage): a West German legal marriage where the couple does not share residence, but merely visits each other (see IAF 1985: 74);

13 *eheähnliches Verhältnis* (relationship resembling a marriage): primarily a West German description used since the sixties to describe partnership forms that resembled 3, the "normal marriage";

14 *gemischt-nationale Ehe* (mixed-nationality marriage): a legal marriage where the partners are of different nationalities, usually employed by West German state bureaucrats;

15  *binationale Ehe* (bi-national marriage): same as 14, except usually employed by people to describe themselves;

16  *Mischehe* (mixed marriages): legal marriages between a German and someone of another nationality, usually applied only when the foreigner has another skin color; became a central category in Nazi marital law and eugenics policy;

17  unnamed – male–male or female–female marriage: where same-sex partners live as a married couple and designate themselves that way but without legal recognition:

18  unnamed – shotgun marriage, or, marriage due to pregnancy: a legal marriage motivated by a pregnancy;

19  unnamed – marriage of an East German citizen with a foreigner not legalized in the GDR; not named by the GDR because its recognition would often mean the move of the GDR citizen to a foreign country;

20  unnamed – dead/missing husband: a marriage of the type where the woman maintains the fiction of a marriage despite the fact that her husband is not physically present; corresponds to the woman whose husband had been killed during or was missing after the war, but where the woman had no proof of that or refused to believe the evidence she had received.

The origin of these twenty marital models can be traced either to historically specific pragmatic practices and tactics or to state strategies. These marriages obey no central rule, fulfill no set of necessary and sufficient conditions to make them a marriage (see Bourdieu 1977:22–30). Instead, they are different historical experiences and articulations, where no single model is able to account for all of the types that go by the name. The central or ideal type around which the others revolve (variously, either 1 *Hausfrauenehe*, 2 *Liebesheirat*, or 3 *normale Ehe*), but which does not encompass them, always belongs to the "calculus of force relations" or "the proper," following de Certeau, and therefore is aligned with authority, including that of the state. Many of the models served disciplinary functions as part of state strategies for internal regulation or external demarcation; others served as individual tactics to undermine or circumvent state discipline; altogether, the multiplicity of types militates against a single normative standpoint. Moreover, the distinction between tactics and strategies took on a new twist over time, in that individual marital practices not covered by state doctrine, not "executing the rule" or belonging to the "calculus of force relations," were often co-opted by the state, incorporated into its own model(s). These variant practices were then absorbed into the fold of state-defined regulatory interests.

The twenty marital models divide themselves basically into three groups: one based on officially acknowledged semantic criteria of necessary and sufficient conditions for internal regulation of group members, a second unnamed and based on regulatory criteria that is socially taboo and not part of public discourse, and a third based on officially acknowledged semantic criteria for the purpose of external demarcations.

During the period of my fieldwork, these types were assigned the following definitions. In West Germany, centrality was assigned to 1, the *Hausfrauenehe*; in East Germany, 2, the *Liebesehe* was central. Both the housewife and love marriages are based on semantic distinctions corresponding to the necessary and sufficient conditions of an official marriage. Marriages 3 *normale Ehe* and 4 *eheliche Gemeinschaft* are other names for this "proper" form, the former more common in East Germany, the latter in West Germany. In all three types, the strategy precedes the practice; the state's goal was to create and propagate the practices described by the name. Nine of the types – 5 *Onkelehe*, 6 *kinderlose Ehe*, 7 *Kriegsehe*, 8 *Namensehe*, 9 *Zweckehe*, 10 *Scheinehe*, 11 *hinkende Scheinehe*, 12 *Besuchsehe*, 13 *eheähnliches Verhältnis* – relate to insufficient or illegitimate grounds for marriage from the state's perspective. They are *ad hoc* categories with pejorative names meant to discredit by bringing under the rule sets of individual practices too close for comfort to the central model.

In contrast to the first two types, which originated in state appropriation of an ideological norm, marital models 5 through 13 grew out of non-standard practices, and only later, after their discovery, were contested by the state. I should mention in this context the contemporary practice of the *Lebensgemeinschaft*, discussed in great length in the chapters on kinship. In many ways both states defined it as anti-marriage, for most members of such a union could theoretically get married if they liked; their refusal to apply for state blessings was a source of concern in both Germanies, since such relationships were therefore controllable only through the household unit. And state control of households, given the associations with Nazi use of this strategy, continually provoked open resistance among the populace.[2] In short, the first twelve models were part of public discourse, useful to the two states for central, internal regulation.

Such was not the case with our last seven types, which spoke more to individual freedom than to state control. Four of the models – 17 same-sex, 18 due to pregnancy, 19 GDR–foreigner, 20 dead/missing husband marriage – are unnamed because they were taboo marriages. Inability or refusal to name a practice relates directly to the severity with which it breaches the norm; silence keeps practice in the realm of *doxa*, defined by Bourdieu as "that which is beyond question" (1977: 169). Bestowing a name would objectively recognize a practice that is best regulated by keeping it unmentionable; namelessness thus prevents the development of a language for description that might bring individual practices into public discourse.

Dead/missing husband marriage was taboo because the woman loved someone dead or missing for reasons embarrassing to the postwar states – lost in a war the Germans had lost and would like to forget. Same-sex marriage broke the taboo against homosexual love, especially strong when such unions are brought into public discourse and represented as alternatives to heterosexual ones. The pregnancy marriage undermined male privilege (based partly on its nonarticulation in public) by granting the woman power over the man to force a legal union. Here, it is important to note the historicality of these models: the dead/missing husband marriage was specific to women of Generation I; the same-sex marriage was becoming more commonplace over time; and the pregnancy marriage in Berlin had, with the development of a feminist discourse and increased legal equality for women, all but died out. Pregnancy may still be a reason for marriage, but the decision between the partners is usually mutual, and the woman can no longer apply social pressures on the man to marry solely because of pregnancy. While taboo may at any particular time be the strongest of all sanctions, it is also the most fragile over time. Marriage 19 between GDR citizens and foreigners was taboo for the state in its efforts at external demarcation. Most GDR citizens who married foreigners chose residence in the foreign country, and were thus lost to the GDR; the state therefore used the most severe strategy it had to prevent the practice from spreading: not to grant it a name.

As opposed to internal regulation, external demarcation concerns four types: 8 *Namensehe*, 14 *gemischt-nationale Ehe*, 15 *binationale Ehe*, 16 *Mischehe*. The *Mischehe* lost its linguistic legitimacy in the Germanies after World War II, because this was the marital category and state strategy (along with the *Namensehe*, which applied in these cases also, but to a wider field) used to deport Jews married to non-Jewish

Germans. The postwar states nonetheless needed categories to regulate the marriage of Germans to foreigners: the GDR kept this category unnamed, as mentioned above; the FRG deployed the mixed-national model, whereas its citizens in these marriages used the bi-national model. With the world territorially divided into socialist and capitalist blocks, marriage to someone outside the block to which one's state belonged posed the greatest challenge for the state's categories. As external demarcators in countries with permeable borders, these marital types remained legally contentious or dangerous categories, for the marriage of a German to a foreigner blurred the relation, essential to states during the Cold War, between nationality and territory. Given the liminal status of West Berlin, and hence an even greater inability to demarcate the group from outsiders, the model's dangerousness is even more marked.

Individuals often experienced more than one of these marriage types in a lifetime, for some partnerships met several criteria simultaneously, and some citizens engaged in a succession of different marriages over a lifetime. Whereas marital *strategies* are legal devices used by the state to regulate its citizens internally and to demarcate them from outsiders, marital *tactics* grow out of individual pragmatics. The former are institutionalized, thus victories of "space over time"; the latter are non-institutionalized, thus victories of "time over space" (de Certeau 1984). To argue for the priority of practices and integrity of non-central marital models, as I am doing, is not to deny state strategies, but to place the latter within the live, dynamic context that gives them their full regulatory meaning. For, when forms of practice lie totally outside state control, states often stretch the legal model to encompass the heterodox category and include it under its umbrella of acceptable marital forms. Since the institution of marriage is the most direct link between the state and the substance of kinship – to the practices of household, childcare, partnership, and self – its strategic importance should come as no surprise. On the one hand, creating people that belong to the nation involves the use of communication and signification techniques to define their residence, their upbringing, their affective life, and their sense of person. On the other hand, individuals as members of generations define themselves through sets of practices using the very same set of terms and techniques as the state. Control over the categories of the lifecourse, then, is central to the state in constructing belonging patterns that reproduce a particular nationness.

**External demarcations**

In addition to the operation of marriage for internal regulation, it also performs the crucial functions of limiting or controlling membership in the group by regulating who can enter. German marriage to non-nationals stretches the boundaries of self-identity by challenging the categories demarcating the group from outsiders. Population movements across political boundaries have long been characteristic of Central Europe, even before the massive shifts following World War II. And since the time of Frederick II, greater Germany, and Berlin in particular, has continually absorbed other European peoples into its midst. Yet alongside these historically permeable borders one finds during the Cold War a recurrent concern about Germans dying out. This group *Angst* speaks less to population decline than to the insecurity of a group unable to establish a firm demarcation between its identity and those of others. In situations of war or declining internal population the group must often open its borders or expand its criteria of membership – solutions difficult for the modern state to adopt, since its legitimacy is dependent on exactly the opposite: territorially fixed borders and a nation belonging to them and only them.[3] For the Germans, this has traditionally meant *ein Volk*.

Between 1944/1949 and 1961, the two German states experienced a 25 percent increase in population in their territories, the vast majority being Germans who had lived outside the pre-1939 boundaries of the German state, coming from the former *Ostgebiete*. After 1961, the labor migration from East to West Germany was stopped by the building of the Wall, whereafter the West Germans began importing Turkish and southern European labor (see chapter 4). The FRG set up its first bureau to recruit foreign labor in 1955 in Italy; recruiting then accelerated in the mid sixties, and stopped altogether with the recession in 1973. East Germany did not begin suffering major labor shortages until the late seventies (outside of certain skilled industries and professions, where the shortage has been constant), whereafter it began importing labor from other socialist countries, primarily from Poland, Cuba, and Vietnam.

For the FRG, the problem of the *Gastarbeiter*, guestworker, has been conceived as one of external demarcation: how to return "guests" eventually to their country of origin, or to prevent family members from joining them. The standard of living in West Germany/West Berlin is far superior to the home country of the guestworker, thus many seek to stay. By the mid eighties, the FRG had settled on a policy of semi-integration (for example, most civil rights but no political enfranchisement) with legal status for guestworkers already residing in Germany. The East German system of labor importation, never so extensive as the West German, did not result in a major problem of integration for the state, largely because most workers wanted to return to their own countries after the labor stint. Moreover, the East German system of labor exchange was regulated by state contacts, and not individual ones as in the FRG, that determined the length of time foreign workers were allowed to remain. This was not the case for West German policy, where recruiting was pursued both by the state and by private companies. Once non-German individuals already resided in either Germany, marriage to a German remained the only secure way of entering the nation on a permanent legal basis.

In a pioneering article on marriage systems and group boundaries, Robert Merton argued that mixed marriages exist where "an endogamous social group . . . operates according to a social definition of 'difference' and accepts the notion of interdict. Mixed marriage, then, is the union between two people who should not have married. Their marriage infringes upon principles considered as important for the survival and cohesion of the group" (1941: 362). Three of the twenty marriage models listed above (all West German) relate directly to German–foreigner marriages and to state strategies for preventing its citizens from marrying-out. The GDR tried to reduce this variation to one simple form, and regulated marriages to foreigners by forcing the couple to declare a "common residence" (see §5, *Eheschließungen von Bürgern der Deutschen Demokratischen Republik mit Ausländern* reprinted in *Der Tagesspiegel*, December 15, 1988, pp. 12–13). In practice, if the couple did not declare a common residence in the GDR, the East German citizen was compelled to give up his/her citizenship. This was, of course, in keeping with the state strategy of universalism and integration: any person could become a national if they joined the socialist community, residence being a prerequisite set forth by the state because of its labor needs.

Four categories of marriage (8, 14, 15, and 16) pertain to the West German state's attempt to prevent foreigners from marrying-in: mixed marriages, mixed-nationality marriages, and bi-national marriages. From 1950 to 1977, 418,000 West German women married foreign men; 184,000 West German men married foreign women. By 1978, the total numbers of kin taking part in such marriages, or their offspring, totaled approximately one million (Müller-Dincu 1981: 6). Berlin has by far the highest percentage of bi-national marriages in the FRG, totaling 14 percent of all such marriages in 1977, whereas the average for the FRG is 7 percent (Müller-Dincu 1981: 23). Bi-national marriages reached a peak in Berlin in 1981, totaling 2,136, declining to 1,631 in 1983 (IAF 1985: 101). The most favored group for German women has been US-Americans, closely followed by Italians; for German men, Austrians and Dutch up until 1970, Yugoslavian thereafter (Müller-Dincu 1981: 26). A 1968 study of such marriages concluded that 90 percent would end in divorce (Zimmer 1968: 6). Furthermore, since the mid sixties, over 10 percent of all children born in the FRG have been to non-German nationals; hence a new generation likely to use this kind of marriage model is already at hand.

This West German legal situation changed more gradually over time than the East German one. As described in chapter 3, by 1950, East German women had obtained citizenship rights equal to those of men. In her 1949 article, Minister of Justice Hilde Benjamin had specifically argued for not limiting equal rights to the economic domain, but extending them to the political. In West Germany, on the other hand, until 1953 German women who married a foreigner automatically lost their citizenship and were forced to take on that of their (foreign) marital partner. German men who married foreign women maintained their citizenship, and could (until 1970) obtain German citizenship for their wives by a simple statement before state authorities (Müller-Dincu 1981: 39). The same set of double standards applied to children born to these unions: children from German mothers and foreign fathers had no right to German citizenship; children from German fathers and foreign mothers had automatic citizenship upon birth.

Changes in family law that took effect in 1976 rectified this process, making all children born to a German father or mother, regardless of where s/he was born, automatically eligible for FRG citizenship. The 1976 law also eliminated the ban on the *Namensehe*, name-marriage, that applied to those who married for a purpose not recognized by the law. The 1933 law had intended to prevent individuals from hiding as "German" when they were in fact "Jewish." It had been passed because many Jewish and Slavic women were marrying men only to take on their names, and not to fulfill the conditions of an *eheliche Gemeinschaft*, marital partnership. After 1976, the state no longer claimed the right to pass judgment on the motivation (*Zweck*) for marriages between German citizens, but the category *Zweckehe* reappeared after 1980, now transformed to *Scheinehe*, sham marriage, still centered around fulfilling the categories of an *eheliche Gemeinschaft*. This time the concept was intended to apply to German–foreign (nationals) marriages. On January 18, 1985, the Berlin Senator for Internal Affairs, Heinrich Lummer, a Christian Democratic Party member, described these bi-national marriages as a "damaging development for the city [for they] can be successfully stopped only if we are able, through respectable control measures, to nip them in the bud." On January 26, 1985, he further claimed that "90% of all marriages [between Germans and foreigners] are only for appearance, *zum Schein*" (IAF 1985: 6, 59).

The two components of a *Scheinehe* were supposedly that (1) the purpose was to obtain a residency permit for the foreigner, and that (2) there was no "marital partnership." Although West German courts had been reluctant to equate explicitly a marital partnership with shared residency and shared sex, these were, in fact, the criteria used to decide which marriages to investigate and prosecute under the label *Scheinehe* (see details of cases in IAF 1985). Interior Senator Lummer admitted in a 1985 letter that state authorities were told to try to hinder the marriages suspected of not becoming true marital partnerships, although since the middle of 1980 authorities have quit deporting suspected individuals who had already fixed a date to marry (IAF 1985: 103).

Some *Länder* in the FRG, such as West Berlin, had their own special police force to investigate "bi-national" marriages. In most cases this special police force, the AGA or Arbeitsgebiet gezielte Ausländerüber-wachung, a task force for directed investigation/observation of foreign-ers, followed a standard procedure. The following account is a summary of reports from the IAF (1985: 43-45), from my own discussion partners, and from women involved in the IAF-Berlin. Nearly always dressed in civilian clothing, AGA-Beamte, civil servants for this task force, pro-ceeded in groups of two to the suspected persons' apartment. They never announced themselves ahead of time, and often even entered the apart-ment without the permission of the residents in order to have a look around. Of most interest to them were the private rooms, where the nature of intimate life is inscribed in such easily observable banalities as table settings in the kitchen, bed size and underwear in the bedroom, number of toothbrushes or types of razors in the bathroom, pictures of the married couple and their friends and parents in the living room. These control police looked for evidence of the *eheliche Gemeinschaft*: were two individuals of the opposite sex actually sharing residence and bed? Neighbors were routinely asked about those under investigation, to identify their everyday routines, friends, and visitors. Although the

AGA-Beamten were not able to obtain search orders from the courts for such fishing expeditions, they nonetheless used their authority as policemen to persuade the residents to cooperate. Those under investigation know that the findings of such police searches were often crucial in determining the legality of their residence status as foreigners in FRG. In one case involving rejection of an unrestricted residence permit, the Berlin police wrote as reason, "The hesitancy of your wife and your own passivity [during the investigation] can only be taken as indication of a *Zweckehe*, marriage for a purpose." The burden of proof in such cases, to show that a proper marital partnership existed, was not on the police, but on the suspected bi-national partners.

In comparison to the other West German *Länder*, West Berlin had one of the most liberal laws pertaining to asylum and residence permits. Those who had legally resided in the FRG for ten years could apply for West German citizenship. Like the GDR and other *Länder* within the FRG, West Berlin's laws concerning the issuance of residence permits prioritized *Familienzusammenführung*, bringing families together, which, since 1965, was limited to married spouse and children. Foreign married people with a legal residency permit to live in the FRG were allowed to bring their foreign partners or children to their German residence after, on the average, three full uninterrupted years of residence. In the case of a divorce of such a couple, the foreign partner must have lived in Germany for at least four uninterrupted years, or two years if s/he had a dependent child of her/his own, in order to retain the residency permit (Ausländerrecht der Bundesländer 1987: 3–59).

How does this account relate to other social-science accounts about marriage and nation-building? My argument has been a dual one. First, I used native linguistic categories in the postwar Berlins to show that only by taking into account the empirical range of marriages and their historical specificity (identified in strategic and tactical discourses) was it possible to illustrate accurately the function of marriage for internal group regulation. Second, I demonstrated that marriage played a vital role in demarcating groups, in this case "nation-states," from one another.

This argument is not totally new. In studies of darker-skinned peoples in the Third World, anthropologists have often maintained that marriage serves the dual functions of facilitating exchange between kin groups and regulating the behavior of kin (more strongly women than men) within groups. I hope to have shown that this also holds true for the two Germanies during the period of the Cold War. What differentiates my account of marriage in the Berlins from those in more traditional anthropological places is my emphasis on the presence of the state, which changes the context of the exchange (now international) and the nature of group boundaries (now territoriality takes precedence over other boundaries). The unit of exchange for both state-regulated and stateless groups remains kin, but the group to which they belong differs. States exchange people that belong to a nation; non-state societies exchange individuals belonging to *ethnie* or ethnic communities. These two types of belonging are intimately related, as Anthony D. Smith (1986) has argued, with the *ethnie* often giving rise to the nation, and then relying on it for further legitimacy. The process in "nation-states" wherein exchange and belonging unfolds is now part of an inter-national order, where the role of agency is more pronounced, the explicitness of rules is greater, and thus the exchange does not follow the kind of automaticity often assumed of non-state communities. What follows from this argument is not that the rise of Western states, with the new signification of nation as the unit to which one belongs, has created a new genus of marriage, but precisely the opposite, that Western marriages should be brought back into the fold of human marital types. Despite the way in which contemporary marriages legitimate themselves with reference to the ideologies of love and individualism, and the fact that they must obtain legal form within states, they do not differ in kind from marriages among other peoples traditionally studied by anthropologists. Why have we indeed come to the conclusion that Western marital types are unique?

At the end of World War II, social scientists and humanists were in nearly unanimous agreement that Western societies had reached a stage in the development of their civilizations – some called it Modernity – that set them apart from the rest of the world. One of the major characteristics of this new stage was said to be an individualization of emotions; in particular, kin groupings were increasingly based on bonds of love. A corollary to this proposition was that the choices made with regard to the practices of marriage and the family were no longer structured by struggles over land or water rights and the exchange of women, as was the case with so-called primitives. In other words, Western marriage systems were not to be described as institutions of group exchange (external demarcation), nor were they primarily a mechanism for internal discipline of members of the group (internal demarcation) in the struggle for property, status, and power. Once love entered the institution of marriage, a new type of family appeared, built around neither exchange nor control, but romantic affective ties. One folk tale of the Cold War – shared in both Germanies – had it that "love, marriage, and the family" were a basic meaning complex characteristic of Western societies (as opposed to non-Western societies, often referred to as African, Asian, or Oriental). Love motivated people to marry, after which the married pair created a family. In this design for life, the centrality and meanings of marriage, sandwiched in the lifecourse between birth and death, were the generative motor of the plot.

The major problem encountered in using this postwar model was that it could not account for forms of marriage other than those character-ized by the model – except by classifying them as deviations from the norm, as a genus or species different from marriage. Another problem encountered was that this regnant model did not reproduce duplicate forms with the consistency expected of a scientific model. It could not predict its offspring. The initial response to these "exceptions" was to ignore them. If that proved impossible, academicians and literary folk would often introduce alternate forms of practice as jokes, for comic relief in the middle of a narrative dealing with some central, undisputed concept of marriage. The logic remained strictly tautological: because marriage equals x set of legal relationships, all relationships not corresponding to x relationships do not equal marriage. Thus the full range of marital types – including forms of alterity – were conveniently placed outside the purview of the researcher, much as they remained outside the protection of the law.

Does not the cluster of meanings attached to love, marriage, and the family, described in detail in this study, demand that we reconsider whether it is wise to continue employing as an analytical tool this particular folk model of marriage in its legal-ideological form? Indeed, whereas marriage as a Western legal institution fits the particular idealized cognitive model outlined above, marriage as practice does not. Uncritically adopting the state's version invariably leads to a repression of how marriage is in fact conceptualized and practiced in everyday life. Actual linguistic and behavioral marital practices in the Berlins indicate an empirical range of types not confined to or always defined in terms of the legal model.[4]

As I have illustrated throughout this book, kinship revolves around this struggle over the institutionalization of practices, of which the marriage complex is one example. Marriage is but a single device, albeit perhaps the central one, through which the state renames and classifies its citizens in a particular way, thereby exerting direct control over the lifecourse. The form and content of the name is politically contested, for citizens do not uniformly and submissively comply with state strategies, as evidenced by the range of marriage tactics and of lifecourse trajectories that are not structured around the "proper" model. That the German states lacked instruments other than marriage so refined and effective at internal regulation is part of the explanation for why marital regulation, despite indications in both Berlins of its loss of monopoly status and effectiveness, remained a strategic part of the states' arsenal. Such classificatory devices define the conditions of group membership; and group memberships index the allegiances of individuals – their categories of belonging – to kin, to nations, and to states.

### Berlin–Berlin exchange

At the time of my initial fieldwork, from September 1986 to February 1989, the preferred state version of writing Berlin was "Berlin, the capital city" for the East German state and "Berlin (West)" for the West German state. Non-official natives in both cities simply said "Berlin." Fashioned into a dual form in 1945/1949 to represent ideological rifts between the two world superpowers, this highly improbable city became captive to its state of geopolitical liminality. Like a weather vane that turns at the slightest indication of wind, Berlin continually shifted its significations to accommodate prevailing winds. Hence its cultural systems, such as the economic and the domestic, or the political and the culinary, always appeared to be losing their putative coherence, not so much blurred by the constant tectonic jarring of different power matrices meeting as subsumed under a succession of political grids, on which they initially took shape, but from which they could not liberate themselves.

In the period covered by this study, the city of Berlin has successively been transformed from a capital into an occupied territory, from an occupied to a so-called protected city, from a frontier city into one known for its border crossings, from an international Iron Curtain city to a bridge between East and West. Even before the autumn revolution of 1989 accelerated the dissolution of its dual organization, Berlin had begun to change and yield in its radical insistence on mirror-imaging. Since the late sixties, Berlin had sought to avoid the marginality assigned to other Central European cities in a world increasingly structured around oppositions other than the Cold War. In contrast to Berlin, the cities of Warsaw, Budapest, and Prague had been totally mired into representing only one face of the Cold War polarity. By early

1989, the Cold War terms of duality were breaking down everywhere faster than they could be reconstructed and maintained. Instead of the fission of identities in Berlin, I was witnessing fusion.

This fusion started, appropriately enough, at the level of kinship, and appropriately enough, was initiated by the states in one of the most significant German–German accords agreed to by GDR head of state and party Erich Honecker during his 1987 visit to West Germany. New respect for "relatives" was thus written into a 1988 law, carefully opening up the way for consanguinal family members – those sharing the same blood – to visit their relatives in the West. The accord legally guaranteed the right for GDR citizens to visit the FRG – provided they had blood relatives there. Legally recognized kin included "close relatives" (meaning nuclear family and grandparents), uncles, aunts, nieces, nephews, cousins, brothers- and sisters-in-law, sons- and daughters-in-law. Possible grounds for a visit included marriages, baptisms, 25th, 50th, 60th, and 65th wedding anniversaries (either state or church ones), 50th, 60th, 65th, 70th, and all birthdays thereafter, life-threatening illnesses, and deaths (*Der Tagesspiegel*, December 15, 1988, pp. 1, 12).

West Germany heralded this "new transparence," for with this law the GDR signaled political acquiescence to the validity of West German legal kin categories, and simultaneously turned its back on that group of its own citizens who had bought into a culturally constructed identity based not on blood but on universal socialist brotherhood. East Germany had in the past always discouraged people from keeping contacts with relatives in the West, requiring most professionals to sign yearly statements agreeing to avoid any such contacts. Adopting an emplotment that had worked so well for the West Germans, the GDR thus turned to satire and "regional art," to ascribed and not learned identities, to particularism and not universalism. Dissatisfaction over restrictions on free travel to the West increasingly posed the major domestic political obstacle to the legitimacy of the GDR leadership. With some estimates that up to 10 percent of the population had officially applied to resettle in West Germany, the ruling elite apparently hoped that this law would let off steam. Whereas conservatives who had rejected the socialist creed, or careerists who had learned to manipulate it cynically, were best able under the new kin rules to take advantage of travel privileges, the most committed socialists, including the majority of Socialist Unity Party members, most of whom had long since – at the prodding of the state – broken off their kin contacts with the West, were ostensibly locked within their utopia. By then, only the state was maintaining that utopia had been reached.

On the West Berlin side, the new, open-door GDR kin regulations confronted them with the consequences of putting their legal ideology into practice. Rather than respond with joy to the anticipated visits of masses of *Ossis*, they reacted with horror to the possibility that their long-lost, poor relatives might overwhelm them with visits. Everybody knows the exquisite tastes of those in the East, I was told. *Ossis* seek out only the best products, never settle for second-best, and they think Western streets are paved with gold. One 27-year-old West Berlin man, a former East German citizen, went so far as to write a letter to the GDR Office for Visits and Travel Opportunities claiming that his 44-year-old half-sister and his niece, both East Berlin residents, intended to visit him in order to flee the republic, *Republikflucht*, a crime that led to imprisonment. In a Moabit–West Berlin hearing regarding the denunciation, the man claimed he had not wished to endanger his relatives, but only to have the GDR state security reject their travel privileges. On earlier visits to the West, his niece had complained that his gifts were "too cheap," and his half-sister called him a *Geizhals*, miser. His other sister, who also lived in the East, testified in his favor. In testimony by telephone, she told the court that every time her relatives returned to the East from a West visit, they complained that he had sent them back with too little money, even though during the visits he had paid for their costs and lodging, as well as given them money to enjoy West Berlin's nightlife. His retired 69-year-old mother traveled from her home in East Berlin to the West Berlin–Moabit court to testify for her daughter and grandchild. Under §241 of the West German Criminal Code, the man could have received ten years' imprisonment for trying to make his relatives politically suspect, thus placing them in a position of possible political persecution. The court gave him a suspended sentence of six months (*Die Tageszeitung*, July 13, 1988, p. 17).

Whereas the reaction of this West Berliner was an exceptional one, his fears of being overrun by his East relatives, or by others officially classified as *deutschstämmig*, coming from Eastern Europe and the Soviet Union, were quite common. This was especially the case among members of Generation II, who often reported disgust and shock at the "materialism" of the resettlers. Of crucial significance to the West Berliners/West Germans in protecting them from the East was the Wall, which for the West Germans kept others out, and for the East Germans kept their own in. Taking it down endangered the dual organization, and given the power asymmetry between the states, one side was threatened with extinction. Everyone knew that its collapse would menace labor markets, social-welfare systems, and the lifecourse design of all citizens. But taking the Wall down symbolically preceded its destruction physically, much as an imagined division preceded a material construction. This process of deconstructing division and duality had its own logic, independent of Cold War structures and state needs.

The Cold War thaw of the mid eighties, set in motion by Mikhail Gorbachev's reforms in the *Ostblock*, released a veritable flood of claims by people in the East asserting *Deutschstämmigkeit*, that they were of German heritage, and thus had a right to enjoy a West German lifecourse.[5] In 1988 alone, 202,673 Soviet and Eastern European immigrants claiming German roots, officially called *Aussiedler*, settled-out, flooded into the Federal Republic, swamping detention centers and refugee camps. Those resettling from the GDR, called *Zuwanderer*, wandered-out, numbered 39,832 in 1988 (18,958 in 1987). This combined total of 242,505 was the largest number of resettlers in a single year in the history of the FRG (see also table 7).[6] The West German practice of granting foreigners social-welfare benefits while assigning them a permanent signification as "foreign" clearly contrasted with the policy of wholehearted acceptance of those *deutschstämmige* (also known as *Aussiedler* or *Volksdeutsche*), Germans by blood who had settled outside. These *Volksdeutsche* often shared only the myth of *Großdeutschland* with their West German peers, a myth that held less and less sway with postwar generations of Germans who had grown up in the FRG. Most contemporary German nationals of Generation II, in both the GDR and FRG, had more in common with foreigners raised in Germany (though still denied the opportunity to integrate) than with the *Aussiedler* from the East. Not only did many of the returning *Aussiedler* often lack rudimentary knowledge of the German language and culture, but they also shared in a different set of lifecourse transformations, those that made a German feel at home among her/his generational counterparts. Belonging is established more through a shared past than an anticipated common future.

The master narrative most often deployed by the new *Aussiedler*, used to claim their membership in the group, was from the not-so-distant German past. It was above all drawn from the "collective conscience" of a national identity based on *Blut und Boden*, which not only remained dear to right-wing nationalists and neo-Nazis, but was also inscribed in the Basic Law of 1949. Hence experience with *die Vergangenheit*, often meaning documented contact with the Nazis – a grandfather who served in the Third Reich, a grandmother who was raped by an SS officer, a relative who made the upper categories of racial purity on one of the lists employed by the Nazis – became a major commodity used by *Aussiedler* to establish that they, too, should have access to German identity and German wealth.

From the very inception of the West German state, its promise of full membership in the FRG polity to any German who had emigrated "East" compelled it to codify Jesuitical definitions of what Germanness entails. Eleven to fifteen categories of potential immigrants (the lists vary according to circumstances) distinguished the degree of Germanness and hence the responsibilities of the state toward the petitioner for citizenship. Poles presented a particularly thorny problem intensified by the German responsibilities left unconfronted since World War II – for West Germany never signed a peace treaty with or paid reparations to Poland.[7]

According to Paragraph 6 of the Refugee Law, Poles could apply to resettle if they could prove that they were known as German in their homeland. The vast majority of Poles who have appealed have done so under what is called Category 3 of the German *Volksgruppe*. During the war the Nazis compiled lists of Slavs who supposedly had no German blood, but were considered capable of racial integration into a Germanized Europe – who were *eindeutschungsfahig*. Up to 1.7 million people could qualify as descendants of these elect few. The next most common basis for appeal, as mentioned above, is documentation of descent from a soldier or bureaucrat who served the Third Reich. The relationships of domination and humiliation encoded in these bureaucratic niceties can be left to the imagination. Despite the obstacles, in 1988 and 1989, 370,000 Poles applied as *Aussiedler* to resettle in the Federal Republic.

While the problem of *Aussiedler* persists, the thorniest problem facing the German republics during the Cold War does not: the exchange of people who wanted to move from the GDR to the FRG, *Zuwanderer*, in the words of the West German authorities. Since West Germany claimed that all East German citizens also belonged to it, and offered them automatic citizenship (East Germany made no such claim to people outside its territory), every move of a citizen to the West severely undermined the legitimacy of the GDR. Exchanges of people can be traced in origin back to the workers' revolt that shook the East

German regime in 1953. At that time, the FRG rather spontaneously bought free, *freigekauft*, some of the imprisoned instigators of the revolt. The building of the Wall in 1961 stopped the free movement of people, even of visits, from East to West, and initiated a regularized exchange system. People to be exchanged were put into two lists: political prisoners *per se* (H-Cases) and family members of West German citizens (F-Cases). The number of family-related exchanges steadily increased relative to the political exchanges. In 1965, there were 1,555 H-Cases traded, and 762 F-Cases. By 1975, the number of H-Cases had dropped to 1,158 while the number of F-Cases increased to 5,635. By 1989, the H-Cases numbered 1,775, while F-Cases had risen to 6,847. Altogether, from 1965 to 1989, 33,755 "political prisoners" and 21,5019 "family members" were bought. The prices went up over time. From 1963 to 1977, each prisoner cost West Germany 40,000 D-Mark ($20,000), thereafter increasing to 95,847 D-Mark ($47,923).

Neither regime could explicitly discuss the bodies-for-money exchanges. Bartering humans like cattle was in blatant violation of international law; and publicizing the system would have had serious domestic repercussions on both sides. When individuals decided to resettle in the West, they petitioned the government, writing an *Ausreiseantrag*, and then normally waited until they were released, a process that averaged several years, but was actually quite arbitrary. The most secure way for an East German to get to the West was to commit a political crime, and if that failed, to contact church groups in the West who would put one on an official but secret West German list of people desired to be bought. Monetary value of bodies increased, and the individuals were also given priority, if they were labelled political prisoners or had desirable occupations (doctors and architects more, unskilled workers less). Such (non)desirables sold to the FRG, in cases individually negotiated, for between 40,000 and 250,000 D-Marks.[8]

Not all people who petitioned to be released were bought by the West; some were released arbitrarily without payment, and some bought their own way out, giving up a car or home or summer house, often to the Stasi. The number of people resettling through legal petitions reached a high of 34,982 in 1984, declined to 18,958 in 1987, and then reached a new high of 39,832 in 1988. The implications of this continuous movement of people to the West were obvious: kinship ties between East and West strengthened.

Visits of East Germans to West Germany were first legalized for *dringende Familienangelegenheiten*, pressing family events, in 1972. The number of visits per year did not exceed 60,000 until 1986, when, in the liberalization coinciding with Honecker's first postwar visit to the West, 573,000 visits were allowed. The number of visits rose to approximately 900,000 in 1987, with the category "family" often broadly (and arbitrarily) extended to friends and acquaintances. Of those who visited the West, only a few decided to stay (1985: 3,484; 1986: 4,660). In addition to money-for-people exchange, other forms of regularized exchanges where the money flowed from West to East included (all numbers for 1986): 525 million D-Marks for the use of transits through the GDR; 208 million D-Marks for mail services; 1 million D-Marks for use of subway tunnels and communication lines; 262 million D-Marks for a new freeway from Berlin to Helmstedt, 1 trillion for Berlin to Hamburg; 268 million D-Marks for the construction work in Wartha-Eisenach and on the Saalebrücke; 150 million investment in train transportation. It is estimated that between 1971 and 1986, the total from gifts, advantages in inner-German trade, and credit totaled 12 trillion D-Marks (*Die Zeit*, no. 29, July 10, 1987, p. 5). Many East Berliners, and not a few West Berliners, looked at these payments not as a subsidy, but as repayment for the *Ausblutung*, bleeding-dry, policy of the FRG up to the building of the Wall, and in the case of transactions for people, as reasonable repayment for the investments in education and training made by the East German society.

**Berlin itself**

This book has focused on how the two German states sought during the Cold War to emplot the lives of their residents, and how their citizens in Berlin told their own life stories. The individual narratives were generation- and often sex-specific; at times they corresponded to the version offered by the state, but more often than not they deviated significantly from the officially envisioned lifecourse. The states' narratives, on the other hand, while authoritarian and discontinuous in practice, were dependent for success on interactive reading strategies that simultaneously demarcated the states from each other. Unlike their citizens, the two states remained quite consistent in the specific ideational and aesthetic form-giving principles they deployed for the reading of their policies, though they consistently changed the content. In point of fact, their elaborately constructed plots often encountered resistance, were ignored, got lost in the execution, or were even abandoned as the state changed its design. I have traced the forty years of processes and patterns of these interactions between the two states and the Germans at the border in Berlin, a process designed to produce a stable dual organization. But history has taken an ironic twist. We may in fact say with some justification that by 1989 there were two German nations, but at the very apotheosis of their difference, they merged under one state. The states have indeed produced differences but not according to plan – for the specific differences they produced were often not the ones desired. Now the ongoing historical project is to suture themselves, the nations, into one.

Berlin, I have argued, was a privileged topos in this narrative construction. Due to its role as the German capital during the Third Reich, it was physically encoded by self-induced scars and internationally prescribed postwar divisions. Berlin's postwar career and character as a hybrid dual organization made it simultaneously an anomaly of history and a cauldron of what was quintessentially Cold War. This period in which the world was organized round two superpowers is, however, over. Nationalist fights and international constraints are part of its future as well as its past, but they are likely to play a subordinate role to supranational frameworks that are currently reorganizing the world of "nation-states" and the ways in which kinship and nationness figure the self. Indeed, as E.J. Hobsbawm (1990: 175–176) predicts, "The basic political conflicts which are likely to decide [its] fate [will] have little to do with nation-states." The status of Berlin, its future as capital city of Germany, lies therefore in its ability not to overcome but to allegorize and transgress the limits of what it has meant to be the *German* city of Berlin.

I recorded my impressions of the divided Berlin in the winter of 1988 as follows: East Berlin has charm, an *Oststadt* with dim, hazed lights, half of them not functioning, so that the streets are selectively lighted. Fog. A kitsch-like phallic-shaped television tower at its center, boxed in by three churches. Art deco residential buildings snuggled next to a former army barracks now housing rusting garden machinery, and friends, private niches, the *Stasi*. West Berlin is a *Jubelstadt*: postmodern architectural facelift, shopping on KuDamm, and nightlife: chat, dance, flirt, and watch. Punks and aging hippies, *Autonome*, widows ordering *Kaffee und Kuchen*, anti-parades, and state-subsidized artist colonies, Turkish kabobs, and *pommes frites mit mayo*. East Berlin strikes me as the aftermath of a romance; West Berlin has more the heart of a cynic waiting for a new crisis, a satirist gasping for breath.

We are at the end of this narrative about narratives, and normally would resort to a closural scene of some sort. Standardized social-science narratives are usually constructed so that they read as if "thoroughly predestined." Such narrative tyranny will produce nothing but "spurious problems for a solution already in place." With such disregard for the reader, it is no wonder that most social-science accounts rarely move outside the circle of people who read them only because they are required to. Since all is settled before the story begins, why read on? Instead, argues narrative scholar D. A. Miller, "closure needs to be a moment . . . where something is 'a little disguised, a little mistaken'" (1980: xii–xiii). In our case, the neat closure provided by the collapse of Cold War division in November 1989, followed by the dissolution of the GDR and its political annexation by West Germany (with its residents overwhelmingly approving), does not end history but displaces it in a new narrative plot involving a renewed struggle over the legitimation of narrative standpoint. Names, categories, and periods are now being recontested with added fervor and new stakes at hand. It is the burden of a final postscript to explain briefly how division ended, and how the process of unification influences the further development of belonging in Berlin.

# Postscript: Unity

Men make their own history, but they do not make it just as they please; they do not make it under circumstances chosen by themselves, but under circumstances directly encountered, given and transmitted from the past. The tradition of all the dead generations weighs like a nightmare on the brain of the living. And just when they seem engaged in revolutionizing themselves and things, in creating something that has never yet existed, precisely in such periods of revolutionary crisis they anxiously conjure up the spirits of the past to their service and borrow from them names, battle cries and costumes in order to present the new scene of world history in this time-honoured disguise and this borrowed language.

Karl Marx, *The 18th Brumaire of Louis Bonaparte*, published in 1852

### Historical accident and the end of division

As is the case with so much History, the events that plunged Germans into their frenetic rush toward unification – a premature, short-sighted, and cynically pursued unity – all began with a misunderstanding. At a press conference on November 9, 1989, East German politburo member Gunter Schabowski was directed to read new visa regulations for travel of GDR citizens to Western countries.[1] For several months, tens of thousands of young East Germans had been fleeing their republic – sneaking into Hungary over the newly opened Hungarian border and climbing West German embassy walls in Prague, Budapest, and Warsaw. They wanted out, by hook or by crook. The new travel regulations (put forth by a reeling, reformist regime that less than a month before had ousted the Erich Honecker-led group) were to address this problem. Instead, a hesitation by Schabowski in response to a journalistic inquiry about the extent of these changes, broadcast live on German television, resulted in a mis-hearing of the new rules. Within minutes, hundreds of people gathered expectantly at both sides of several of the

Berlin border crossings. Uninformed and taken aback by the sudden and growing crowds, the border guards gave way to the masses and opened all gates. Berlin was one again.

The accidental opening of the Berlin Wall accelerated the tempo of collapse in the already disintegrating East German state and society; it made apparent the fragility of Cold War structures by rendering transparent the ideological and material props for the dual organization of Berlin and Germany. This unraveling, initially referred to as "unification," has continued unchecked, now consciously driven by the West Germans in a process that has since become known as *die Abwicklung der ehemaligen DDR*. *Abwickeln* means to unwind or unreel. Thus imaged like an antiquated clock whose internal coils have sprung, the former GDR is being unwound, set back in a prior time. *Abwickeln* also means, figuratively that is, an orderly and step-by-step winding down, or bringing to completion as in a finishing of business or settling of accounts. These definitions capture two of the fundamental aspects of German unification: first, the GDR as a social formation, with its own unique sets of practices and dispositions, will be unrolled and deconstructed to its thinnest, most unadorned and elementary units; second, this orderly and step-by-step unraveling is a final settling of Cold War accounts.

Among the many legacies of the Cold War – only slowly and reluctantly acknowledged by the whole world – is a *de facto* divided Germany, with two distinct nations. That these nations do not precisely correspond to the images the two postwar states sought to construct and represent in no way denies their distinctiveness. As I have demonstrated throughout this book, their trajectories have been unique, if erratic and unforeseeable, unfolding in interaction with but not according to plan. This interaction was, of course, more distorted in the East, where the state was less successful in legitimating its policies and its concept of Germanness. Not only was the East German state much less cunning than its West counterpart in its control of German symbology, but it also failed to deliver its promised utopia. Thus the satirical-lapsarian West German state form (constitutionality), *Westintegration*, prosperity, automobiles, and vacations abroad – the generative symbols of West Germanness – were the goods desired by the East Germans after the opening.[2] Germans on both sides quickly seemed to reach agreement on the future goals. The East Germans initially considered this moment, as Habermas (1990: 3–23) argues from a more limited perspective, a *nachholende* revolution, a catching up. They sought to rectify the last forty years by recovering what was already achieved in the West. For the West Germans, the revolution served as a confirmation for who they are and what they have. With this compromise in mind, formal political and economic unity were completed within a year of the autumn revolution.

The speed and facility of this fusion seems to undermine my statement that the people in fact constitute two nations, not one. If this were the case, then why should unity have been perceived and presented initially as so natural and unproblematic? Built into this breakneck pace to political unity lies a riddle of a more profound character, for the unity consummated at the state level by a simple, swift annexation must now produce a cultural unification that will be anything but quick. Within six months of unity, the assumption that a uniform, undifferentiated policy could unify such differently made peoples proved bankrupt. The new German state, the enlarged Federal Republic, began acknowledging that this revolutionary moment and the new formal unity could not efface, to paraphrase Marx, the quite different nightmares on the brain of the living, given and transmitted from the immediate past.

An ideal unity in a state is all about equal life chances, about standardizing the lifecourse to the point where people, despite their inescapable genetic and historical differences, perceive themselves as mastering the social order to the extent that resulting differences can be explained by individual choices or chance rather than attributed to external, social-structural causes. German unity entails making real in the present this fantasy of a past unity. It is a process that will preoccupy Germany through this century and into the next. Before entering into the details of unification, and their consequences for the German state, for Berlin, and the Germanness of the citizens, let us briefly deal with the sequence of events between the end of division and the present, from the autumn revolution of 1989 through March 1991.

**The fall of the Wall**
"We were speechless," so many of them said, the East and West Berliners; they said it over and over, describing their experience on November 9 of what they called *Verbrüderung*, an instant sense of kinship. "We were speechless," they said, making speech of their own silence. All Germans, who before the opening had coexisted in complex, tense, and carefully mediated relations, were suddenly, spontaneously loving brothers. And then they added, "It was all *Wahnsinn*!" – insane or, more literally, crazy sense.

Because the Wall was steeped in symbolism, because it summed up and condensed the whole system of oppositions – local, national, and international – that constituted the Cold War, its opening, more than any other particular event in Eastern Europe in 1989, accelerated the pace and affirmed the inevitability of the collapse of Cold War divisions. It served to undermine the old and disorient the present, more for the East than the West Germans given that their release from physical containment produced a more immediate rush. Old categories of East and West, communist and capitalist, friend and foe, lost their meaning – replaced by a speechless *Verbrüderung*.

Hence the opening of the Wall, being an object "saturated with emotional quality," in the words of Benjamin Sapir (1934: 492–493), undermined the tranquility of quotidian life in the divided city, producing a sense of immediacy in unity, a sense of "homogeneous, empty time" (phrase from Walter Benjamin, cited in Anderson 1983: 30) that one might call a national "communitas." All social relations were simplified as conventional categories of everyday behavior were ignored and replaced with mythic constructs – brotherhood, Germanness, freedom. On the one hand, there was an exaggerated appeal to the mediating influence of myth, to the concept of *Gesamtdeutschland*, the entire Germany. On the other, there was an elaboration of banal rituals to serve as material support for the mythic concepts. Drinking, buying, visiting, the repeated rites that accompanied a general increase in sociability, served to imprint the grand new unity unconsciously on its practitioners.

### Elections and ritualizing legitimacy

That week of *Verbrüdering* killed any realistic expectation that the dual organization of Berlin and Germany could survive in its political and economic manifestations. For it became obvious to everyone on the street, in the home, at work, or in the shopping center, that the myth of the dual economic and political base, of its infrastructural determinacy and superstructural significance, had lost its force. What replaced everyday division was a collective misrecognition of another sort: culture, in the form of a pan-German nation, appeared to have survived forty years of political and economic division. And it was above all this myth – of cultural continuity, cultural unity, cultural coherence – that initially sustained the political leaders in East and West who pushed for unification, as well as nourishing the people's own ecstasy in their newfound ether of an imagined but profound and deeply felt nationness.

This myth of cultural unity, in turn, found a means of ritual legitimation, and thus a way of representing itself as the really real, in the election process.

In the year following the revolution East Germans marched three times to the polls. All three elections were elaborately staged public spectacles, with the concomitant politicians, media, polling experts, and election analysts there to affirm they were conducted according to the new rules. Twenty-four parties competed in the first bout, declining in number with each successive round as the spectrum of represented public interest narrowed. Shrinking this base of representable interest, molding political will into West German form, were West German political professionals. Yet with each secretly marked "X" on a ballot, neatly folded and placed in a ballot box with those marked similarly by other citizens, East Germans – and West Germans in two of the three elections – consecrated the series of unification steps resulting in the complete dissolution of the GDR. By means of the magical vote in these ritual elections, Germans bestowed legitimacy on the liberal-democratic regime of the Federal Republic and the entire capitalist cultural order it purports to represent. Thereby East Germans and their territory were incorporated into the West German order.

Before these elections, from November 1989 to March 1990, the interim East German regime under Hans Modrow had groped from crisis to crisis. Suffering a series of humiliations and snubs by the Helmut Kohl-led West German government, as well as internal scandals and an expanding economic crisis (further facilitated by the Kohl government), it seemed barely to make it to the March 18, 1990 election, the first fully free election on East German territory since 1933, and the first in Eastern Europe since World War II. For most citizens – 92 percent of the voting-age population went to the polls – it was their first experience with a secret ballot. Over 48 percent supported a conservative coalition headed by the Christian Democratic Union – the parties most forcefully arguing for quick political reunification. The Social Democratic Party, heavily favored only the week before, won a mere 21 percent of the vote. The restructured Communist Party, renamed the Party of Democratic Socialism, surprised many with a showing of 16 percent. Those people who started the revolutionary process, united in a coalition called Bündnis '90, won the support of 2.9 percent of the people.

Above all, beyond its immediate winners and losers, this election signified the end of the revolution that had begun with the mass flights across the Hungarian border in the summer of 1989 and the mass protests in East German cities following them. It closed the brief, and very open, liminal period of social questioning, democratic will formation, and attempted revolutionary renewal. The revolution, started as a struggle to revitalize socialism by making it more democratic, culminated in its abolition and the triumph of consumer culture. This election in March 1990 transformed the question from one about ends or goals to one about means or procedures, from *whether* to *how* to assimilate East Germans into the norms, class structure, and habits of West Germany.

In contrast to the alacrity of the March election in the GDR, the first pan-German election, on December 2, 1990, was a rather somber affair, with little enthusiasm and very little at stake.[3] The ruling coalition of Christian Democrats and Free Democrats won an absolute majority (54.8 percent) by promising relatively painless and quick cultural and economic unity: the East Germans would be better off than before, but this improvement would not cost the West Germans anything.[4] They also appealed strongly to the idea of a German nation, whereas their major opponent, Oskar Lafontaine of the Social Democrats (who made a dismal showing at 33.5 percent), predicted a painful, costly unity and refused to make appeals to the nation. (Journalist to Lafontaine: "What do you think of the nation?" Lafontaine: "Ask Helmut Kohl.") Given the tendency of German politicians in the past to use the idea of the nation to demarcate themselves from who they are not – from, for example, the Slavs, Jews, and Gypsies – Lafontaine's fear and avoidance of German nationalism was understandable, though politically simplistic. For such an imagined community at the political level is a precondition for an economic and social nation. As a member of West German Generation II, Lafontaine, torn between the historical alternatives of identities as *Weltbürger* or provincials tied to a place, remained silent on the issue of the nation, yielding the mapping of its terrain to his opponents. Kohl, on the other hand, represented the nation as an enlarged and prosperous West German political-legal order, avoiding references to *Blut und Boden* that might have alarmed the international community. Rather, he pleaded for territorial unity by using the quaint term *Landsleute*, fellow countrymen, as well as insisting on a concurrent *Westintegration*, integration into Western Europe.

Why bother to bring these elections into this postscript when I have largely ignored those that preceded them? After all, I have dealt quite perfunctorily with the regular elections with massive participation held by both German states during the Cold War. In this case, however, due to the uncertainty of unification as to when and how it would be realized, the new elections in 1990 performed a ritual function that is most critical for the functioning of capitalist, liberal republics. They would have been altogether superfluous for the praxis of unification had it not been for this essential ceremonial function: legitimating the new system of rules, the principles of domination in the symbolic order, that enable corporate capitalism to work in cursive tandem with liberal-democratic political institutions. Elections in liberal republics function not to change but to stabilize political orders by legitimating the cultural order from which they take their form. Indeed, the elimination of the regime in the East did not precede but followed dramatic changes in everyday life. And, as I have been arguing in this study, everyday life is structured less directly by the content of policies of actual regimes than by their long-term forms of legality and legitimacy. This is not to deny the significance of the state and its agents in its institutional and formal representational forms, but rather to call attention to the fact that its ability to influence everyday life is contingent on the very fact that its system of legality and legitimacy, which represents itself as beyond question and indeed taken-for-granted, predates and prefigures actual policy. By the successful strategic framing of policy in aesthetic, ideational, and teleological emplotments, states constitute policy as intelligible, thus enabling its possible consecration through "correct" appropriation by the citizen.

The elections after the collapse of the Wall, unlike those imposed on the residents of Berlin and Germany by the Allies following the war, were, in effect, free. Yet this freedom was highly circumscribed by other non-election structures (above all, by the power asymmetry between the symbolic order of the two sides and the superior economic capital of the West) that largely predetermined the outcome. Let us return then to the restructuring of daily life in Berlin following the collapse of dual organization, and its consequences for the two generations in the two halves.

### The reaction of the people

Ein Teil der Menschen rotiert, die Mehrzahl sitzt wie das Kaninchen vor der Schlange – unfähig, das Tempo mitzuhalten. (Some of the people are rotating, but the majority sit like a rabbit before a snake. They are unable to keep up with the tempo.) *Letter from an East Berlin friend, January 16, 1991*

With the collapse of their state and social system, East Germans lost their time and space coordinates. The quickened tempo of life in the capitalist West replaced the petrified sense of time cultivated by the conservative regime in the East. Under these circumstances, people sought for something to hold on to, a rudder that might enable their sinking life-boat to resist being overturned by errant waves, and thus enable a resumption of movement in a particular direction. At first this rudder seemed to be identified with nothing other than the person of Helmut Kohl. Not exactly a charismatic leader, Kohl nonetheless personifies some of the most significant traits of Germanness: his mammoth size alone (approximately 6′4″ and 230 pounds) denotes to the Germans prosperity, much as the Samoans or Tahitians identify well-being with a well-fed princess (the German word *dick* means not only the slightly negative "fat" but also the very positive "stout"). His major campaign posters presented him from behind, with a wide-angle lens highlighting his broad back and his gaze over the landscape.

Also Kohl's arrogant inarticulateness appeals to the relatively unsophisticated mentality of the West German *Spießbürger* and the East German *Kleinbürger* – much of life need not be expressed or defended for it is ruled by common sense; his attention to local happening and detail – accidents, deaths, births – endears him to the proud provinciality and ties to place of the non-cosmopolitan; and finally, when he finds his self-interest at stake, he is incredibly and self-righteously *stur*, stubborn, stolid, intransigent – yet he shows great flexibility and willingness to change firm positions if practical necessities seem to warrant that. For all these reasons, Helmut Kohl appeared to a large number of Germans, East and West, as a rudder and anchor, the right man to weather stormy times.

What Helmut Kohl promised to East Germans was the D-Mark and (soon to follow) West German living standards; what he promised to West Germans was a maintenance of their living standards while at the same time increasing the size of their country, opening a new frontier for their markets and administrative skills. Representing himself as the new Bismarck uniting the unjustly divided nation, Kohl personally set the speed and tempo of unity, a simple act effected by a vote of East German politicians according to Article 23 of the Basic Law. Thus the negotiation of the Unification Treaty, finally signed on August 31, 1990, was a deal forged and ratified not by the people (as would have been required by Article 146 of the Basic Law), but by German bureaucrats and politicians, in a manner similar to the unities achieved in 1648, 1815, 1866, and 1871. And, as Klaus Offe has argued, Kohl was supported on this by a political and intellectual elite.[5] Thus the impatience and *rush* to unity were due less to popular pressure than to strategic manipulation of national feeling by West German elites.

In the days and weeks after the opening, East Germans gorged themselves on the symbolic goods of West German nationness. They crossed out the first "D" and the "R" in the acronym "DDR", leaving only a "D," heretofore acronym for *Deutschland* (West), and they waved West German flags. They flocked to the shopping centers and stores in a consumptive orgy that kept West German businesses open long after the state-mandated (and sacred) closing hours, and they sought those items that most define the West German self: cars indexing power and prosperity, pornography symbolizing pleasure and free time, travel out of their country, jeans of the sort identifying one as *westlich*. Parallel to the process of state-dissolution, they began a personal process of self-dissolution that mirrored the self-effacement formerly demanded of them by the East German state. In the old GDR, public space had been so colonized by the state, so constrained in form, that any attempt to speak the self in public became an exercise in self-effacement. Thus people's primary investments were in private lives, private niches, private selves. In the new FRG, expression in public required dissolution of this highly prized, cultivated, and intricately constructed private self – followed by the adoption of a consumer self oriented to public display (see Borneman 1991a).

Nearly all West Germans gained from unity, initially at least, in both cultural and economic capital. In the following year, West German production increased by 12 percent; East German production declined 40 percent and unemployment rose from 0 percent to levels exceeding those at the height of the Great Depression in 1932 (approaching 40 per cent by mid year 1991). Many West Berliners did not experience unity as something positive, for, as East Germans crowded into their S-Bahn and stores, riding public transportation and shopping became more stressful. And with severely reduced federal subsidies in store for West Berlin, most individuals will be experiencing an actual decline in their standard of living. Over time West Berlin is certain to resemble more its eastern surroundings than those characterizing West Germany. Moreover, unity means ending the special status of West Berlin: eliminating federal subsidies and the peculiar right of young male residents to avoid military service. Yet for both West Germans and West Berliners, unification has served to confirm the values of (West)

Germanness, though experienced in generation and gender-specific ways.

## The search for a metaphor

How does one describe the merging of these two halves, asymmetrical in landmass, population size, military power, productive capacity, and technological sophistication? Their unification is a many-sided process, proceeding disjunctively over time, with divergent tempos in different domains of life. Our ability to make such processes intelligible is limited by our choice of metaphors. While in Berlin in December 1990, I heard three metaphors – the initial metaphor of fraternity had long since perished – all of which I would argue have some, but limited, explanatory power.

*Anschluss*, political annexation, employed most often to describe Hitler's takeover of the Sudetenland and Austria, is of limited utility, for it is incapable of depicting the sundry and shifting forms of economic and cultural adjustments and interdigitations; in particular, it shifts attention away from specific instances of resistance, complicity, and exploitation. Rape, the metaphor used by the United States to justify the 1991 Gulf War (Kuwait as the raped woman; Iraq as the rapist; the United States as the male hero who saves the victim), is inappropriate because the majority of East and West Germans freely voted for unification. The third metaphor, colonialism, has some utility, since unification partakes of aspects of internal colonization true of, for example, Wales under England, or the Mezzogiorno against the Italian north. Yet German unity differs from most colonial situations in both the way in which the two sides share a language and multiple kinship ties (eliminating the basis for the racial differentiation), and in the lack of extreme educational discrepancies between the two sides. In addition to employing all these terms in various contexts to describe what is happening in German–German relations, people also use the more specific verb, *abwickeln* (to unwind), to which I referred earlier; they have no correspondingly specific term for processes resulting from unity in the Federal Republic. The development of a new nomenclature that fails to name the actual agents responsible for and the benefits they obtain from unity parallels, of course, one mode of domination in all such asymmetrical relationships: to name but not be named in return (see Long and Borneman 1991).

I might suggest a metaphor for comparison that, to my knowledge, the Germans themselves have not yet employed, one from the American experience: post Civil War reconstruction. History is unfolding in a process similar to American reconstruction, when carpetbaggers, boot-leggers, jural administrators, and politicians from the north went to the south to do business with those willing to do their bidding.[6] This particular configuration of dominator/dominated was made possible by the new spaces opened up in the accelerated pace of unification.

In order to execute the political unity supported by voters in the March 1990 election, politicians began negotiating a unity treaty, eventually signed in August 1990. But before the actual signing, the two negotiating sides, made up of politicians and bureaucrats, had to agree upon a currency union. The date agreed upon, July 1, 1990, seemed to have more to do with the timing of summer vacations (to allow East Germans to vacation in the West) than with economic savvy. Much like the Currency Reform of 1948, which set the tenor of division, the 1990 reform set the tenor of unity. Both had symbolic value beyond their narrow economic and legal import; both introduced with a single stroke and by fiat the new system of domination – the manner in which objects obtain value – peculiar to capitalism.

East Germans seemed to be pleased that their negotiating side had obtained for them an immediate favorable exchange rate of 1:1 (on private accounts up to certain maximums) to 3:1 Marks (East) for D-Marks (West). In return, the West German negotiators obtained a settlement favorable to them on longer-term monetary agreements; accumulated East German debts did not automatically belong to the Federal Republic – the issue was to be decided in a united parliament where the West German *Länder* had disproportionate strength; the equalization law that strives for parity between the different West German *Länder* (taxing the richer ones for the benefit of the poorer) would not be applied to the East until 1994; administrative property belonging to the GDR would be turned over to the FRG (instead of to the five new *Länder*).[7]

The immediate effect of the currency reform was to revalue East German goods – increasing their prices by 300 percent. One should scarcely be surprised, then, that following the introduction of this new system of valuation, nobody would want to buy East German goods. Neither should it be surprising that this price inflation for East German goods would enhance the value of and desire for West German goods, whose prices remained stable. In what was a modern historical prece-dent, a national economy was subjected to a brutal and sudden resignifying of value. Other factors added to the negative effects of the Currency Reform on the East German economy. Whereas in the 1948 reform, property rights were unquestioned, the 1990 reform was accompanied by the introduction of a new system of property rights. With the takeover of West German property law, all contracts made from 1945 to 1989 under Soviet occupation and East German law were immediately opened to contestation (Borneman 1991b).

Settlement of these disputes over property was a necessary precondition for investment in the East. Why would a businessman invest in disputed property without securely knowing with whom he was negotiating? By the end of 1990, over one million complaints concerning property disputes had been registered. Moreover, settling these legal claims on property was made difficult because of the lack of judges capable of adjudicating claims and of lawyers to represent contestants in court. Of the 1,000 judges and 800 state prosecutors in the GDR, most were released from their functions by the latter half of 1990. In Berlin, the Justice Minister Jutta Limbach dismissed all judges, replacing most with professionals from West Berlin. This radical restructuring was unavailable to the rest of the former GDR, given the difficulty in recruiting *Wessies* to work at such distance from West German cities. Most judges were given the opportunity to reapply for their positions, based on three evaluative criteria: (1) Had they shown exceptional obedience to the system? (2) Had they displayed uncalled-for severity? (3) Had they exhibited execution of unprincipled forms of judicial independence? Disqualification would result only when judges met all three criteria, since nearly every judge is assumed to have been "guilty" of at least one.[8]

Retraining of East judges remained a hypothetical solution, since very few training courses of any sort were made available. Private attorneys, *Rechtsanwälte*, have been allowed to continue to practice provided they complete an expensive training course or registered before January 1991 an intent to practice under the new legal system. Several of the lawyers I know claim that most could not afford to complete the course, and paradoxically, few availed themselves of the opportunity to register to practice under the new rules. Yet, for those legal professionals who are trying to make the adjustment, they will have great difficulty adjudicating disputes according to a foreign law that was not meant to apply to the cases at hand. East and West German laws varied radically with respect to, e.g., contracts, rental agreements, inheritance, property, marriage, and divorce. GDR law was simplified, meant to be read by laymen, whereas FRG law was written in an arcane, technical language intended for professionals only. Thus, for example, in the domain of inheritance in civil law, GDR law contains 66 paragraphs; FRG law contains 464. In trial law, GDR law contains 209 paragraphs; FRG law contains 1,048. With insufficient numbers of qualified judges and administrators to adjudicate legal disputes, decisions during this "reconstruction" concerning redistribution of wealth are left with local power brokers.

Hence reports of corruption have been rampant ever since the opening of the Wall. The currency union itself provided a big windfall for some: swindlers in the GDR and other East European countries earned a reported 100 billion D-Marks through the illegal sale of goods, and by establishing "fake" bank accounts. Yet the wealth exchanged, lost, and gained, in the currency union was minimal compared to the wealth at stake in the redistribution of different forms of property (see Borneman 1991a). At the center of public attention in this redistribution is the former East German Stasi.

Even before it was officially dissolved in February 1990, groups of Stasi members reorganized into business ventures. In a clear case of conversion of social into economic capital, Stasi exploited their contacts with businesses and licensing agencies, as well as their information about others for possible blackmail, to establish a new (and now legitimate) power matrix, based no longer on the use of force or production of fear but rooted in the economy. Their exchange items tend to be fourfold: illegally accumulated cash, information, physical property including land and buildings, and armaments. Over the years the Stasi (among coworkers always called "the company") accumulated a great deal of property forcefully expropriated from *Ausreisende*, individuals who wanted to leave the GDR and resettle in West Germany; they also had numerous schemes to create foreign currency, much of which circulated back to them.

One issue in this "reconstruction" unites the two Germanies: both want to be freed of the legacy of their loss in World War II. This new context of unity has left the two Cold War superpowers in a state of shock, reducing them to clients of the new German patron. The Soviet Union was by far the more reluctant of the two powers to accept the dissolution of its East German state, understandably so since the terms of unity represented humiliation on a grand scale. Helmut Kohl arranged the deal in a meeting with Mikhail Gorbachev on July 15, 1990: German unification and the withdrawal of all Soviet troops within three to four years in return for 15–16 billion D-Marks ($9–$11 billion), of which 5.5 billion D-Marks are earmarked to resettle Soviet troops back in the USSR; an agreement not to station atomic weapons or foreign troops on East German territory; reduction of the united German troop level to 370,000; and renunciation of territorial claims on land lost in World War II. And by February 1991 the Soviets had even given in to the demands of their allies to dissolve the Warsaw Pact.

It stretches the imagination to envision accurately the situation for the Soviets in which German unity is unfolding: forty-five years after World War II, a war in which the winning Soviets lost 22 million people compared to 6 million for the losing Germans, the victorious army and their dependents (totaling over 500,000 people) are now humiliatingly forced to leave their occupied territory, returning home to a chaotic political situation, widening national–ethnic conflict, a disgraced ideological program, and an abysmal economy. Quite aware of what awaited them at home, Soviet soldiers stationed in the former GDR reportedly deserted in droves. Despite threats of deportation and the miniscule chances of obtaining political asylum, living in Germany under any circumstances – in the army or a refugee camp – was considered preferable to a return to the USSR as it was dissolved.

Meanwhile, the United States, apparent victor of the Cold War, was faced with an equally improbable scenario. Even before formal unity was completed, the United States regime, engulfed by a deteriorating economy and explosive domestic political situation, began planning a military adventure in the Persian Gulf. "Operation Desert Shield" quickly expanded into "Operation Desert Storm," the largest military display in the history of the world, as the United States drove an imperialist Iraq out of Kuwait, restoring the monarchy and redistributing power in the Gulf as part of President George Bush's proposed New World Order. In this effort, the United States successfully enlisted the support and compliance of most of the world, including both Germany and Japan. Yet it was forced to fight the war largely with its own troops acting as mercenaries, reliant on German and Japanese capital to finance the action. Instead of displaying strength, the United States revealed weakness in its actual dependence on the countries it had occupied after World War II. The refusal of Germany and Japan to send troops to the Gulf, along with the tremendous popular domestic dissatisfaction with the war, were signs that they would both be more agents than pawns in this post Cold War Order.

### Constitutionality and unity

Unification was quickened by integrating the territory of the GDR into the FRG by means of Article 23 rather than Article 146 of the Basic

Law.[9] According to Article 23, which was aggressively pushed by Chancellor Helmut Kohl, the GDR reorganized itself into the old *Länder* from 1945, and, by means of a single parliamentary vote and signing of the Unification Treaty, acceded into the Federal Republic. In the months immediately after the opening of the Wall, however, it was generally assumed that unity would take place according to Article 146, which would have meant a slow process of negotiation between the two Germanies, considering specific proposals from both sides, followed by citizen ratification and eventually complete unification. Instead, Article 23 was utilized, meaning that the entire corpus of law and political structure of the Federal Republic was supplanted onto East Germany. The elections in 1990 were interpreted as legitimating this quick annexation.

Throughout unification, scholars and statesmen in both Germanies hotly contested the issue of constitutionality. As I have argued in this book, during the Cold War the *Grundgesetz* became somewhat of a holy grail for the West Germans, a mark of stability and symbol of a successful social charter. It is from this satiric-lapsarian position of superior virtue, reinforced by the collapse of the GDR, that the West German state (and statesmen) justify their actions. Thus many prominent West Germans have appealed to *Verfassungspatriotismus*, constitutional patriotism, as both the basic glue that holds the Federal Republic together, and as the major achievement of the Federal Republic over past (and other) German socio-political formations. Unity, and the chaos surrounding it, provoked a new round of these appeals. For example, in November 1990, the Berlin Christian Democrat Heinrich Lummer, former Minister of the Interior, recommended that a new ethics be introduced into the schools, whereby the Federal Republic and its constitution would be "internalized" by youth. This constitutional ethics, he argued, would stop the escalation of violence and criminality that accompanied unity (*Die Tageszeitung*, November 12, 1990, p. 1). Moreover, as I have explained in the preceding pages, the *Grundgesetz* is considered the instance of final appeal in questions concerning right and wrong, so that the fate reserved for the most despicable of all criminals in the Federal Republic is to be labelled a *Verfassungsfeind*, enemy of the constitution.[10]

Unification posed a challenge to this entire cognitive schema, as it threatened to replace the system of legality and legitimacy based on the authority of the *Grundgesetz* with a new, pan-German system.[11] Buttressing this threat was the fact that the authors of the Basic Law explicitly acknowledged the document to be provisional, "to give new order to life in this state for a transitional period" (see Strauch 1985: 39–46; Seifert 1989: 40–70). Furthermore, a clause in the preamble states, "The entire German Volk is summoned in free self-determination to complete the unity and freedom of Germany." After unification, the constitution was to be renegotiated and legitimated by the people. Primarily due to Kohl's leadership, this popular legitimation came only after it was beside the point, after the terms of unity were already cast in a particular form.

Many people (members of Generation II in the West, and of both generations in the East) see unity being used as an excuse to expand *Verfassungsschutz*, with its organization of informants, police, and legal experts. Immediately following political unification, in October 1990, the Office of Constitutional Protection began arresting former members of the Red Army Faction (RAF), who had taken on pseudonyms and were leading new lives in East Germany. Sensational stories about the RAF appeared daily in the press, with revelations about their contacts and organization, ideology, and daily life as normal citizens in small East German towns. Preceding these stories in time, and later coterminous with them, were ones about the continued existence and corruption of the East German Stasi.

The question of constitutionality and unity, then, concerns both eliminating the Stasi, the former control arm of the East German regime of fear, and expanding the West German Office of Constitutional Protection. Supposedly, the Stasi were officially dissolved by the Hans Modrow-led regime in January 1990. That dissolution was made possible through a pay-off system, where agents were paid to keep quiet as well as to secure them financially during the transition to other forms of work. Some Stasi groups transferred a great deal of money into private or collective foreign accounts. Full-time workers were apparently awarded severance pay ranging anywhere from 10,000 and 90,000 D-Marks ($6,666 – $60,000). It is now assumed that the Modrow regime actually protected the Stasi by serving as a cover for the illegal activities during the most chaotic period in the dissolution of the GDR.

Between the March and December 1990 elections, the coalition regime led by the Christian Democrat Lothar de Maiziére (since revealed as an unofficial Stasi agent himself) completed the dissolution of the state and the Stasi. Peter-Michael Diestel, the son of an army general, served as Minister of the Interior, and, according to Matthias Büchner of the Erfurt committee to eliminate the Stasi, he will probably become known as "the last great protector of the Stasi in the history of the GDR." Diestel took under his wing over 1,000 "former" Stasi, and proved very uncooperative with the local citizen committees set up to investigate and dissolve local police units. During this interim period, many Stasi obtained civil service and teaching jobs, some went to the Soviet KGB and some to the West German BKA (Federal Ministry of Crime). Given their expertise in information-gathering and wide networks in the East, multinational concerns also employed some. The majority, however, probably moved into competition in the local economy – considering their severance pay, from an advantageous starting position.

Meanwhile, the West German Office of Constitutional Protection has been moving into the East, expanding like any conglomerate that sees a new field ripe for development. Given the experiences of East Germans with the Stasi, the president of the West German *Verfassungschutz*, Gerhard Boeden, admitted that he could not "work in the five new *Länder* like [we] work in the Federal Republic. I think first we have to win their trust." Trust is certainly the immediate issue. The question is whether this can be established using the same authoritative methods – based, I have argued, on a satiric-lapsarian, past-oriented state narrative – as deployed in West Germany. These methods, including identification of the enemy, harassment, then differential exclusion and inclusion, were quite transparently used against West German Generation II after 1968.

While Boeden seems to acknowledge the need for less aggressive methods in the East, he defended the old tactics of his organization in an interview in late 1990. Much like leaders of other disciplinary and paramilitary organizations that grew out of the Cold War, he argued that the constitutional police were "continually controlled by parliament, by experts responsible for the protection of data, and by the public. We are not police and also not a child of the Cold War. We're a legitimate child of democracy." However, approximately one month after this interview, on November 11, 1990, in the first confrontation between West German/West Berlin police and East German citizens, the Berlin police stormed a squatters' settlement in the East Berlin Mainzer Straße, terrorizing the neighborhood in a show of force reminiscent of police actions against West Berlin squatters at the end of the seventies.[12] This overly dramatic use of force seems to indicate a continuity in state strategies and methods, rather than, as Boeden suggests, the formulation of a new strategy for the united Germany.

**Everyday life in the New Berlin**

Rather than eliminating division, the reunification of Germany has reformulated its terms: quickening time, refiguring space, and introducing alternate principles of legitimate domination. Old distinctions between East and West, that during the Cold War constituted a dual organization of territorial, political, cultural, and economic mirror-imaging, are now being reduced to the principles of domination peculiar to late-twentieth-century capitalism. A post Civil War type of reconstruction has replaced mirror-imaging as the dominant generative metaphor. Rather than displaying the self with, for example, the Trabant and Wartburg on one side and the Mercedes and Volkswagen on the other, only West German automobile brands are available as signifiers. Thus a new subjectivity is being fashioned in the united Germany, one based on the West German model focused around West German signs of self. That these symbols are unequally distributed in no way detracts from their significance, but rather reinforces their distinctiveness and ability to distinguish by constituting an economy of practices. The state has available to it an infinite array of more spatially based strategies, of semiotic technologies, capable of articulating and reinforcing these principles of domination, much as the individual has available more temporally based tactics to resist or appropriate these marks of distinction.

Refiguring the new state has once again repositioned Berlin. While the unity treaty forced politicians to recognize Berlin as the capital city of Germany, the decision as to whether it would have more than a symbolic function, as well as to where the regime would sit, were left to the new, united German parliament. Many West Germans did not want the capital relocated to Berlin, where they would be reminded of the heavy costs the East Germans paid for World War II, still visible in the many dilapidated buildings and backward infrastructure. Yet, initial hesitancy about moving the capital from Bonn to Berlin was overcome when Chancellor Kohl threw his support behind the move. The solution agreed upon, however, made metropolitan Berlin an immediate capital in name only, with Bonn remaining the place where politics is made – at least through this century. Whereas the timetable for the physical move of various branches of government is still being negotiated, contours of the new gestalt are already clear. The *Finanzamt* and *Verfassungsschutz* were re-located in privileged and unchallenged spaces; their competitors in the East – the Stasi and Socialist Unity Party – had been dissolved. And West German alter-egos – the East Germans – are being unwound and set back in a prior time. This is the new, united, democratic, capitalist Germany.

Mapping out the terms of this new unity, inscribing the political agreements in everyday life, goes on in all fields of practices. East German cultural capital – academic degrees, technical diplomas, literary production – has all been tremendously devalued *vis-à-vis* West German counterparts. Moving to the East to take advantage of this resignification within a single market of signs, in addition to West German jural experts and West German laws, are pedagogues, businessmen, entrepreneurs, and academics.

Responsibility for "privatizing" state and communal property went to the West German Detlev Rohwedder, a fiduciary who headed the Treuhandanstalt, a parapublic agency set up for this task. Rohwedder had under his control 40 percent of all property in the former GDR. With even more power over individual destinies than Erich Honecker, he was responsible for the fate – modernize and sell, or close – of 800 *Kombinaten*, state-owned trusts, including 40,000 companies. In March 1991, his office had sold merely 1,000 of these companies. Furthermore, the Treuhand had originally estimated that 80 percent of all jobs in the former GDR would be eliminated, and that only a fraction of the estimated 500 billion D-Marks ($33.3 billion) worth of the GDR national economy would be salvageable. In this atmosphere of bitterness, helplessness, and desperation, Rohwedder was assassinated, reportedly by a rejuvenated Red Army Faction.

Not only objects of new value, such as cars and consumer goods, but also objects devoid of value, are being shipped from West to East. Drug dealers and new mafias are now operating in the East. Perhaps most significant symbolically in this new exchange, the policy of receiving much of the garbage of Western Europe, developed by leaders of the GDR to obtain foreign currency, has now been expanded. Paradoxically, protest against environmental poisoning was one of the reasons most often given by former GDR citizens for participating in the demonstrations of 1989. And indeed, all of the Eastern European socialist states lacked environmental protection policies. Before the revolution of 1989 their ability to poison systematically their citizens and territories was attributed to the lack of democratic control over policy. Yet given the choice between unemployment or pollution, even democratically elected East German politicians are choosing pollution. Thus Klaus Töpfer, Christian Democratic Minister of the Environment in the united Germany, planned converting former East German coal mines into dumps for up to 70 billion cubic meters of toxic wastes, making East Germany the largest depository for such wastes in Europe. Five new East German sites are planned. When those dumps fill, it is expected western European garbage will move further East, to either Poland or the former USSR.

But unity has not only dumped additional garbage on the East Germans. It has made them complicitous in their own poisoning by participation as consumers of West German goods with their elaborate disposable packaging. Thus since the opening of the Wall, East Germans have been overwhelmed by plastic and paper containers from the capitalist West. West Germans produce three times as much personal garbage as East Germans. With no federal commitment in the united Germany to an environmentally friendly disposal system, East Germany's own ascetic system of minimal packaging and well-organized disposal was shut down on October 1, 1990. On that date in East Berlin, authorities closed the 137 collecting stations and 14 mobile stations for sorted garbage. Half of the 800 employees were then reduced to "zero hours part-time work," official language for being fired with pay for a limited period.

Not all exchange in the united Germany runs from West to East. Continuing unabated since autumn 1989 is the flow of skilled, young people emigrating to the West – over 300,000 yearly. These bodies are, of course, the very labor the former GDR needs to develop the "blooming" economy West German conservatives and liberals had promised them. Instead, it seems likely that well into the next century the East will be permanently demarcated as the inferior, the less valuable, the garbage dump not only of Germany but of Western Europe. What they can extract from their West German lords, not in terms of welfare rights, but in terms of political guarantees of equal chances, might be considered a test of the democratic aspirations of liberal-capitalist regimes in this post Cold War period.

Beyond the internal differentiation within the new unity, Germans will now act as one with regard to external states and peoples. As explained in the final chapter of this book, external demarcation is affected primarily through immigration and asylum policy. Both areas are now hotly contested, with more conservative forces focusing on changing Article 16 of the *Grundgesetz*, which specifies rights of asylum for politically persecuted individuals, and more liberal forces focusing on changing Article 116, which grants an automatic right to *Deutschstämmige*, individuals of German origin (blood), to become

*Bundesbürger.*[13] Regardless of which article is changed, it appears likely that the new Germany will exhibit more xenophobia than either of the two states during the Cold War.

### Final reflections

My reader may want to know how all this affects what s/he has read. In many ways, unification provides the ultimate test of my various hypotheses concerning politics and everyday life in the divided Berlin. An effortless unity would make the entire set of questions this study posed, questions that often ignored or challenged conventional social science wisdoms, seem in error at worst, misplaced at best. I asked: How did the two German states regulate the lifecourse during the Cold War by defining the particular categories of the self which can be said to signify Germanness? How did citizens in the two Berlins appropriate, in their own experiences, the aesthetic and ideational frameworks provided by these states? Was *Abrenzungspolitik* about more than the holding of contrary political opinions? In other words, were aspects of policy on *both* sides of the Cold War totalistic in their goals of constituting meaningful subjects?

And as to their efficacy, did the political division enforced by the two German states, specifically with respect to their policies of mirror-imaging, institutionalize different lifecourses? Were East and West everyday relationships and interaction routines unique so that the distinctive features for belonging, for being at home, to one side excluded one from belonging to the other? I think we must conclude that not only were the questions appropriate to the object of study, but that the answers to them now provide us with a perspective from which one can begin formulating the kinds of questions necessary to explain the process of unity.

To be sure, no single explanation can account for the difficulties of unity. I have repeatedly argued for an approach that takes into consideration the many levels at which reality is constructed. This said, not all levels are equally significant. Included in any explanation, I would argue, must be a recognition of the effects of different nation-building policies in the two states, of the Cold War context in which these policies unfolded, and of the asymmetrical structures carried into unity derived from the dual organization that characterized division. In the East, state-making took precedence over nation-building, so that, to paraphrase Brecht, leaders built a state instead of a community. And without community there can be no nation. In the West, on the other hand, the two – state- and nation-building – went hand-in-hand, however uneasily and precariously. We might predict that a more complete unity will depend precisely upon the extent to which these processes continue to go hand-in-hand: the extent to which the security interests of the state are balanced against and made accountable to the multiplicity of needs of personal articulation in the public spaces of everyday life.

Perhaps one reason why unity is so difficult, from the West German perspective, lay in resentment at the disintegration of their mirror-image, and the collapse of a moral order that always ascribed to them superiority – at least over the *Ossies*. And perhaps, from the East German perspective, the difficulty lay in their ignorance of and inability to decipher and manipulate a sign system whose construction, in part, was predicated on this very ignorance and inability; in other words, on the very inferiority they bring with them into every interaction with West Germans. Given these initial terms of unity, it appears that durable forms of division have now been built into the East–West distinction.

In any case, the new German nation will be constructed in a process not totally dissimilar to that of nation-building during the Cold War. Legal ordinances in the new unity will be appropriated in generation- and gender-specific ways, and rarely as they were intended, since the situation of interaction will be different from the one that generated the legal code (and logic for its efficacy) in the first place. Thus a delay in time (between enactment of rule and act of appropriation), as well as a shift in the recipient (a person unlike the one imagined at the time of enactment) will build into policy an inescapable logic of misrecognition. Nonetheless, I would expect that specific symbols will play central generative roles in any construction of practices, and that these symbols will be readily identifiable given that actors always begin with prejudices inherited from a tradition, or, as Marx so perspicaciously wrote, "in . . . time-honoured disguise[s] and . . . borrowed language[s]."

# Notes

## Introduction

1 By the late 1950s anthropologists began having problems explaining empirical systems of classification that resembled dual organization because many of them exhibited anomalous features, thus not perfectly conforming to the expectations of the model. Their actual confusion lay, as Lévi-Strauss has pointed out, in believing that all reciprocal exchanges implied equality, whereas many moieties exhibited regularized unequal exchange, and they probably changed over time: "The inequality of the moieties came to be treated as an irregularity of the system. And – much more serious – the striking anomalies that were discovered later were completely neglected" (1967: 158–159). It would seem as if inequality and asymmetry are the norm in exchange relationships. Hence differences between dual organizations regarding the degree of reciprocity (and thus the perfection of the structural symmetry) should not lead one to reject the basic model, but to reformulate its relation to practices in different historical contexts.

2 *The Attraction of Opposites* (1989), a collection of essays edited by David Maybury-Lewis and Uri Almagor, makes an important contribution to the redefinition of dual organization. Almagor specifically argues for conceptualizing "different kinds of dual organizations," which should not be tied to a structuralist paradigm, but also studied "from other perspectives, such as those of conflict and power relations, exchange theory" (1989: 20, 31). Maybury-Lewis seeks to redefine the study as one of explaining "the attraction of dualistic philosophies," and makes the argument: "Dualistic practice seeks to institutionalize the balance of contending forces in order to maintain that harmony in society." This study of Berlin does not focus on understanding dualistic philosophy, but rather examines dualistic practices and their relation to ideology and power. Maybury-Lewis insists that dual organization existed "before a process of modernization" produced "intellectual and social fragmentation of a kind that even a dualistic system is unable to synthesize" (1989: 2, 14, 16). According to his model, Berlin obviously does not qualify as a type of dual organization, for duality in Berlin (which was "modern" before it was dual) increased the fragmentation instead of

regularizing conflict so as to institutionalize harmony. The duality of Berlin and the Cold War might have reached some kind of asymmetrical equilibrium in the future had it developed long enough; after a mere forty years, it already enjoyed regularized features of duality (see the list by Almagor 1989: 144). Yet, its breakdown in the late 1980s had more to do with growing asymmetry in power relations than with the "social fragmentation" characteristic of modernity.

3 I am not thereby suggesting that all dual organizations grew out of a single group which later divided into two. It may very well be that some began as two independent groups and over time established a moiety relationship with each other while sharing the same physical space.

4 The terms "mirror-imaging" and "misrecognition" are taken from Jacques Lacan's psychoanalytic theory (1977). Lacan, drawing upon Hegel's theory of recognition, initially formulated these notions to explain the process of human development from infancy on; I will be employing them more in the Hegelian sense, at the level of the development of political and social organization as well as at the individual level.

5 Johannes Fabian (1983) has eloquently criticized the employment of devices of time to substantiate a false objectivity and thus avoid considering how ethnographer and native are coeval cultural constructs. Marc Augé (1982: 105) also problematized the "relation between questioner and questioned," proposing that "'modern' society of the Western type [is] an object that can and must be studied from the anthropological point of view."

**1 Naming, categorizing, periodizing**

1 Scholars working in the French structuralist tradition have long been preoccupied with the importance of classificatory systems for history. See Emile Durkheim and Marcel Mauss (1963), Claude Lévi-Strauss (1962), Roland Barthes (1967), and Michel Foucault (1966). This line of thought has been most recently elaborated upon by Pierre Bourdieu (1972; 1979).

2 The syllogistic reasoning on the part of the Allies – Germans = fascism, fascism = evil, therefore Germans = evil – deserves further research and a separate discussion, especially in the context of an account of the reception of Nazism by the two superpowers, the United States and the Soviet Union.

3 The work of reeducation had already begun in the Soviet Union during the war. A group called "Nationalkomitees Freies Deutschland," organized by, among others, Wilhelm Pieck, Johannes R. Becher, and Walter Ulbricht, worked there to train German soldiers held in prisoner-of-war camps about the evils of Nazism. They hoped to recruit them for fighting with the resistance. Once back in Germany, this committee worked together with other groups under Soviet authority to reeducate all Germans.

4 Denazification in West Germany varied greatly from region to region, for the French, British, and Americans differed greatly among themselves regarding policy. See the detailed study of American policy in Bavaria by Tent (1982).

5 Cf. Dotterweich (1979) and Niethammer (1988a).

6 Cf. Wolfgang Mommsen (1987).

7 As David Clay Large (1987: 79–113) writes, by 1950 West German Chancellor Adenauer, with near-unanimous support across the political spectrum, even argued for integration of elite units of the Waffen-SS into the society. Former leaders of such units were often welcomed back in their home towns with parades. By the mid 1960s silence over the Nazi period and the relation of the Federal Republic to the Third Reich became a matter for some public debate. A controversy erupted again in 1987, provoked by a letter by Jürgen Habermas. This debate is well documented in *Historiker-streit* (1987). For an informative collection of essays in historical and cultural analysis of identity formation in the two Germanies, see Weidenfeld (1983).

8 Cf. *DDR Handbuch* (1985).

9 Two important critiques of kinship studies in non-Western cultures have been made within anthropology by Rodney Needham and David Schneider. After devoting several decades of his life to kinship theory, Needham (1971) came to the conclusion that because he could not find a similar set of characteristics to identify as kin in every society, he (and others) had misidentified their object of study. Thus kinship theory, for him (by which he meant primarily kinship algebra – relationships that can be represented by genealogical grids), is not an appropriate domain for analysis. Schneider wrote at approximately the same time that kinship was a "non-subject since it does not exist in any culture known to me" (1972: vii). But Schneider's cultural critique was far more radical than Needham's, namely, that kinship theory, based on Western cultural assumptions that relations between humans arise out of sexual reproductive needs, can make no universal claims since not all cultures share these assumptions. "Robbed of its grounding in biology, kinship is nothing; robbed of its grounding in the supernatural, religion is everyday life" (1984: 120). After showing how the Yaps have no system that can be ordered according to the universalistic criteria of kinship theory, Schneider dissolved kinship as a "privileged system" because we cannot explain what such a system would be without the Western cultural assumption of a biological relationship.

My goal in this study is not to resurrect kinship as conventionally conceptualized, but to follow up on Schneider's implicit suggestion to *redefine* kinship independent of biological essentialism, or, as he suggests for religion, in terms of categories of everyday life. A study of kin need yield neither to granting it the autonomy of a "system" nor to ontologizing it by imputing some ahistorical essence (in his words, "Blood Is Thicker Than Water," or the "blood-and-mud" thesis). My redefinition follows in the text.

10 Even in the construction of the Ur-text (published in 1880) on kinship categorization, the kinship terminology of the Australian aborigines, Lori-mer Fison and A.W. Howitt artificially superimposed their own idea of a kinship system on native linguistic usage. Fison comments about the aborigine: "When asked to define the relationship in which he stands to other persons, [he] frequently takes into consideration matters other than relation-ship, and so gives words which are not specific terms of kinship. After years of inquiry into this matter, the humiliating confession must be made that I am hopelessly puzzled" (quoted in Kuper 1988: 97).

11 I define nationness as a subjectivity, not contingent on an opinion or attitude, but derived from lived experience within a state. See chapter 3.

12 On June 17, 1953, workers in most large cities in the GDR protested against new work norms leading to a chaotic political rebellion of sorts put down by Russian tanks. This uprising is commemorated as a national holiday in West Germany, and a major street in West Berlin that ran perpendicular to the Wall has been named after it, the "17th of June."

13 Cited in Conradt and Heckmann-Janz (1987).

14 *Abgrenzungspolitik*, demarcation policy, had in fact been very successful in West Berlin/West Germany, but a big failure in the East. A 1988 study by Richard Hilmar found that 80 percent of West German youths between the ages of 14 and 29 thought that travel in the GDR was like travel in a foreign country. Of those who had not visited the GDR, only 23 percent indicated any interest in doing so, and only 17 percent indicated any feelings of solidarity with people in the GDR. These indicators changed dramatically after a mere two visits to the GDR – increasing from 23 to 29 percent for those indicating interest, and from 17 to 40 percent for those feeling solidarity (1988: 1,091–1,100). It was well known that the FRG often fostered false awareness of East Germany. This misinformation policy had its greatest effect on school children, even those in Berlin (West). For example, during my fieldwork, the civic book used for school classes in West Berlin, entitled *Berlin Berlin*, published by Diesterweg Verlag in Frankfurt, maintained (falsely) that school classes were not allowed to visit East Berlin. In addition, the book omitted the names of certain cities in the GDR ("Heimatkundebuch trotz einer Reihe von Fehlern zugelassen," *Der Tagesspiegel*, November 17, 1987, p. 12).

15 The GDR led the world in the amount of garbage it received from other countries for processing and storing. The environmental organization Greenpeace estimates that, between 1986 and 1988, 3.65 million tons of garbage were exported in the world, of which the GDR received 3 million. West Berlin alone was responsible for 300,000 tons of the garbage that went to the GDR. Because of fewer technical controls and the inability of the public to oversee the dumps, the GDR could process West-garbage for 5–10 percent of the cost (40 DM per ton) that a West German company charged (see Gerd Thorns, "Giftmüllhalde DDR," *Zitty* 18, 1987, p.18, 19; "Giftmülle-Exporte: Die Verlockung ist groß," *Volksblatt* 43, November 9, 1988, p.2).

16 Morgan very succinctly states his case: "It may be here premises that all forms of government are reducible to two general plans, using the world plan in its scientific sense. In these bases the two are fundamentally distinct. The first, in the order of time, is founded upon persons, and upon relations purely personal, and may be distinguished as a society [*societas*]. The gens is the unit of this period, the gens, the phratry, the tribe, and the confederacy of tribes, which constituted a people or nation [*populus*]. At a later period a coalescence of tribes in the same area into a nation took the place of a confederacy of tribes occupying independent areas. Such, through prolonged ages, after the gens appeared, was the substantially universal organization of ancient society; and it remained among the Greeks and Romans after

civilization supervened. The second is founded upon territory and upon property, and may be distinguished as a state" (1877: 6–7).

17 See the important critical history of the use of "primitive society" in anthropological analysis by Adam Kuper (1988).

18 To cite some of the earliest proponents of such an approach, intimately tied to the establishment of survey research as the paradigm of political science data-gathering techniques, see Gabriel Almond and Sidney Verba (1963), Almond and G. Bingham Powell (1966) and Lucian W. Pye and Verba (1965). For an early critique of these approaches, see Charles Taylor (1979: 24–72).

19 Gellner (1983) concentrates on nationalism, what he calls "willed adherence" to a community, rather than nationness, or what I would call the praxis of belonging. Thus he argues that "nations can be defined only in terms of the age of nationalism, rather than . . . the other way around" (1983: 55). If he means that modern nations can be defined only in terms of the age of state-building, then I am in total agreement with him – but he does not. His voluntaristic or idealist definition suits the purposes of analyzing types of contemporary nationalism, but is not helpful for understanding nationness. Nationalism is a phenomenon that comes and goes (hence, opinion polls can, to some extent, measure it), whereas nationness is fundamentally tied to identity structures and has a tenuous relationship to opinion. Gellner's concern with how high culture diffuses to produce social homogeneity shifts our analytical focus away from where it should be: on the heterogeneity of multicultural states, the actual norm in praxis even if not in the ideology and forms of representation of most modern states.

Moreover, the diversity of cultural forms within a state does not preclude a shared set of lifecourse transformations; these transformations are, I would argue, more crucial for the legitimacy of the state than is the standardization of literary norms or cultural grammar, as Gellner argues. Otherwise, how do we explain the actual planned illiteracy or planned linguistic incompetence of certain sectors of the (national) population in Western states such as France, the United States, and England? These states do, in fact, systematically offer different educations to various groups and subcategories of their populations. A frequent example Gellner uses, the education system, is indeed part of the state apparatus and does systematize the lifecourse, but it does not track every life identically. The kind of high cultural competence that Gellner focuses upon is simply beside the point for state legitimacy. For analyses along these lines, see Bourdieu and Passeron (1977); Bourdieu (1984); Willis (1977); Bernstein (1972).

20 For a theoretical review of the shifts in contemporary sociological theory regarding the nature of "the social," see Heinz Bude (1988: 4–17).

21 Many contemporary theorists prefer to speak of the family, reserving the word "kinship" for so-called primitive societies. Yet what they understand to be the family is quite similar to the way in which I am using kinship. Jacques Donzelot, for example, maintains that the family in the modern Western world is "both queen and prisoner" of the social. It remains a privileged site in (re)producing society. The exact place of the family in this social schema

must not, however, be posited "as a point of departure, as a manifest reality," argues Donzelot, "but as a moving resultant, an uncertain form whose intelligibility can only come from studying the system of relations it maintains with the sociopolitical level" (1979: xxv). Researchers have staked out a variety of positions regarding the conceptualization and role of state intervention in the family. See, for example, the conservative defense of "the family" by Bane (1976), liberal defenses by Lasch (1977) and Berger and Berger (1983), a liberal critique by Freeman (1984), radical critiques by Barrett and McIntosh (1982) and Olsen (1984).

22 In this important paper, Kohli asks that we move beyond looking at the lifecourse as a mere result of other social and economic structures, and that we consider the lifecourse itself a structuring and structured object of study, much as we look at, for example, gender and class. Whereas Kohli restricts himself to empirical (primary demographic) indicators of lifecourse development, I am in this study defining the lifecourse as a series of transformations in experiential meaning, and focusing much more on fights over classification of demographic indicators than on the nature of demographic change itself. See also Mayer and Müller (1986: 217–245), and John W. Meyer (1986: 199–216).

23 In both East and West, the initial term used was *Opfer des Faschismus*, shortened to *OpF*. The East has stuck to this label, whereas the West soon dropped the *Opfer*, victim, label for the special group who would get reparation payments, and relabeled these *Verfolgte*, persecuted. By 1949, the time of the founding of the two states, many in the West, especially members of the ruling Christian Democratic Party, were insisting that nearly all Germans had also been victims of the Nazis (now fascism was also too general and inclusive a term), thus they needed another label for those singled out for special persecution as opposed to victimization during the Third Reich. *Opfer des Nationalsozialismus*, victims of National Socialism, was also a commonly used phrase in the West, but over time *Verfolgte* has become more common than *Opfer*. (See Engelmann 1981: 162–165; "Berliner Synode fordert Aufhebung des Erbgesundheitsgesetzes," *Der Tagesspiegel*, November 17, 1987, p. 10.)

## 2 Clarification of concepts

1 This "turn" to interpretation within anthropology had much to do with the rediscovery, or recovery, of the interpretive work of Max Weber in the early seventies, following a period when structuralism had reached a paradigm in some parts of the academy. I see this turn more as a growth out of structuralism than a rejection of it. Of course, each university has its own trajectory of literary appropriation, and disciplines also have national specificities. See the collection of essays by Paul Rabinow and William M. Sullivan (1979).

2 Among some of the more articulate proponents of a dialogic anthropology, see work by Clifford (1988), Marcus and Fischer (1986), Dwyer (1982), and Fabian (1979: 1–26).

3 For Hegel, as for myself, the state is an abstraction, referring to a system of

law based on principles of legality and legitimacy. It is a historical possibility that grows out of specific communities, where, Hegel writes, "[T]he state is not the abstract confronting the citizens; they are parts of it, like members of an organic body, where no member is end and none is means" (1953: 51–52). As White notes, Hegel was most interested in the "conflict between desire, on the one side, and the law, on the other. Where there is no rule of law, there can be neither a subject nor the kind of event which lends itself to narrative representation" (1981: 12). Here I am interested in the state as a system of formal authority that has a culturally specific character, and not in the state as a system of organization – that is, not in its, e.g., feudal, absolutist, socialist, welfare-capitalist forms.

4  I thank Terri O'Nell for making me aware of this difference.

5  I have rejected official historiographical texts as "data" in favor of actual legal and policy texts of the state primarily because of their secondhand nature. For the same reason, I have rejected purely literary accounts of life histories, despite the fact that they as well as historiography are cultural artifacts that might reveal the same story as I am about to tell. See Benedict Anderson's (1983) imaginative use of literary accounts in examining nation-building, as well as a volume edited by Homi K. Bhabha (1990) that follows Anderson's lead in analyzing literary accounts from this perspective.

6  White's use of trope, as a formal, universal linguistic mechanism that figures narrative, has since become linguistic convention among academics. His tendency to theoretical ahistoricism has often been criticized. David Carroll argues that White has difficulty keeping his tropes from "shading into one another [a remark taken from Kenneth Burke] and often his determination of a *dominant trope* at the end of an analysis in which several tropes have been in question seems purely arbitrary" (1976: 61). In a criticism reminiscent of Vico, Fredric Jameson chides White for his cyclical view of history, his reinventing a "tropological cycle" that is more concerned with universal typology than with the concrete historicity of texts (1976: 2–9).

7  I would agree with Fernandez that the "sensation of wholeness" is obtained for individuals through the use of tropes, but this metaphoric function of tropes does not exhaust their "mission." His focus on expressive culture and religious experience leads him to concentrate on individual appropriation of metaphor, and therefore the coherence of a cosmology. My focus is not on the individual "sensation of wholeness" but on the coherence provided by the whole, in this case, of generational belonging. Cultural integration at the group level, I would maintain, is not accomplished by single tropes, but rather made possible through the metonymic relation of tropes to one another. This integration is performed not by tropes themselves but by their ability to appeal to master narratives that are derived not from personal experience but from social constructs.

8  Lakoff (1987) has illustrated how objectivist assumptions based on an Aristotelian or classical theory of cognition, the regnant theory of classification in the social sciences, hold true only for certain propositional models of thought, and are unable to account for a wide range of category systems found by anthropologists in different societies. An "experiential view of the

mind," Lakoff argues, must necessarily go beyond a propositional model of truth. It is not that this model is false or wrong, simply that there are other, more inclusive principles of categorization also operative at any moment in time.

9  See the 1978 issue of *Daedalus*, 107 (4), devoted to the concept generation, especially the essays by Laura Nash, Matilda White Riley, and Annie Kriegel.

10  The distinction, widely used in literary study, between *fabula* and *sjuzet*, is often translated as the difference between story and discourse. See the discussion by Peter Brooks (1984: 12–30).

11  See the brilliant essays on ethnographic authority by James Clifford (1988: 1–92).

### 3  Demographics of production and reproduction

1  The argument was often made that women in the GDR decided to have their first baby without a husband only in order to take advantage of social welfare benefits, and that they would marry the father later. Yet 28.8 percent of all single mothers in the GDR never married; it is unlikely that this decision was due solely to rational calculations about welfare benefits. The meaning of marriage and the motivation for having a child, as we shall see in the following chapters, were not reducible to a single cause.

2  Statistics reveal that 80 percent of all West Berlin women became mothers, but this number is inflated for German women because it includes the many Mediterranean women in Berlin who rarely abstain from having children.

### 4  State strategies and kinship

1  See Jacques Lacan (1977) and Pierre Bourdieu (1977), who apply these terms in quite different contexts.

2  This concept of law owes much to Sally Falk Moore (1978: 214–256).

3  The study of the state as a semi-autonomous organization is perhaps the ruling paradigm within political science. There are, however, many different types of analyses of the state that try to incorporate a concept of "society" or "culture" into their framework. For a historical sociology of the state, see Badie and Birnbaum (1983); for a political critique of the capitalist state, see Offe (1988; 1985), and of the socialist state, see Arato (1981) and Jowitt (1975); for an anthology of different perspectives by political scientists, see the volume edited by Held and Krieger (1983). Despite their sophistication, these authors rarely reach the level of everyday practices in their analyses, rather focusing on culture or "civil society" as an abstraction *vis-à-vis* the state; their major interest is ultimately not culture or belonging as nation-building but political change or state-building *per se*. For a very innovative attempt to move beyond the state versus civil society approach within political science, to understand the state in "its spatial and temporal dimensions," see the essays by Held (1989).

4  While all aspects of the lifecourse written into the law are relevant to this discussion, I have omitted a discussion of those embedded in legal codes that carry us too far away from kinship regulations. Thus, I have regretfully omitted a discussion of legal codes mandating compulsory military duty (or

civilian service) for men, although this does come up in autobiographical accounts presented in chapters 5 and 6. Also I have omitted a discussion of formal taxation and housing codes, which are equally central to kinship formation, and which are also discussed in the autobiographies.

5 See Borneman (1992) for an initial sketch of a history of kinship understood as the categories of belonging in Germany.

6 In a purely textual reading of Marx, White has linked his narrative to a comic archetype and romantic paradigm (1973: 281–282). Actual legal texts of the postwar socialist republics reveal more of the romantic paradigm and less of the comic, although there may be additional forms of differentiation among socialist republics if their use of literary genres is historicized, as Jameson (1981) argues should be done, by considering them in their specific national-cultural contexts over time. This analysis limits itself to socialist state narratives in the GDR.

7 This particular attitude to legitimate authority is clearly explicated by Kant (1991: 41–54; 93–125) in his political writings, where he argues that republican (constitutional) government is the only rightful form, and that, while citizens should have the right to criticize the state, they do not have the right to rebel and are obligated to be loyal to the constitution. The state's authority is thus based on a priori, transcendental principles of right (*Recht*).

8 For a useful summary of the relation of West German political insitutions to the principles of constitutionality, see Jesse (1986: 35–68).

9 There is, of course, variance among liberal as well as socialist states. For example, the act of foundation in the United States is itself regarded as more basic than the constitution as document, whereas for the West Germans, the Basic Law is more revered. (Hence in the United States, for example, the importance of the Bill of Rights is constantly questioned, and opinion polls often indicate that, if subject to a popular vote, a majority of citizens would vote against some of these rights.) In part, this is to be explained by the historical context of the act of state formation: the West German state did not result from a popular revolution against a foreign enemy, as did the American, but grew out of increased enmity between the Allied Occupation Forces. In addition, the founding act divided the nation in Germany; in the United States, as in France, it united the people. See the discussion by Arendt (1963).

10 It seems as if the *Hausfrauenehe* was also carried into Japanese legal codes through the influence of Prussian legal reform at the end of the nineteenth century, and then further reproduced with American encouragement after World War II. On the role of the good wife and wife/mother in Japan, see the article by Jennifer Robertson (1989: 50–69).

11 I thank Scott Long for helping me to clarify this idea, which I first encountered in Habermas (1987). For a more complete exposition of the notion of the colonization of public and private space see Borneman (1991a: 57–81).

12 The first step of the Russian occupiers involved the dismissal of all National Socialist Party members and sympathizers involved in administration and state bureaucracy. The vast majority of these Nazi bureaucrats, as the GDR

has consistently maintained, went West, and after 1950, most regained comparable jobs in West Germany/West Berlin. The reform was perhaps most thorough in the area of justice. Approximately 85 percent of the 2,467 judges, lawyers and prosecutors were immediately fired, necessitating the education of a new generation of legal experts to take over the administration of the organs of justice (see H. Weber 1985).

The Western Allies and West Germany, on the other hand, because they claimed continuity with the past and relied on a lapsarian form of legitimation, were caught in the dilemma of integrating Nazi subjects into the republic without also incorporating the Nazi past. What this meant, in fact, was that not a single judge who sat in the notorious *Volksgerichtshof*, local courts responsible for applying Nazi laws (including sending people to the death camps), was tried after 1945. Moreover, of the regular members of the judiciary, slightly more than 7 percent were actually sentenced in the postwar period, with approximately 67 percent of these prosecutions taking place before the founding of the West German state (see the volume edited by J. Weber and P. Steinbach 1988; Lübbe 1988). Only in 1958 did the Adenauer regime set up a special prosecutor to oversee criminal action against former Nazis throughout central Europe, and, even then, the Cold War justified lack of cooperation between East and West in gathering evidence for trials.

13  Cf. Uwe-Jens Heuer (1986: 182–206).

14  Particularly stressed in the relation of law to the citizen is the "overcoming of isolated conflict situations" and the reaching of a stage where conflict does not arise. See H. Kellner (1969: 81).

15  Friedrich Engels' formal theory in *Origins of the Family, Private Property and the State* (1884) was derived from Lewis Henry Morgan's postulates, drawn from Morgan's work (1871) with American Indian populations. This work was regularly cited in GDR texts.

16  For an extensive review of these texts, see Obertreis (1985: 31–47).

17  Women did in fact reach approximate parity in educational competence and occupational training. Yet, for a variety of reasons including, e.g., becoming primary (and often sole) childcare providers, assuming traditional marital roles, and underperforming due to lack of self-worth, the majority of women performed in the lower rungs of the labor hierarchy. See chapter 5.

18  An additional law was passed in 1977, called *Radikalenerlaß*, which declared many of the intellectual leaders of the "68 generation" to be "enemies of the constitution." This effectively blacklisted them for life in public employment, which, of course, also affected private employment in the FRG, since the two forms of employment were not so easily separable. About "one-third of the total population are largely dependent on state-provided incomes for longer periods of their lives" (Mayer and Müller 1986: 240).

19  Among the goals of Clara Zetkin (1984) were the following: full legal rights and equality of men and women, fully equal conditions for women and men in the workplace (the workplace defined by women and men alike as center of identity), state support for the care and education of children, equal division of housework between marital partners, and easing the burden of housework through the construction of state-supported institutions.

20 Above all, the Mother and Child Protection Act (MCPL) from September 27, 1950 accelerated the development of institutions such as Krippe (for babies), Horte (for after-school), Heim (longer-term homes, daily, weekly, and yearly), and of free time organizations such as, e.g., the Pioniere (for children) and Freie Deutsche Jugend, FDJ, (for youth).

21 The West German Ministry of the Family founded in 1953 did not consider itself responsible for "youth work" until 1957, when it first incorporated the word "youth" into its title.

22 Obertreis (1985: 321) maintains that the initial plans to issue a family law book in 1954 were delayed because of the ruling Party's insecurity *vis-à-vis* its political base. Scholars within the GDR whom I know agreed in part with this explanation, readily admitting that publication would have not been accepted by a majority of the public; they also stressed that the ruling SED wanted to hold open the possibility for reunification. Between 1954 and 1965, policy had more specific goals, e.g., integrating women into the workforce, counteracting influences of the church, refuting West German media propaganda, redressing gender- and class-based privileges, and developing a socialist youth policy.

23 Unification has politicized this issue for both Germanies, resulting in the take-over of West German Law into the East, as well as more stringent enforcement of abortion law in the West.

24 Some critics of the regime interpreted this law as another attempt to strengthen the housewife marriage. Now full-time housewives are extended the same benefits as are single mothers and working women. In order to qualify under the law, one of the partners must practically quit working, which in the majority of cases means the woman (see Malzahn 1985: 184–192).

25 See detailed accounts of naming practices by Helwig (1982) and Korinth (1988: 32).

26 As Mary Ann Glendon (1989) points out, beginning in the 1960s, family law in all Western industrial societies has changed along these lines. "Indeed, in countries that are culturally quite diverse, there has been a remarkable coincidence of similar legal developments produced at about the same time, in apparent independence from one another" (1989: 1). I have sought to sketch in this chapter how this process of transformation took place in the two German states, in "apparent independence from one another," as she says but, I would emphasize, only apparent. Each state had its own *raison d'état* at any particular time, though this reason of state grew out of a highly charged, international Cold War context.

**5 Victimization, political reconstruction, and kinship transformations: Generation I in East Berlin**

1 In a 1987 study of GDR industrial workers, directed by Lutz Niethammer (1988b: 283–345), researchers found that the majority of people had "made an arrangement" with the regime, and were not motivated by a political consensus. Using methods of oral history, Niethammer concluded that the committed communists were not opportunistic enough, perhaps too principled, to maintain leadership positions after the war, most of which went to

more politically compliant individuals. My own study based on fieldwork confirms his findings.

2 I am using the convention of "women" and "men" without meaning to imply that all German or Berliner women and men had the same experience. My account is limited to biographies of discussion partners of my acquaintance and to already published autobiographical texts. Sources are discussed in more detail in chapter 2. In particular, I have often drawn on the excellent life histories of women in Berlin published by Meyer and Schulze (1984; 1985). Several of the women they interviewed lived in the East after the war, though all currently live in West Berlin. In descriptions of the immediate postwar years, their accounts are similar in detail to those I gathered in both Berlins. Hence I draw on their biographies for both East and West, and bring in autobiographies gathered by other researchers as well as myself only when they differ from Meyer and Schulze's interviewees. I cite only residents currently living in East Berlin for accounts of the years following 1952.

3 Instability was a characteristic of Berlin domestic life during the entire war years, though more pronounced after 1943. Between 1939 and 1943 over 700,000 Berliners left the city, among whom were numbered 86,000 children and youths under eighteen years of age. In the first three months of the accelerated, planned evacuation, from August to November 1943, approximately 823,000 Berliners, including 442,000 children and youths, were transported to other areas of the Reich. At war's end, more than 25 percent of Berlin residents were either foreigners or so-called non-Germans, the majority of whom were forced laborers in the armaments industry (Heimann 1985: 110). From January 1943 to December 1944, the number of Berliner *Versorgten*, people with food-ration cards, sank from 4.07 to 2.82 million. Sixty percent of all children and youths had been evacuated between July 1943 and October 1944, the largest group being children under three years of age (Meyer and Schulze 1985: 29).

4 Accusations of war crimes do not always mean guilt, for many POWs insist that Soviet authorities conveniently placed them in the "war criminals" category in order to legitimize retaining them for forced labor. The last such POWs were released from Soviet prisons in 1956.

5 People outside Berlin, particularly those in the country and small cities, report different experiences for the years 1944–1948, claiming that food became scarce by 1944 and that it improved at war's end in some occupied regions. It may be either that Berliners had better provisions than others during the Third Reich or that Berliners themselves were more clever at exploiting official delivery systems. In any case, the radical worsening of the situation in Berlin immediately after the war does not correspond to most accounts of those living outside Berlin.

6 For an interesting comparison, see the now classic interpretation of the American "New Woman" of the 1920s by Caroll Smith-Rosenberg (1985: 245–296).

7 See the account of the use of homosexual stereotyping by Sander Gilman (1985); on homosexuality and nationalism, see George Mosse (1985); on

the meaning of homosexuality in East Germany, see Borneman (1987); Steakley (1976).

8 The close link between the state and the workplace, and the use of the workplace to structure the rhythms of everyday life is common to some degree in all industrial countries. Within the anthropological literature, Japan is perhaps the most interesting example of such a pattern (see Nakane (1970), Plath (1983), Noguchi (1990), and Kondo (1990).

9 These statistics are taken from *Die Zeit*, no. 1, "Politik," January 1, 1988, p. 5; *Die Zeit*, no. 29, "Politik," July 10, 1987, p. 5.

10 It is difficult to distinguish statistically between visits and visitors. The two numbers were often confused in reporting. Retired people were allowed sixty days per year in the West, not sixty visits, as often reported. The one exception was when they got a visa for a longer residence period in a foreign country. This meant, for counting purposes, that someone who stayed for twenty days on a single visit to West Berlin had only another forty days in that year at their disposal to travel abroad.

11 The Allied Occupation Forces were more stringent in their control of the civilian population in Berlin than in other cities, due in large part to mutual control of each other. All of the Allies required certain forms of forced labor in their separate zones, not only for former soldiers, but also for former Nazi Party members, their wives, and often their daughters. Those women not required to perform rubble clean-up work, *Trümmerarbeit*, but who nonetheless volunteered for the work, were paid for their labor; those required to work were given food-ration coupons in return.

Rationing cards for food and essential goods gave preference to those involved in heavy manual labor. Of the five classificatory groups, housewives were given the least. Therefore many mothers and housewives performed hard manual labor, such as crane operation, excavation, dock work, clock repair, and of course, *Trümmerarbeit*, in order to obtain better provisions. Meyer and Schulze (1985) estimate that, in 1946, between 5 and 10 percent of the adult women in Berlin worked in construction. The status of housewives changed on March 1, 1947, as they were elevated in rank from fifth to third in the hierarchy of the needy. In September 1945, 371,409 women officially worked in Berlin, almost 50 percent of the total eligible for rations. In September 1946 the total had nearly doubled, to 705,397. These figures are also much higher for Berlin than for the other German zones.

12 Helmut K. may have exaggerated his plight. The official pay ratio during this period was 60:40 East/West money for East Berlin residents who worked in West Berlin.

13 Compare my account of the *Kumpel* with Kapferer's description of "mateship" in Australia (1988). Kapferer ties mateship to egalitarianism, sociability, and ultimately nationalism. He describes how mutual drinking patterns among males result in forms of bonding. Of particular note is how he links "piss" with the drinking ritual, which, I would suggest, should be seen as mutual consumption of an ecstasy-producing fluid that is then often collectively and publicly excreted. This oral consumption and public emission lessens inhibitions to the point where not merely an abstract social

identity (nationalism) is shared, but the participants also open up to each other physically, in ways that the double play on the social experiencing of "piss" (drinking and emitting) perhaps best captures. Physical bonding, in turn, forms the basis for longer-term attachments of the participants to each other.

14 For an analysis of the importance of blood, and liquids generally, in German metaphors, see Linke (1986).

**6  Sentimentalization, fear, and alternate domestic form in East Berlin: Generation II**

1 Among those most responsible for constructing the theory of totalitarianism, though with quite different goals in mind, see Friedrich A. von Hayek (1944), Hanna Arendt (1951), and Carl Friedrich and Zbigniew Brzezinski (1965); also the recent more critical discussion of use of the concept by Jacques Rupnik (1988: 224–248).

2 In 1949, the regime founded a Worker and Farmer Faculty, ABF, at each university to train a new generation of children from the families of workers, farmers, and the "working intelligentsia." Except for small faculties at Halle and Freiberg, the program was dissolved in 1963. Between 1951 and 1963, 33,729 persons received degrees and with them a chance of social mobility (*DDR Handbuch* 1985: 52–53).

3 See the classic study on cargo cults by Peter Worsley (1957).

4 The official interpretation of Marxism in the GDR is, of course, only one of many possible readings this corpus of work can be given. The leadership's stress on the utopian element was by no means a necessary emphasis, for Marx and Engels emphasized equally, depending on which of their texts one reads, the illusion contained within any utopia, and the aspects of reification that enhance and sustain its appeal.

5 I thank Michael Weck (personal communication) for bringing this relationship to my attention.

6 See the study by Elizabeth Bott (1957) on the importance to British couples of networks outside the partnership.

7 Male–male friendships for Generation II form a kind of radial pattern centered around the *Kumpel* relationship of working-class men. The possible meanings of *Kumpel*, as I have described in chapter 5, have increased from the time when it narrowly referred to coal-miner relationships and from its early appropriation by blue-collar workers of Generation I. In 1989 it was widely used in domains outside of work, although still less among some professional classes (especially Party professionals, *Reisekader*, people approved for official travel to the West), where the expectations to conform to a exclusive, married, heterosexual pair model were the strongest.

8 In discussing the social mechanisms that broke down leading to the revolution of 1989, Lutz Niethammer points to different generational expectations as one of the primary factors. Specifically, he argues that women of Generation II see their mothers (using my categories) as "a miracle phenomenon out of another world, more as a horror than a model"

(1990: 257). He maintains that the women of Generation II see their own contributions as undervalued, and no longer think of their work as a field for self-discovery.

## 7 *Hausfrauenehe* and kinship restoration in West Berlin: Generation I

1 The way in which the socially privileged classes and groups quickly reestablished their privileges is well documented in two studies of Darmstadt families by Gerhart Baumert (1954: 91–117; 1952: 157). One can assume these processes were similar in West Berlin.

2 See Borneman (1992).

3 I analyze the different gradations of Germanness in chapter 9.

4 Under the decentralized federal form of government in West Germany, West Berlin had a special status, partially integrated at some levels, fully at others. From 1946 to 1953, a coalition led by a Social Democratic mayor ruled Berlin, replaced from 1953 to 1955 with a Christian-Democratic-led coalition. From 1955 to 1957, a "Grand Coalition" of Social and Christian Democrats ruled, replaced in 1957 by a Social Democratic coalition, alternating with their sole rule, until 1981, when the Christian Democrats again took over. My purpose here is not to trace the differences in the way the political parties represent themselves, nor in the substantial conflicts between the federal government and the city of Berlin. The laws I have dealt with, concerning housing, family, and taxation policies, as well as policies regarding the church, are federal laws that held true for all *Länder* within the Federal Republic and for the city of West Berlin. I note when Berlin had a unique status *vis-à-vis* the federal law, either obtaining special privileges or negating in some fashion the federal will. Up until Willy Brandt initiated the *Ostpolitik* in 1970, the Social Democrats that ruled Berlin were in basic agreement with, or at least deferred to, the Christian Democrats about Cold War strategies discussed in this book. A Treaty on the Basis of Relations between the two German states was signed in East Berlin on December 21, 1972, marking the beginning of normalization of Cold War divisions.

5 Unless stated otherwise in the notes, most of the following information is taken from a 1987–1988 exhibition in West Berlin, *Von Interbau '57 zu IBA '87 – 30 Jahre Wohnen in Berlin* 1987–1988. See also Hauptstadt Berlin (1990).

6 Houses were occupied already in the early seventies, but since the occupiers did not form a movement they did not attract media attention. I am told that in Frankfurt, the other major German city where social movements started, the first squatters occupied a large, bourgeois house in 1970. Moreover, the squatters were not all students, but also included people from the working class.

7 For a review article of the celebration, see Trumpener (1989: 79–108).

8 I am primarily concerned here with social science and not with the humanities. For excellent accounts of the role of historiography see Hans Mommsen (1984: 263–283; 1987: 174–189), H.U. Wehler (1984: 221–262), and Wolfgang Mommsen (1987: 300–321).

9 For a critique of Schelsky's generalizations, see Baumert (1954: 184–189). Baumert argues, among other things, that Schelsky overexaggerates the influence of the war on the German family structure, and, contrary to Schelsky, he claims that the processes influencing family construction are reversible since the family itself is an unstable unit.

10 For a discussion of how women experienced and in part internalized this model, see the different aspects in the volume edited by Dellile and Grohn (1985).

11 See Habermas (1961), where he also argues that domination in Western democracies is rooted in a hidden politicization of private life coupled with an appearance of openness in the political domain.

12 See the detailed analysis of family policy in the Third Reich by Mühlfeld and Schönweiss (1989).

13 These ideas are fully in agreement with those expressed in the insightful essays on West German demarcation from the East by Rainer Lepsius (1981: 419) and on German national identity by Wolfgang Mommsen (1987: 300–321), where the tropes of anti-communism and prosperity are discussed.

14 Not all political leaders were content with the state's satirical strategy of encouraging demarcation from the East in and through an unabashed materialism in everyday life in the West. The Christian Democrat Ludwig Erhard, for example, who as the "father of the *Wirtschaftswunder*" followed Adenauer as Chancellor from 1963 to 1966, called for a return to an idealism (a social-market economy and a *formierte Gesellschaft*) that could compete with the idealism of the GDR. As Michael Weck (1989) demonstrates, Erhard felt uncomfortable with the "Lutheran-Protestant orgiastic" behavior of his fellow West Germans, embodied above all in the *Freßwelle*. Erhard thought that prosperity alone was insufficient to legitimate the new state. Weck notes, however, that those Germans who had lived through the idealism of the Nazis were skeptical of idealism of any sort. By the late sixties, Generation II began precisely where Erhard had left off, with a critique of West German materialism.

15 See Heinz Bude's (1987: 86–142) fascinating biography-based analysis of German self-flight, from which I have taken much inspiration.

**8 Politicized kinship in West Berlin: Generation II**

1 See the interesting ethnography of a musical conservatory by Kingsbury (1988), where he discusses the political context of ascertaining talent.

2 In archival work on this period, one is also confronted with the influence of French existentialist philosophy on the German "beat" culture of the fifties, though I was not able to document this in life reconstructions. From today's standpoint, the American influence is selectively emphasized.

3 For West Germans as of 1988, there was disincentive to avoid military service because West German companies tended to discriminate against men without a service record, and it was increasingly difficult to obtain a training/university position without a record of military or civilian service.

4 Protection of the state, often translated into persecution of Lefties or Communist Party members, was indeed the major argument authorities used since 1949. In the year 1953 alone, 1,634 persons were sentenced to prison terms for "endangering the state," with the justification that this was necessary to protect democracy (Jesse 1986: 28).

5 See the evocative article on the *Autonome* by Jane Kramer (1989: 67–100).

6 One should not overlook the fact that during this period of state repression, the state was governed by a Social Democratic coalition. Throughout the 1970s the Social Democrats, as the most reform-oriented of the major parties, were "forced" to prove their loyalty to the ideas of the state by reacting in an authoritarian and extremely repressive manner toward dissidents.

7 Despite the existence of class-based models, there was a leveling of class in kin-related aspects of nationness. This is supported by Lüschen (1988: 167–168), who writes that studies since the late sixties show that family relations, support systems, interaction routines, and urban structures are independent of occupation and income. In other words, class-specific aspects of family life have been declining since the late sixties.

8 Descriptions in my own interviews contradict more controlled studies (based on polling, for example), such as the one quoted by Schütze (1988: 124), where few people list children as belonging to a marriage, and the majority of women claim to have children for "joy" or "sense of life." Another way of interpreting the responses to this poll would be that the respondents mean partnership does not belong to having children; instead, they consider children part of a personal relationship, related to fulfilling a concept of self independent of a partner. The questioners in such polls are confusing, and conflating – in response to questions that, I suspect, also confuse and conflate – marriage with partnership. Whereas marriage is, in fact, intimately connected to securing a socially recognized relationship between the individual and the state regarding parental authority and childcare, partnership, on the other hand, does not require a legal status. Marriage is, as pointed out above, usually consummated upon pregnancy or in its anticipation; it is not usually entered into merely because the people want to become partners.

9 Similar claims are made in a collection of interpretive essays on the history of socialization techniques since World War II (Preuss-Lausitz, Büchner, and Fischer-Kowalski 1983). The volume is structured around the argument that three generations of children, organized successively around *Krieg*, *Konsum* and *Krisen* (war, consumerism, and crisis), have typified youth in the postward period.

10 For women of Generation II, opportunities for fulfillment in work, while greater than for their mothers, were still substantially limited due to the structure of the labor market. Despite gains made in the late sixties/early seventies in opening up education and employment for women, their position was still not equal to that of men of the same rank. For example, when unemployment increased from 3.8 to 9.3 percent from 1980 to 1985, women consistently showed 0.9 to 2.5 percent higher unemployment rates than did men (Süßmuth 1988: 231). Women in the eighties partook in the

educational system to the same degree as men did, although this did not translate into the same employment opportunities. This gender-specific employment pattern was especially marked for mothers. While 20 percent of all mothers with children under fifteen were working in 1950, the rate in 1982 had risen to 42.6 percent (Sommerkorn 1988: 117; Claessens, Klönne, and Tschoepe 1985: 409–416), a substantial gain, but still less than half the number in the GDR. Lack of educational opportunities in the fifties left many of the older women of Generation II underemployed or working at jobs rather than in occupations, and their pensions will also be correspondingly low (Claessens, Klönne, and Tschoepe 1985: 360–371). Nonetheless, women and men alike held to the distinction between work and vacation described above.

## 9 Marriage, family, nation

1 The fact of nationness, of belonging to the nation in the sense defined in this book, does not always translate into nationalism, which involves subjective devotion to the nation. These terms are often confused. States frequently turn to policies that foment nationalism, manipulating the opinions of their citizenry in times of crises to bolster governmental legitimacy, but this type of devotion, often manifested equally in newcomers to the nation as well as longtime members, is as unstable as are all subjective opinions. Nationness, on the other hand, is a subjectivity, not contingent on an opinion or attitude, but derived from lived experience within a state.

2 A household census in East Germany in the early eighties and one in West Germany in 1987 were not entirely successful affairs. Most of my discussion partners in both Berlins reported falsifying or refusing to answer the questionnaires. The fight against the census in West Berlin was led by the Alternative Liste (Greens), who called for a boycott. The state declared this action "against the Constitution," and threatened resisters with monetary fines and imprisonment. All such resisters, estimated at about 25 percent of the total adult population in West Berlin, are now on state-security computer lists under the category "suspected terrorist" or "enemy of the state" (for a manual on West German resistance, see Hauck-Scholz 1987).

3 See the historical study on nations and nationalism by E. J. Hobsbawm (1990).

4 An examination of postwar marriages in the two Berlins illustrates that marriage is the classic example of a non-classic categorization; it simply cannot be described or accounted for in Aristotelian terms. According to Aristotle, concepts are internal representations of external reality. Since concepts correspond to an external, coherent, stable, objective reality, cognitive models have fixed boundaries. Membership within a category is determined by a set of necessary and sufficient conditions that specify elements, their properties, and the relations between them. Whereas marriage as a Western legal concept fits this particular cognitive model, marriage as practice does not. Actual linguistic and cultural practice in the Berlins indicate a range of marriage types much broader than the legal model.

Postwar marriage types in Berlin appear nonsensical, in fact, if looked at in terms of one essential or ideal type, if, in other words, examined as an

Aristotelian category system. Drawing on recent advances in prototype theory by Lakoff (1987:74–76, 91–96), we can describe the marriage complex in Berlin in terms of cognitive processes that partake of a cluster model, where a number of models combine to form a complex cluster that is more basic to marriage than the models taken individually. This phenomenon is beyond the scope of classical theory, for marriage is organized not according to a set of "necessary and sufficient conditions," but rather structured radially with respect to a number of its subcategories: there may at any time be one central subcategory (depending on the time and state, the housewife marriage or the love marriage), defined by a cluster of converging cognitive models, but there are also noncentral extensions or variants of the central subcategory (uncle marriage, war marriage, sham marriage, etc.). A single type can not account for the other types that comprise the whole pattern.

5 See the interesting discussion of degrees of Germanness by Forsythe (1989).

6 The two largest group of *Aussiedler* in 1988, followed by 1987 in parenthesis, were the 140,000 (48,423) from Poland, and 47,572 (14,488) from the USSR (*Süddeutsche Zeitung*, No. 3, January 4, 1989, p. 2).

7 Under pressure from the international community, the ruling West German Christian Democrats negotiated and signed an agreement with Poland shortly before the completion of formal political unification in 1990.

8 These numbers were obtained in 1988 from several conversations with two West Berlin lawyers, who work on such cases. Also see *Der Spiegel* 14, 1991: 65.

### Postscript: unity

1 See the protocols about the opening by Schabowski and Egon Krenz (politburo members at that time heading the government) in *Der Spiegel* 43, 1990: 103. Unless otherwise noted, all quotations and statistics in this postscript have been verified in issues of *Der Spiegel*, the recognized magazine of record in Germany, from October 1989 through April 1991. A lengthier description and analysis of these events can be found in Borneman (1991a).

2 The realization of these desires is, of course, a quite different process from their formulation. It is estimated that only 10 percent of all East Germans vacationed outside the new Germany during 1990. Among Berliners during this period, the number and type of automobiles increased dramatically, from 719,000 to 1.2 million. It is safe to assume that most of these purchases were by East Germans. Paradoxically, buying the West German cars, one-third of which go 50 to 110 percent faster than the GDR speed limit, is killing the East Germans. Accompanying the massive introduction in 1990 of West German autos into the former GDR is an increase in the number of accidents, up 83 percent, with a threefold increase in the deaths of children.

3 Municipal elections held on October 2, 1990 formally absorbed the GDR into the FRG, creating the Five New *Länder* at the same time. These were seen as a prelude to the federal elections two months later.

4 Kohl said on July 1, 1990, the day of the currency union, "For the people in

the Federal Republic this means: Nobody will have to give up something because of the unification of Germany. It is really about making available to our countrymen in the GDR a portion of what we additionally are able to earn in the coming years – as help for self-help" (Rudolph Augstein, "Es gilt das gebrochene Wort," *Der Spiegel* 48/1990: 21). By February 1991, Kohl was proposing major tax increases.

5 "Vom taktischen Gebrauchswert nationaler Gefühle," *Die Zeit* No. 51, December 14, 1990, p. 42.

6 Two salient examples of new East German politicans willing to do the bidding of their West German counterparts are the Christian Democrat Günther Krause, one of the three East Germans pulled into the first all-German cabinet by Helmut Kohl, and Hans-Michael Diestel, the Minister of the Interior under the de Maiziére regime. Diestel purchased a Gründerzeit house in Berlin for 189,000 D-Marks that was apparently worth minimally one million. Krause obtained for rent a relatively new, luxurious house designed for a handicapped person (for Günter Mittag, former politburo member who had his legs amputated), when the house was supposed to go to the organization for the handicapped. Benefits from holding office or position since the autumn revolution have not been limited, of course, to conservative politicians, but extend to members of all large parties, including and perhaps from November 1989 through March 1990 most pronounced by some members of the renamed Socialist Unity Party (SED). Since March 1990, the Christian Democrats, who formerly had cooperated with the SED, have ruled (in a coalition with several other parties), and it seems likely that they personally benefited most from their positions and the confusion during unification.

7 The unity treaty also avoided any incorporation of the more progressive East German laws. Instead of equal rights for women in the state and society, included in the GDR constitution, a general appeal was made to make possible the "unity of family and occupation." The more liberal East German abortion law was not extended to West Germany; rather, in 1991 the government started checking women on the German–Netherlands border to ascertain if they had obtained abortions in the more liberal Holland, in which case they were subject to criminal prosecution. No mention was made in the unity treaty about the right to education or living quarters or work, as in the GDR constitution, and local voting rights for foreigners residing in Germany was also omitted. Even the issue of ratifying the treaty in a popular vote, as seemingly required by Article 146 of the *Grundgesetz*, was omitted.

8 A related problem is how to deal with legal claims against harm perpetrated by the Stasi. By January 1991 over 10,000 legal claims had been made demanding personal rehabilitation or restitution for crimes committed by the state security.

9 The people of Saarland, for example, voted in 1957 to secede from France to become one of the West German *Länder*. This was effected in a series of steps through Article 23 of the Basic Law.

10 Loyalty to the *Grundgesetz* seems to be, in fact, a precondition for the right to engage in political activity in the united Germany. Even the renamed

Socialist Unity Party (now the Party of Democratic Socialism) formally declared to the Cologne Office for *Verfassungsschutz* in December 1990 that they were "without reservation in agreement with the goals and efficacy" of the *Grundgesetz* (*Süddeutsche Zeitung*, No. 294, 1990, p. 3).

11 West German political parties took quite different positions on how to unify. The SPD favored use of Article 146, while the CDU pushed for Article 23. The SPD also argued for a new constitution, with planks about environmental protection and equal rights for women (rather than just forbidding their discrimination). The Greens and civil rights movement in the GDR wanted more direct democracy, referendums, and civilian intiatives written into the constitution. The FDP initially wanted a majority vote on the consitution and possible changes before the election on December 2, 1990, but finally yielded to the CDU. The CDU wanted simply to extend the Basic Law to all of East Germany.

12 The fight over these occupied houses was a complicated event with many issues at stake. At one level it was a fight between forces of order and Generation II, but at another level it also demonstrated a basic conflict between Generation II in East and West Berlin. The East Autonome wanted to negotiate with the authorities, whereas the West Autonome, seasoned veterans of street fights with West Berlin police, refused any negotiation or resolution of the conflict other than through the use of force. Even at this particular political extreme, Generation II in West Berlin imagined itself autonomous from and in complete antagonism to the state, whereas the East German Autonome did not see the state as a natural enemy.

13 This issue may be more important for the ideological self-representation of Germans than for individuals applying to enter the polity. For example, of the approximately 200,000 people who applied for asylum in 1990 – the majority from Romania, Turkey, and Yugoslavia – only 3 percent or 6,000 were granted the right to stay. Other groups of foreigners have even less of a chance: of 12,000 Indians who applied in the last three years, only one was granted asylum.

# References

Adorno, Theodor. 1984 [1951]. *Minima Moralia*. Transl. by E. F. N. Jephcott. London: Verso Press

Albrecht, Heinz. 1986. *Die Kriegsopferversorgung in Berlin (West) 1945 bis 1985 – Bestandsaufnahme und historischer Rückblick Berliner Statistik*. Statistisches Landesamt Berlin 12/86: 202–221. Berlin: Kulturbuch-Verlag

Almagor, Uri. 1989. Dual Organization Reconsidered. In *The Attraction of Opposites*, eds. David Maybury-Lewis and Uri Almagor. Cambridge, Mass: Harvard University Press, pp. 19–32

Almond, Gabriel and G. Bingham Powell. 1966. *Comparative Politics: A Developmental Approach*. Boston and Toronto: Little, Brown

Almond, Gabriel and Sidney Verba. 1963. *The Civic Culture: Political Attitudes and Democracy in Five Nations*. Princeton: Princeton University Press

Anderson, Benedict. 1983. *Imagined Communities: Reflections on the Origin and Spread of Nationalism*. London: Verso Press

Ansorg, Linda. 1967. *Leitfaden, Familienrecht der DDR*. Berlin: Staatsverlag der DDR

1986. Interview with John Borneman, unpublished.

Arato, Andrew. 1981. Civil Society against the State: Poland 1980–81. *Telos* 47: 23–47

Arendt, Hannah. 1951. *The Origins of Totalitarianism*. New York: Harcourt Brace Jovanovich

1985 [1963]. *On Revolution*. New York: Penguin Books

Aßmann, Georg and Gunner Winkler, eds. 1987. *Zwischen Alex und Marzahn. Studie zur Lebensweise in Berlin*. Berlin: Dietz Verlag

Auden, W. H. 1979. *Selected Poems*. Ed. Edward Mendelson. New York: Vintage Books, pp. 190–195

Aue, Herbert. 1976. *Die Jugendkriminalität in der DDR*. Berlin: Berlin Verlag

Augé, Marc. 1982 [1979]. *The Anthropological Circle*. Cambridge: Cambridge University Press

Ausländerrecht der Bundesländer. 1987. *Die Beauftragten der Bundesregierung für die Integration der ausländischen Arbeitnerhmer und ihrer Familienangehörigen*. Bonn: BdB

Aust, Stefan. 1989. *Der Baader Meinhof Komplex*. Munich: Knaur

Badie, Bertrand and Pierre Birnbaum. 1983. *The Sociology of the State*. Transl. by Arthur Goldhammer. Chicago: University of Chicago Press

Bane, Mary Jo. 1976. *American Families in the Twentieth Century*. New York: Basic Books

Barrett, Michelle and Mary McIntoch. 1982. *The Anti-Social Family*. London: Verso Books

Barthes, Roland. 1981 [1967]. Le Discours d'histoire. In *Rhetoric and History: Comparative Criticism Yearbook*, ed. Elmore Schaffner. Cambridge: Cambridge University Press

Bartholmai, Bernd und Manfred Melzer. 1987. Zur Entwicklung des Wohungsbaus in der DDR und in der Bundesrepublik Deutschland. *Deutschland Archiv* 2: 180–187

Bathke, Gustav-Wilhelm. 1985. Unpublished thesis (Diss. B). Sozialstrukturelle Herkunftsbedingungen und Persönlichkeitsentwicklung von Hochschulstudenten. Leipzig: Akademie für Gesellschaftswissenschaften beim Zentralkomitee der SED

Baumert, Gerhard. 1952. *Jugend in der Nachkriegszeit. Lebensverhältnisse und Reaktionsweisen*. Darmstadt: Roether

1954. *Deutsche Familie nach dem Kriege*. Darmstadt: Roether

Benjamin, Hilde. 1966. Die Kontinuität in der Entwicklung des Familienrechts der Deutschen Demokratischen Republik. *Wissenschaftliche Zeitschrift der Humboldt-Universität zu Berlin, Gesellschafts- und Sprachwissenschaftliche Reihe* 6: 271–279

1982. *Aus Reden und Aufsätzen*. Berlin: Staatsverlag der DDR

Benjamin, Walter. 1978. *Karl Kraus*. Transl. by Edmund Jephcott, in *Reflections*, ed. Peter Demetz. New York: Harcourt Brace Jovanovich

Berger, Peter and Brigitte Berger. 1983. *The War over the Family: Capturing the Middle Ground*. New York: Doubleday

*Berlin ABC*. 1965. Eds. Wilhelm Luize and Richard Höpfner. Berlin: Presse- und Informationsamtes des Landes Berlin

*Berlin im Überblick*. 1988. Berlin: Informationszentrum Berlin

*Berlin in Zahlen*. 1947. Berlin: Berliner Kulturbuch-Verlag

*Berliner Statistik* 1950–1989 Statistisches Landesamt Berlin. Berlin: Kulturbuch-Verlag

Bernstein, Basil. 1972. Social Class, Language, and Social Action. In *Language and Social Context*, ed. Pier Paolo Giglioli. New York: Penguin Books

Bhabha, Homi, ed. 1990. *Nation and Narration*. London and New York: Routledge

Bock, Gisela. 1986. *Zwangssterilisation im Nationalsozialismus. Studien zur Rassen- und Frauenpolitik*. Opladen: Westdeutscher Verlag

Böll, Heinrich, ed. 1985. *Niemandsland: Kindheitserinnerungen an die Jahre 1945 bis 1949*. Bornheim-Merten: Lamuz Verlag

Bondy, Kurt. 1957. *Jugendliche stören die Ordnung: Bericht und Stellungnahme zu den Halbstarkenkrawallen*. Munich: Schriftenreihe der Arbeitsgemeinschaft für Jugendpflege und Jugendfürsorge

Borneman, John. 1987. Sexual Aufklärung and Sexual Practices in the German

Democratic Republic. In *Homosexuality, Which Homosexuality?* Conference papers, Social Science, vol. II. Amsterdam: Free University

1991a. *After the Wall: East Meets West in the New Berlin.* New York: Basic Books

1991b. *Uniting The German Nation: Law and Narrations of History.* Cornell Project of Comparative Institutional Analysis, Working Papers, no. 91.2. Ithaca: Cornell University

1992. State, Territory, and Identity Formation in the Postwar Berlins, 1945–1989. In *Culture, Power, Place: Explorations in Critical Anthropology*, ed. R. Rouse, J. Ferguson, and A. Gupta. Boulder, Col.: Westview

Bott, Elizabeth. 1957. *Family and Social Network.* London: Tavistock Publications

Bourdieu, Pierre. 1977 [1972]. *Outline of a Theory of Practice.* Cambridge: Cambridge University Press

1984 [1979]. *Distinction.* Cambridge, Mass.: Harvard University Press

Bourdieu, Pierre and Jean-Claude Passeron. 1977. *Reproduction in Education, Society and Culture.* Beverly Hills: Sage Publications

Brooks, Peter. 1984. *Reading for the Plot: Design and Intention in Narrative.* New York: Alfred A. Knopf

Brückner, Peter. 1976. *Ulrike Marie Meinhof und die deutschen Verhältnisse.* Berlin: Wagenbach

Brügge, Peter. 1988. Träume im Kopf, Sturm auf den Straße, *Der Spiegel* 18: 78–96

Brunhöber, Hannelore. 1985. Wohnen. In *Die Bundesrepublik Deutschland*, vol. II: *Gesellschaft*, ed. Wolfgang Benz, pp. 183–208

Bude, Heinz. 1987. *Lebenskonstruktionen sozialer Aufsteiger aus der Flakhelfer-Generation.* Frankfurt am Main: Suhrkamp Verlag

1988. Auflösung des Socialen: Die Verflüssigung des soziologischen "Gegenstandes" im Fortgang de soziologis̓chen Theorie. *Soziale Welt* 39 (1): 4–17

Büttner, Thomas. 1987. *Geburtenentwicklung in der DDR.* In Wulfram Speigner, ed., *Kind und Gesellschaft.* Berlin: Akademie Verlag, pp. 22–46

Carroll, David. 1976. On Tropology: The Forms of History. *Diacritics* 6 (3): 58–64

Chaussy, Ulrich. 1985. Jugend. In *Die Bundesrepublik Deutschland*, vol. II, ed. W. Benz. Frankfurt am Main: Fischer

CILIP 9/10 (Civil Liberties and Police). 1981. *Politik, Protest und Polizei.* Eds. W.-D. Narr, A. Funk, H. Busch, V. Kauß, C. Kunze, Th. v. Zabern, and F. Werkentin. Berlin: Verlag CILIP

Claessens, Dieter, Arno Klönne, and Armin Tschoepe. 1985 [1978]. *Sozialkunde der Bundesrepublik.* Reinbek bei Hamburg: Rowohlt

Clifford, James. 1988. *The Predicament of Culture.* Cambridge, Mass.: Harvard University Press

Conradt, Sylvia and Kirsten Heckmann-Janz. 1987. *Reichstrümmerstadt: Leben in Berlin 1945–1961.* Darmstadt: Luchterhand

*DDR Handbuch.* 1985. Bundesministerium für innerdeutsche Beziehungen. Cologne: Verlag Wissenschaft und Politik

de Certeau, Michel. 1984. *The Practice of Everyday Life*. Berkeley: University of California Press

Dellile, Angela and Andrea Grohn, eds. 1985. *Perlon Zeit*. Berlin: Elefanten Press

*Demographische Prozesse und Bevölkerungspolitik in der Deutschen Demokratischen Republik*. 1984. Institut für Soziologie und Sozialpolitik der Akademie der Wissenschaft der DDR. Berlin: Akademie der Wissenschaft der DDR

Dietz, Gabrielle. 1985. Halbstarke Mädchen. In *Perlon Zeit*, ed. A. Delille and A. Grohn. Berlin: Elefanten Press, pp. 32–36

Donzelot, Jacques. 1979. *The Policing of Families*. New York: Random House, Inc.

Dorbritz, Jürgen. 1987. Geburtenfördernde Bevölkerungspolitik und die Wirkungsweise der social- und bevölkerungspolitischen Maßnahmen. In *Kind und Gesellschaft*, ed. Wulfram Speigner. Berlin: Akademie Verlag, pp. 143–165

Dotterweich, Volker. 1979. Die Entnazifizierung. In *Vorgeschichte der Bundesrepublik*, ed. Josef Becker, Theo Stammen, and Peter Waldmann. Munich: Wilhelm Fink Verlag

Douglas, Mary. 1966. *Purity and Danger*. London: Ark

Dwyer, Kevin. 1982. *Moroccan Dialogues: Anthropology in Question*. Baltimore: The Johns Hopkins University Press

Durkheim, Emile and Marcel Mauss. 1903 [1963]. *Primitive Classification*. Chicago: University of Chicago Press

Eckart, Gabriella. 1984. *So Sehe ick die Sache*. Cologne: Kiepenhauer & Witsch

Edding, Friedrich. 1952. *Die Flüchtling als Belastung und Antrieb der westdeutschen Wirtschaft*. Kiel: Institut für Weltwirtschaft

Elias, Norbert. 1978 [1939]. *The Civilizing Process*, vol. I. New York: Pantheon Books

Engelmann, Bernt. 1981. *Wir Sind Wieder Wer: Auf dem Weg ins Wirtschaftswunderland*. Munich: Goldmann Verlag

Engels, Fredrich. 1972 [1884]. *Origins of the Family, Private Property and the State*. London: Lawrence and Wishart

Esser, Hartmut. 1985. Gastarbeiter. In *Die Bundesrepublik Deutschland*, vol. II: *Gesellschaft*, ed. Wolfgang Benz. Frankfurt: Fischer Verlag, pp. 127–156

Fabian, Johannes. 1979. Rule and Process: Thoughts on Ethnography as Communication. *Philosophy of Social Science* 9: 1–26

    1983. *Time and the Other: How Anthropology Makes its Object*. New York: Columbia University Press

*Familienbericht: Bericht über die Situation der Familien in Berlin*. 1987. Berlin: Senator für Jugend und Familie

*Familiengesetzbuch der Deutschen Demokratischen Republik vom 20. Dezember 1965*. 1966. Ministerium der Justiz. Berlin: Staatsverlag der DDR

*Der Familienlastenausgleich: Eine Denkschrift des Bundesministers für Familienfragen*. 1955. Bonn: Bundesministerium für Familienfragen

*Familienrecht. Lehrbuch*. 1981. Ed. Anita Grandke. Berlin: Staatsverlag der DDR

Fernandez, James W. 1986. *Persuasions and Performances.* Bloomington: Indiana University Press

Fischer-Kowalski, Marina. 1983. Halbstarke 1958, Studenten 1968: Eine Generation und zwei Rebellionen. In *Kriegskinder,* eds. Ulf Preuss-Lausitz, Peter Büchner, and Marina Fischer-Kowalski. Weinheim and Basle: Beltz Verlag, pp. 53–70

Forsythe, Diana. 1989. German Identity and the Problem of History. In *History and Ethnicity,* ed. Elizabeth Tonkin, Maryon McDonald, and Malcolm Chapman. London: Routledge

Fortes, Meyer and E. E. Evans-Pritchard, eds. 1940. *African Political Systems.* Oxford: Oxford University Press

Foucault, Michel. 1972 [1969]. *The Archaeology of Knowledge.* Transl. by A.M. Sheridan Smith. New York: Harper Colophon

1973 [1966]. *The Order of Things.* New York: Vintage/Random House

1979 [1975]. *Discipline and Punish: The Birth of the Prison.* New York: Vintage/Random House

1981. Sexuality and Solitude. Seminar in the Institute for the Humanities. Discussion with Richard Sennett. *London Review of Books,* May 21–June 3

Freeman, Michael D.A. 1984. *State, Law, and the Family.* New York: Tavistock

Friedrich, Carl and Zbigniew Brzezinski. 1965. *Totalitarian Dictatorship and Autocracy.* Cambridge, Mass.: Harvard University Press

Friedrich, Heinz, ed. 1988. *Mein Kopfgeld: Die Währungsreform – Rückblicke nach vier Jahrzehnten.* Munich: C.H. Beck

Frye, Northrop. 1957. *Anatomy of Criticism.* Princeton: Princeton University Press

Furet, François. 1984. *In the Workshop of History.* Transl. by Jonathan Mandelbaum. Chicago: University of Chicago Press

Füssl, Karl-Heinz and Christian Kubina. 1981. *Zuegen zur Berliner Schulgeschichte (1951–1961).* Berlin: Marhold

1982. *Dokumente zur Berliner Schulgeschichte (1948–1965).* Berlin: Marhold

Gadamer, Hans Georg. 1975. *Truth and Method.* New York: Crossroad Press

1979. The Problem of Historical Consciousness. In *Interpretive Social Science Reader,* ed. Paul Rabinow and William Sullivan. Berkeley: University of California Press, pp. 103–162

Gaus, Günter. 1981. Die Elbe – ein deutscher Strom, nicht Deutschlands Grenze: Ein Zeit-Interview. *Die Zeit,* February 6

Geertz, Clifford. 1973. *The Interpretation of Cultures.* New York: Basic Books

1974. From the Native's Point of View: On the Nature of Anthropological Understanding. In *Meaning in Anthropology,* ed. Keith Basso and Henry Selby, Albuquerque: University of New Mexico Press, pp. 221–238

1980. Blurred Genres: The Refiguration of Social Thought. *The American Scholar* 29 (2): 165–179

Gellner, Ernest. 1983. *Nations and Nationalism.* Ithaca: Cornell University Press

Gilman, Sander. 1985. *Difference and Pathology: Stereotypes of Sexuality, Race, and Madness.* Ithaca: Cornell University Press

Glendon, Mary Ann. 1989. *The Transformation of Family Law: State, Law, and*

*Family in the United States and Western Europe.* Chicago: University of Chicago Press

Goffman, Erving. 1961. *Asylums.* Garden City, New York: Anchor Books

Grandke, Anita. 1978. Zur Geschichte des Familienrechts in der DDR. *XXVII Wissenschaftliche Zeitschrift der Humboldt Universität,* pp. 155–159. Berlin: Humbold-Universität-Berlin

1986. Zur Ehe als Rechtsverhältnis und Institution des Rechts. *Bericht* 6(11): 129–149. Berlin: Humboldt-Universität-Berlin

Greschat, Martin. 1985. Die Evangelische Kirche. In *Die Bundesrepublik Deutschland,* vol. II: *Gesellschaft,* ed. Wolfgang Benz. Frankfurt: Fischer Verlag, pp. 265–296

Gysi, Jutta and Wulfram Speigner. 1983. *Changes in the Life Patterns of Families in the German Democratic Republic.* Berlin: Institut für Soziologie und Sozialpolitik an der Akademie der Wissenschaften der Deutschen Demokratischen Republik

Habermas, Jürgen. 1961. Über den Begriff der politischen Beteiligung. In *Student and Politik,* ed. J. Habermas. Berlin: Neuwied

1986. The New Obscurity: The Crisis of the Welfare State and the Exhaustion of Utopian Energies. *Philosophy and Social Criticism* N2 (11): 1–18

1987. *The Theory of Communicative Action,* vol. II. Transl. by Thomas MacCarthy. Boston: Beacon Press

1990. What Does Socialism Mean Today? The Rectifying Revolution and the Need for New Thinking on the Left. *New Left Review* 183: 3–22

Hauck-Scholz, Peter. 1987. *Rechtsschutzfibel zur Volkszählung.* Berlin: Elefanten Press

*Hauptstadt Berlin. Internationaler städtebaulicher Ideenwettberwerb 1957/58.* 1990. Berlinische Galerie e. V. Berlin: Berlinische Galerie

Hayek, Friedrich A. von. 1944. *The Road to Serfdom.* Chicago: University of Chicago Press

Hegel, G. W. F. 1953. *Reason In History.* Transl. by Robert S. Hartman. New York: Macmillan

Heider, Ulrike. 1989. The West German Student Movement and the Sexual Revolution. *Zeder Magazine* 7:125–130

Heimann, Siegfried. 1985. Das Überleben organisieren: Berliner Jugend und Berliner Jugendbanden in den vierziger Jahren. In *Vom Lagerfeuer zur Musikbox: Jugendkulturen 1900–1960,* ed. Berliner Geschichtswerkstatt e.V. Berlin: Elefanten Press, pp. 137–170

Held, David. 1989. *Political Theory and the Modern State.* Stanford: Stanford University Press

Held, David and Joel Krieger, eds. 1983. *States and Societies.* New York: New York University Press

Helwig, Gisela. 1982. *Frau und Familie in beiden deutschen Staaten.* Cologne: Verlag Wissenschaft und Politik

Herzberg, Wolfgang. 1987. *Ich bin doch wer: Arbeiter und Arbeiterinnen des VEB Berliner Glühlampenwerk erzählen ihr Leben 1900–1980.* Darmstadt u. Neuwied: Luchterhand

Herzfeld, Michael. 1987. *Anthropology Through the Looking-Glass*. Cambridge: Cambridge University Press

Heuer, Uwe-Jens. 1986. Zur Geschichte des marxistisch-leninistischen Demokratiebegriffs. In *Politische Theorie und sozialer Fortschritt*, ed. Karl-Heinz Röder. Berlin: Staatsverlag der DDR

Heyl, Wolfgang. 1986. Förderung und Festigung von Ehe und Familie – Anliegen christlicher Demokraten. In *Bürgerpflicht und Christenpflicht*. Berlin: Sekretariat der CDU

Hille, Barbara. 1985. *Familie und Sozialisation in der DDR*. Opladen: Leske and Budrich

Hilmar, Richard. 1988. DDR und die Deutsche Frage: Antworten jungen Generation. *Deutschland Archiv* 10: 1,091–1,100

*Historikerstreit*. 1987. Ed. R. Piper. Munich: Piper Verlag

Hobsbawm, E. J. 1990. *Nations and Nationalism Since 1780: Programme, Myths, Reality*. New York: Cambridge University Press

Hoffmann, Elke. 1987. Kinderwunsch – subjektiver Faktor reproduktiven Verhaltens. In *Kind und Gesellschaft*, ed. Wulfram Speigner. Berlin: Akademie Verlag, pp. 98–115

Hollenstein, Günter. 1985. Die Katholische Kirche. In *Die Bundesrepublik Deutschland*, ed. Wolfgang Benz, pp. 234–264

IAF (Interessengemenschaft der mit Ausländern verheirateten Frauen e.V.). 1985. Bulletin: ART. 6I GG: *Ehe und Familie stehen unter dem besonderen Schutz der staatlichen Ordnung*. Berlin: Selbstverlag

Iser, Wolfgang. 1974. *The Implied Reader*. Transl. by David Henry Wilson. Baltimore: The Johns Hopkins University Press
    1989. The Reading Process: A Phenomenological Approach. In *Contemporary Critical Reader*, ed. Dan Latimer. New York: Harcourt, Brace, and Jovanovich

Jaide, Walter. 1988. *Generationen eines Jahrhunderts*. Opladen: Leske and Budrich

Jameson, Fredric. 1976. Figural Relativism, or the Poetics of Historiography. *Diacritics* 6 (3): 58–64
    1981. *The Political Unconscious: Narrative as a Socially Symbolic Art*. Ithaca: Cornell University Press

Jauss, Hans Robert. 1970. Literary History as a Challenge to Literary Theory. *New Literary History* 2 (1): 7–37

Jeremias, U. 1956. *Die Jugendweihe in der Sowjetzone*. Bonn: Deutscher Bundesverlag

Jesse, Eckhard. 1986. *Die Demokratie der Bundesrepublik*. Berlin: Colloquium Verlag

Jowitt, Kenneth. 1975. Inclusion and Mobilization in European Leninist Regimes. *World Politics* 28 (1): 69–96

Jugendwerk der Deutschen Shell. 1981. *Jugend '81, Lebensentwürfe, Alltagskulturen, Zukunftsbilder*, vol. III. Hamburg: JdDS

Kant, Immanuel. 1991. *Kant: Political Writings*, ed. Hans Reiss. Cambridge: Cambridge University Press

Kapferer, Bruce. 1988. *Legends of People, Myths of State: Violence, Intoler-*

ance, and Political Culture in Sri Lanka and Australia. Washington, D.C.: Smithsonian Institution Press

Katzenstein, Peter J. 1990. *West Germany's Internal Security Policy: State and Violence in the 1970s and 1980s*. Western Societies Program Occasional Paper 28, Cornell University Center for International Studies. Ithaca: Cornell University

Keiderling, Gerhard. 1987. *Berlin 1945–1986: Geschichte der Haupstadt der DDR*. Berlin: Dietz Verlag

Keil, Siegfried. 1988. Veränderungen im Verhältnis von Kirche und Familie seit den Anfängen der Bundesrepublik Deutschland am Beispiel der evangelischen Kirche. In *Wandel*, ed. R. Nave-Herz. Stuttgart: Enke Verlag, pp 198–219

Kellner, H. 1969. Zu den Aufgaben und zur Stellung der Rechtsprechung in Rechtsverwirklichungs- und Rechtsbildungsprozessen. *Annales Universitatis Scientarium Budapestinensis*. Budapest: Secto Juridica, vol. X

Kershaw, Ian. 1983. *Popular Opinion and Political Dissent in the Third Reich, Bavaria 1933–1945*. Oxford: Clarendon Press

Keuerleber, Gisela. 1987. Jung und anmutig . . . vor 65 Jahren wurden Frauen in der Justiz zugelassen. *Die Zeit*, 13 July, p. 49

Kingsbury, Henry A. 1988. *Music, Talent, and Performance*. Philadelphia: Temple University Press

*Kleines Politisches Wörterbuch*. 1986. Editorial collective Gerhard Schütz, Walfraud Böhm, and Sigrid Dominik. Berlin: Dietz Verlag

Kligman, Gail. 1988. *The Wedding of the Dead*. Berkeley: University of California Press

Kohli, Martin. 1985. Die Institutionalisierung des Lebenslaufs. *Kölner Zeitschrift für Soziologie und Sozialpsychologie* 37 (1): 1–29

Kohli, Martin and J. Wolf. 1986. Altersgrenzen im Schnittpunkt von betrieblichen Interressen und individueller Lebensplanung: Das Beispiel des Vorruhestands. *Soziale Welt* 34 (4)

Kondo, Dorine. 1990. *Crafting Selves: Power, Gender, and Discourses of Identity in a Japanese Workplace*. Chicago: University of Chicago Press

König, René. 1946 [1974]. *Materialien zu einer Soziologie der Familie*. Cologne: Kiepenheuer & Witsch

Korinth, Michael H. 1988. Rechts und Steuerwesen: Zwang zum gemeinsamen Ehenamen verstößt nicht gegen das Persönlichkeitsrecht. *Der Tagesspiegel*, July 31, p. 32

Korte, Hermann. 1985. Bevölkerungsstruktur und -entwicklung. In *Die Bundesrepublik Deutschland*, ed. Benz, pp. 13–34

Kramer, Jane. 1989. Letter From Europe. *The New Yorker*. November 28, 1989, pp. 67–100

Kuper, Adam. 1988. *The Invention of Primitive Society*. New York: Routledge

Lacan, Jacques. 1977. *Ecrits, A Selection*. Transl. by Alan Sheridan. New York: Norton Press

Lakoff, George. 1987. *Women, Fire, and Dangerous Things: What Categories Reveal about the Mind*. Chicago: University of Chicago Press

Lampert, Heinz. 1988. Die soziale Marktwirtschaft in der Bundesrepublik Deutschland. *Aus Politik und Zeitgeschichte*. B 17: 3–14

Lange, M.G. 1954. *Totalitäre Erziehung – Das Erziehungssystem der Sowjetzone Deutschlands*. Frankfurt am Main: Frankfurter Hefte XLVIII

Langer, Ingrid. 1985. Familienpolitik – ein Kind der 50er Jahre; In letzer Konsequenz . . . Uranberg Werk. In *Perlon Zeit*, eds. A. Delille and A. Grohn. Berlin: Elefanten Press, pp. 72–81; 109–119

Large, David Clay. 1987. Reckoning With The Past: The HIAG of the Waffen-SS and the Politics of Rehabilitation in the Bonn Republic, 1950–1961. *Journal of Modern History* 59: 79–113

Lasch, Christopher. 1977. *Haven in a Heartless World*. New York: Basic Books

Lehr, Ursula. 1984. *Auf dem Weg zu einer Fünf-Generationen-Gesellschaft. Veröffentlichung d. Hanns-Martin-Schleyer-Stiftung*. Cologne: Bachem Verlag

Lemke, Christiane. 1980. *Persönlichkeit und Gesellschaft: zur Theorie der Persönlichkeit in der DDR*. Opladen: Westdeutschen Verlag

Lepsius, Rainer. 1981. Die Teilung Deutschlands und die Deutsche Nation. In Lothar Albertin and Werner Link, eds., *Politische Parteien auf dem Weg zur Parlamentarischen Demokratie in Deutschland*. Düsseldorf: Druste

Levi, Carlo. 1962. *The Linden Trees*. Transl. by Joseph M. Bernstein. New York: Knopf

Lévi-Strauss, Claude. 1966 [1962]. *The Savage Mind*. Chicago: University of Chicago Press
    1967 [1958]. *Structural Anthropology*. New York: Anchor Books
    1969 [1949]. *The Elementary Structures of Kinship*. Boston: Beacon Press

Limbach, Jutta. 1988. Die Entwicklung des Familienrechts seit 1949. In *Wandel*, ed. R. Nave-Herz. Stuttgart: Enke Verlag, pp. 11–33

Lindholm, Charles. 1988. Lovers and Leaders: A Comparison of Social and Psychological Models of Romance and Charisma. *Social Science Information* 27 (1): 3–45

Linke, Ulrike. 1986. "Where Blood Flows, A Tree Grows": A Study of Root Metaphors in German Culture. Ph.D. Dissertation. Berkeley: University of California

Long, Scott and John Borneman. 1990. Power, Objectivity, and the Other: Studies in the Creation of Sexual Species in Anglo-American Discourse. *Dialectical Anthropology* 15: 285–314

Lübbe, Herman. 1988. Der National Sozialismus im politischen Bewusstsein der Gengenwart. In *Deutschlands Weg in die Diktatur*, Martin Broszat, ed. Berlin: Siedler

Luhmann, Niklas. 1982. *Liebe als Passion – Zur Codierung von Intimität*. Frankfurt am Main: Suhrkamp

Lukes, Steven. 1982. Relativism in its Place. In *Rationality and Relativism*, ed. Martin Hollis and Steven Lukes. Cambridge, Mass.: MIT Press

Lukesch, Helmut. 1988. Von der "radio-Hörenden" zur "verkabelten" Familie – Mögliche Einflüsse der Entwicklung von Massenmedien auf das Familienleben und die familiale Sozialisation. In *Wandel*, ed. R. Nave-Herz. Stuttgart: Enke Verlag, pp. 279–308

Lüschen, Günther. 1988. Familial-verwandtschaftliche Netzwerke. In *Wandel*, ed. R. Nave-Herz. Stuttgart: Enke Verlag, pp. 145–169

Lüscher, Kurt and Franz Schultheis. 1988. Die Entwicklung von Familienpolitik – Soziologische Überlegungen anhand eines regionalen Beispiels. In *Wandel*, ed. R. Nave-Herz, pp. 235–256

Maase, Kaspar. 1985. Freizeit. In *Die Bundesrepublik Deutschland*, ed. N. Benz. Munich: Fischer Verlag, pp. 209–233

Malkki, Liisa. 1992. National Geographic: The Rooting of Peoples and the Territorialization of National Identity among Scholars and Refugees. In *Culture, Power, Place: Explorations in Critical Anthropology*, eds. R. Rouse, J. Ferguson, A. Gupta. Boulder, Colo.: Westview

Malzahn, Marion. 1985. Erziehungsgeld – Ministers Beitrag Zur Frauenemanizipation. *Kritische Justiz* 18: 184–192

Mandel, Ruth. 1988. We Called For Manpower, But People Came Instead: The Foreigner Problem and Turkish Guestworkers in West Germany. Ph.D. Dissertation. Chicago: University of Chicago

Mannheim, Karl. 1928. Das Problem der Generationen. In Karl Mannheim, *Wissenssoziologie* (1964). Berlin/Neuwied: Luchterhand, pp. 509–565

Marcus, James and Michael Fischer. 1986. *Anthropology as Cultural Critique: An Experimental Moment in the Human Sciences*. Chicago: University of Chicago Press

*Materialien zum Bericht zu Lage der Nation im geteilten Deutschland*. 1974. Berlin: Bundesministerium für innerdeutsche Beziehungen

1987. Bonn: Bundesministerium für innerdeutsche Beziehungen

Mauss, Marcel. 1967 [1925]. *The Gift*. New York: Routledge and Kegan Paul

Maybury-Lewis, David and Uri Almagor. 1989. *The Attraction of Opposites*. Cambridge, Mass.: Harvard University Press

Mayer, Karl Ulrich and Walter Müller. 1986. The State and the Structure of the Life Course. In *Human Development and the Life Course*, eds. Aaege B. Sørensen, Franz E. Weinert, and Lonnie R. Sherrod. Hillsdale, N.J.: Lawrence. Erlbaum Associates, Publishers, pp. 217–245

Mehlan, Karl-Heinz. 1980. Zwanzig Jahre Abortbekämpfung in Europa. In *Partnerschaft und Familienplanung*, vol. I, eds. Karl-Heinz Mehlan, Alfred Geißler, and Beate Wegner. Rostock: Wilhelm-Pieck-Universität, pp. 53–62

Merton, Robert K. 1941. Intermarriage and the Social Structure: Fact and Theory. *Psychiatry* 4: 361–374

Meyer, Dagmar. 1987. Wertorientierungen in ihrem Einfluß auf die Herausbildung und Realisierung des Kinderwunsches. In *Kind und Gesellschaft*, ed. Wulfram Speigner, pp. 79–97

Meyer, John W. 1986. The Self and the Life Course: Institutionalization and its Effects. In *Human Development and the Life Course*, eds. Aage B. Sørensen, Franz E. Weinert, and Lonnie R. Sherrod, pp. 199–216. Hillsdale, N.J.: Lawrence Erlbaum Associates

Meyer, Sibylle and Eva Schulze. 1984. *Wie Wir das alles geschafft haben: Alleinstehende Frauen berichten über ihr Leben nach 1945*. Munich: Deutscher Taschenbuch Verlag

1985. *Von Liebe Sprach damals Keiner – Familienalltag in der Nachkriegs-zeit*. Munich: C.H. Beck

1988. Nichteheliche Lebensgemeinschaften. Eine Möglichkeit zur Veränder-ung des Geschlechterverhältnisses? *Kölner Zeitschrfit für Soziologie und Sozialpsychologie* 2 (40): 337–356

Miller, D.A. 1981. *Narrative and its Discontents*. Princeton: Princeton University Press

Mink, Louis O. 1978. Narrative Form as a Cognitive Instrument. In *The Writing of History: Literary Form and Historical Understanding*, eds. Robert H. Canary and Henry Kozicki, Madison: University of Wisconsin Press, pp. 129–149

*Miteinander Leben: Ausländerbericht*. 1986. Ausländerbeauftragte des Senats beim Senator für Gesundheit und Soziales. Berlin: SGS

Mitter, Armin and Stefan Wolle. 1990. *Iche liebe euch doch alle! Befehle und Lagerberichte des MfS*. Berlin: BasisDruck

Mommsen, Hans. 1984 [1979]. The Burden of the Past. In *Observations on "The Spiritual Situation of the Age,"* ed. Jürgen Habermas. Cambridge, Mass.: MIT Press, pp. 263–282

1987. Suche nach der "verlorenen Geschichte"? In *Historikerstreit*, ed. R. Piper. Munich: Piper Verlag, pp. 156–173

Mommsen, Wolfgang. 1987. Weder Leugnen noch Vergessen befreit von der Vergangenheit: Die Harmonisierung des Geschichtsbildes gefährdet die Freiheit. In *Historikerstreit*. Munich: Piper Verlag, pp. 300–321

Moore, Sally Falk. 1978. *Law as Process: An Anthropological Approach*. Boston: Routledge & Kegan Paul

Morgan, Lewis Henry. 1871. *Systems of Consanguinuity and Affinity of the Human Family*. Smithsonian Contributions to Knowledge, 218. Washington D.C.: Smithsonian Institution

1877. *Ancient Society*. New York: Holt

Mosse, George. 1985. *Nationalism and Sexuality; Respectability and Abnormal Sexuality in Modern Europe*. New York: H. Fertig

Mühlfeld, Claus and Friedrich Schönweiss. 1989. *Nationalsozialistische Familien-politik*. Stuttgart: Enke Verlag

Müller, K. Valentin. 1953. *Heimatvertriebene Jugend*. Beiheft zum Jahrbuch der Albertus Universität zu Königsberg, no. 2. Kitzeingen: BzJ

Müller-Dincu, Barbara. 1981. *Gemischt-nationale Ehen zwischen deutschen Frauen und Ausländern in der Bundesrepublik*. Materialien zur Bevölker-ungswissenschaft 22. Wiesbaden: Bundesinstitut für Bevölkerungsforschung

Nakane, Chie. 1970. *Japanese Society*. Berkeley: University of California Press

Nathan, Hans. 1949. Zur Gestaltung des Familienrechts. *Neue Justiz* 1: 102–103

Nave-Herz, Rosemarie, ed. 1988. *Wandel und Kontinuität in der Bundesrepublik Deutschland*. Stuttgart: Enke Verlag

Needham, Rodney. 1971. Remarks on the Analysis of Kinship and Marriage. In *Rethinking Kinship and Marriage*, ed. R. Needham. London: Tavistock Publications

Neumann, Franz. 1942. *Behemoth: The Structure and Practice of National Socialism*. Oxford: Oxford University Press

Niethammer, Lutz. 1988a. Entnazifizierung: Nachfragen eines Historikers. In *Von der Gnade der geschenkten Nation*, eds. Hajo Funke and W.-D. Narr. Berlin: Rotbuch Verlag, pp. 115–131

— 1988b. Annäherung an den Wandel. Auf der Suche nach der volkseigenen Erfahrung in der Industrieprovinz der DDR. *Bios*. 1: 19–66

— 1990. Das Volk der DDR und die Revolution. In *Wir sind das Volk!*, ed. Charles Schüddekopf. Reinbek bei Hamburg: Rowohlt, pp. 251–279

Noguchi, Paul. 1990. *Delayed Departures, Overdue Arrivals: Industrial Familialism and the Japanese National Railways*. Honolulu: University of Hawaii Press

Obertreis, Regina. 1985. *Familienpolitik in der DDR 1945–1980*. Opladen: Leske and Budrich

Offe, Claus. 1985. *Disorganized Capitalism*, ed. John Keane. Cambridge, Mass.: MIT Press

— 1988. Das Dilemma der Sicherheit. *Die Zeit* 49, December 2, p. 24

Olsen, Fran. 1984. The Politics of Family Law. *Harvard Law Review* 2: 1–19

Ortner, Sherry B. 1973. On Key Symbols. *American Anthropologist* 75: 1,338–1,346

Parsons, Talcott. 1951. *The Social System*. New York: The Free Press

Plath, David. 1983. *Work and Lifecourse in Japan*. Albany: State University of New York Press

Preuss-Lausitz, Ulf, Peter Büchner, and Marina Fischer-Kowalski, eds. 1983. *Kriegskinder, Konsumkinder, Krisenkinder: Zur Sozialisationsgeschichte seit dem Zweiten Weltkrieg*. Weinheim and Basle: Beltz Verlag

Pye, Lucian W. and S. Verba, eds. 1965. *Political Culture and Political Development*. Princeton: Princeton University Press

Rabinow, Paul and William M. Sullivan, eds. 1979. *Interpretive Social Science Reader*. Berkeley: University of California Press

Renan, Ernest. 1990. What is a Nation? In *Nation and Narration*, ed. Homi Bhabha. London and New York: Routledge, pp. 8–23

Ricoeur, Paul. 1981. *Hermeneutics and the Human Sciences*. Cambridge: Cambridge University Press

Robertson, Jennifer. 1989. Gender-Bending in Paradise: Doing "Female" and "Male" in Japan. *Genders* 5:50–69

Rodnick, David. 1948. *Postwar Germans*. New Haven: Yale University Press

Rosenbaum, Heidi. 1978. *Familie als Gegenstruktur zur Gesellschaft*. Stuttgart: Enke Verlag

Royal Anthropological Institute of Great Britain and Ireland. 1951. *Notes and Queries on Anthropology* 6th edn. London: Routledge and Kegan Paul

Ruhl, Klaus-Jörg, ed. 1988. *Frauen in der Nachkriegszeit 1945–1963*. Munich: Deutscher Taschenbuch Verlag

Runge, Irene. 1985. *Ganz in Familie*. Berlin: Dietz Verlag

Rupnik, Jacques. 1988. *The Other Europe*. London: Weidenfeld and Nicolson

Rytlewski, Ralf. 1972. Hochschulen und Studenten in der DDR. *Deutschland Archiv* 5: 734–742

Sahlins, Peter. 1988. The Nation in the Village: State-Building and Communal

Struggle in the Catalan Borderland during the Eighteenth and Nineteenth Centuries. *Journal of Modern History* 60 (2): 234–263

Said, Edward. 1983. *The World, the Text, and the Critic.* Cambridge, Mass.: Harvard University Press

Sapir, Edward. 1934. Symbolism. *Encyclopedia of the Social Sciences* XIV. New York: The Macmillan Co., pp. 492–493

Schaffner, Bertram. 1949. *Fatherland.* New York: Columbia University Press

Schelsky, Helmut. 1951. Flüchtlingsfamilien. In *Kölner Zeitschrift für Soziologie* 3, 1950/51: 159–177

1954. *Wandlungen der deutschen Familie in der Gegenwart.* Stuttgart: Enke Verlag

Schmidt, Klaus-Dieter and R. Rose. 1985. Germany: The Expansion of an Active State. In *Public Employment in Western Nations*, ed. Richard Rose. Cambridge: Cambridge University Press, pp. 126–162

Schmidt-Harzbach, Ingrid. 1985. Rock 'n Roll in Hanau. In *Perlon Zeit*, ed. A. Delille and A. Grohn. Berlin: Elefanten Press, pp. 37–81

Schneider, David. 1972. What is Kinship All About. In *Kinship Studies in the Morgan Centennial Years*, ed. P. Reining. Seattle: Anthropological Society of Washington

1980. *American Kinship.* Chicago: University of Chicago Press

1984. *A Critique of the Study of Kinship.* Ann Arbor: University of Michigan Press

Schöll, Ingrid. 1985. Frauenprotest gegen die Wiederbewaffnung. In *Perlon Zeit*, eds. A. Delille and A. Grohn. Berlin: Elefanten Press, pp. 82–91

Schütz, Yvonne. 1988. Zur Veränderung im Eltern-Kind-Verhältnis seit der Nachkriegszeit. In *Wandel*, ed. R. Nave-Herz. Stuttgart: Enke Verlag, pp. 95–112

Schwarz, Karl. 1988. Die Haushalte und Familie in Hamburg, Bremen und Berlin (West) im Vergleich zu einen des gesamten Bundesgebietes. *Berliner Statistik* 5: 998–102. Berlin: Kulturbuch Verlag

Seifert, Jürgen. 1989. Die Verfassung. In *Die Geschichte der Bundesrepublic Deutschland*, vol. I: *Politik*, ed. W. Benz. Frankfurt: Fischer Verlag

Smith, Anthony D. 1986. *The Ethnic Origin of Nations.* Oxford and New York: Basil Blackwell

Smith-Rosenberg, Carroll. 1985. *Disorderly Conduct.* New York: Alfred A. Knopf

Sommerkorn, Ingrid N. 1988. Die Erwerbstätige Mutter in der Bundesrepublik: Einstellungs- und Problemveränderungen. In *Wandel*, ed. R. Nave-Herz. Stuttgart: Enke Verlag, pp. 115–140

Speigner, Wulfram. 1987. *Kind und Gesellschaft.* Berlin: Akademie Verlag

*Statistisches Jahrbuch-Berlin.* 1946–1989. Statistisches Landesamt Berlin. Berlin: Statistisches Kulturbuck Verlag

*Statistisches Jahrbuch der Deutschen Demokratischen Republik.* 1955–1988. Eds. Staatliche Zentralverwaltung für Statistik. Berlin: Staatsverlag der DDR

*Statistisches Jahrbuch für die Bundesrepublik.* 1955–1989. Ed. Statistisches Bundesamt. Stuttgart: Metzler Poeschel

Steakley, Jim. 1976. Gays under Socialism: Male Homosexuality in GDR. *The Body Politic* 29: 15–18

Stolpe, Ilona. 1986. Erziehungsrecht, unpublished manuscript

Sträter, Winfried. 1985. Das konnte ein Erwachsener nicht mit ruhigen Augen beobachten: Die Halbstarken. In *Vom Lagerfeuer zur Musikbox: Jugendkulturen 1900–1960*, ed. Berliner Geschichtswerkstatt e.V. Berlin: Elefanten Press, pp. 137–170

Strauch, Rudolf. 1985. Die Entstehung des Grundgesetzes. In *Die Bundesrepublik Deutschland und die Deutsche Demokratische Republik*, ed. E. Jesse. Berlin: Colloquium

Süßmuth, Rita. 1988. Wandlungen in der Struktur der Erwerbstätigkeit und ihr Einfluß auf das Familienleben. In *Wandel*, ed. R. Nave-Herz. Stuttgart: Enke Verlag, pp. 222–234

Tambiah, Stanley J. 1984. *The Buddhist Saints of the Forest and the Cult of Amulets*. Cambridge: Cambridge University Press

Taylor, Charles. 1979. Interpretation and the Science of Man. In *Interpretive Social Science Reader*, eds. Paul Rabinow and William M. Sullivan. Berkeley: University of California Press, pp. 24–72

Tent, James F. 1982. *Mission on the Rhine: Reeducation and Denazification in American-Occupied Germany*. Chicago: University of Chicago Press

Thurnwald, Hilde. 1948. *Gegenwartsprobleme Berliner Familien*. Berlin: Weidemann Verlag

Trumpener, Katie. 1989. Goethe in Chains. West Berlin "at 750": The Politics of Commemoration. *Telos*: 79, 79–109

Tucker, Robert C., ed. 1972. *The Marx-Engels Reader*. New York: W.W. Norton

Turner, Victor. 1969. *The Ritual Process*. Ithaca: Cornell University Press

Unruh, Trude, ed. 1987. *Trümmerfrauen: Biografien einer betrogenen Generation*. Essen: Klartext-Verlag

Vaskovics, Lazlo A. 1988. Veränderungen der Wohn- und Wohnumweltbedingungen in ihren Auswirkungen auf Sozializationsleistung der Familie. In *Wandel*, ed. R. Nave-Herz. Stuttgart: Enke Verlag, pp. 36–58

*Vierter Familienbericht: Die Situation der älteren Menschen in der Familie*. 1986. Bonn: Der Bundesministerium für Jugend, Familie, Frau und Gesundheit

Vogel, Angela. 1985. Familie. In *Die Bundesrepublik Deutschland*, ed. W. Benz. Munich: Fischer Verlag, pp. 98–127

Walther, Rosemarie. 1971. Die Erziehung in der Familie als Bestandteil sozialistischer Lebensweise. *Einheit* 9: 986–997

1986. Interview with John Borneman, unpublished

Wander, Maxie. 1978. *Guten Morgen, du Schöne*. Darmstadt und Neuwied: Luchterhand

Weber, Hermann. 1986 [1985]. *Geschichte der DDR*. Munich: Deutscher Taschenbuch Verlag

Weber, Jürgen and Peter Steinbach, eds. 1988. *Vergangenheitsbewältigung durch Strafverfahren? NS-Prozesse in der Bundesrepublik Deutschland*. Munich: G. Olzog

Weber, Max. 1968. *The Methodology of the Social Sciences*. New York: The Free Press

370    *References*

1978. *Economy and Society*, vol. I eds. Guenther Roth and Claus Wittich. Berkeley: University of California Press

Weck, Michael. 1989. Das Staatsverständnis der Erhardschen Konzeption von der Formierten Gesellschaft. Unpublished manuscript

Wehler, Hans-Ulrich. 1984 [1979]. Germany Today. In *Observations on "The Spiritual Situation of the Age,"* ed. Jürgen Habermas, pp. 221–262

Weidenfeld, Werner, ed. 1983. *Die Identität der Deutschen*. Bonn: Bundeszentrale für politische Bildung

Weiß, Elisabeth. 1976. *Zur politisch-erzieherischen Grundhaltung der Eltern*. Berlin: Pädagogische Dissertation, Humboldt Universität-Berlin

1986. Interview with John Borneman, unpublished

Welzk, Stefan. 1987. Made in Germany. Deutsche Mark und deutsche Macht. *Kursbuch* 89: 15–34

White, Hayden. 1973. *Metahistory. The Historical Imagination in Nineteenth-Century Europe*. Baltimore: Johns Hopkins University Press

1978a. *Tropics of Discourse: Essays in Cultural Criticism*. Baltimore: Johns Hopkins University Press

1978b. The Historical Text as Literary Artifact. In *The Writing of History: Literary Form and Historical Understanding*, eds. Robert H. Canary and Henry Kozicki. Madison: University of Wisconsin Press

1981. The Value of Narrativity in the Representation of Reality. In *On Narrative*, ed. W.J.T. Mitchell. Chicago: University of Chicago Press, pp. 1–24

1984. The Question of Narrative in Contemporary Historical Theory. *History and Theory* 23 (1): 33

Willenbacher, Barbara. 1988. Thesen zur rechtlichen Stellung der Frau. In *Frauensituation*, eds. Uta Gerhardt and Yvonne Schütze. Frankfurt: Suhrkamp, pp. 141–165

Willis, Paul. 1977. *Learning to Labor*. New York: Columbia University Press

Winkelmann, Ingeburg. 1986. *Jugendweihe als Bestandteil sozialistischer Lebensweise in der DDR*. Documentatio Ethnographica 11. Budapest: MTA Neprajzi Kutató csoport

Winkler, Gunnar, ed. 1990. *Sozialreport '90: Daten und Fakten zur sozialen Lage in der DDR*. Berlin: Verlag Die Wirtschaft

Worsley, Peter. 1957. *The Trumpet Shall Sound*. New York: Schocken Books

Wurzbacher, Gerhard. 1954. *Leitbilder gegenwärtigen deutschen Familienlebens*. Dortmund: Ardey

*Zahlenspiegel*. 1985. Bundesministerium für innerdeutsche Beziehungen. Bonn: Gesamtdeutsches Institut

1988. Bundesministerium für innerdeutsche Beziehungen. Bonn: Gesamtdeutsches Institut

Zetkin, Clara. 1984. *Selected Writings*, ed. Philip S. Foner. New York: International Publishers

Ziegenhagen, Ilse. 1987. Geht Nämlich Die Liebe Verloren: mit Jutta Gysi sprach Ilse Ziegenhagen, *Sonntag* 34: 7–8

Zimmer, Norbert. 1968. *Heirat mit Ausländern. Afrika und Asien.* Schriften des Auslandskurier 5. Hofheim/Taunus

Zinnecker, Jürgen. 1987. *Jugendkultur 1940–1985.* Opladen: Leske and Budrich

*Zur Sozialpolitik in der antifaschistisch-demokratischen Umwälzung 1945–1949.* 1984. Editorial collective Helene Fiedler, Marita Beier, and Helga Reichelt. Berlin: Dietz Verlag

# Index

# Cambridge Studies in Social and Cultural Anthropology

Editors: Ernest Gellner, Jack Goody, Stephen Gudeman, Michael Herzfeld, Jonathan Parry

* available in paperback